CIMA
STUDY TEXT

Foundation Paper 2

Management Accounting Fundamentals

BPP's NEW STUDY TEXTS FOR CIMA's NEW SYLLABUS

- Targeted to the **syllabus** and **learning outcomes**

- Quizzes and questions to check your understanding

- Incorporates CIMA's new Official Terminology

- Clear layout and style designed to save you time

- Plenty of exam-style questions

- Chapter Roundups and summaries to help revision

- Mind Maps to integrate the key points

BPP Publishing
July 2000

First edition July 2000

ISBN 0 7517 3132 3

British Library Cataloguing-in-Publication Data
A catalogue record for this book
is available from the British Library

Published by

BPP Publishing Ltd
Aldine House, Aldine Place
London W12 8AW

www.bpp.com

Printed in Great Britain by W M Print
Frederick Street
Walsall
West Midlands, WS2 9NE

We are grateful to the Chartered Institute of Management Accountants for permission to reproduce past examination questions and questions from the pilot paper. The suggested solutions to the illustrative questions have been prepared by BPP Publishing Limited.

Page

THE BPP STUDY TEXT

HELP YOURSELF STUDY FOR YOUR CIMA EXAMS
The right approach - suggested study sequence - developing your
personal Study Plan

SYLLABUS AND LEARNING OUTCOMES

THE EXAM PAPER

WHAT THE EXAMINER MEANS

TACKLING OBJECTIVE TEST QUESTIONS

PART A: COST DETERMINATION

PART B: COSTING AND ACCOUNTING SYTEMS

PART C: MARGINAL COSTING AND DECISION MAKING

PART D: STANDARD COSTING AND BUDGETING

EXAM QUESTION BANK

EXAM ANSWER BANK

LIST OF KEY TERMS

INDEX

REVIEW FORM & FREE PRIZE DRAW

ORDER FORM

Multiple choice questions form a large part of the exam. To go with the Study Text, we have produced a bank of **multiple choice question cards**, covering the syllabus. This bank contains exam style questions in a format to help you revise on the move.

THE BPP STUDY TEXT

Aims of this Study Text

To provide you with the knowledge and understanding, skills and application techniques that you need if you are to be successful in your exams

This Study Text has been written around the **Management Accounting Fundamentals** syllabus.

- It is **comprehensive**. It covers the syllabus content. No more, no less.

- It is written at the **right level**. Each chapter is written with CIMA's precise learning outcomes in mind.

- It is targeted to the **exam**. We have taken account of the pilot paper, questions put to the examiners at the recent CIMA conference and the assessment methodology.

To allow you to study in the way that best suits your learning style and the time you have available, by following your personal Study Plan (see page (x))

You may be studying at home on your own until the date of the exam, or you may be attending a full-time course. You may like to (and have time to) read every word, or you may prefer to (or only have time to) skim-read and devote the remainder of your time to question practice. Wherever you fall in the spectrum, you will find the BPP Study Text meets your needs in designing and following your personal Study Plan.

To tie in with the other components of the BPP Effective Study Package to ensure you have the best possible chance of passing the exam (see page (vi))

BPP PUBLISHING

Recommended period of use	Elements of the BPP Effective Study Package
Three to twelve months before the exam	**Study Text** Use the Study Text to acquire knowledge, understanding, skills and the ability to use application techniques.
One to six months before the exam	**Practice & Revision Kit** Attempt the tutorial questions and complete the interactive checklists which are provided for each topic area in the Kit. Then try the numerous examination questions, for which there are realistic suggested solutions prepared by BPP's own authors.
From three 3 months before the exam until the last minute	**Passcards** Work through these short, memorable notes which are focused on what is most likely to come up in the exam you will be sitting.
One to six months before the exam	**Success Tapes** These cover the vital elements of your syllabus in less than 90 minutes per subject with these audio cassettes. Each tape also contains exam hints to help you fine tune your strategy.
Three to twelve months before the exam	**Breakthrough Videos** Use a Breakthrough Video to supplement your Study Text. They give you clear tuition on key exam subjects and allow you the luxury of being able to pause or repeat sections until you have fully grasped the topic.

HELP YOURSELF STUDY FOR YOUR CIMA EXAMS

Exams for professional bodies such as CIMA are very different from those you have taken at college or university. You will be under **greater time pressure before** the exam - as you may be combining your study with work. There are many different ways of learning and so the BPP Study Text offers you a number of different tools to help you through. Here are some hints and tips: they are not plucked out of the air, but **based on research and experience.** (You don't need to know that long-term memory is in the same part of the brain as emotions and feelings - but it's a fact anyway.)

The right approach

1   **The right attitude**

Believe in yourself	Yes, there is a lot to learn. Yes, it is a challenge. But thousands have succeeded before and you can too.
Remember why you're doing it	Studying might seem a grind at times, but you are doing it for a reason: to advance your career.

2   **The right focus**

Read through the Syllabus and learning outcomes	These tell you what you are expected to know and are supplemented by Exam Focus Points in the text.
Study the Exam Paper section	The pilot paper is likely to be a reasonable guide of what you should expect in the exam.

3   **The right method**

The big picture	You need to grasp the detail - but keeping in mind how everything fits into the big picture will help you understand better. • The **Introduction** of each chapter puts the material in context. • The **Syllabus content, learning outcomes** and **Exam focus points** show you what you need to **grasp.** • **Mind Maps** show the links and key issues in key topics.
In your own words	To absorb the information (and to practise your written communication skills), it helps **put it into your own words.** • **Take notes.** • Answer the **questions** in each chapter. As well as helping you absorb the information you will practise your written communication skills, which become increasingly important as you progress through your CIMA exams. • Draw **mind maps.** We have some examples. • Try 'teaching' to a colleague or friend.

BPP PUBLISHING

Give yourself cues to jog your memory	The BPP Study Text uses **bold** to **highlight key points** and **icons** to identify key features, such as **Exam focus points** and **Key terms.** • Try **colour coding** with a highlighter pen. • Write **key points** on cards.

4   **The right review**

Review, review, review	It is a **fact** that regularly reviewing a topic in summary form can **fix it in your memory**. Because **review** is so important, the BPP Study Text helps you to do so in many ways. • **Chapter roundups** summarise the key points in each chapter. Use them to recap each study session. • The **Quick quiz** is another review technique to ensure that you have grasped the essentials. • Use the **Key term** index as a quiz. • Go through the **Examples** in each chapter a second or third time.

Suggested study sequence

Tackle the chapters in the order you find them in the Study Text. Taking into account your individual learning style, you could follow this sequence.

Key study steps	Activity
Step 1 **Topic list**	Each numbered topic is a numbered section in the chapter.
Step 2 **Introduction**	This gives you the **big picture** in terms of the **context** of the chapter, the **content** you will cover, and the **learning outcomes** the chapter assesses - in other words, it sets your **objectives for study.**
Step 3 **Knowledge brought forward boxes**	In these we highlight information and techniques that it is assumed you have 'brought forward' with you from your earlier studies. If there are topics which have changed recently due to legislation for example, these topics are explained in more detail.
Step 4 **Explanations**	Proceed methodically through the chapter, reading each section thoroughly and making sure you understand.
Step 5 **Key terms and Exam focus points**	• **Key terms** can often earn you *easy marks* if you state them clearly and correctly in an appropriate exam answer (and they are indexed at the back of the text). • **Exam focus points** give you a good idea of how we think the examiner intends to examine certain topics.
Step 6 **Note taking**	Take brief notes if you wish, avoiding the temptation to copy out too much.
Step 7 **Examples**	Follow each through to its solution very carefully.
Step 8 **Case examples**	Study each one, and try to add flesh to them from your own experience - they are designed to show how the topics you are studying come alive (and often come unstuck) in the real world.
Step 9 **Questions**	Make a very good attempt at each one.
Step 10 **Answers**	Check yours against ours, and make sure you understand any discrepancies.
Step 11 **Chapter roundup**	Work through it very carefully, to make sure you have grasped the major points it is highlighting.
Step 12 **Quick quiz**	When you are happy that you have covered the chapter, use the **Quick quiz** to check how much you have remembered of the topics covered.

BPP PUBLISHING

Key study steps	Activity
Step 13 **Question(s) in the Question bank**	Either at this point, or later when you are thinking about revising, make a full attempt at the **Question(s)** suggested at the very end of the chapter. You can find these at the end of the Study Text, along with the **Answers** so you can see how you did. We highlight those that are introductory, and those which are of the standard you would expect to find in an exam.

Developing your personal Study Plan

Preparing a Study Plan (and sticking closely to it) is one of the key elements in learning success.

Step 1. How do you learn?

First you need to be aware of your style of learning. There are four typical learning styles. Consider yourself in the light of the following descriptions and work out which you fit most closely. You can then plan to follow the key study steps in the sequence suggested.

Learning styles	Characteristics	Sequence of key study steps in the BPP Study Text
Theorist	Seeks to understand principles before applying them in practice	1, 2, 3, 4, 7, 8, 5, 9/10, 11, 12, 13 (6 continuous)
Reflector	Seeks to observe phenomena, thinks about them and then chooses to act	
Activist	Prefers to deal with practical, active problems; does not have much patience with theory	1, 2, 9/10 (read through), 7, 8, 5, 11, 3, 4, 9/10 (full attempt), 12, 13 (6 continuous)
Pragmatist	Prefers to study only if a direct link to practical problems can be seen; not interested in theory for its own sake	9/10 (read through), 2, 5, 7, 8, 11, 1, 3, 4, 9/10 (full attempt), 12, 13 (6 continuous)

Step 2. How much time do you have?

Work out the time you have available per week, given the following.

- The standard you have set yourself
- The time you need to set aside later for work on the Practice & Revision Kit and Passcards
- The other exam(s) you are sitting
- Very importantly, practical matters such as work, travel, exercise, sleep and social life

Note your time available in box A.

A [　　　　　] Hours

Step 3. Allocate your time

- Take the time you have available per week for this Study Text shown in box A, multiply it by the number of weeks available and insert the result in box B.

B [　　　　　]

- Divide the figure in Box B by the number of chapters in this text and insert the result in box C.

C [　　　　　]

Step 4. Implement

Set about studying each chapter in the time shown in box C, following the key study steps in the order suggested by your particular learning style.

This is your personal **Study Plan**.

Short of time: *Skim study technique?*

You may find you simply do not have the time available to follow all the key study steps for each chapter, however you adapt them for your particular learning style. If this is the case, follow the **skim study** technique below (the icons in the Study Text will help you to do this).

- Study the chapters in the order you find them in the Study Text.

- For each chapter, follow the key study steps 1-3, and then skim-read through step 4. Jump to step 11, and then go back to step 5. Follow through steps 7 and 8, and prepare outline answers to questions (steps 9/10). Try the Quick quiz (step 12), following up any items you can't answer, then do a plan for the Question (step 13), comparing it against our answers. You should probably still follow step 6 (note-taking), although you may decide simply to rely on the BPP Passcards for this.

Moving on...

However you study, when you are ready to embark on the practice and revision phase of the BPP Effective Study Package, you should still refer back to this Study Text, both as a source of **reference** (you should find the list of key terms and the index particularly helpful for this) and as a **refresher** (the Chapter roundups and Quick quizzes help you here).

And remember to keep careful hold of this Study Text - you will find it invaluable in your work.

BPP PUBLISHING

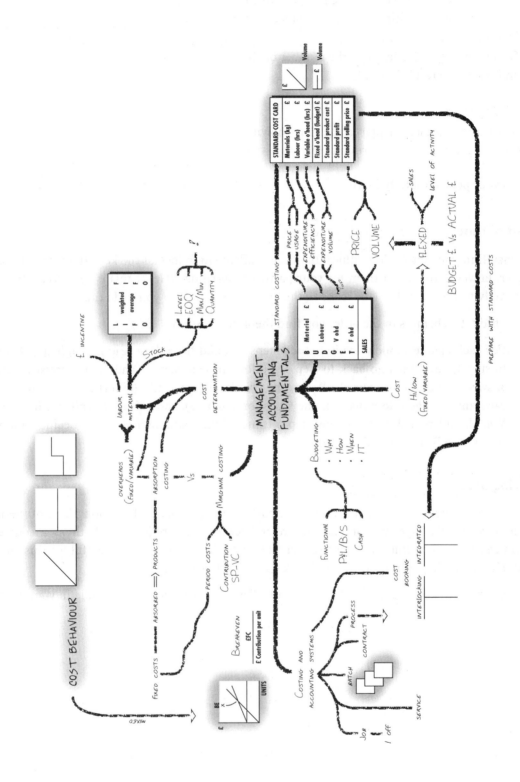

SYLLABUS AND LEARNING OUTCOMES

Syllabus overview

Management Accounting is an introduction to management accounting for students with limited knowledge or no knowledge of this subject While this paper focuses on the application of fundamental methods and techniques, students are also expected to have an understanding of when and when not to use them. Students must also appreciate the contribution made by information technology to management accounting.

Aims

This syllabus aims to test the student's ability to:

- Explain the basic concepts and processes used to determine product and service costs
- Explain absorption cost, marginal cost, opportunity cost, notional cost and relevant cost concepts
- Apply CVP analysis and interpret the results
- Apply a range of costing and accounting systems
- Explain the role of budgets and standard costing within organisations
- Prepare and interpret budgets, standard costs and variance statements

Assessment

There will be a written paper of 3 hours. Section A will use objective testing and will contain 50% of the marks. Section B will be a compulsory question for 25% of the marks. Section C will offer a choice of one question from two for 25% of the marks.

Learning outcomes and syllabus content

2(i) Cost determination – 30%

Learning outcomes

On completion of their studies students should be able to:

- Explain why organisations use costing systems

- Explain raw material accounting and control procedures

- Explain and calculate re-order quantity, re-order level, maximum stock, minimum stock and economic order quantity

- Explain FIFO, LIFO and weighted average stock valuation methods

- Calculate stock, cost of sales and gross profit under LIFO, FIFO and weighted average

- Explain labour accounting and control procedures

- Discuss and calculate factory incentive schemes for individuals and groups

- Explain absorption costing

- Prepare cost statements for allocation and apportionment of overheads including reciprocal service departments

- Calculate and discuss overhead absorption rates

- Calculate under/over recovery of overheads
- Calculate products costs under absorption and marginal costing
- Compare and contrast absorption and marginal costing

Syllabus content

	Covered in chapter
• Classification of costs	1
• Materials: accounting and control procedures	3
• Labour: accounting and control procedures	4
• Factory incentive schemes for individuals and groups	4
• Overhead costs: allocation, apportionment, re-appointment and absorption of overhead costs	5
NB. the repeated distribution method only will be used for reciprocal service department costs	
• Absorption costing	5
• Marginal costing	6
• Materials: re-order quantity, re-order level, maximum stock, minimum stock, economic order quantity	3

2(ii) Standard costing – 15%

Learning outcomes

On completion of their studies students should be able to:

- Explain the principles of standard costing
- Prepare the standard cost for a product/service
- Calculate and interpret variances for sales, materials, labour, variable overheads and fixed overheads
- Prepare a report reconciling budget gross profit/contribution with actual profit

Syllabus content

	Covered in chapter
• Principles of standard costing	15
• Preparation of standard costs under absorption and marginal costing	15
• Variances: materials: total, price and usage; labour: total, rate and efficiency; variable overhead: total, expenditure and efficiency; fixed overhead: total, expenditure and volume (absorption costing); fixed overhead: expenditure (marginal costing); sales: total sales margin variance	16, 17

(xiv)

2(iii) Costing and accounting systems – 20%

Learning outcomes

On completion of their studies students should be able to:

- Compare and contrast job , batch, contract and process costing systems

- Prepare ledger accounts for job, batch, contract (in accordance with SSAP 9) and process costing systems NB the average cost method will only be used for process costing and students must be able to calculate normal losses and abnormal loss/gains and deal with opening and closing stocks

- Prepare and contrast cost statements for service and manufacturing organisations

- Prepare profit and loss accounts from the same data under absorption and marginal costing and reconcile and explain the differences in reported profits

- Prepare accounting entries for an integrated accounting system using standard costs

- Explain the difference between integrated and interlocking accounting systems

Syllabus content

	Covered in chapter
• Job, batch, contract and process costing	8, 9
• Cost accounting statements for services and service industries	10
• Marginal and absorption costing profit and loss accounts	6
• Accounting entries for an integrated accounting system	7, 17
• Interlocking accounting	7

2(iv) Marginal costing and decision making – 15%

Learning outcomes

On completion of their studies students should be able to:

- Identify relevant costs and revenues

- Identify cost behaviour

- Explain the contribution concept

- Calculate and interpret the break even point, profit target, margin of safety and profit/volume ratio for a single product

- Prepare breakeven charts and profit/volume graphs for a single product

- Calculate the profit-maximising sales mix for a company with a single resource constraint which has total freedom of action

- Discuss CVP analysis

BPP PUBLISHING

Syllabus content

	Covered in chapter
• Relevant cost concepts, including sunk costs, committed costs and opportunity costs	11
• Fixed, variable and semi-variable costs	2
• Contribution concept	6
• Break even charts, profit volume graphs, break even point, profit target, margin of safety, contribution/sales ratio	12
• Limiting factor analysis	11

2(v) Budgeting – 20%

Learning outcomes

On completion of their studies students should be able to:

- Explain why organisations prepare budgets
- Explain how organisations prepare budgets
- Explain the use of IT in the budget process
- Prepare functional budgets, profit and loss account, balance sheet and a simple cash budget
- Calculate simple cost estimates using high-low method and line of best fit
- Prepare simple reports showing actual and budgeted results
- Explain the differences between fixed and flexible budgets
- Prepare a fixed and flexible budget
- Calculate expenditure, volume and total budget variances

Syllabus content

	Covered in chapter
• Budget theory	13
• Budget preparation	13
• IT and budgeting	14
• Cost estimation and estimating techniques	2
• Reporting of actual against budget	14
• Fixed and flexible budgeting	14

THE EXAM PAPER

Format of the paper

		Number of marks
Section A:	objective test questions	50
Section B:	one compulsory question	25
Section C:	one question from two	25
		100

Time allowed: 3 hours

Analysis of pilot paper

Section A

1   Twenty five objective test questions covering various management accounting fundamentals topics

Section B

2   Marginal costing and absorption costing, breakeven analysis

Section C

3   Flexible budgets and budget variances
4   Limiting factor decision making

BPP PUBLISHING

WHAT THE EXAMINER MEANS

The table below has been prepared by CIMA to help you interpret exam questions.

Learning objective	Verbs used	Definition
1 Knowledge What you are expected to know	• List • State • Define	• Make a list of • Express, fully or clearly, the details of/facts of • Give the exact meaning of
2 Comprehension What you are expected to understand	• Describe • Distinguish • Explain • Identify • Illustrate	• Communicate the key features of • Highlight the differences between • Make clear or intelligible/state the meaning of • Recognise, establish or select after consideration • Use an example to describe or explain something
3 Application Can you apply your knowledge?	• Apply • Calculate/compute • Demonstrate • Prepare • Reconcile • Solve • Tabulate	• To put to practical use • To ascertain or reckon mathematically • To prove with certainty or to exhibit by practical means • To make or get ready for use • To make or prove consistent/compatible • Find an answer to • Arrange in a table
4 Analysis Can you analysis the detail of what you have learned?	• Analyse • Categorise • Compare and contrast • Construct • Discuss • Interpret • Produce	• Examine in detail the structure of • Place into a defined class or division • Show the similarities and/or differences between • To build up or compile • To examine in detail by argument • To translate into intelligible or familiar terms • To create or bring into existence
5 Evaluation Can you use your learning to evaluate, make decisions or recommendations?	• Advise • Evaluate • Recommend	• To counsel, inform or notify • To appraise or assess the value of • To advise on a course of action

TACKLING OBJECTIVE TEST QUESTIONS

Of the total marks available for this paper, objective test questions comprise:
A   25%
B   50%
C   75%
D   100%

The answer is on page (xvii)

The objective test questions (OTs) in your exam contain four possible answers. You have to **choose the option that best answers the question**. The three incorrect options are called distracters. There is a skill in answering OTs quickly and correctly. By practising OTs you can develop this skill, giving you a better chance of passing the exam.

You may wish to follow the approach outlined below, or you may prefer to adapt it.

Step 1.   Skim read all the OTs and identify what appear to be the easier questions.

Step 2.   Attempt each question - **starting with the easier questions** identified in Step 1. Read the question thoroughly. You may prefer to work out the answer before looking at the options, or you may prefer to look at the options at the beginning. Adopt the method that works best for you.

Step 3.   Read the four options and see if one matches your own answer. Be careful with numerical questions, as the distracters are designed to match answers that incorporate common errors. Check that your calculation is correct. Have you followed the requirement exactly? Have you included every stage of the calculation?

Step 4.   You may find that none of the options matches your answer.

- Re-read the question to ensure that you understand it and are answering the requirement

- Eliminate any obviously wrong answers

- Consider which of the remaining answers is the most likely to be correct and select the option

Step 5.   If you are still unsure make a note and continue to the next question. (You have an average 1.8 minutes per question. If you average 2 minutes per question, this will leave you with 20 minutes at the end of the exam in which to revisit problem questions.)

Step 6.   Revisit unanswered questions. When you come back to a question after a break you often find you are able to answer it correctly straight away. If you are still unsure have a guess. You are not penalised for incorrect answers, so **never leave a question unanswered!**

Exam focus. After extensive practice and revision of MCQs, you may find that you recognise a question when you sit the exam. Be aware that the detail and/or requirement may be different. If the question seems familiar read the requirement and options carefully - do not assume that it is identical.

Part A
Cost determination

Chapter 1

COST ACCOUNTING AND COST CLASSIFICATION

Topic list		Syllabus reference	Ability required
1	What is cost accounting?	(i)	Comprehension
2	The organisation, cost centres and cost units	(i)	Comprehension
3	Cost classification	(i)	Comprehension
4	Cost classification for stock valuation and profit measurement	(i)	Comprehension
5	Cost classification for decision making	(i)	Comprehension
6	Cost classification for control	(i)	Comprehension

Introduction

Welcome to the Foundation level of CIMA's new syllabus, and in particular to **Management Accounting Fundamentals.** This chapter will introduce the subject of cost accounting and explain what cost accounting is and what a **cost accountant** does. We will briefly consider how an organisation is structured from the point of view of the cost accountant and we will then turn our attention to costs and look at the various ways in which they can be classified to assist the work of the cost accountant.

Your study of cost behaviour in Chapter 2 will use the knowledge gained from this chapter on how costs can be divided into fixed and variable components.

Learning outcomes covered in this chapter

- Explain why organisations use costing systems

Syllabus content covered in this chapter

- Classification of costs

1 WHAT IS COST ACCOUNTING?

1.1 Who can provide the answers to the following questions?

- What was the cost of goods produced or services provided last period?
- What was the cost of operating a department last month?
- What revenues were earned last week?

Yes, you've guessed it, the cost accountant.

1.2 Knowing about costs incurred or revenues earned enables management to do the following.

  (a) **Assess the profitability of a product**, a service, a department, or the whole organisation.

  (b) Perhaps, **set selling prices** with some regard for the costs of sale.

  (c) **Put a value to stocks of goods** (raw materials, work in progress, finished goods) that are still held in store at the end of a period, for preparing a balance sheet of the company's assets and liabilities.

1.3 That was quite easy. But who could answer the following questions?

  (a) What are the future costs of goods and services likely to be?

  (b) How do actual costs compare with planned costs?

  (c) What information does management need in order to make sensible decisions about profits and costs?

  Well, you may be surprised, but again it is the cost accountant.

1.4 Originally cost accounting did deal with ways of accumulating historical costs and of charging these costs to units of output, or to departments, in order to establish stock valuations, profits and balance sheet items. It has since been extended into **planning, control** and **decision making**, so that the cost accountant is now able to answer the second set of questions. In today's modern industrial environment, the role of cost accounting in the provision of management information is therefore almost indistinguishable from that of management accounting, which is basically concerned with the **provision of information to assist management** with **planning**, **control** and **decision making**.

1.5 The managers of a business have the responsibility of planning and controlling the resources used. To carry out this task effectively they must be provided with **sufficiently accurate** and **detailed information**, and the cost accounting system should provide this. **Cost accounting is a management information system which analyses past, present and future data to provide the basis for managerial action.**

1.6 It would be wrong to suppose that cost accounting systems are restricted to manufacturing operations. Cost accounting information is also used in service industries, government departments and welfare organisations. Within a manufacturing organisation, the cost accounting system should be applied not only to manufacturing operations but also to administration, selling and distribution, research and development and so on.

1.7 Cost accounting is concerned with providing information to assist the following.

  • Establishing stock valuations, profits and balance sheet items
  • Planning
  • Control
  • Decision making

The relationship with financial accounting

1.8 The financial accounting and cost accounting systems in a business both record the same basic data for income and expenditure, but each set of records may analyse the data in a different way. This is because each system has a **different purpose**.

1.9 **Financial accounting versus cost accounting**

(a) **Financial accounts** are prepared for individuals **external** to an organisation eg shareholders, customers, suppliers, the Inland Revenue and employees.

(b) **Management accounts** are prepared for **internal** managers of an organisation.

1.10 The data used to prepare financial accounts and management accounts are the same. The differences between the financial accounts and the management accounts arise because the data is analysed differently.

Financial accounts	Management accounts
Financial accounts detail the performance of an organisation over a defined period and the state of affairs at the end of that period.	Management accounts are used to aid management record, plan and control the organisation's activities and to help the decision-making process.
Limited companies must, by law, prepare financial accounts.	There is no legal requirement to prepare management accounts.
The format of published financial accounts is determined by law (mainly the Companies Acts), by Statements of Standard Accounting Practice and by Financial Reporting Standards. In principle the accounts of different organisations can therefore be easily compared.	The format of management accounts is entirely at management discretion: no strict rules govern the way they are prepared or presented. Each organisation can devise its own management accounting system and format of reports.
Financial accounts concentrate on the business as a whole, aggregating revenues and costs from different operations, and are an end in themselves.	Management accounts can focus on specific areas of an organisation's activities. Information may be produced to aid a decision rather than to be an end product of a decision.
Most financial accounting information is of a monetary nature.	Management accounts incorporate non-monetary measures. Management may need to know, for example, tons of aluminium produced, monthly machine hours, or miles travelled by salesmen.
Financial accounts present an essentially historic picture of past operations.	Management accounts are both a historical record and a future planning tool.

2 THE ORGANISATION, COST CENTRES AND COST UNITS

2.1 An organisation, whether it is a manufacturing company, a provider of services (such as a bank or a hotel) or a public sector organisation (such as a hospital), may be divided into a number of different **functions** within which there are a number of **departments**. A manufacturing organisation might be structured as follows.

BPP
PUBLISHING

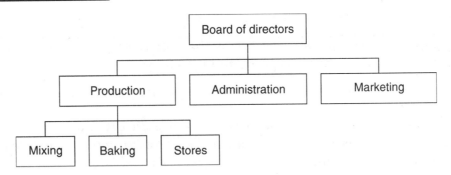

2.2 Suppose the organisation above produces chocolate cakes for a number of supermarket chains. The production function is involved with the making of the cakes, the administration department with the preparation of accounts and the employment of staff and the marketing department with the selling and distribution of the cakes.

2.3 Within the production function there are three departments, two of which are production departments (the mixing department and the baking department) which are actively involved in the production of the cakes and one of which is a service department (stores department) which provides a service or back-up to the production departments.

Cost centres

2.4 *In general*, for cost accounting purposes, departments are termed **cost centres** and the product produced by an organisation is termed the **cost unit**. In our example, the cost centres of the production function could be the mixing department, the baking department and the stores department and the organisation's cost unit could be one chocolate cake.

2.5 When costs are incurred, they are generally allocated to a **cost centre**. A cost centre acts as a **collecting place** for certain costs before they are analysed further. Cost centres may include the following.

- A **department** (as in our example above)
- A **machine** or group of machines
- A **project** (eg the installation of a new computer system)
- A **new product** (to enable the costs of development and production to be identified)

Cost units

2.6 Once costs have been traced to cost centres, they can be further analysed in order to establish a **cost per cost unit**. Alternatively, some items of costs may be charged directly to a cost unit, for example direct materials and direct labour costs, which you will meet later in this text.

KEY TERM

A **cost unit** is 'A unit of product or service in relation to which costs are ascertained'.

CIMA *Official Terminology*

2.7 Different organisations use different cost units. Here are some suggestions.

Organisation	Possible cost unit
Steelworks	Tonne of steel produced
	Tonne of coke used
Hospital	Patient/day
	Operation
	Out-patient visit
Freight organisation	Tonne/kilometre
Passenger transport organisation	Passenger/kilometre
Accounting firm	Audit performed
	Chargeable hour
Restaurant	Meal served

2.8 One of the principal purposes of cost accounting is therefore to **determine the cost of a single cost unit** (for stock valuation, cost planning and control and profit reporting purposes).

3 COST CLASSIFICATION

3.1 Before any attempt is made to establish stock valuations and measure profits, to plan, make decisions or exercise control (in other words, do any cost accounting), costs must be classified. **Classification** involves **arranging costs into groupings of similar items** in order to make stock valuation, profit measurement, planning, decision making and control easier.

4 COST CLASSIFICATION FOR STOCK VALUATION AND PROFIT MEASUREMENT

4.1 For the purposes of stock valuation and profit measurement, the cost accountant must calculate the cost of one unit. The total cost of a cost unit is made up of the following three elements of cost.

- Materials
- Labour
- Other expenses (such as rent and rates, interest charges and so on)

Cost elements can be classified as **direct** costs or **indirect** costs.

Direct cost

> **KEY TERM**
>
> A **direct cost** is a cost that can be traced in full to the product, service, or department that is being costed.

4.2 (a) **Direct materials costs** are the costs of materials that are known to have been used in making and selling a product (or providing a service).

(b) **Direct labour costs** are the specific costs of the workforce used to make a product or provide a service. Direct labour costs are established by measuring the time taken for a job, or the time taken in 'direct production work'.

(c) **Other direct expenses** are those expenses that have been incurred in full as a direct consequence of making a product, or providing a service, or running a department.

Indirect cost/overhead

> **KEY TERM**
>
> An **indirect cost** or overhead is a cost that is incurred in the course of making a product, providing a service or running a department, but which cannot be traced directly and in full to the product, service or department. Examples might be the cost of supervisors' wages, cleaning materials and buildings insurance.

4.3 Total expenditure may therefore be analysed as follows.

Materials cost	=	Direct materials cost	+	Indirect materials cost
+		+		+
Labour cost	=	Direct labour cost	+	Indirect labour cost
+		+		+
Expenses	=	Direct expenses		Indirect expenses
Total cost	=	Direct cost	+	Overhead cost

4.4 **Total direct cost** is often referred to as **prime cost** ie the total cost of direct material, direct labour and direct expenses.

4.5 You should be able to specify whether an item of expenditure is classed as a direct materials cost, a direct labour cost, a production overhead and so on. Further information on such cost items is given below.

Direct material

> **KEY TERM**
>
> **Direct material** is all material becoming part of the product (unless used in negligible amounts and/or having negligible cost).

4.6 Direct material costs are charged to the product as part of the **prime cost**. Examples of direct material are as follows.

(a) **Component parts** or other materials specially purchased for a particular job, order or process.

(b) **Part-finished work** which is transferred from department 1 to department 2 becomes finished work of department 1 and a direct material cost in department 2.

(c) **Primary packing materials** like cartons and boxes.

4.7 Materials used in negligible amounts and/or having negligible cost can be grouped under indirect materials as part of overhead.

KEY TERM

Direct wages are all wages paid for labour (either as basic hours or as overtime expended on work on the product itself.

4.8 **Direct wages** costs are charged to the product as part of the **prime cost**.

Examples of groups of labour receiving payment as direct wages are as follows.

(a) Workers engaged in **altering** the condition, conformation or composition of the product.

(b) Inspectors, analysts and testers **specifically required** for such production.

Question 1

Classify the following labour costs as either direct or indirect.

(a) The basic pay of direct workers (cash paid, tax and other deductions)
(b) The basic pay of indirect workers
(c) Overtime premium, ie the premium above basic pay, for working overtime
(d) Bonus payments under a group bonus scheme
(e) Employer's National Insurance contributions
(f) Idle time of direct workers, paid while waiting for work
(g) Work on installation of equipment

Answer

(a) The basic pay of direct workers is a direct cost to the unit, job or process.

(b) The basic pay of indirect workers is an indirect cost, unless a customer asks for an order to be carried out which involves the dedicated use of indirect workers' time, when the cost of this time would be a direct labour cost of the order.

(c) Overtime premium paid to both direct and indirect workers is usually an indirect cost because it is 'unfair' to charge the items produced in overtime hours with the premium. Why should an item made in overtime be more costly just because, by chance, it was made after the employee normally clocks off for the day?

There are two particular circumstances in which the overtime premium might be a direct cost.

(i) If overtime is worked at the specific request of a customer to get his order completed, the overtime premium paid is a direct cost of the order.

(ii) If overtime is worked regularly by a production department in the normal course of operations, the overtime premium paid to direct workers could be incorporated into the (average) direct labour hourly rate.

(d) Bonus payments are generally an indirect cost.

(e) Employer's national insurance contributions (which are added to employees' total pay as a wages cost) are normally treated as an indirect labour cost.

(f) Idle time is an overhead cost, that is an indirect labour cost.

(g) The cost of work on capital equipment is incorporated into the capital cost of the equipment.

Direct expenses

> **KEY TERM**
>
> **Direct expenses** are any expenses which are incurred on a specific product other than direct material cost and direct wages

4.9 **Direct expenses** are charged to the product as part of the **prime** cost. Examples of direct expenses are as follows.

- The cost of **special** designs, drawings or layouts
- The **hire of tools** or equipment for a particular job
- **Maintenance costs** of tools, jigs, fixtures and so on

Direct expenses are also referred to as **chargeable expenses.**

Production overhead

> **KEY TERM**
>
> **Production (or factory) overhead** includes all indirect material cost, indirect wages and indirect expenses incurred in the factory from receipt of the order until its completion.

4.10 Production overhead includes the following.

(a) **Indirect materials** which cannot be traced in the finished product.

- Consumable stores, eg material used in negligible amounts

(b) **Indirect wages**, meaning all wages not charged directly to a product.

- Salaries of non-productive personnel in the production department, eg foremen

(c) **Indirect expenses** (other than material and labour) not charged directly to production.

- Rent, rates and insurance of a factory
- Depreciation, fuel, power and maintenance of plant and buildings

Administration overhead

> **KEY TERM**
>
> **Administration overhead** is all indirect material costs, wages and expenses incurred in the direction, control and administration of an undertaking.

4.11 Examples of administration overhead are as follows.

- **Depreciation** of office equipment.
- **Office salaries**, including salaries of secretaries and accountants.
- Rent, rates, insurance, telephone, heat and light costs of general offices.

Selling overhead

> **KEY TERM**
>
> **Selling overhead** is all indirect materials costs, wages and expenses incurred in promoting sales and retaining customers.

4.12 Examples of selling overhead are as follows.

- **Printing** and **stationery,** such as catalogues and price lists.
- **Salaries** and **commission** of sales representatives and sales department staff.
- **Advertising** and **sales promotion**, market research.
- Rent, rates and insurance of sales offices and showrooms, bad debts and so on.

Distribution overhead

> **KEY TERM**
>
> **Distribution overhead** is all indirect material costs, wages and expenses incurred in making the packed product ready for despatch and delivering it to the customer.

4.13 Examples of distribution overhead are as follows.

- Cost of packing cases.
- Wages of packers, drivers and despatch clerks.
- Depreciation and running expenses of delivery vehicles.

Question 2

A direct labour employee's wage in week 5 consists of the following.

		£
(a)	Basic pay for normal hours worked, 36 hours at £4 per hour =	144
(b)	Pay at the basic rate for overtime, 6 hours at £4 per hour =	24
(c)	Overtime shift premium, with overtime paid at time-and-a-quarter	
	¼ × 6 hours × £4 per hour =	6
(d)	A bonus payment under a group bonus (or 'incentive') scheme -	
	bonus for the month =	30
	Total gross wages in week 5 for 42 hours of work	204

What is the direct labour co0st for this employee in week 5?

A £144   B £168   C £198   D £204

Answer

Let's start by considering a general approach to answering multiple choice questions (MCQs). In a numerical question like this, the best way to begin is to ignore the available options and work out your own answer from the available data. If your solution corresponds to one of the four options then mark this as your chosen answer and move on. Don't waste time working out whether any of the other options might be correct. If your answer does not appear among the available options then check your workings. If it still does not correspond to any of the options then you need to take a calculated guess. Never leave a question out because CIMA does not penalise an incorrect MCQ answer.

Do not make the common error of simply selecting the answer which is closest to yours. The best thing to do is to first eliminate any answers which you know or suspect are incorrect. For example you could eliminate C and D because you know that group bonus schemes are usually indirect costs. You are then left with a choice between A and B, and at least you have now improved your chances if you really are guessing.

The correct answer is B because the basic rate for overtime is a part of direct wages cost. It is only the overtime premium that is usually regarded as an overhead or indirect cost.

Product costs and period costs

KEY TERMS

- **Product costs** are costs identified with a finished product. Such costs are initially identified as part of the value of stock. They become expenses (in the form of cost of goods sold) only when the stock is sold.

- **Period costs** are costs that are deducted as expenses during the current period without ever being included in the value of stock held.

4.14 Consider a retailer who acquires goods for resale without changing their basic form. The only product cost is therefore the purchase cost of the goods. Any unsold goods are held as stock, valued at the lower of purchase cost and net realisable value and included as an asset in the balance sheet. As the goods are sold, their cost becomes an expense in the form of 'cost of goods sold'. A retailer will also incur a variety of selling and administration expenses. Such costs are **period costs** because they are **deducted from revenue** without ever being regarded as part of the **value of stock.**

4.15 Now consider a manufacturing firm in which direct materials are transformed into saleable goods with the help of direct labour and factory overheads. All these costs are **product costs** because they are allocated to the value of stock until the goods are sold. As with the retailer, selling and administration expenses are regarded as **period costs.**

Functional costs

4.16 In a 'traditional' costing system for a manufacturing organisation, costs are classified as follows.

- Production or manufacturing costs
- Administration costs
- Marketing, or selling and distribution costs

Many expenses fall comfortably into one or other of these three broad classifications. Manufacturing costs are associated with the factory, selling and distribution costs with the sales, marketing, warehousing and transport departments and administration costs with general office departments (such as accounting and personnel). Classification in this way is known as **classification by function**. Other expenses that do not fall fully into one of these classifications might be categorised as **general overheads** or even classified on their own (for example **research and development costs**).

Question 3

Within the costing system of a manufacturing company the following types of expense are incurred.

Reference number

1	Cost of oils used to lubricate production machinery
2	Motor vehicle licences for lorries
3	Depreciation of factory plant and equipment
4	Cost of chemicals used in the laboratory
5	Commission paid to sales representatives
6	Salary of the secretary to the finance director
7	Trade discount given to customers
8	Holiday pay of machine operatives
9	Salary of security guard in raw materials warehouse
10	Fees to advertising agency
11	Rent of finished goods warehouse
12	Salary of scientist in laboratory
13	Insurance of the company's premises
14	Salary of supervisor working in the factory
15	Cost of typewriter ribbons in the general office
16	Protective clothing for machine operatives

Required

Place each expense within the following classifications.

(a) Production costs
(b) Selling and distribution costs
(c) Administration costs
(d) Research and development costs

Each type of expense should appear only once in your answer. You may use the reference numbers in your answer.

Answer

The reference number for each expense can be classified as follows.

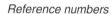

		Reference numbers
(a)	Production costs	1, 3, 8, 9, 14, 16
(b)	Selling and distribution costs	2, 5, 7, 10,11
(c)	Administration costs	6, 13, 15
(d)	Research and development costs	4, 12

5   COST CLASSIFICATION FOR DECISION MAKING

5.1   Decision making is concerned with **future events** and hence management require information on **expected future costs and revenues**. Although cost accounting systems are designed to accumulate **past costs and revenues** this historical information may provide a starting point for **forecasting future events.**

Fixed costs and variable costs

5.2   A knowledge of how costs will **vary at different levels of activity** (or volume) is essential for decision making.

KEY TERMS

- A **fixed cost** is a cost which is incurred for a particular period of time and which, within certain activity levels, is unaffected by changes in the level of activity.

- A **variable cost** is a cost which tends to vary with the level of activity.

5.3 Some examples are as follows.

(a) Direct material costs are **variable costs** because they rise as more units of a product are manufactured.

(b) Sales commission is often a fixed percentage of sales turnover, and so is a **variable cost** that varies with the level of sales.

(c) Telephone call charges are likely to increase if the volume of business expands, and so they are a **variable overhead cost.**

(d) The rental cost of business premises is a constant amount, at least within a stated time period, and so it is a **fixed cost.**

5.4 Note that costs can be classified as direct costs or indirect costs/overheads, or as fixed costs or variable costs. These alternative classifications are not, however, mutually exclusive, but are complementary to each other, so that we can find some direct costs that are fixed costs (although they are commonly variable costs) and some overhead costs that are fixed and some overhead costs that are variable.

6 COST CLASSIFICATION FOR CONTROL

Controllable and uncontrollable costs

6.1 One of the purposes of cost accounting is to provide control information to management who wish to know whether or not a particular cost item can be controlled by management action.

KEY TERMS

- A **controllable cost** is a cost which can be influenced by management decisions and actions.

- An **uncontrollable cost** is any cost that cannot be affected by management within a given time span.

Exam focus point

The topics covered in this chapter are most likely to be examined in Section A (the multiple choice questions section) of the **Management Accounting Fundamentals** paper. For example, candidates might be asked to choose the correct definition of a cost accounting term from four provided.

Chapter roundup

- **Cost accounting** is a method of establishing stock valuations, profits and balance sheet items as well as a system for planning, control and decision making.

- In general terms, **financial accounting** is for **external** reporting whereas **cost accounting** is for **internal** reporting.

- **Cost centres** are **collecting places** for costs before they are further analysed, and **cost units** are the **basic control units** for costing purposes.

- A **direct cost** is a cost that can be traced in full to the product, service or department being costed. An **indirect cost** (or overhead) is a cost that is incurred in the course of making a product, providing a service or running a department, but which cannot be traced directly and in full to the product, service or department.

- For the preparation of financial statements, costs are often classified as either **product costs** or **period costs**. Product costs are costs identified with goods produced or purchased for resale. Period costs are costs deducted as expenses during the current period.

- **Classification by function** involves classifying costs as production/manufacturing costs, administration costs or marketing/selling and distribution costs.

- A different way of analysing and classifying costs is into **fixed costs** and **variable costs**. Many items of expenditure are part-fixed and part-variable and hence are termed **semi-fixed**, **semi-variable** or **mixed**. We will look at such costs in more detail in Chapter 2.

- For control purposes, costs can be analysed as **controllable** or **uncontrollable**.

Quick quiz

1   How is cost accounting distinguished from financial accounting?

2   (a)   A .... is a unit of product or service to which costs can be related, it is the basic control unit for costing purposes.

      (b)   A .... acts as a collecting place for certain costs before they are analysed further.

3   There are a number of different ways in which costs can be classified.

      (a)   .... and .... (or overhead) costs.

      (b)   .... costs (production costs, distribution and selling costs, administration costs and financing costs).

      (c)   Fixed......... and ....costs.

4   A fixed cost is a cost which tends to vary with the level of activity.

      True   ☐

      False   ☐

5   Categorise these costs:

      Sales commission   Functional costs

      Rent   ?   Fixed cost

      Research and development costs   Variable cost

6   Which of the following would be classed as indirect labour?

      A   Assembly workers in a company manufacturing televisions
      B   A stores assistant in a factory store
      C   Plasterers in a construction company
      D   An audit clerk in a firm of auditors

Answers to quick quiz

1   Cost accounting is mainly concerned with the preparation of management accounts for **internal** managers of an organisation.

Financial accounts are prepared for individuals **external** to an organisation eg shareholders, customers and so on.

2   (a)   Cost unit
    (b)   Cost centre

3   (a)   Direct, indirect (overhead) costs
    (b)   Functional
    (c)   Variable

4   False. Fixed costs are unaffected by changes in the level of activity.

5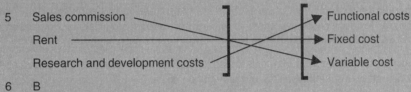

Sales commission

Rent

Research and development costs

Functional costs

Fixed cost

Variable cost

6   B

Now try the question below from the Exam Question Bank

Number	Level	Marks	Time
Q1	Introductory	n/a	30 mins

BPP PUBLISHING

Chapter 2

COST BEHAVIOUR

Topic list	Syllabus reference	Ability required
1 Cost behaviour and levels of activity	(iv)	Comprehension
2 Cost behaviour patterns	(iv)	Comprehension
3 Determining the fixed and variable elements of semi-variable costs	(iv),(v)	Comprehension, application

Introduction

In Chapter 1 we introduced you to the subject of cost accounting and explained, in general terms, what it is and what it does. We then considered the principal methods of classifying costs. In particular we introduced the concept of the division of costs into those that vary directly with changes in activity levels (**variable costs**) and those that do not (**fixed costs**). This chapter examines further this particular two-way split of **cost behaviour** and explains two methods of splitting total costs into these two elements, the **scattergraph (line of best fit)** method and the **high-low** method.

You will need to rely on concepts covered in this chapter and the previous chapter in the remainder of your management accounting studies both at the Foundation level and at future examination levels.

Learning outcomes covered in this chapter

- **Identify** cost behaviour
- **Calculate** simple cost estimates using high-low method and line of best fit

Syllabus content covered in this chapter

- Fixed, variable and semi-variable costs
- Cost estimation and estimating techniques

1   COST BEHAVIOUR AND LEVELS OF ACTIVITY

> **KEY TERM**
>
> **Cost behaviour** is 'The variability of input costs with activity undertaken.'
>
> CIMA *Official Terminology*

1.1   The level of activity refers to the amount of work done, or the number of events that have occurred. Depending on circumstances, the level of activity may refer to measures such as the following.

- The volume of production in a period.
- The number of items sold.
- The value of items sold.
- The number of invoices issued.
- The number of units of electricity consumed.

Basic principles of cost behaviour

1.2 **The basic principle of cost behaviour is that as the level of activity rises, costs will usually rise.** It will probably cost more to produce 2,000 units of output than it will cost to produce 1,000 units; it will usually cost more to make five telephone calls than to make one call and so on. The problem for the accountant is to determine, for each item of cost, the way in which costs rise and by how much as the level of activity increases.

1.3 For our purposes in this chapter, the level of activity will generally be taken to be the volume of production/output.

2 COST BEHAVIOUR PATTERNS

Fixed costs

2.1 We discussed fixed costs briefly in Chapter 1. A **fixed cost** is a cost which tends to be unaffected by increases or decreases in the volume of output. Fixed costs are a **period charge**, in that they relate to a span of time; as the time span increases, so too will the fixed costs. A sketch graph of a fixed cost would look like this.

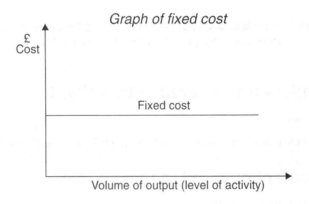

2.2 Examples of a fixed cost would be as follows.

- The salary of the managing director (per month or per annum)
- The rent of a single factory building (per month or per annum)
- Straight line depreciation of a single machine (per month or per annum)

> **KEY TERM**
>
> A **step cost** is a cost which is fixed in nature but only within certain levels of activity.

2.3 Consider the depreciation of a machine which may be fixed if production remains below 1,000 units per month. If production exceeds 1,000 units, a second machine may be required, and the cost of depreciation (on two machines) would go up a step. A sketch graph of a step cost could look like this.

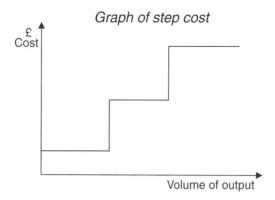

Other examples of step costs are as follows.

(a) Rent is a step cost in situations where accommodation requirements increase as output levels get higher.

(b) Basic pay of employees is nowadays usually fixed, but as output rises, more employees (direct workers, supervisors, managers and so on) are required.

Variable costs

2.4 We discussed variable costs briefly in Chapter 1. A **variable cost** is a cost which tends to vary directly with the volume of output. The variable cost **per unit** is the same amount for each unit produced whereas **total** variable cost increases as volume of output increases. A sketch graph of a variable cost would look like this.

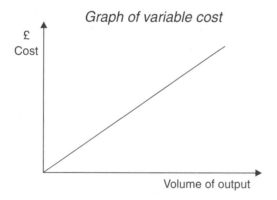

2.5 Examples of variable costs are as follows.

(a) The cost of raw materials (where there is no discount for bulk purchasing since bulk purchase discounts reduce the unit cost of purchases).

(b) Direct labour costs are, for very important reasons which you will study in Chapter 4, usually classed as a variable cost even though basic wages are often fixed.

(c) Sales commission is variable in relation to the volume or value of sales.

Semi-variable costs (or semi-fixed costs or mixed costs)

KEY TERM

A **semi-variable/semi-fixed/mixed cost** is 'A cost containing both fixed and variable components and which is thus partly affected by a change in the level of activity'.

CIMA *Official Terminology*

2.6 Examples of semi-variable costs include the following.

(a) **Electricity and gas bills**. There is a basic charge plus a charge per unit of consumption.

(a) **Sales representative's salary**. The sales representative may earn a basic monthly amount of, say, £1,000 and then commission of 10% of the value of sales made.

The behaviour of a semi-variable cost can be presented graphically as follows.

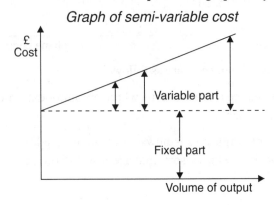

Graph of semi-variable cost

Cost behaviour and total and unit costs

2.7 If the variable cost of producing a unit is £5 per unit then it will remain at that cost per unit no matter how many units are produced. However if the business's fixed costs are £5,000 then the fixed cost *per unit* will decrease the more units are produced: one unit will have fixed costs of £5,000 per unit; if 2,500 are produced the fixed cost per unit will be £2; if 5,000 are produced the fixed cost per unit will be only £1. Thus as the level of activity increases the total costs *per unit* (fixed cost plus variable cost) will decrease.

In sketch graph form this may be illustrated as follows.

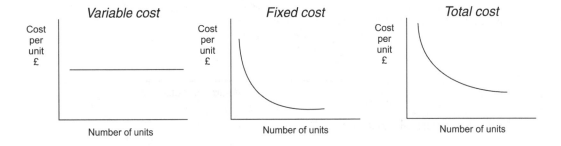

Question 1

Are the following likely to be fixed, variable or mixed costs?

(a) Telephone bill
(b) Annual salary of the chief accountant
(c) The management accountant's annual membership fee to CIMA (paid by the company)
(d) Cost of materials used to pack 20 units of product X into a box

Answer

(a) Mixed
(b) Fixed
(c) Fixed
(d) Variable

Assumptions about cost behaviour

2.8 It is often possible to assume that, within the normal or relevant range of output, costs are either fixed, variable or semi-variable.

3 DETERMINING THE FIXED AND VARIABLE ELEMENTS OF SEMI-VARIABLE COSTS

3.1 There are several ways in which fixed cost elements and variable cost elements within semi-variable costs may be ascertained. Each method only gives an estimate, and can therefore give differing results from the other methods. The main methods that you need to know about for the Management Accounting Fundamentals examination are the **high-low method** and the **scattergraph** method.

High-low method

3.2 (a) Records of costs in previous periods are reviewed and the costs of the following two periods are selected.

- The period with the **highest** volume of activity
- The period with the **lowest** volume of activity

(b) The difference between the total cost of these two periods will be the **variable cost** of the difference in activity levels (since the same fixed cost is included in each total cost).

(c) The variable cost per unit may be calculated from this (difference in total costs ÷ difference in activity levels), and the **fixed cost** may then be determined by substitution.

3.3 EXAMPLE: THE HIGH-LOW METHOD

The costs of operating the maintenance department of a computer manufacturer, Bread and Butter Ltd, for the last four months have been as follows.

Month	Cost £	Production volume Units
1	110,000	7,000
2	115,000	8,000
3	111,000	7,700
4	97,000	6,000

Required

Calculate the costs that should be expected in month five when output is expected to be 7,500 units. Ignore inflation.

3.4 SOLUTION

(a)		Units		£
	High output	8,000	total cost	115,000
	Low output	6,000	total cost	97,000
	Variable cost of	2,000		18,000

Variable cost per unit   £18,000/2,000 = £9

(b) Substituting in either the high or low volume cost:

		High £		Low £
Total cost		115,000		97,000
Variable costs	(8,000 × £9)	72,000	(6,000 × £9)	54,000
Fixed costs		43,000		43,000

(c) Estimated maintenance costs when output is 7,500 units:

	£
Fixed costs	43,000
Variable costs (7,500 × £9)	67,500
Total costs	110,500

Question 2

The Valuation Department of a large firm of surveyors wishes to develop a method of predicting its total costs in a period. The following past costs have been recorded at two activity levels.

	Number of valuations (V)	Total cost (TC)
Period 1	420	82,200
Period 2	515	90,275

The total cost model for a period could be represented as follows.

A TC = £46,500 + 85V
B TC = £42,000 + 95V
C TC = £46,500 – 85V
D TC = £51,500 – 95V

Answer

Although we only have two activity levels in this question we can still apply the high-low method.

	Valuations V	Total cost £
Period 2	515	90,275
Period 1	420	82,200
Change due to variable cost	95	8,075

∴ Variable cost per valuation = £8,075/95 = £85.

Period 2: fixed cost = £90,275 – (515 × £85)

= £46,500

Using good MCQ technique, you should have managed to eliminate C and D as incorrect options straightaway. The variable cost must be added to the fixed cost, rather than subtracted from it. Once you had calculated the variable cost as £85 per valuation (as shown above), you should have been able to select option A without going on to calculate the fixed cost (we have shown this calculation above for completeness).

Exam focus point

The high-low method was examined in the multiple choice section of the **Management Accounting Fundamentals** Pilot paper. The information in the question related to **two** activity levels only. The high-low method is still an appropriate method for identifying the fixed and variable elements of costs where two levels of activity are concerned – you still have a **high** and a **low** activity level.

Scattergraph method

3.5 A scattergraph of costs in previous periods can be prepared (with cost on the vertical axis and volume of output on the horizontal axis). A **line of best fit,** which is a line drawn **by judgement** to pass through the middle of the points, thereby having as many points above the line as below it, can then be drawn and the fixed and variable costs determined.

3.6 A scattergraph of the cost and volume data in Paragraph 3.3 is shown below.

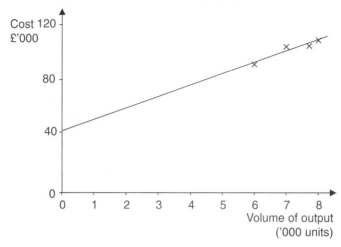

The point where the line cuts the vertical axis (approximately £40,000) is the fixed cost (the cost if there is no output). If we take the value of one of the plotted points which lies close to the line and deduct the fixed cost from the total cost, we can calculate the variable cost per unit.

Total cost for 8,000 units   = £115,000
Variable cost for 8,000 units = £(115,000 – 40,000) = £75,000
Variable cost per unit   = £75,000/8,000 = £9.375

Exam focus point

Remember that you can pick up easy marks in an examination for drawing a graph neatly. Always use a ruler, label your axes and use an appropriate scale.

Chapter roundup

- This chapter has considered the way in which costs are affected by changes in the level of activity.

- Costs which are not affected by the level of activity are **fixed costs** or **period costs**.

- **Step costs** are fixed within a certain range of activity.

- **Variable costs** increase or decrease with the level of activity

- **Semi-fixed**, **semi-variable** or **mixed costs** are costs which are part fixed and part variable.

- It is often possible to assume that, within the normal or relevant range of output, costs are either variable, fixed or semi-variable.

- The fixed and variable elements of semi-variable costs can be determined by the **high-low method** or the **scattergraph** method.

Quick quiz

1   Cost behaviour is ....

2   The basic principle of cost behaviour is that as the level of activity rises, costs will usually rise/fall.

3   Fill in the gaps for each of the graph titles below.

(a)

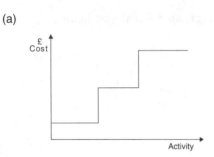

Graph of a ....cost

Example:

(b)

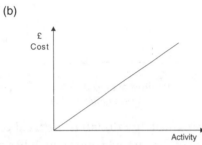

Graph of a ....cost

Example:

(c)

Graph of a ....cost

Example:

(d)

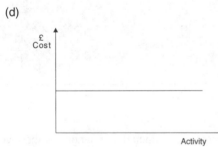

Graph of a...............................cost

Example

4   Costs are assumed to be either fixed, variable or semi-variable within the normal or relevant range of output.

True   ☐

False   ☐

5   The costs of operating the canteen at 'Eat a lot Company' for the past three months is as follows.

Month	Cost £	Employees
1	72,500	1,250
2	75,000	1,300
3	68,750	1,175

Variable cost (per employee per month) =
Fixed cost per month =

Answers to quick quiz

1   The variability of input costs with activity undertaken.

2   Rise

3   (a)   Step cost. Example: rent, supervisors' salaries
     (b)   Variable cost. Example: raw materials, direct labour
     (c)   Semi-variable cost. Example: electricity and telephone
     (d)   Fixed. Example: rent, depreciation (straight-line)

4   True

5   Variable cost = £50 per employee per month
     Fixed costs = £10,000 per month

	Activity	Cost £
High	1,300	75,000
Low	1,175	68,750
	125	6,250

Variable cost per employee = £6,250/125 = £50

For 1,175 employees, total cost = £68,750

Total cost	= variable cost + fixed cost
£68,750	= (1,175 × £50) + fixed cost
∴ Fixed cost	= £68,750 − £58,750
	= £10,000

Now try the question below from the Exam Question Bank

Number	Level	Marks	Time
Q2	Introductory	n/a	15 mins

BPP PUBLISHING

Chapter 3

MATERIAL COSTS

Topic list	Syllabus reference	Ability required
1 What is stock control?	(i)	Comprehension
2 The ordering, receipt and issue of raw materials	(i)	Comprehension
3 The storage of raw materials	(i)	Comprehension
4 Stock control levels	(i)	Comprehension, application
5 Stock valuation	(i)	Comprehension, application
6 FIFO (first in, first out)	(i)	Comprehension, application
7 LIFO (last in, first out)	(i)	Comprehension, application
8 Cumulative weighted average pricing	(i)	Comprehension, application
9 Other methods of pricing and valuation	(i)	-
10 Stock valuation and profitability	(i)	Comprehension, application

Introduction

The investment in stock is a very important one for most businesses, both in terms of monetary value and relationships with customers (no stock, no sale, loss of customer goodwill). It is therefore vital that management establish and maintain an **effective stock control system** and that they are aware of the major costing problem relating to materials, that of pricing materials issues and valuing stock at the end of each period.

The first half of this chapter will concentrate on a **stock control system** for materials, but similar problems and considerations apply to all forms of stock. In the second half of the chapter we will consider the methods for **pricing materials issues/valuing stock**. We will look at the various methods, their advantages and disadvantages and their impact on profitability.

Learning outcomes covered in this chapter

- **Explain** raw material accounting and control procedures
- **Explain** and **calculate** reorder quantity, reorder level, maximum stock, minimum stock and economic order quantity
- **Explain** FIFO, LIFO and weighted average stock valuation methods
- **Calculate** stock, cost of sales and gross profit under LIFO, FIFO and weighted average

Syllabus content covered in this chapter

- Materials: accounting and control procedures
- Materials: reorder quantity, reorder level, maximum stock, minimum stock, economic order quantity

1 WHAT IS STOCK CONTROL?

1.1 The stocks held in any organisation can generally be classified under four main headings.

- Raw materials
- Work in progress
- Spare parts/consumables
- Finished goods

Not all organisations will have stock of all four general categories.

1.2 This chapter will concentrate on a **stock control system** for materials, but similar problems and considerations apply to all forms of stock. Controls should cover the following functions.

- The **ordering** of stock
- The **purchase** of stock
- The **receipt** of goods into store
- **Storage**
- The **issue** of stock and maintenance of stock at the most appropriate level

Qualitative aspects of stock control

1.3 We may wish to **control stock** for the following reasons.

- Holding costs of stock may be expensive.
- Production will be disrupted if we run out of raw materials.
- Unused stock with a short shelf life may incur unnecessary expenses.

1.4 If manufactured goods are made out of low quality materials, the end product will be of low quality also. It may therefore be necessary to control the quality of stock, in order to maintain a good reputation with consumers.

2 THE ORDERING, RECEIPT AND ISSUE OF RAW MATERIALS

Ordering and receiving materials

2.1 Proper records must be kept of the physical procedures for ordering and receiving a consignment of materials to ensure the following.

- That enough stock is held
- That there is no duplication of ordering
- That quality is maintained
- That there is adequate record keeping for accounts purposes

A typical series of procedures might be as follows.

(a) Current stocks run down to the level where a reorder is required. The stores department issues a **purchase requisition** which is sent to the purchasing department, authorising the department to order further stock. An example of a purchase requisition is shown below.

```
┌─────────────────────────────────────────────────────────────────────┐
│              PURCHASE REQUISITION   Req. No.                          │
│                                                                       │
│  Department/job number:                      Date                     │
│  Suggested Supplier:                                                   │
│                                                                       │
│                                          Requested by:                │
│                                          Latest date required:        │
├──────────┬─────────┬──────────────────────┬───────────────────┤
│          │ Code    │                      │   Estimated Cost  │
│ Quantity │ number  │    Description       ├──────────┬────────┤
│          │         │                      │   Unit   │   £    │
│          │         │                      │          │        │
│          │         │                      │          │        │
│          │         │                      │          │        │
│          │         │                      │          │        │
├──────────┴─────────┴──────────────────────┴──────────┴────────┤
│ Authorised signature:                                                 │
└─────────────────────────────────────────────────────────────────────┘
```

(b) The purchasing department draws a **purchase order** which is sent to the supplier. (The supplier may be asked to return an acknowledgement copy as confirmation of his acceptance of the order.) Copies of the purchase order must be sent to the accounts department and the storekeeper (or receiving department).

```
┌────────────────────────────────────────────────────────┐
│  Purchase Order/Confirmation                            │
│                                                         │
│                                                         │
│  Our Order Ref:            Date                         │
│  To                                                     │
│  ┌(Address)              ┐   Please deliver to the above address │
│                              Ordered by:                │
│                              Passed and checked by:     │
│                              Total Order Value £        │
│  └                      ┘                               │
├──────┬──────┬──────────────────┬──────────┬──────────┤
│      │      │                  │          │          │
│      │      │                  │          │          │
│      │      │                  │          │          │
│      │      │                  │          │          │
│      │      │                  │          │          │
│      │      │     Subtotal     │          │          │
│      │      │     VAT          │          │          │
│      │      │     ( @ 17.5%)   │          │          │
│      │      │     Total        │          │          │
└──────┴──────┴──────────────────┴──────────┴──────────┘
```

(c) The purchasing department may have to obtain a number of quotations if either a new stock line is required, the existing supplier's costs are too high or the existing supplier no longer stocks the goods needed. Trade discounts (reduction in the price per unit given to some customers) should be negotiated where possible.

(d) The supplier delivers the consignment of materials, and the storekeeper signs a **delivery note** for the carrier. The packages must then be checked against the copy of the purchase order, to ensure that the supplier has delivered the types and quantities of materials which were ordered. (Discrepancies would be referred to the purchasing department.)

(e) If the delivery is acceptable, the storekeeper prepares a **goods received note (GRN)**, an example of which is shown below.

```
┌─────────────────────────────────────────────────────────────┐
│                                          WAREHOUSE COPY        │
│        GOODS RECEIVED NOTE                  NO  5565           │
│  DATE: _ _ _ _ _ _ _ _ _ _ _ _ _. TIME: _ _ _ _ _ _ _ _ _ _ _ │
│                                          WAREHOUSE A          │
│  OUR ORDER NO: _ _ _ _ _ _ _ _ _ _ _ _ _ _ _ _ _ _ _ _ _ _ _. │
│  SUPPLIER AND SUPPLIER'S ADVICE NOTE NO: _ _ _ _ _ _ _ _ _ _ _.│
├─────────────┬───────────┬───────────────────────────────────┤
│  QUANTITY   │  CAT NO   │  DESCRIPTION                        │
│             │           │                                     │
│             │           │                                     │
│             │           │                                     │
│             │           │                                     │
│             │           │                                     │
│             │           │                                     │
├─────────────┴───────────┴───────────────────────────────────┤
│  RECEIVED IN GOOD CONDITION:                     (INITIALS)   │
└─────────────────────────────────────────────────────────────┘
```

(f)   A copy of the **GRN** is sent to the accounts department, where it is matched with the copy of the purchase order. The supplier's invoice is checked against the purchase order and GRN, and the necessary steps are taken to pay the supplier. The invoice may contain details relating to discounts such as trade discounts, quantity discounts (order in excess of a specified amount) and settlement discounts (payment received within a specified number of days).

Question 1

What are the possible consequences of a failure of control over ordering and receipt of materials?

Answer

(a)   Incorrect materials being delivered, disrupting operations
(b)   Incorrect prices being paid
(c)   Deliveries other than at the specified time (causing disruption)
(d)   Insufficient control over quality
(e)   Invoiced amounts differing from quantities of goods actually received or prices agreed

You may, of course, have thought of equally valid consequences.

Issue of materials

2.2   Materials can only be issued against a **materials/stores requisition**. This document must record not only the quantity of goods issued, but also the cost centre or the job number for which the requisition is being made. The materials requisition note may also have a column, to be filled in by the cost department, for recording the cost or value of the materials issued to the cost centre or job.

	Materials requisition note			
Date required _ _ _ _ _ _ _ _ .		Cost centre No/ Job No _ _ _ _ _ _ _ _ _ _ _ .		
Quantity	Item code	Description		£
Signature of requisitioning Manager/ Foreman _			Date _ _ _ _ _ _	

Materials transfers and returns

2.3 Where materials, having been issued to one job or cost centre, are later transferred to a different job or cost centre, without first being returned to stores, a **materials transfer note** should be raised. Such a note must show not only the job receiving the transfer, but also the job from which it is transferred. This enables the appropriate charges to be made to jobs or cost centres.

2.4 Material returns must also be documented on a **materials returned note**. This document is the 'reverse' of a requisition note, and must contain similar information. In fact it will often be almost identical to a requisition note. It will simply have a different title and perhaps be a distinctive colour, such as red, to highlight the fact that materials are being returned.

Impact of computerisation

2.5 Many stock control systems these days are computerised. Computerised stock control systems vary greatly, but most will have the features outlined below.

(a) **Data must be input into the system**. For example, details of goods received may simply be written on to a GRN for later entry into the computer system. Alternatively, this information may be keyed in directly to the computer: a GRN will be printed and then signed as evidence of the transaction, so that both the warehouse and the supplier can have a hard copy record in case of dispute. Some systems may incorporate the use of devices such as bar code readers.

Other types of transaction which will need to be recorded include the following.

(i) **Transfers** between different categories of stock (for example from work in progress to finished goods)

(ii) **Despatch**, resulting from a sale, of items of finished goods to customers

(iii) **Adjustments** to stock records if the amount of stock revealed in a physical stock count differs from the amount appearing on the stock records

(b) **A stock master file is maintained**. This file will contain details for every category of stock and will be updated for new stock lines. A database file may be maintained.

Question 2

What type of information do you think should be held on a stock master file?

Answer

Here are some examples.

(a) Stock code number, for reference
(b) Brief description of stock item
(c) Reorder level
(d) Reorder quantity
(e) Cost per unit
(f) Selling price per unit (if finished goods)
(g) Amount in stock
(h) Frequency of usage

The file may also hold details of stock movements over a period, but this will depend on the type of system in operation. In a **batch system**, transactions will be grouped and input in one operation and details of the movements may be held in a separate transactions file, the master file updated in total only. In an **on-line system**, transactions may be input directly to the master file, where the record of movements is thus likely to be found. Such a system will mean that the stock records are constantly up to date, which will help in monitoring and controlling stock.

The system may generate orders automatically once the amount in stock has fallen to the reorder level.

(c) **The system will generate outputs**. These may include, depending on the type of system, any of the following.

   (i) **Hard copy** records, for example a printed GRN, of transactions entered into the system.

   (ii) Output on a **VDU** screen in response to an enquiry (for example the current level of a particular line of stock, or details of a particular transaction).

   (iii) Various **printed reports**, devised to fit in with the needs of the organisation. These may include stock movement reports, detailing over a period the movements on all stock lines, listings of GRNs, despatch notes and so forth.

2.6 A computerised stock control system is usually able to give more up to date information and more flexible reporting than a manual system but remember that both manual and computer based stock control systems need the same types of data to function properly.

3 THE STORAGE OF RAW MATERIALS

3.1 Storekeeping involves storing materials to achieve the following objectives.

- Speedy **issue** and **receipt** of materials
- Full **identification** of all materials at all times
- Correct **location** of all materials at all times
- **Protection** of materials from damage and deterioration
- Provision of **secure stores** to avoid pilferage, theft and fire
- **Efficient** use of storage space
- **Maintenance** of correct stock levels
- Keeping correct and up-to-date **records** of receipts, issues and stock levels

Recording stock levels

3.2 One of the objectives of storekeeping is to maintain accurate records of current stock levels. This involves the accurate recording of stock movements (issues from and receipts into stores). The most frequently encountered system for recording stock movements is the use of bin cards and stores ledger accounts.

Bin cards

3.3 A **bin card** shows the level of stock of an item at a particular stores location. It is kept with the actual stock and is updated by the storekeeper as stocks are received and issued. A typical bin card is shown below.

Bin card

Part code no _ _ _ _ _ _ _ _ _ _ _ _ _ _ _ _			Location _ .			
Bin number _ _ _ _ _ _ _ _ _ _ _ _ _ _ _ _ _			Stores ledger no _ _ _ _ _ _ _ _ _ _ _ _ _ _ _ _ _ _ _			
Receipts			*Issues*			Stock balance
Date	Quantity	G.R.N. No.	Date	Quantity	Req. No.	

The use of bin cards is decreasing, partly due to the difficulty in keeping them updated and partly due to the merging of stock recording and control procedures, frequently using computers.

Stores ledger accounts

3.4 A typical stores ledger account is shown below. Note that it shows the value of stock.

Stores ledger account

Material _ _ _ _ _ _ _ _ _ _ _ _ _ _ _ _ _ _ .				Maximum Quantity _ _ _ _ _ _ _ _ _ _ _ _ _ _ _						
Code _				Minimum Quantity _ _ _ _ _ _ _ _ _ _ _ _ _ _						
Date	Receipts			Issues				Stock		
	G.R.N. No.	Quantity	Unit Price £	Amount £	Stores Req. No.	Quantity	Unit Price £	Amount £	Quantity	Unit Price £	Amount £

3.5 The above illustration shows a card for a manual system, but even when the stock records are computerised, the same type of information is normally included in the computer file. The running balance on the stores ledger account allows stock levels and valuation to be monitored.

Free stock

3.6 Managers need to know the **free stock balance** in order to obtain a full picture of the current stock position of an item. Free stock represents what is really **available for future use** and is calculated as follows.

Materials in stock	X
+ Materials on order from suppliers	X
− Materials requisitioned, not yet issued	(X)
Free stock balance	X

3.7 Knowledge of the level of physical stock assists stock issuing, stocktaking and controlling maximum and minimum stock levels: knowledge of the level of free stock assists ordering.

Question 3

A wholesaler has 8,450 units outstanding for Part X100 on existing customers' orders; there are 3,925 units in stock and the calculated free stock is 5,525 units.

How many units does the wholesaler have on order with his supplier?

A 9,450   B 10,050   C 13,975   D 17,900

Answer

Free stock balance	=	units in stock + units on order – units ordered, but not yet issued
5,525	=	3,925 + units on order – 8,450
Units on order	=	10,050

The correct answer is B.

Identification of materials: stock codes (materials codes)

3.8 Materials held in stores are **coded** and **classified**. Advantages of using code numbers to identify materials are as follows.

(a) Ambiguity is avoided.

(b) Time is saved. Descriptions can be lengthy and time-consuming.

(c) Production efficiency is improved. The correct material can be accurately identified from a code number.

(d) Computerised processing is made easier.

(e) Numbered code systems can be designed to be flexible, and can be expanded to include more stock items as necessary.

The digits in a code can stand for the type of stock, supplier, department and so forth.

Stocktaking

3.9 Stocktaking involves counting the physical stock on hand at a certain date, and then checking this against the balance shown in the stock records. There are two methods of carrying out this process, **periodic stocktaking** and **continuous stocktaking**.

> **KEY TERMS**
>
> - **Periodic stocktaking** is a 'process whereby all stock items are physically counted and valued at a set point in time, usually at the end of an accounting period' (CIMA *Official Terminology*).
>
> - **Continuous stocktaking** is 'the process of counting and valuing selected items at different times on a rotating basis' (CIMA *Official Terminology*). This involves a specialist team counting and checking a number of stock items each day, so that each item is checked at least once a year. Valuable items or items with a high turnover could be checked more frequently.

3.10 The **advantages of continuous stocktaking compared to periodic stocktaking** are as follows.

    (a) The annual stocktaking is unnecessary and the disruption it causes is avoided.

    (b) Regular skilled stocktakers can be employed, reducing likely errors.

    (c) More time is available, reducing errors and allowing investigation.

    (d) Deficiencies and losses are revealed sooner than they would be if stocktaking were limited to an annual check.

    (e) Production hold-ups are eliminated because the stores staff are at no time so busy as to be unable to deal with material issues to production departments.

    (f) Staff morale is improved and standards raised.

    (g) Control over stock levels is improved, and there is less likelihood of overstocking or running out of stock.

Stock discrepancies

3.11 There will be occasions when stock checks disclose discrepancies between the physical amount of an item in stock and the amount shown in the stock records. When this occurs, the cause of the discrepancy should be investigated, and appropriate action taken to ensure that it does not happen again.

Perpetual inventory

3.12 **A perpetual inventory system involves recording every receipt and issue of stock as it occurs on bin cards and stores ledger accounts.** This means that there is a continuous record of the balance of each item of stock. The balance on the stores ledger account therefore represents the stock on hand and this balance is used in the calculation of closing stock in monthly and annual accounts. In practice, physical stocks may not agree with recorded stocks and therefore continuous stocktaking is necessary to ensure that the perpetual inventory system is functioning correctly and that minor stock discrepancies are corrected.

Obsolete, deteriorating and slow-moving stocks and wastage

3.13 **Obsolete stocks are those items which have become out-of-date and are no longer required.** Obsolete items are written off to the profit and loss account and disposed of.

3.14 Stock items may be wasted because, for example, they get broken. All **wastage** should be noted on the stock records immediately so that physical stock equals the stock balance on records and the cost of the wastage written off to the profit and loss account.

3.15 **Slow-moving stocks are stock items which are likely to take a long time to be used up.** For example, 5,000 units are in stock, and only 20 are being used each year. This is often caused by overstocking. Managers should investigate such stock items and, if it is felt that the usage rate is unlikely to increase, excess stock should be written off as for obsolete stock, leaving perhaps four or five years' supply in stock.

4 STOCK CONTROL LEVELS

Why hold stock?

4.1 The costs of purchasing stock are usually one of the largest costs faced by an organisation and, once obtained, stock has to be carefully controlled and checked.

4.2 The main reasons for holding stocks can be summarised as follows.

- To ensure sufficient goods are available to meet expected demand
- To provide a buffer between processes
- To meet any future shortages
- To take advantage of bulk purchasing discounts
- To absorb seasonal fluctuations and any variations in usage and demand
- To allow production processes to flow smoothly and efficiently
- As a necessary part of the production process (such as when maturing cheese)
- As a deliberate investment policy, especially in times of inflation or possible shortages

Holding costs

4.3 If stocks are too high, **holding costs** will be incurred unnecessarily. Such costs occur for a number of reasons.

(a) **Costs of storage and stores operations.** Larger stocks require more storage space and possibly extra staff and equipment to control and handle them.

(b) **Interest charges.** Holding stocks involves the tying up of capital (cash) on which interest must be paid.

(c) **Insurance costs.** The larger the value of stocks held, the greater insurance premiums are likely to be.

(d) **Risk of obsolescence.** The longer a stock item is held, the greater is the risk of obsolescence.

(e) **Deterioration.** When materials in store deteriorate to the extent that they are unusable, they must be thrown away with the likelihood that disposal costs would be incurred.

Costs of obtaining stock

4.4 On the other hand, if stocks are kept low, small quantities of stock will have to be ordered more frequently, thereby increasing the following **ordering or procurement costs**.

(a) **Clerical and administrative costs** associated with purchasing, accounting for and receiving goods

(b) **Transport costs**

(c) **Production run costs**, for stock which is manufactured internally rather than purchased from external sources

Stockout costs

4.5 An additional type of cost which may arise if stocks are kept too low is the type associated with running out of stock. There are a number of causes of **stockout costs**.

- Lost contribution from lost sales
- Loss of future sales due to disgruntled customers

- Loss of customer goodwill
- Cost of production stoppages
- Labour frustration over stoppages
- Extra costs of urgent, small quantity, replenishment orders

Objective of stock control

4.6 The overall objective of stock control is, therefore, to maintain stock levels so that the total of the following costs is minimised.

- Holding costs
- Ordering costs
- Stockout costs

Stock control levels

4.7 Based on an analysis of past stock usage and delivery times, a series of control levels can be calculated and used to maintain stocks at their optimum level (in other words, a level which minimises costs). These levels will determine 'when to order' and 'how many to order'.

(a) **Reorder level**. When stocks reach this level, an order should be placed to replenish stocks. The reorder level is determined by consideration of the following.

- The maximum rate of consumption
- The maximum lead time

The maximum lead time is the time between placing an order with a supplier, and the stock becoming available for use

FORMULA TO LEARN

Reorder level = maximum usage × maximum lead time

(b) **Minimum level**. This is a warning level to draw management attention to the fact that stocks are approaching a dangerously low level and that stockouts are possible.

FORMULA TO LEARN

Minimum level = reorder level – (average usage × average lead time)

(c) **Maximum level**. This also acts as a warning level to signal to management that stocks are reaching a potentially wasteful level.

FORMULA TO LEARN

Maximum level = reorder level + reorder quantity – (minimum usage × minimum lead time)

Question 4

A large retailer with multiple outlets maintains a central warehouse from which the outlets are supplied. The following information is available for Part Number SF525.

Average usage   350 per day
Minimum usage   180 per day
Maximum usage   420 per day
Lead time for replenishment   11-15 days
Re-order quantity   6,500 units
Re-order level   6,300 units

(a) Based on the data above, what is the maximum level of stock?

    A 5,250   B 6,500   C 10,820   D 12,800

(b) Based on the data above, what is the approximate number of Part Number SF525 carried as buffer stock?

    A 200   B 720   C 1,680   D 1,750

Answer

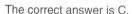

(a) Maximum stock level = reorder level + reorder quantity − (min usage × min lead time)
                          = 6,300 + 6,500 − (180 × 11)
                          = 10,820

The correct answer is C.

Using good MCQ technique, if you were resorting to a guess you should have eliminated option A. The maximum stock level cannot be less than the reorder quantity.

(b) Buffer stock   = minimum level

Minimum level = reorder level − (average usage × average lead time)
              = 6,300 − (350 × 13) = 1,750.

The correct answer is D.

Option A could again be easily eliminated. With minimum usage of 180 per day, a buffer stock of only 200 would not be much of a buffer!

(d) **Reorder quantity**. This is the quantity of stock which is to be ordered when stock reaches the reorder level. If it is set so as to minimise the total costs associated with holding and ordering stock, then it is known as the economic order quantity.

(e) **Average stock**. The formula for the average stock level assumes that stock levels fluctuate evenly between the minimum (or safety) stock level and the highest possible stock level (the amount of stock immediately after an order is received, ie safety stock + reorder quantity).

FORMULA TO LEARN

Average stock = safety stock + ½ reorder quantity

Question 5

A component has a safety stock of 500, a re-order quantity of 3,000 and a rate of demand which varies between 200 and 700 per week. The average stock is approximately

A 2,000   B 2,300   C 2,500   D 3,500

Answer

Average stock	= safety stock + ½ reorder quantity
	= 500 + (0.5 × 3,000)
	= 2,000

The correct answer is A.

Economic order quantity (EOQ)

4.8 **Economic order theory assumes that the average stock held is equal to one half of the reorder quantity** (although as we saw in the last section, if an organisation maintains some sort of buffer or safety stock then average stock = buffer stock + half of the reorder quantity). We have seen that there are certain costs associated with holding stock. These costs tend to increase with the level of stocks, and so could be reduced by ordering smaller amounts from suppliers each time.

4.9 On the other hand, as we have seen, there are costs associated with ordering from suppliers: documentation, telephone calls, payment of invoices, receiving goods into stores and so on. These costs tend to increase if small orders are placed, because a larger number of orders would then be needed for a given annual demand.

4.10 Suppose a company purchases raw material at a cost of £16 per unit. The annual demand for the raw material is 25,000 units. The holding cost per unit is £6.40 and the cost of placing an order is £32.

4.11 We can tabulate the annual relevant costs for various order quantities as follows.

Order quantity (units)		100	200	300	400	500	600	800	1,000
Average stock (units)	(a)	50	100	150	200	250	300	400	500
Number of orders	(b)	250	125	83	63	50	42	31	25
		£	£	£	£	£	£	£	£
Annual holding cost	(c)	320	640	960	1,280	1,600	1,920	2,560	3,200
Annual order cost	(d)	8,000	4,000	2,656	2,016	1,600	1,344	992	800
Total relevant cost		8,320	4,640	3,616	3,296	3,200	3,264	3,552	4,000

Notes

(a) Average stock = Order quantity ÷ 2 (ie assuming no safety stock)
(b) Number of orders = annual demand ÷ order quantity
(c) Annual holding cost = Average stock × £6.40
(d) Annual order cost = Number of orders × £32

4.12 You will see that the economic order quantity is 500 units. At this point the total annual relevant costs are at a minimum.

4.13 We can present the information tabulated in Paragraph 4.11 in graphical form. The vertical axis represents the relevant annual costs for the investment in stocks, and the horizontal axis can be used to represent either the various order quantities or the average stock levels; two scales are actually shown on the horizontal axis so that both items can be incorporated. The graph shows that, as the average stock level and order quantity increase, the holding cost increases. On the other hand, the ordering costs decline as stock levels and order quantities increase. The total cost line represents the sum of both the holding and the ordering costs.

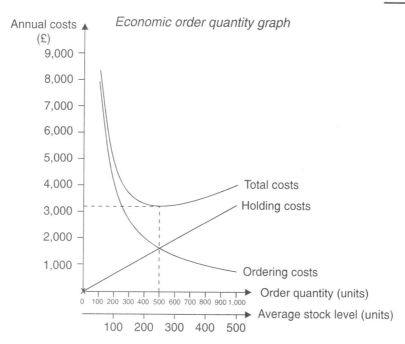

Economic order quantity graph

4.14 Note that the total cost line is at a minimum for an order quantity of 500 units and occurs at the point where the ordering cost curve and holding cost curve intersect. **The EOQ is therefore found at the point where holding costs equal ordering costs.**

4.15 There is also a formula for the EOQ. Note that this is the *only* formula that will be provided in your examination for this paper.

EXAM FORMULA

$$EOQ = \sqrt{\frac{2C_0D}{Ch}}$$

where
- Ch = cost of holding one unit of stock for one time period
- C_0 = cost of ordering a consignment from a supplier
- D = demand during the time period

Question 6

Calculate the EOQ using the formula and the information in Paragraph 4.10.

Answer

$$EOQ = \sqrt{\frac{2 \times £32 \times 25,000}{£6.40}}$$

$$= \sqrt{250,000}$$

$$= 500 \text{ units}$$

Other systems of stores control and reordering

4.16 (a) **Under the order cycling method, quantities on hand of each stores item are reviewed periodically** (every 1, 2 or 3 months). For low-cost items, a technique called the 90-60-30 day technique can be used, so that when stocks fall to 60 days' supply, a fresh order is placed for a 30 days' supply so as to boost stocks to 90 days' supply. For high-cost items, a more stringent stores control procedure is advisable so as to keep down the costs of stock holding.

(b) **The two-bin system of stores control (or visual method of control) is one whereby each stores item is kept in two storage bins.** When the first bin is emptied, an order must be placed for re-supply; the second bin will contain sufficient quantities to last until the fresh delivery is received. This is a simple system which is not costly to operate but it is not based on any formal analysis of stock usage and may result in the holding of too much or too little stock.

(c) **Materials items may be classified as expensive, inexpensive or in a middle-cost range.** Because of the practical advantages of simplifying stores control procedures without incurring unnecessary high costs, it may be possible to segregate materials for selective stores control.

  (i) Expensive and medium-cost materials are subject to careful stores control procedures to minimise cost.

  (ii) Inexpensive materials can be stored in large quantities because the cost savings from careful stores control do not justify the administrative effort required to implement the control.

  This selective approach to stores control is sometimes called the **ABC method** whereby materials are classified A, B or C according to their expense-group A being the expensive, group B the medium-cost and group C the inexpensive materials.

(d) A similar selective approach to stores control is the **Pareto (80/20) distribution** is based on the finding that in many stores, 80% of the value of stores is accounted for by only 20% of the stores items, and stocks of these more expensive items should be controlled more closely.

5 STOCK VALUATION

5.1 You may be aware from your studies for the Financial Accounting Fundamentals paper that, for financial accounting purposes, stocks are valued at the **lower of cost and net realisable value**. In practice, stocks will probably be valued at cost in the stores records throughout the course of an accounting period. Only when the period ends will the value of the stock in hand be reconsidered so that items with a net realisable value below their original cost will be revalued downwards, and the stock records altered accordingly.

Charging units of stock to cost of production or cost of sales

5.2 It is important to be able to distinguish between the way in which the physical items in stock are actually issued. In practice a storekeeper may issue goods in the following way.

- The oldest goods first
- The latest goods received first
- Randomly
- Those which are easiest to reach

5.3 By comparison the cost of the goods issued must be determined on a **consistently applied basis,** and must ignore the likelihood that the materials issued will be costed at a price different to the amount paid for them.

5.4 This may seem a little confusing at first, and it may be helpful to explain the point further. Suppose that there are three units of a particular material in stock.

Units	Date received	Purchase cost
A	June 20X1	£100
B	July 20X1	£106
C	August 20X1	£109

In September, one unit is issued to production. As it happened, the physical unit actually issued was B. The accounting department must put a value or cost on the material issued, but the value would not be the cost of B, £106. The principles used to value the materials issued are not concerned with the actual unit issued, A, B, or C. Nevertheless, the accountant may choose to make one of the following assumptions.

(a) The unit issued is valued as though it were the earliest unit in stock, ie at the purchase cost of A, £100. This valuation principle is called **FIFO**, or **first in, first out**.

(b) The unit issued is valued as though it were the most recent unit received into stock, ie at the purchase cost of C, £109. This method of valuation is **LIFO**, or **last in, first out**.

(c) The unit issued is valued at an average price of A, B and C, ie £105.

5.5 In the following sections we will consider each of the pricing methods detailed above (and a few more), using the following transactions to illustrate the principles in each case.

TRANSACTIONS DURING MAY 20X3

	Quantity	Unit cost	Total cost	Market value per unit on date of transaction
	Units	£	£	£
Opening balance, 1 May	100	2.00	200	
Receipts, 3 May	400	2.10	840	2.11
Issues, 4 May	200			2.11
Receipts, 9 May	300	2.12	636	2.15
Issues, 11 May	400			2.20
Receipts, 18 May	100	2.40	240	2.35
Issues, 20 May	100			2.35
Closing balance, 31 May	200			2.38
			1,916	

6 FIFO (FIRST IN, FIRST OUT)

6.1 **FIFO assumes that materials are issued out of stock in the order in which they were delivered into stock:** issues are priced at the cost of the earliest delivery remaining in stock.

Using **FIFO**, the cost of issues and the closing stock value in the example would be as follows.

Date of issue	Quantity issued	Value	£	£
	Units			
4 May	200	100 o/s at £2	200	
		100 at £2.10	210	
				410
11 May	400	300 at £2.10	630	
		100 at £2.12	212	
				842
20 May	100	100 at £2.12		212
Cost of issues				1,464
Closing stock value	200	100 at £2.12	212	
		100 at £2.40	240	
				452
				1,916

Notes

(a) The cost of materials issued plus the value of closing stock equals the cost of purchases plus the value of opening stock (£1,916).

(b) The market price of purchased materials is rising dramatically. In a period of inflation, there is a tendency with FIFO for materials to be issued at a cost lower than the current market value, although closing stocks tend to be valued at a cost approximating to current market value.

6.2   The advantages and disadvantages of the **FIFO** method are as follows.

Advantages	Disadvantages
It is a logical pricing method which probably represents what is physically happening: in practice the oldest stock is likely to be used first.	FIFO can be cumbersome to operate because of the need to identify each batch of material separately.
It is easy to understand and explain to managers.	Managers may find it difficult to compare costs and make decisions when they are charged with varying prices for the same materials.
The stock valuation can be near to a valuation based on replacement cost.	In a period of high inflation, stock issue prices will lag behind current market value.

Question 7

Draw up an extract from a stores ledger account using the columns shown below. Complete the columns in as much details as possible using the information in Paragraphs 5.5 and 6.1.

	STORES LEDGER ACCOUNT											
Date	Receipts				Issues				Stock			
	GRN No	Quantity	Unit price £	Amount £	Stores Req No	Quantity	Unit price £	Amount £	Quantity	Unit price £	Amount £

Answer

	Receipts			Issues				Stock		
Date	GRN No.	Quantity	Unit price £	Amount £	Stores Req. No.	Quantity	Unit price £	Amount £	Quantity	Unit price £	Amount £

STORES LEDGER ACCOUNT (extract)

Date	GRN No.	Quantity	Unit price £	Amount £	Stores Req. No.	Quantity	Unit price £	Amount £	Quantity	Unit price £	Amount £
1.5.X3									100	2.00	200.00
3.5.X3		400	2.10	840.00					100	2.00	200.00
									400	2.10	840.00
									500		1,040.00
4.5.X3						100	2.00	200.00			
						100	2.10	210.00	300	2.10	630.00
9.5.X3		300	2.12	636.00					300	2.10	630.00
									300	2.12	636.00
									600		1,266.00
11.5.X3						300	2.10	630.00			
						100	2.12	212.00	200	2.12	424.00
18.5.X3		100	2.40	240.00					200	2.12	424.00
									100	2.40	240.00
									300		664.00
20.5.X3						100	2.12	212.00	100	2.12	212.00
									100	2.40	240.00
31.5.X3									200		452.00

7 LIFO (LAST IN, FIRST OUT)

7.1 **LIFO assumes that materials are issued out of stock in the reverse order to which they were delivered:** the most recent deliveries are issued before earlier ones, and are priced accordingly.

Using LIFO, the cost of issues and the closing stock value in the example above would be as follows.

Date of 000issue	Quantity issued Units	Valuation	£	£
4 May	200	200 at £2.10		420
11 May	400	300 at £2.12	636	
		100 at £2.10	210	
				846
20 May	100	100 at £2.40		240
Cost of issues				1,506
Closing stock value	200	100 at £2.10	210	
		100 at £2.00	200	
				410
				1,916

Notes

(a) The cost of materials issued plus the value of closing stock equals the cost of purchases plus the value of opening stock (£1,916).

(b) In a period of inflation there is a tendency with **LIFO** for the following to occur.

43

(i)   Materials are issued at a price which approximates to current market value.

(ii)   Closing stocks become undervalued when compared to market value.

7.2   The advantages and disadvantages of the **LIFO** method are as follows.

Advantages	Disadvantages
Stocks are issued at a price which is close to current market value.	The method can be cumbersome to operate because it sometimes results in several batches being only part-used in the stock records before another batch is received.
Managers are continually aware of recent costs when making decisions, because the costs being charged to their department or products will be current costs.	LIFO is often the opposite to what is physically happening and can therefore be difficult to explain to managers.
	As with FIFO, decision making can be difficult because of the variations in prices.

8   CUMULATIVE WEIGHTED AVERAGE PRICING

8.1   The cumulative weighted average pricing method calculates a **weighted average price** for all units in stock. Issues are priced at this average cost, and the balance of stock remaining would have the same unit valuation. The average price is determined by dividing the total cost by the total number of units.

A new weighted average price is calculated whenever a new delivery of materials into store is received. This is the key feature of cumulative weighted average pricing.

8.2   In our example, issue costs and closing stock values would be as follows.

Date	Received Units	Issued Units	Balance Units	Total stock value £	Unit cost £	£
Opening stock			100	200	2.00	
3 May	400			840	2.10	
			* 500	1,040	2.08	
4 May		200		(416)	2.08	416
			300	624	2.08	
9 May	300			636	2.12	
			* 600	1,260	2.10	
11 May		400		(840)	2.10	840
			200	420	2.10	
18 May	100			240	2.40	
			* 300	660	2.20	
20 May		100		(220)	2.20	220
						1,476
Closing stock value			200	440	2.20	440
						1,916

* A new stock value per unit is calculated whenever a new receipt of materials occurs.

Notes

(a)   The cost of materials issued plus the value of closing stock equals the cost of purchases plus the value of opening stock (£1,916).

(b)   In a period of inflation, using the cumulative weighted average pricing system, the value of material issues will rise gradually, but will tend to lag a little behind the current market value at the date of issue. Closing stock values will also be a little below current market value.

8.3 The advantages and disadvantages of **cumulative weighted average pricing** are these.

Advantages	Disadvantages
Fluctuations in prices are smoothed out, making it easier to use the data for decision making.	The resulting issue price is rarely an actual price that has been paid, and can run to several decimal places.
It is easier to administer than FIFO and LIFO, because there is no need to identify each batch separately.	Prices tend to lag a little behind current market values when there is gradual inflation.

9 OTHER METHODS OF PRICING AND VALUATION

Periodic weighted average pricing

9.1 Under the periodic weighted average pricing method, a retrospective average price is calculated for *all* materials issued during the period. The average issue price is calculated for our example as follows.

$$\frac{\text{Cost of all receipts in the period } + \text{ Cost of opening stock}}{\text{Number of units received in the period } + \text{ Number of units of opening stock}} = \frac{£1,716 + £200}{800 + 100}$$

Issue price = £2.129 per unit

Closing stock values are a balancing figure.

9.2 The issue costs and closing stock values are calculated as follows.

Date of issue	Quantity issued	Valuation
	Units	£
4 May	200 × £2.129	426
11 May	400 × £2.129	852
20 May	100 × £2.129	213
Cost of issues		1,491
Value of opening stock plus purchases		1,916
Value of 200 units of closing stock (at £2.129)		425

9.3 The periodic weighted average pricing method is easier to calculate than the cumulative weighted average method, and therefore requires less effort, but it must be applied retrospectively since the costs of materials used cannot be calculated until the end of the period.

Standard cost pricing

9.4 **Under the standard cost pricing method, all issues are at predetermined standard price.** Such a method is used with a system of standard costing, which will be covered later in this text.

Replacement cost pricing

9.5 Arguments for **replacement cost pricing** include the following.

BPP PUBLISHING

(a) When materials are issued out of stores, they will be replaced with a new delivery; issues should therefore be priced at the current cost to the business of replacing them in stores.

(b) Closing stocks should be valued at current replacement cost in the balance sheet to show the true value of the assets of the business.

9.6 The advantages and disadvantages of **replacement costing** are as follows.

Advantages	Disadvantages
Issues are at up-to-date costs so that managers can take recent trends into account when making decisions based on their knowledge of the costs being incurred.	The price may not be an actual price paid, and a difference will then arise on issues.
It is recommended as a method of accounting for inflation.	It can be difficult to determine the replacement cost.
It is easy to operate once the replacement cost has been determined.	The method is not acceptable to the Inland Revenue or for SSAP 9, although this should not be a major consideration in internal cost accounts.

Question 8

Which pricing method can be used as a practical alternative to replacement cost pricing?

Answer

LIFO is a reasonably accurate method of accounting for inflation provided that closing stock values are periodically reviewed and revalued.

Highest in, first out (HIFO)

9.7 This method values issues at the highest price of the items in stock at the time of issue. Although prudent it is an approach which does not follow any particular chronological order.

Next in, first out (NIFO)

9.8 This method values issues at the price to be paid for the next delivery, which may or may not be the same as replacement cost. This method does value issues at the most up-to-date price but it is administratively difficult.

Specific price

9.9 This method values issues at their individual price and the stock balance is made up of individual items valued at individual prices. It is only really suitable for expensive stock lines where stock holdings and usage rates are low.

10 STOCK VALUATION AND PROFITABILITY

10.1 In the previous descriptions of FIFO, LIFO, average costing and so on, the example used raw materials as an illustration. Each method produced different figures for both the value of closing stocks and also the cost of material issues. Since raw materials costs affect the cost of production, and the cost of production works through eventually into the cost of sales, it follows that different methods of stock valuation will provide different profit figures. The following example will help to illustrate the point.

10.2 EXAMPLE: STOCK VALUATION AND PROFITABILITY

On 1 November 20X2, Delilah's Dresses (Haute Couture Emporium) held 3 pink satin dresses with orange sashes, designed by Freda Swoggs. These were valued at £120 each. During November 20X2, 12 more of the dresses were delivered as follows.

Date	Units received	Purchase cost per dress
10 November	4	£125
20 November	4	£140
25 November	4	£150

A number of the pink satin dresses with orange sashes were sold during November as follows.

Date	Dresses sold	Sales price per dress
14 November	5	£200
21 November	5	£200
28 November	1	£200

Required

Calculate the gross profit (sales – (opening stock + purchases – closing stock)) from selling the pink satin dresses with orange sashes in November 20X2, applying the following principles of stock valuation.

(a) FIFO
(b) LIFO
(c) Cumulative weighted average pricing

10.3 SOLUTION

(a) **FIFO**	Date	Cost of sales	Total £	Closing stock £
	14 November	3 units × £120 + 2 units × £125	610	
	21 November	2 units × £125 + 3 units × £140	670	
	28 November	1 unit × £140	140	
	Closing stock	4 units × £150		600
			1,420	600

(b) **LIFO**

Date	Cost of sales	Total £	Closing stock £
14 November	4 units × £125 + 1 unit × £120		
		620	
21 November	4 units × £140 + 1 unit × £120		
		680	
28 November	1 unit × £150	150	
Closing stock	3 units × £150 + 1 unit × £120		
			570
		1,450	570

(c) **Cumulative weighted average pricing**

		Unit cost £	Balance in stock £	Cost of sales £	Closing stock £
1 November	3	120.00	360		
10 November	4	125.00	500		
	7	122.86	860		
14 November	5	122.86	614	614	
	2		246		
20 November	4	140.00	560		
	6	134.33	806		
21 November	5	134.33	672	672	
	1		134		
25 November	4	150.00	600		
	5	146.80	734		
28 November	1	146.80	147	147	
30 November	4	146.80	587	1,433	587

Profitability	FIFO £	LIFO £	Weighted average £
Opening stock	360	360	360
Purchases	1,660	1,660	1,660
	2,020	2,020	2,020
Closing stock	600	570	587
Cost of sales	1,420	1,450	1,433
Sales (11 × £200)	2,200	2,200	2,200
Gross profit	780	750	767

10.4 In the example above, **different stock valuation methods produced different costs of sale and hence different profits. As opening stock values and purchase costs are the same for each method, the different costs of sale are due to different closing stock valuations. The differences in profits therefore equal the differences in closing stock valuations.**

10.5 The profit differences are only **temporary**. In the example, the opening stock in December 20X2 will be £600, £570 or £587, depending on the stock valuation method used. Different opening stock values will affect the cost of sales and profits in December, so that in the long run, inequalities in costs of sales each month will even themselves out.

Exam focus point

The Pilot paper for **Management Accounting Fundamentals** included two multiple choice questions on topics covered in this chapter (worth a total of 4%).

Firstly candidates were required to value stock issues using the FIFO method and secondly, to calculate an economic order quantity using data supplied in the question.

Stock valuation and stock control levels are likely to be examined in the multiple choice sections of this paper, but look out for these topics in longer questions also.

Chapter roundup

- **Stock control** includes the functions of stock ordering and purchasing, receiving goods into store, storing and issuing stock and controlling the level of stocks.

- Every movement of material in a business should be documented using the following as appropriate: purchase requisition, purchase order, GRN, materials requisition note, materials transfer note and materials returned note.

- **Perpetual inventory** refers to a stock recording system whereby the records (bin cards and stores ledger accounts) are updated for each receipt and issue of stock as it occurs.

- Stocktaking can be carried out on a **continuous** or **periodic** basis.

- **Free stock balance** calculations take account of stock on order from suppliers, and of stock which has been requisitioned but not yet delivered.

- **Stock costs** include purchase costs, holding costs, ordering costs and stockout costs.

- **Stock control levels** can be calculated in order to maintain stocks at the optimum level. The three critical control levels are reorder level, minimum level and maximum level. The economic order quantity is the order quantity which minimises stock costs. The EOQ can be calculated using a table, graph or formula.

- The correct pricing of issues and valuation of stock are of the utmost importance because they have a direct effect on the calculation of profit. Several different methods can be used in practice.

- **FIFO** assumes that materials are issued out of stock in the order in which they were delivered into stock: issues are priced at the cost of the earliest delivery remaining in stock. **LIFO** assumes that materials are issued out of stock in the reverse order to which they were delivered: the most recent deliveries are issued before earlier ones and issues are priced accordingly.

- There are two weighted average methods of pricing: **cumulative weighted average** and **periodic weighted average**.

- Under the **standard costing method**, all issues are at a predetermined standard price.

- Although **replacement costing** is recommended as a method of accounting for inflation, in many instances it is impractical because of the difficulty of maintaining records of replacement market values.

Quick quiz

1 List six objectives of storekeeping.

- ....
- ....
- ....
- ....
- ....
- ....

2 Free stock represents...

3 Free stock is calculated as follows. (Delete as appropriate)

(a)	+ −	Materials in stock	X
(b)	+ −	Materials in order	X
(c)	+ −	Materials requisitioned (not yet issued)	X
		Free stock balance	X

4 How does periodic stocktaking differ from continuous stocktaking?

5 Match up the following.

Reorder level ─────────────► Maximum usage × maximum lead time

Minimum level   Safety stock + $^{1}/_{2}$ reorder level

Maximum level   **?**   Reorder level − (average usage × average lead time)

Average stock   Reorder level + reorder quantity − (minimum usage × minimum lead time)

6 $EOQ = \sqrt{\dfrac{2C_oD}{C_h}}$

Where

(a) C_h = ...

(b) C_o = ...

(c) D = ...

7 Which of the following are true?

I With FIFO, the stock valuation will be very close to replacement cost.

II With LIFO, stocks are issued at a price which is close to the current market value.

III Decision making can be difficult with both FIFO and LIFO because of the variations in prices.

IV A disadvantage of the weighted average method of stock valuation is that the resulting issue price is rarely an actual price that has been paid and it may be calculated to several decimal places.

A I and II only
B I, II and III only
C I and III only
D I, II, III and IV

Answers to quick quiz

1 • Speedy **issue** and **receipt** of materials
 • Full **identification** of all materials at all times
 • Correct **location** of all materials at all times
 • **Protection** of materials from damage and deterioration
 • Provision of **secure stores** to avoid pilferage, theft and fire
 • **Efficient** use of storage space
 • **Maintenance** of correct stock levels
 • Keeping correct and up-to-date **records** of receipts, issues and stock levels

2 Stock that is readily available for future use.

3 (a) +
 (b) +
 (c) –

4 **Periodic stocktaking.** All stock items physically counted and valued, usually annually.

 Continuous stocktaking. Counting and valuing selected items at different times of the year (at least once a year).

5
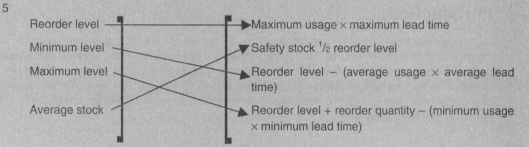

Reorder level — Maximum usage × maximum lead time

Minimum level — Safety stock $^1/_2$ reorder level

Maximum level — Reorder level – (average usage × average lead time)

Average stock — Reorder level + reorder quantity – (minimum usage × minimum lead time)

6 (a) Cost of holding one unit of stock for one time period
 (b) Cost of ordering a consignment from a supplier
 (c) Demand during the time period

7 D

Now try the questions below from the Exam Question Bank

Number	Level	Marks	Time
Q3	Introductory	n/a	30 mins
Q4	Introductory	n/a	40 mins

BPP PUBLISHING

Chapter 4

LABOUR COSTS

Topic list	Syllabus reference	Ability required
1 Remuneration methods	(i)	Application, analysis
2 Labour cost behaviour	(i)	Comprehension
3 Recording labour costs	(i)	Comprehension

Introduction

Just as management need to control stocks and operate an appropriate valuation policy in an attempt to control material costs, so too must they be aware of the most suitable **remuneration policy** for their organisation. We will be looking at a number of methods of remuneration and will consider the various types of **incentive scheme** that exist. We will also examine the procedures and documents required for the accurate **recording and control of labour costs**. Labour cost behaviour will be studied too.

Learning outcomes covered in this chapter

- **Explain** labour accounting and control procedures

- **Discuss** and **calculate** factory incentive schemes for individuals and groups

Syllabus content covered in this chapter

- Labour: accounting and control procedures

- Factory incentive schemes for individuals and groups

1   REMUNERATION METHODS

1.1   Labour remuneration methods need to be considered very carefully as they will affect the following.

- The cost of finished products or services
- The morale and efficiency of employees

1.2   There are three basic groups of remuneration method.

- Time work
- Piecework schemes
- Bonus/incentive schemes

We will discuss each of these in the next few paragraphs.

Time work

> **FORMULA TO LEARN**
>
> The most common form of **time work** is a **day-rate system** in which wages are calculated by the following formula.
>
> Wages = Hours worked × Rate of pay per hour

1.3 If an employee works for more hours than the basic daily requirement he may be entitled to an **overtime payment**. Hours of overtime are usually paid at a premium rate. For instance, if the basic day-rate is £4 per hour and overtime is paid at time-and-a-quarter, eight hours of overtime would be paid the following amount.

	£
Basic pay (8 × £4)	32
Overtime premium (8 × £1)	8
Total (8 × £5)	40

1.4 The **overtime premium** is the extra rate per hour which is paid, not the whole of the payment for the overtime hours. Overtime can be at any agreed rate; common examples are time-and-a-half or double time.

1.5 If employees work unsocial hours, for instance overnight, they may be entitled to a **shift allowance or premium**. This is similar to an overtime premium and means that the employee is paid an increased hourly rate. The extra amount paid per hour, above the basic hourly rate, is the shift premium.

1.6 **Day-rate systems** may be summarised as follows.

(a) They are easy to understand.

(b) They do not lead to very complex negotiations when they are being revised.

(c) They are most appropriate when the quality of output is more important than the quantity, or where there is no basis for payment by performance.

(d) There is no incentive for employees who are paid on a day-rate basis to improve their performance.

Piecework schemes

> **FORMULA TO LEARN**
>
> In a **piecework scheme**, wages are calculated by the following formula.
>
> Wages = Units produced × Rate of pay per unit

1.7 Suppose for example, an employee is paid £1 for each unit produced and works a 40 hour week. Production overhead is added at the rate of £2 per direct labour hour.

Weekly production	Pay (40 hours)	Overhead	Conversion cost	Conversion cost per unit
Units	£	£	£	£
40	40	80	120	3.00
50	50	80	130	2.60
60	60	80	140	2.33
70	70	80	150	2.14

As his output increases, his wage increases and at the same time unit costs of output are reduced.

1.8 It is normal for pieceworkers to be offered a **guaranteed minimum wage,** so that they do not suffer loss of earnings when production is low through no fault of their own.

1.9 If an employee makes several different types of product, it may not be possible to add up the units for payment purposes. Instead, a **standard time allowance** is given for each unit to arrive at a total of piecework hours for payment.

1.10 EXAMPLE: PIECEWORK

An employee is paid £3 per piecework hour produced. In a 40 hour week he produces the following output.

	Piecework time allowed per unit
15 units of product X	0.5 hours
20 units of product Y	2.0 hours

Required

Calculate the employee's pay for the week.

1.11 SOLUTION

Piecework hours produced are as follows.

Product X	15×0.5 hours	7.5 hours
Product Y	20×2.0 hours	40.0 hours
Total piecework hours		47.5 hours

Therefore employee's pay = $47.5 \times £3 = £142.50$ for the week.

1.12 **Differential piecework schemes** offer an incentive to employees to increase their output by paying higher rates for increased levels of production. For example:

up to and including 80 units, rate of pay per unit in this band	=	£1.00
81 to 90 units, rate of pay per unit in this band	=	£1.20
above 90 units, rate of pay per unit in this band	=	£1.30

An employee producing 97 units would therefore receive $(80 \times £1.00) + (10 \times £1.20) + (7 \times £1.30) = £101.10$.

Employers should obviously be careful to make it clear whether they intend to pay the increased rate on all units produced, or on the extra output only.

1.13 **Piecework schemes** may be summarised as follows.

(a) They enjoy fluctuating popularity.

(b) They are occasionally used by employers as a means of increasing pay levels.

(c) They are frequently condemned as a means of driving employees to work too hard to earn a satisfactory wage.

(d) Careful inspection of output is necessary to ensure that quality is maintained as production increases.

Bonus/incentive schemes

1.14 In general, bonus schemes were introduced to compensate workers paid under a time-based system for their inability to increase earnings by working more efficiently. Various types of incentive and bonus schemes have been devised which encourage greater productivity. The characteristics of such schemes are as follows.

(a) A target is set and actual performance is compared with target.

(b) Employees are paid more for their efficiency.

(c) In spite of the extra labour cost, the unit cost of output is reduced and the profit earned per unit of sale is increased; in other words the profits arising from productivity improvements are shared between employer and employee.

(d) Morale of employees should be expected to improve since they are seen to receive extra reward for extra effort.

1.15 Whatever scheme is used, it must satisfy certain conditions to operate successfully.

(a) Its **objectives** should be **clearly stated** and **attainable** by the employees.

(b) The **rules** and conditions of the scheme should be **easy to understand** and not liable to be misinterpreted.

(c) It must win the full **acceptance** of everyone concerned including, of course, trade union negotiators and officials.

(d) It should be seen to be **fair to employees and employers**. Other groups of employees should not feel unjustly excluded from the scheme, as their work might be affected by their dissatisfaction.

(e) The bonus should ideally be **paid soon after the extra effort has been made** by the employees, to associate the ideas of effort and reward.

(f) **Allowances** should be made for external factors outside the employees' control which reduce their productivity such as machine breakdowns or raw materials shortages.

(g) Only those employees who make the extra effort should be rewarded. It would not be an incentive, for example, to institute a scheme in all factories in a country-wide organisation and to pay a productivity bonus to employees in London for work done by employees in a factory in the North of England (especially if these North of England employees fail to get an adequate bonus for their efforts as a result of this sharing).

(h) The scheme must be **properly communicated** to employees.

1.16 There are many possible types of incentive schemes. Some organisations employ a variety of incentive schemes. A scheme for a production labour force may not necessarily be appropriate for clerical workers. An organisation's incentive schemes may be regularly reviewed, and altered as circumstances dictate.

(a) A **high day-rate system** is an incentive scheme where employees are paid a high hourly wage rate in the expectation that they will work more efficiently than similar employees on a lower hourly rate in a different company.

(b) Under an **individual bonus scheme**, individual employees qualify for a bonus on top of their basic wage, with each person's bonus being calculated separately.

(c) Where individual effort cannot be measured, and employees work as a team, an individual incentive scheme is impractical but a **group bonus scheme** is feasible.

(d) In a **profit sharing scheme**, employees receive a certain proportion of their company's year-end profits (the size of their bonus being related to their position in the company and the length of their employment to date).

(e) Companies operating **incentive schemes involving shares** use their shares, or the right to acquire them, as a form of incentive.

1.17 Note that an employer may provide other bonuses and benefits (company cars, non-contributory pension schemes, subsidised canteen). Such benefits do not improve production so much as reduce labour turnover.

Labour turnover

1.18 Labour turnover is a measure of the rate at which employees are leaving an organisation. It is usually calculated as follows.

FORMULA TO LEARN

$$\text{Labour turnover for the period} = \frac{\text{number of employees leaving and replaced}}{\text{average workforce}} \times 100$$

1.19 A high turnover can be costly for an organisation. For example new employees must be recruited and trained, they may work at a slower rate and there may be a loss of output due to a delay in the new labour becoming available.

1.20 The level of labour turnover should obviously be minimised and well-designed remuneration and incentive schemes can contribute towards this.

1.21 EXAMPLE: INCENTIVE SCHEMES

Elliot Frederick Ltd manufactures a single product. Its work force consists of 10 employees, who work a 36-hour week exclusive of lunch and tea breaks. The standard time required to make one unit of the product is two hours, but the current efficiency (or productivity) ratio being achieved is 80%. No overtime is worked, and the work force is paid £4 per attendance hour.

Because of agreements with the work force about work procedures, there is some unavoidable idle time due to bottlenecks in production, and about four hours per week per person are lost in this way.

The company can sell all the output it manufactures, and makes a 'cash profit' of £20 per unit sold, deducting currently achievable costs of production but *before* deducting labour costs.

An incentive scheme is proposed whereby the work force would be paid £5 per hour in exchange for agreeing to new work procedures that would reduce idle time per employee per week to two hours and also raise the efficiency ratio to 90%. Evaluate the incentive scheme from the point of view of profitability.

1.22 SOLUTION

The current situation

Hours in attendance $\qquad 10 \times 36 = 360$ hours

Hours spent working $\qquad 10 \times 32 = 320$ hours

Units produced, at 80% efficiency $\dfrac{320}{2} \times \dfrac{80}{100} = 128$ units

	£
Cash profits before deducting labour costs ($128 \times £20$)	2,560
Less labour costs ($£4 \times 360$ hours)	1,440
Net profit	1,120

The incentive scheme

Hours spent working $\qquad 10 \times 34 = 340$ hours

Units produced, at 90% efficiency $\dfrac{340}{2} \times \dfrac{90}{100} = 153$ units

	£
Cash profits before deducting labour costs ($153 \times £20$)	3,060
Less labour costs ($£5 \times 360$)	1,800
Net profit	1,260

In spite of a 25% increase in labour costs, profits would rise by £140 per week. The company and the workforce would both benefit provided, of course, that management can hold the work force to their promise of work reorganisation and improved productivity.

Exam focus point

The syllabus for the **Management Accounting Fundamentals** paper specifically states that candidates need to be able to **discuss** and **calculate** factory incentive schemes for individuals and groups. Study the contents of this section of the chapter very carefully and have a go at the following questions.

Question 1

(a) List five ways in which a company might reward extra effort by its employees.
(b) What is differential piecework?
(c) Why might a company operate a group bonus scheme?

Answer

(a) • Overtime
    • Piecework
    • Bonus for saving time
    • Discretionary bonus to individuals
    • Group bonus
    • Profit sharing schemes

(b) **Piecework** is a system of payments according to the amount of work performed. Differential piecework involves paying a different rate for different levels of production.

(c) A **group bonus scheme** is appropriate where each individual's contribution to overall performance is highly diverse and overall performance is not within any one person's control. Group bonuses are likely to encourage team effort. They are simpler to administer than individual bonuses.

Question 2

The following data relate to work at a certain factory.

Normal working day	8 hours
Basic rate of pay per hour	£6
Standard time allowed to produce 1 unit	2 minutes
Premium bonus	75% of time saved at basic rate

What will be the labour cost in a day when 340 units are made?

A £48 B £51 C £63 D £68

Answer

Standard time for 340 units (× 2 minutes)	680 minutes
Actual time (8 hours per day)	480 minutes
Time saved	200 minutes

	£
Bonus = 75% × 200 minutes × £6 per hour	15
Basic pay = 8 hours × £6	48
Total labour cost	63

Therefore the correct answer is C.

Using basic MCQ technique you can eliminate option A because this is simply the basic pay without consideration of any bonus. You can also eliminate option D, which is based on the standard time allowance without considering the basic pay for the eight-hour day. Hopefully your were not forced to guess, but had you been you would have had a 50% chance of selecting the correct answer (B or C) instead of a 25% chance because you were able to eliminate two of the options straightaway.

2 LABOUR COST BEHAVIOUR

2.1 (a) When employees are paid on a **piecework basis** their pay is a variable cost.

   (b) When employees are paid a **basic day-rate wage**, their pay per week is fixed, regardless of the volume of output. The high cost of redundancy payments and the scarcity of skilled labour will usually persuade a company to retain its employees at a basic wage even when output is low.

   (c) Because of productivity bonuses, overtime premium, commission and so on, labour costs are often mixed semi-variable costs.

2.2 Labour costs tend to behave in a **step cost** fashion.

   (a) Where the steps are short (that is where extra labour is needed for small increases in output volumes), the labour costs tend to approximate a variable cost.

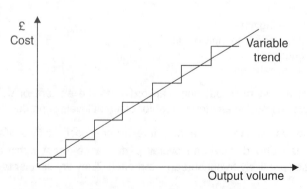

In this graph, the short steps approximate closely to a variable cost line, and for most purposes, it will be sufficiently accurate to treat labour as a purely variable cost.

(b) If, on the other hand, the labour force is static for wide ranges of output, the cost tends to be fixed in nature.

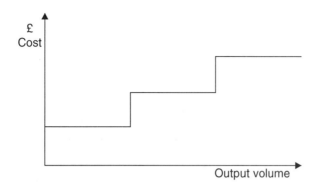

2.3 The cost accountant has to treat labour costs as fixed or variable.

(a) Direct labour is usually regarded as being a variable cost in labour-intensive work. In highly automated industries it may be regarded as a fixed cost.

(b) For control purposes, direct labour is regarded as a variable cost so that measures of efficiency or productivity can be obtained.

3   RECORDING LABOUR COSTS

Organisation for controlling and measuring labour costs

3.1 Several departments and management groups are involved in the collection, recording and costing of labour. These include the following.

- Personnel
- Production planning
- Timekeeping
- Wages
- Cost accounting

3.2 From a cost accounting point of view, the **timekeeping department** provides the most important information to facilitate the recording of labour cost. The timekeeping department is responsible for accurately recording the time spent in the factory by each worker and time spent by each worker on each job or operation: attendance time and job time respectively. Such timekeeping provides basic data for statutory records, payroll preparation, labour costs of an operation or overhead absorption (where based on wages or labour hours) and statistical analysis of labour records for determining productivity and control of labour costs.

Attendance time

3.3 The bare minimum record of employees' time is a simple **attendance record** showing days absent because of holiday, sickness or other reason. A typical record of attendance would look like this.

NAME: A.N. OTHER								DEPT: 072								NI REF: WD 4847 41C								LEAVE ENTITLEMENT: 20					
	1	2	3	4	5	6	7	8	9	10	11	12	13	14	15	16	17	18	19	20	21	22	23	24	25	26	27	28	29	30	31
JAN																															
FEB																															
MAR																															
APR																															
MAY																															
JUNE																															
JULY																															
AUG																															
SEPT																															
OCT																															
NOV																															
DEC																															

Illness: I	Leave: L	Training: T	*Note overleaf:* (1) The reasons for special leave (eg bereavement).
Industrial Accident: IA	Unpaid Leave: UL	Jury Service: J	
Maternity: M	Special Leave: SL		(2) Ensure training is noted on personnel card.

RECORD OF ATTENDANCE

3.4 It is also necessary to have a record of the following.

- Time of arrival
- Time of breaks
- Time of departure

These may be recorded as follows.

- In a signing-in book
- By using a time recording clock which stamps the time on a clock card
- By using swipe cards (which make a computer record)

An example of a clock card is shown below.

No				Ending	
Name					
HOURS	RATE	AMOUNT	DEDUCTIONS		
Basic			Income Tax		
O/T			NI		
Others			Other		
			Total deduction		
Total					
Less deductions					
Net due					
Time	Day			Basic time	Overtime
1230 T					
0803 T					
1700 M					
1305 M					
1234 M					
0750 M					
Signature _ _ _ _ _ _ _ _ _ _					

Job time

3.5 The next step is to analyse the hours spent at work according to what was done during those hours. The method adopted depends upon the size of the organisation, the nature of the work and the type of incentive scheme in operation.

3.6 **Continuous production.** Where **routine, repetitive** work is carried out it might not be practical to record the precise details. For example if a worker stands at a conveyor belt for seven hours his work can be measured by keeping a note of the number of units that pass through his part of the process during that time.

3.7 **Job costing.** When the work is not of a repetitive nature the records required might be one or several of the following.

(a) **Daily time sheets.** A time sheet is filled in by the employee as a record of how their time has been spent. The total time on the time sheet should correspond with time shown on the attendance record. Times are recorded daily and so there is less risk that they will be forgotten or manipulated, but this system does produce considerable volumes of paperwork. It is most appropriate if the worker deals with a number of small jobs.

(b) **Weekly time sheets.** These are similar to daily time sheets but are passed to the cost office at the end of the week, although entries must be made by employees on a daily basis to avoid error. Paperwork is reduced and weekly time sheets are particularly suitable where there are just a few job changes in a week. An example is shown below.

Time Sheet No. _____							
Employee Name _____ Clock Code _____ Dept _____							
Date _____ Week No. _____							
Job No.	Start Time	Finish Time	Qty	Checker	Hrs	Rate	Extension

The time sheet will be filled in by the employee, for hours worked on each job (job code) or area of work (cost code). The cost of the hours worked will be entered at a later stage in the accounting department.

(c) **Job cards.** Cards are prepared for each job or batch, unlike time sheets which are made out for each employee and which may contain bookings relating to numerous jobs. When employees work on a job they record on the job card the time spent on that job and so job cards are likely to contain entries relating to numerous employees. On completion of the job it will contain a full record of the times involved in the job or batch. The problem of job cards, however, is that the reconciliation of job time and attendance time can be a difficult task, especially for jobs which stretch over several weeks. It is therefore difficult to incorporate them directly into wage calculation procedures. They do, however, reduce the amount of writing to be done by the employee and therefore the possibility of error. A typical job card is shown below.

```
                          JOB CARD

  Department _ _ _ _ _ _ _ _ _ _     Job no  _ _ _ _ _ _ _ _ _ _ _ _ _ _ _ .

  Date  _ _ _ _ _ _ _ _ _ _ _ _ _    Operation no _ _ _ _ _ _ _ _ _ _ _ _ _


  Time allowance _ _ _ _ _ _ _ _ _   Time started  _ _ _ _ _ _ _ _ _ _ _ _

                                     Time finished _ _ _ _ _ _ _ _ _ _ _ _

                                     Hours on the job _ _ _ _ _ _ _ _ _ _ _

  Description of job                          Hours     Rate      Cost




  Employee no_ _ _ _ _ _ _ _ _ _ _ _ _ _     Certified by _ _ _ _ _ _ _ _ _ _ _ _ _ _ .

  Signature _ _ _ _ _ _ _ _ _ _ _ _ _ _ _
```

3.8   **Piecework.** The wages of pieceworkers and the labour cost of work done by them is
        determined from what is known as a **piecework ticket** or an **operation card**. The card
        records the total number of items (or 'pieces') produced and the number of rejects. Payment
        is only made for 'good' production. A typical operation card is shown below.

```
                       OPERATION CARD

  Operator's Name _ _ _ _ _ _ _ _ _ _ _ _ _ _    Total Batch Quantity _ _ _ _ _ _ _ _ _ _

  Clock No . _ _ _ _ _ _ _ _ _ _ _ _ _ _ _ _     Start Time _ _ _ _ _ _ _ _ _ _ _ _ _ _

  Pay week No _ _ _ _ _ _ _ Date _ _ _ _ _ _ _   Stop Time _ _ _ _ _ _ _ _ _ _ _ _ _ _


  Part No _ _ _ _ _ _ _ _ _ _ _ _ _ _ _ _ _ _    Works Order No _ _ _ _ _ _ _ _ _ _ _ _

  Operation _ _ _ _ _ _ _ _ _ _ _ _ _ _ _ _ _    Special Instructions _ _ _ _ _ _ _ _ _ _

  Quantity Produced    No Rejected     Good Production      Rate        £




  Inspector _ _ _ _ _ _ _ _ _ _ _ _ _ _ _ _    Operative _ _ _ _ _ _ _ _ _ _ _ _ _ _ _

  Foreman - - - - - - - - - - - - - - - - - -  Date - - - - - - - - - - - - - - - - - -

  PRODUCTION CANNOT BE CLAIMED WITHOUT A PROPERLY SIGNED CARD
```

        Note that the attendance record of a pieceworker is still required for calculations of
        holidays, sick pay and so on.

Salaried labour

3.9   Even though salaried staff are paid a flat rate monthly, they may be required to complete
        timesheets. The reasons are as follows.

        (a)   Timesheets provide management with information (eg product costs).

        (b)   Timesheet information may provide a basis for billing for services provided, for
              example, a firm of solicitors or accountants may bill clients based on the number of
              hours work done.

        (c)   Timesheets are used to record hours spent and so support claims for overtime
              payments by salaried staff.

3.10   An example of the type of time sheet which can be found in large firms in the service sector
        of the economy is as follows.

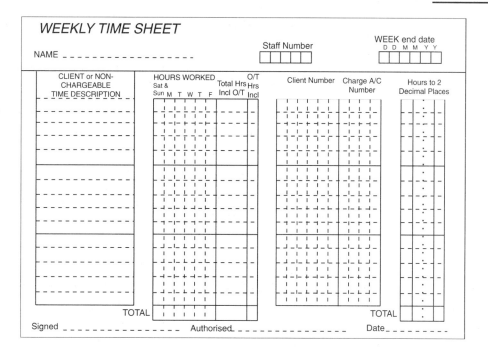

Idle time

3.11 In many jobs there are times when, through no fault of their own, employees cannot get on with their work. They may be waiting for another department to finish its contribution to a job, or a machine may break down or there may simply be a temporary shortage of work.

3.12 **Idle time** has a cost because employees will still be paid their basic wage or salary for these unproductive hours and so there should be a record of idle time. This may simply comprise an entry on time sheets coded to 'idle time' generally, or separate idle time cards may be prepared. A supervisor might enter the time of a stoppage, its cause, its duration and the employees made idle on an idle time record card. Each stoppage should have a separate reference number which can be entered on time sheets or job cards as appropriate.

Cost accounting department

3.13 The cost accounting department has the following responsibilities.

(a) The accumulation and classification of all cost data (which includes labour costs).

(b) Preparation of cost data reports for management.

(c) Analysing information on time cards and payroll to obtain details of direct and indirect labour, overtime and so on.

3.14 In order to establish the labour cost involved in products, operations, jobs and cost centres, the following documents are used.

- Clock cards
- Job cards
- Idle time cards
- Payroll

3.15 Analyses of labour costs are used for the following.

(a) Charging wages directly attributable to production to the appropriate job or operation.

(b) Charging wages which are not directly attributable to production as follows.

(i) **Idle time of production workers** is charged to indirect costs as part of the overheads.

(ii) **Wages costs of supervisors,** or store assistants are charged to the overhead costs of the relevant department.

(c) Producing idle time reports which show a summary of the hours lost through idle time, and the cause of the idle time. Idle time may be analysed as follows.

- **Controllable** eg lack of materials.
- **Uncontrollable** eg power failure.

FORMULA TO LEARN

$$\text{Idle time ratio} = \frac{\text{Idle hours}}{\text{Total hours}} \times 100\%$$

3.16 The idle time ratio is useful because it shows the proportion of available hours which were lost as a result of idle time.

Chapter roundup

- **Labour** is a major cost in many businesses and it is therefore vital that you have understood this chapter's topics, a summary of them being set out below.

- There are three basic groups of **remuneration** method - **time work**, **piecework** schemes and **bonus/incentive** schemes.

- Although labour costs tend to behave in a step cost fashion, cost accountants usually treat labour costs as **fixed** or **variable**.

- **Labour turnover** is the rate at which employees leave a company and this rate should be kept as low as possible.

- Labour attendance time is recorded on, for example, an **attendance record** or clock card. Job time may be recorded on **daily time sheets**, **weekly time sheets** or **job cards**.

- The labour cost of pieceworkers is recorded on a **piecework ticket/operation card**.

- **Idle time** has a cost and must therefore be recorded.

Quick quiz

1   What is a differential piecework scheme?

2   List five types of incentive scheme.

3   List four types of document used in recording job time.

4   What is idle time?

5   What is the idle time ratio?

Answers to quick quiz

1   A scheme that offers an incentive to employees to increase their output by paying higher rates for increased levels of production.

2   • High day-rate system
    • Individual bonus scheme
    • Group bonus scheme
    • Profit sharing scheme
    • Incentive schemes involving shares

3   • Daily timesheets
    • Weekly timesheets
    • Job cards
    • Piecework ticket/operation card

4   Idle time occurs when, through no fault of their own, employees cannot get on with their work (eg machine breakdown or shortage of work).

5   Idle time ratio $= \dfrac{\text{Idle hours}}{\text{Total hours}} \times 100\%$

Now try the question below from the Exam Question Bank

Number	Level	Marks	Time
Q5	Introductory	n/a	30 mins

BPP PUBLISHING

Chapter 5

OVERHEAD APPORTIONMENT AND ABSORPTION

Topic list	Syllabus reference	Ability required
1 Overhead allocation	(i)	Comprehension, application
2 Overhead apportionment	(i)	Comprehension, application
3 Overhead absorption	(i)	Comprehension, application
4 Blanket absorption rates and departmental absorption rates	(i)	Comprehension, application
5 Over and under absorption of overheads	(I)	Application

Introduction

There are basically two schools of thought as to the correct method of dealing with overheads, **marginal costing** (which we will be looking at in the next chapter) and **absorption costing**, the topic of this chapter.

Absorption costing is a method for sharing overheads between a number of different products on a fair basis. The chapter begins by looking at the three stages of absorption costing: **allocation, apportionment and absorption**. We then move on to the important issue of **over/under absorption**.

Learning outcomes covered in this chapter

- **Explain** absorption costing

- **Prepare** cost statements for allocation and apportionment of overheads including reciprocal service departments

- **Calculate** and **discuss** overhead absorption rates

- **Calculate** under/over recovery of overheads

- **Calculate** product costs under absorption costing

Syllabus content covered in this chapter

- Overhead costs: allocation, apportionment, reapportionment and absorption of overhead costs

  NB. The repeated distribution method only will be used for reciprocal service department costs

- Absorption costing

1 OVERHEAD ALLOCATION

KEY TERM

Allocation is the process by which whole cost items are charged direct to a cost unit or cost centre.

1.1 Cost centres may be one of the following types.

(a) A **production department**, to which production overheads are charged

(b) A **production area service department**, to which production overheads are charged

(c) An **administrative department**, to which administration overheads are charged

(d) A **selling** or a **distribution department**, to which sales and distribution overheads are charged

(e) An **overhead cost centre**, to which items of expense which are shared by a number of departments, such as rent and rates, heat and light and the canteen, are charged

1.2 The following are examples of costs which would be charged direct to cost centres via the process of allocation.

(a) The cost of a warehouse security guard will be charged to the warehouse cost centre.

(b) Paper on which computer output is recorded will be charged to the computer department.

1.3 As an example of overhead allocation, consider the following costs of a company.

Wages of the supervisor of department A	£200
Wages of the supervisor of department B	£150
Indirect materials consumed in department A	£50
Rent of the premises shared by departments A and B	£300

The cost accounting system might include three cost centres.

Cost centre:	101	Department A
	102	Department B
	201	Rent

Overhead costs would be allocated directly to each cost centre, ie £200 + £50 to cost centre 101, £150 to cost centre 102 and £300 to cost centre 201. The rent of the factory will be subsequently shared between the two production departments, but for the purpose of day to day cost recording in this particular system, the rent will first of all be charged in full to a separate cost centre.

2 OVERHEAD APPORTIONMENT

First stage: apportioning general overheads

2.1 Overhead apportionment follows on from overhead allocation. The first stage of overhead apportionment is to identify all overhead costs as production department, production service department, administration or selling and distribution overhead. This means that the costs for heat and light, rent and rates, the canteen and so on (that is, costs which have been allocated to general overhead cost centres) must be shared out between the other cost centres.

Bases of apportionment

2.2 Overhead costs should be shared out on a fair basis. You will appreciate that because of the complexity of items of cost it is rarely possible to use only one method of apportioning costs to the various departments of an organisation. The bases of apportionment for the most usual cases are given below.

Overhead to which the basis applies	Basis
Rent, rates, heating and light, repairs and depreciation of buildings	Floor area occupied by each cost centre
Depreciation, insurance of equipment	Cost or book value of equipment
Personnel office, canteen, welfare, wages and cost offices, first aid	Number of employees, or labour hours worked in each cost centre
Heating, lighting (see above)	Volume of space occupied by each cost centre

Exam focus point

If an examination question calls for the apportionment of overhead items, the basis to be used will be obvious in the majority of cases. But you may encounter one or two items for which two (or more) bases may appear to be equally acceptable. In such circumstances, do not take too much time trying to weigh up the merits of each: use the method you prefer. Always indicate the basis of apportionment you have chosen, and in any case of doubt explain why you chose one basis in preference to another.

2.3 EXAMPLE: OVERHEAD APPORTIONMENT

McQueen Ltd has incurred the following overhead costs.

	£'000
Depreciation of factory	100
Factory repairs and maintenance	60
Factory office costs (treat as production overhead)	150
Depreciation of equipment	80
Insurance of equipment	20
Heating	39
Lighting	10
Canteen	90
	549

Information relating to the production and service departments in the factory is as follows.

	Department			
	Production 1	Production 2	Service 100	Service 101
Floor space (square metres)	1,200	1,600	800	400
Volume (cubic metres)	3,000	6,000	2,400	1,600
Number of employees	30	30	15	15
Book value of equipment	£30,000	£20,000	£10,000	£20,000

Required

Determine how the overhead costs should be apportioned between the four departments.

2.4   SOLUTION

Costs are apportioned using the following general formula.

$$\frac{\text{Total overhead cost}}{\text{Total value of apportionment base}} \times \text{value of apportionment base of cost centre}$$

For example, heating for department 1 $= \dfrac{£39,000}{13,000} \times 3,000 = £9,000$

Item of cost	Basis of apportionment	Total cost £	To Department 1 £	2 £	100 £	101 £
Factory depreciation	(floor area)	100	30.0	40	20.0	10.0
Factory repairs	(floor area)	60	18.0	24	12.0	6.0
Factory office costs	(number of employees)	150	50.0	50	25.0	25.0
Equipment depreciation	(book value)	80	30.0	20	10.0	20.0
Equipment insurance	(book value)	20	7.5	5	2.5	5.0
Heating	(volume)	39	9.0	18	7.2	4.8
Lighting	(floor area)	10	3.0	4	2.0	1.0
Canteen	(number of employees)	90	30.0	30	15.0	15.0
Total		549	177.5	191	93.7	86.8

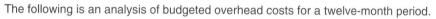

Question 1

Pippin Ltd has three production departments (forming, machines and assembly) and two service departments (maintenance and general).

The following is an analysis of budgeted overhead costs for a twelve-month period.

	£	£
Rent and rates		8,000
Power		750
Light, heat		5,000
Repairs, maintenance:		
Forming	800	
Machines	1,800	
Assembly	300	
Maintenance	200	
General	100	
		3,200
Departmental expenses:		
Forming	1,500	
Machines	2,300	
Assembly	1,100	
Maintenance	900	
General	1,500	
		7,300
Depreciation:		
Plant		10,000
Fixtures and fittings		250
Insurance:		
Plant		2,000
Buildings		500
Indirect labour:		
Forming	3,000	
Machines	5,000	
Assembly	1,500	
Maintenance	4,000	
General	2,000	
		15,500
		52,500

Part A: Cost determination

Other available data are as follows

	Floor area sq.ft	Plant value £	Fixtures & fittings £	Effective horse-power	Direct cost for year £	Labour hours worked	Machine hours worked
Forming	2,000	25,000	1,000	40	20,500	14,400	12,000
Machines	4,000	60,000	500	90	30,300	20,500	21,600
Assembly	3,000	7,500	2,000	15	24,200	20,200	2,000
Maintenance	500	7,500	1,000	5	-	-	-
General	500	-	500	-	-	-	-
	10,000	100,000	5,000	150	75,000	55,100	35,600

Required

Using the data provided apportion overheads to the five departments.

Answer

	Basis	Forming £	Machines £	Assembly £	Maint'nce £	General £	Total £
Directly allocated overheads:							
Repairs, maintenance		800	1,800	300	200	100	3,200
Departmental expenses		1,500	2,300	1,100	900	1,500	7,300
Indirect labour		3,000	5,000	1,500	4,000	2,000	15,500
Apportionment of other overheads:							
Rent, rates	1	1,600	3,200	2,400	400	400	8,000
Power	2	200	450	75	25	0	750
Light, heat	1	1,000	2,000	1,500	250	250	5,000
Dep'n of plant	3	2,500	6,000	750	750	0	10,000
Dep'n of F & F	4	50	25	100	50	25	250
Insurance of plant	3	500	1,200	150	150	0	2,000
Insurance of buildings	1	100	200	150	25	25	500
		11,250	22,175	8,025	6,750	4,300	52,500

Basis of apportionment:

1 floor area
2 effective horsepower
3 plant value
4 fixtures and fittings value

Second stage: service cost centre cost apportionment

2.5 The second stage of overhead apportionment concerns the treatment of **service cost centres**. A factory is divided into several production departments and also a number of service departments, but only the production departments are directly involved in the manufacture of the units. In order to be able to add production overheads to unit costs, it is necessary to have all the overheads charged to (or located in) the production departments. The next stage in absorption costing is, therefore, to apportion the costs of service cost centres to the production cost centres. Examples of possible apportionment bases are as follows.

Service cost centre	Possible basis of apportionment
Stores	Number of materials requisitions
Maintenance	Hours of maintenance work done for each cost centre
Production planning	Direct labour hours worked in each production cost centre

2.6   There are two main methods of apportioning the costs of service cost centres to production cost centres (**reapportionment**).

- Direct method of reapportionment
- Repeated distribution method of reapportionment

2.7   EXAMPLE: DIRECT METHOD OF REAPPORTIONMENT

A company has two production and two service departments (stores and maintenance). The following information about activity in the recent costing period is available.

	Production departments		Stores department	Maintenance department
	A	B		
Overhead costs	£10,030	£8,970	£10,000	£8,000
Cost of material requisitions	£30,000	£50,000	-	£20,000
Maintenance hours needed	8,000	1,000	1,000	-

(a)   If service department overheads were apportioned **directly** to production departments, the apportionment would be as follows.

Service department	Basis of apportionment	Total cost		A		B
		£		£		£
Stores	Material requisitions	10,000	(3/8)	3,750	(5/8)	6,250
Maintenance	Maintenance hours	8,000	(8/9)	7,111	(1/9)	889
		18,000		10,861		7,139
Overheads of departments A and B		19,000		10,030		8,970
		37,000		20,891		16,109

(b)   If, however, recognition is made of the fact that the stores and maintenance department do work for each other, and the basis of apportionment remains the same, we ought to apportion service department costs as follows.

	Dept A	Dept B	Stores	Maint-enance
Stores (100%)	30%	50%	-	20%
Maintenance (100%)	80%	10%	10%	-

This may be done using the **repeated distribution method of apportionment** which is perhaps best explained by means of an example.

2.8   EXAMPLE: REPEATED DISTRIBUTION METHOD OF REAPPORTIONMENT

	Production dept A	Production dept B	Stores	Maintenance
	£	£	£	£
Overhead costs	10,030	8,970	10,000	8,000
First stores apportionment (see note (a))	3,000	5,000	(10,000)	2,000
			0	10,000
First maintenance apportionment	8,000	1,000	1,000	(10,000)
			1,000	0
Second stores apportionment	300	500	(1,000)	200
Second maintenance apportionment	160	20	20	(200)
Third stores apportionment	6	10	(20)	4
Third maintenance apportionment	4	-	-	(4)
	21,500	15,500	0	0

Notes

(a) The first apportionment could have been the costs of maintenance, rather than stores; there is no difference to the final results.

(b) When the repeated distributions bring service department costs down to small numbers (here £4) the final apportionment to production departments is an approximate rounding.

2.9 You should note the difference in the final overhead apportionment to each production department using the different service department apportionment methods. Unless the difference is substantial, the **direct apportionment method** might be preferred because it is clerically simpler to use.

Exam focus point

You must never ignore the existence of reciprocal services unless the question clearly instructs you to do so. The question will usually indicate clearly if you are required to use a specific method of reciprocal apportionment.

2.10 Apportioning service department overheads is only useful if the resulting product costs reflect accurately the amounts expended by service departments. If, however, the apportionment is arbitrary or ill-considered, the absorption of service department costs into product costs may be misleading.

Question 2

Using your answer to Question 1 and the following information, apportion the overheads of the two service departments using the repeated distribution method.

Service department costs are apportioned as follows

	Maintenance	General
	%	%
Forming	20	20
Machines	50	60
Assembly	20	10
General	10	-
Maintenance	-	10
	100	100

Answer

Apportionment of service department overheads to production departments, using the repeated distribution method.

	Forming	Machines	Assembly	Maintenance	General	Total
	£	£	£	£	£	£
Overheads	11,250	22,175	8,025	6,750	4,300	52,500
Apportion maintenance (2:5:2:1)	1,350	3,375	1,350	(6,750)	675	
Apportion general (2:6:1:1)					4,975	
Apportion maintenance (2:5:2:1)	995	2,985	498	497	(4,975)	
Apportion general (2:6:1:1)	99	249	99	(497)	50	
Apportion maintenance (2:5:2:1)	10	30	5	5	(50)	
	1	3	1	(5)		
	13,705	28,817	9,978	0	0	52,500

3   OVERHEAD ABSORPTION

3.1   Having allocated and/or apportioned all overheads, the next stage in absorption costing is to add them to, or **absorb them into,** the cost of production or sales.

(a)   **Production overheads** are added to the prime cost (direct materials, labour and expenses), the total of the two being the factory cost, or full cost of production. Production overheads are therefore included in the value of stocks of finished goods.

(b)   **Administration and selling and distribution overheads** are then added, the sum of the factory cost and these overheads being the total cost of sales. These overheads are therefore not included in the value of closing stock.

Use of a predetermined absorption rate

3.2   Overheads are not absorbed on the basis of the actual overheads incurred but on the basis of estimated or budgeted figures (calculated prior to the beginning of the period). The rate at which overheads are included in cost of sales (**absorption rate**) is predetermined before the accounting period actually begins for a number of reasons.

(a)   Goods are produced and sold throughout the year, but many actual overheads are not known until the end of the year. It would be inconvenient to wait until the year end in order to decide what overhead costs should be.

(b)   An attempt to calculate overhead costs more regularly (such as each month) is possible, although estimated costs must be added for occasional expenditures such as rent and rates (incurred once or twice a year). The difficulty with this approach would be that actual overheads from month to month would fluctuate randomly; therefore, overhead costs charged to production would depend on a certain extent on random events and changes. A unit made in one week might be charged with £4 of overhead, in a subsequent week with £5, and in a third week with £4.50. Only units made in winter would be charged with the heating overhead. Such charges are considered misleading for costing purposes and administratively and clerically inconvenient to deal with.

(c)   Similarly, production output might vary each month. For example actual overhead costs might be £20,000 per month and output might vary from, say, 1,000 units to 20,000 units per month. The unit rate for overhead would be £20 and £1 per unit respectively, which would again lead to administration and control problems.

3.3   Overhead absorption rates are therefore predetermined as follows.

(a)   The overhead **likely to be incurred** during the coming year is estimated.

(b)   The total hours, units, or direct costs on which the overhead absorption rates are to be based (activity level) are estimated.

(c)   The estimated overhead is divided by the budgeted activity level to arrive at an absorption rate.

Selecting the appropriate absorption base

3.4   There are a number of different **bases of absorption** (or 'overhead recovery rates') which can be used. Examples are as follows.

- A percentage of direct materials cost
- A percentage of direct labour cost
- A percentage of prime cost

- A rate per machine hour
- A rate per direct labour hour
- A rate per unit

3.5 The choice of an absorption basis is a matter of judgement and common sense. There are no strict rules or formulae involved, although factors which should be taken into account are set out below. What is required is an absorption basis which realistically reflects the characteristics of a given cost centre and which avoids undue anomalies.

3.6 It is safe to assume, for example, that the overhead costs for producing brass screws are similar to those for producing steel screws. The cost of brass is, however, very much greater than that of steel. Consequently, the overhead charge for brass screws would be too high and that for steel screws too low, if a percentage of cost of materials rate were to be used.

3.7 Using prime cost as the absorption base would lead to anomalies because of the inclusion of the cost of material, as outlined above.

3.8 If the overhead actually attributable to units was incurred on, say a time basis, but one highly-paid employee was engaged on producing one item, while a lower-paid employee was producing another item, the overhead charged to the first item using a percentage of wages rate might be too high while the amount absorbed by the second item might be too low. This method should therefore only be used if similar wage rates are paid to all direct employees in a production department. A direct labour hour rate might be considered 'fairer'.

3.9 It is for this reason that many factories use a **direct labour hour rate** or **machine hour rate** in preference to a rate based on a percentage of direct materials cost, wages or prime cost.

   (a) A **direct labour** hour basis is most appropriate in a **labour intensive** environment.

   (b) A **machine hour** rate would be used in departments where production is controlled or dictated by **machines**. This basis is becoming more appropriate as factories become more heavily automated.

3.10 A **rate per unit** would be effective only if all units were identical.

3.11 EXAMPLE: OVERHEAD ABSORPTION

The budgeted production overheads and other budget data of Calculator Ltd are as follows.

Budget	*Production dept 1*	*Production dept 2*
Overhead cost	£36,000	£5,000
Direct materials cost	£32,000	
Direct labour cost	£40,000	
Machine hours	10,000	
Direct labour hours	18,000	
Units of production		1,000

Required

Calculate the absorption rate using the various bases of apportionment.

3.12 SOLUTION

(a) Department 1

(i) Percentage of direct materials cost = $\dfrac{£36,000}{£32,000} \times 100\% = 112.5\%$

(ii) Percentage of direct labour cost = $\dfrac{£36,000}{£40,000} \times 100\% = 90\%$

(iii) Percentage of prime cost = $\dfrac{£36,000}{£72,000} \times 100\% = 50\%$

(iv) Rate per machine hour = $\dfrac{£36,000}{10,000 \text{ hrs}} = £3.60$ per machine hour

(v) Rate per direct labour hour = $\dfrac{£36,000}{18,000 \text{ hrs}} = £2$ per direct labour hour

(b) The department 2 absorption rate will be based on units of output.

$\dfrac{£5,000}{1,000 \text{ units}} = £5$ per unit produced

3.13 The choice of the basis of absorption is significant in determining the cost of individual units, or jobs, produced. Using the previous example, suppose that an individual product has a material cost of £80, a labour cost of £85, and requires 36 labour hours and 23 machine hours to complete. The overhead cost of the product would vary, depending on the basis of absorption used by the company for overhead recovery.

(a) As a percentage of direct materials cost, the overhead cost would be
112.5% × £80   = £90.00

(b) As a percentage of direct labour cost, the overhead cost would be
90% × £85   = £76.50

(c) As a percentage of prime cost, the overhead cost would be 50% × £165   = £82.50

(d) Using a machine hour basis of absorption, the overhead cost would be
23 hrs × £3.60   = £82.80

(e) Using a labour hour basis, the overhead cost would be 36 hrs × £2   = £72.00

3.14 In theory, each basis of absorption would be possible, but the company should choose a basis for its own costs which seems to be 'fairest'. In our example, this choice will be significant in determining the cost of individual products, as the following summary shows, but the **total cost** of production overheads is the budgeted overhead expenditure, no matter what basis of absorption is selected. It is the relative share of overhead costs borne by individual products and jobs which is affected by the choice of overhead absorption basis.

3.15 A summary of the product costs in the previous example is shown below.

Basis of overhead recovery

	Percentage of materials cost	Percentage of labour cost	Percentage of prime cost	Machine hours	Direct labour hours
	£	£	£	£	£
Direct material	80	80.00	80.00	80.00	80
Direct labour	85	85.00	85.00	85.00	85
Production overhead	90	76.50	82.50	82.80	72
Total production cost	255	241.50	247.50	247.80	237

Question 3

Using your answer to Question 2 and the following information, determine suitable overhead absorption rates for Pippin Ltd's three production departments.

	Forming	Machines	Assembly
Budgeted direct labour hours per annum	5,482	790	4,989
Budgeted machine hours per annum	1,350	5,240	147

Answer

Forming (labour intensive) $\dfrac{£13,705}{5,482}$ = £2.50 per direct labour hour

Machines (machine intensive) $\dfrac{£28,817}{5,240}$ = £5.50 per machine hour

Assembly (labour intensive) $\dfrac{£9,978}{4,989}$ = £2 per direct labour hour

4 BLANKET ABSORPTION RATES AND DEPARTMENTAL ABSORPTION RATES

> **KEY TERM**
>
> A **blanket overhead absorption rate** is an absorption rate used throughout a factory and for all jobs and units of output irrespective of the department in which they were produced.

4.1 For example, if total overheads were £500,000 and there were 250,000 direct machine hours during the period, the **blanket overhead rate** would be £2 per direct machine hour and all units of output passing through the factory would be charged at that rate.

4.2 Such a rate is not appropriate, however, if there are a number of departments and units of output do not spend an equal amount of time in each department.

4.3 It is argued that if a single factory overhead absorption rate is used, some products will receive a higher overhead charge than they ought 'fairly' to bear, whereas other products will be under-charged. By using a separate absorption rate for each department, charging of overheads will be equitable and the full cost of production of items will be more representative of the cost of the efforts and resources put into making them. An example may help to illustrate this point.

4.4 EXAMPLE: SEPARATE ABSORPTION RATES

AB Ltd has two production departments, for which the following budgeted information is available.

	Department 1	Department 2	Total
Budgeted overheads	£360,000	£200,000	£560,000
Budgeted direct labour hours	200,000 hrs	40,000 hrs	240,000 hrs

If a single factory overhead absorption rate is applied, the rate of overhead recovery would be:

$$\frac{£560,000}{240,000 \text{ hours}} = £2.33 \text{ per direct labour hour}$$

4.5 If separate departmental rates are applied, these would be:

Department 1   *Department 2*

$$\frac{£360,000}{200,000 \text{ hours}} = £1.80 \text{ per direct labour hour} \qquad \frac{£200,000}{40,000 \text{ hours}} = £5 \text{ per direct labour hour}$$

Department 2 has a higher overhead cost per hour worked than department 1.

Now let us consider two separate products.

(a) Product A has a prime cost of £100, takes 30 hours in department 2 and does not involve any work in department 1.

(b) Product B has a prime cost of £100, takes 28 hours in department 1 and 2 hours in department 2.

4.6 What would be the factory cost of each product, using the following rates of overhead recovery.

(a) A single factory rate of overhead recovery
(b) Separate departmental rates of overhead recovery

4.7 **SOLUTION**

			Product A		*Product B*
(a)	**Single factory rate**		£		£
	Prime cost		100		100
	Factory overhead ($30 \times £2.33$)		70		70
	Factory cost		170		170
(b)	**Separate departmental rates**		£		£
	Prime cost		100		100.00
	Factory overhead: department 1		0	($28 \times £1.80$)	50.40
	department 2	($30 \times £5$)	150	($2 \times £5$)	10.00
	Factory cost		250		160.40

4.8 Using a single factory overhead absorption rate, both products would cost the same. However, since product A is done entirely within department 2 where overhead costs are relatively higher, whereas product B is done mostly within department 1, where overhead costs are relatively lower, it is arguable that product A should cost more than product B. This will occur if separate departmental overhead recovery rates are used to reflect the work done on each job in each department separately.

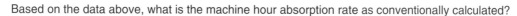

Question 4

The following data relate to one year in department A.

Budgeted machine hours	25,000
Actual machine hours	21,875
Budgeted overheads	£350,000
Actual overheads	£350,000

Based on the data above, what is the machine hour absorption rate as conventionally calculated?

A £12   B £14   C £16   D £18

Answer

Don't forget, if your calculations produce a solution which does not correspond with any of the options available, then eliminate the unlikely options and make a guess from the remainder. Never leave out a multiple choice question.

A common pitfall is to think 'we haven't had answer A for a while, so I'll guess that'. The examiner is *not* required to produce an even spread of A, B, C and D answers in the examination. There is no reason why the answer to *every* question cannot be D!

The correct answer in this case is B.

$$\text{Overhead absorption rate} = \frac{\text{Budgeted overheads}}{\text{Budgeted machine hours}} = \frac{£350,000}{25,000} = £14 \text{ per machine hour}$$

5 OVER AND UNDER ABSORPTION OF OVERHEADS

5.1 The rate of overhead absorption is based on **estimates** (of both numerator and denominator) and it is quite likely that either one or both of the estimates will not agree with what *actually* occurs. Actual overheads incurred will probably be either greater than or less than overheads absorbed into the cost of production.

(a) **Over absorption** means that the overheads charged to the cost of production are greater than the overheads actually incurred.

(b) **Under absorption** means that insufficient overheads have been included in the cost of production.

5.2 Suppose that the budgeted overhead in a production department is £80,000 and the budgeted activity is 40,000 direct labour hours. The overhead recovery rate (using a direct labour hour basis) would be £2 per direct labour hour.

Actual overheads in the period are, say £84,000 and 45,000 direct labour hours are worked.

	£
Overhead incurred (actual)	84,000
Overhead absorbed (45,000 × £2)	90,000
Over-absorption of overhead	6,000

In this example, the cost of produced units or jobs has been charged with £6,000 more than was actually spent. An adjustment to reconcile the overheads charged to the actual overhead is necessary and the over-absorbed overhead will be written as a credit to the **profit and loss account** at the end of the accounting period.

Exam focus point

You can always work out whether overheads are under- or over-absorbed by using the following rule.

- If **Actual** overhead incurred − **Absorbed** overhead = **NEGATIVE** (N), then overheads are **over-absorbed** (O) (NO)

- If **Actual** overhead incurred − **Absorbed** overhead = **POSITIVE** (P), then overheads are **under-absorbed** (U) (PU)

So, remember the **NOPU** rule when you go into your examination and you won't have any trouble in deciding whether overheads are under- or over-absorbed!

The reasons for under-/over-absorbed overhead

5.3 The overhead absorption rate is **predetermined from budget estimates** of overhead cost and the expected volume of activity. Under or over recovery of overhead will occur in the following circumstances.

- Actual overhead costs are different from budgeted overheads.
- The actual activity level is different from the budgeted activity level.
- Both actual overhead costs and actual activity level are different from budget.

5.4 EXAMPLE: UNDER AND OVER ABSORPTION OF OVERHEADS

Rioch Havery Ltd is a small company which manufactures two products, A and B, in two production departments, machining and assembly. A canteen is operated as a separate production service department.

The budgeted production and sales in the year to 31 March 20X3 are as follows.

	Product A	Product B
Sales price per unit	£50	£70
Sales (units)	2,200	1,400
Production (units)	2,000	1,500
Material cost per unit	£14	£12

	Product A Hours per unit	Product B Hours per unit
Direct labour:		
Machining department (£4 per hour)	2	3
Assembly department (£3 per hour)	1	2
Machine hours per unit:		
Machining department	3	4
Assembly department	$^1/_2$	

Budgeted production overheads are as follows.

	Machining department £	Assembly department £	Canteen £	Total £
Allocated costs	10,000	25,000	12,000	47,000
Apportionment of other general production overheads	26,000	12,000	8,000	46,000
	36,000	37,000	20,000	93,000
Number of employees	30	20	1	51
Floor area (square metres)	5,000	2,000	500	7,500

Required

(a) Calculate an absorption rate for overheads in each production department for the year to 31 March 20X3 and the budgeted cost per unit of products A and B.

(b) Suppose that in the year to 31 March 20X3, 2,200 units of Product A are produced and 1,500 units of Product B. Direct labour hours per unit and machine hours per unit in both departments were as budgeted.

Actual production overheads are as follows.

	Machining department £	Assembly department £	Canteen £	Total £
Allocated costs	30,700	27,600	10,000	68,300
Apportioned share of general production overheads	17,000	8,000	5,000	30,000
	47,700	35,600	15,000	98,300

Calculate the under- or over-absorbed overhead in each production department and in total.

5.5 SOLUTION

(a) **Choose absorption rates**

Since machine time appears to be more significant than labour time in the machining department, a machine hour rate of absorption will be used for overhead recovery in this department. On the other hand, machining is insignificant in the assembly department, and a direct labour hour rate of absorption would seem to be the basis which will give the fairest method of overhead recovery.

Apportion budgeted overheads

Next we need to apportion budgeted overheads to the two production departments. Canteen costs will be apportioned on the basis of the number of employees in each department. (Direct labour hours in each department are an alternative basis of apportionment, but the number of employees seems to be more directly relevant to canteen costs.)

	Machining department £	Assembly department £	Total £
Budgeted allocated costs	10,000	25,000	35,000
Share of general overheads	26,000	12,000	38,000
Apportioned canteen costs (30:20)	12,000	8,000	20,000
	48,000	45,000	93,000

Calculate overhead absorption rates

The overhead absorption rates are predetermined, using budgeted estimates. Since the overheads are production overheads, the budgeted activity relates to the volume of production, in units (the production hours required for volume of sales being irrelevant).

	Product A	Product B	Total
Budgeted production (units)	2,000	1,500	
Machining department: machine hours	6,000 hrs	6,000 hrs	12,000 hrs
Assembly department: direct labour hours	2,000 hrs	3,000 hrs	5,000 hrs

The overhead absorption rates will be as follows.

	Machining department	Assembly department
Budgeted overheads	£48,000	£45,000
Budgeted activity	12,000 hrs	5,000 hrs
Absorption rate	£4 per machine hour	£9 per direct labour hour

Determine a budgeted cost per unit

The budgeted cost per unit would be as follows.

	Product A		Product B	
	£	£	£	£
Direct materials		14		12
Direct labour:				
Machining department	8		12	
Assembly department	3		6	
		11		18
Prime cost		25		30
Production overhead:				
Machining department	12		16	
Assembly department	9		18	
		21		34
Full production cost		46		64

(b) Apportion actual service department overhead to production departments

When the actual costs are analysed, the 'actual' overhead of the canteen department (£15,000) would be split between the machining and assembly departments.

	Machining department £	Assembly department £	Total £
Allocated cost	30,700	27,600	58,300
Apportioned general overhead	17,000	8,000	25,000
Canteen (30:20)	9,000	6,000	15,000
	56,700	41,600	98,300

Establish the over- or under-absorption of overheads

There would be an over- or under-absorption of overheads as follows.

		Machining department £		Assembly department £	Total £
Overheads absorbed					
Product A (2,200 units)	(× £4 × 3hrs)	26,400	(× £9 × 1hr)	19,800	46,200
Product B (1,500 units)	(× £4 × 4hrs)	24,000	(× £9 × 2hrs)	27,000	51,000
		50,400		46,800	97,200
Overheads incurred		56,700		41,600	98,300
Over-/(under)-absorbed overhead		(6,300)		5,200	(1,100)

The total under-absorbed overhead of £1,100 will be written off to the profit and loss account at the end of the year, to compensate for the fact that overheads charged to production (£97,200) were less than the overheads actually incurred (£98,300).

Question 5

Using your answer to Question 3 and the following information, determine the under-/over-absorbed overhead in each of the three production departments of Pippin Ltd for the twelve-month period.

	Forming	Machines	Assembly
Actual direct labour hours	5,370	950	5,400
Actual machine hours	1,300	6,370	100
Actual overhead	£13,900	£30,300	£8,500

Answer

Forming	£
Overhead absorbed (£2.50 × 5,370)	13,425
Overhead incurred	13,900
Under-absorbed overhead	475

Machines	£
Overhead absorbed (£5.50 × 6,370)	35,035
Overhead incurred	30,300
Over-absorbed overhead	4,735

Assembly	£
Overhead absorbed (£2 × 5,400)	10,800
Overhead incurred	8,500
Over-absorbed overhead	2,300

5.6 It is important that you should be completely confident in handling under- and over-absorption of overheads. This question will demonstrate that the techniques which you have just learned can also be applied in a service organisation.

Question 6

A management consultancy recovers overheads on chargeable consulting hours. Budgeted overheads were £615,000 and actual consulting hours were 32,150. Overheads were under-recovered by £35,000.

If actual overheads were £694,075 what was the budgeted overhead absorption rate per hour?

A £19.13   B £20.50   C £21.59   D £22.68

Answer

	£
Actual overheads	694,075
Under-recoverable overheads	35,000
Overheads recovered for 32,150 hours at budgeted overhead absorption rate (x)	659,075

$$32,150x = 659,075$$

$$x = \frac{659,075}{32,150} = £20.50$$

The correct option is B.

Chapter roundup

- Product costs are built up using **absorption costing** by a process of **allocation**, **apportionment** and **absorption**.

- In absorption costing, it is usual to add overheads into product costs by applying a **predetermined overhead absorption rate**. The predetermined rate is set annually, in the budget.

- To work out the **absorption rate**, budgeted overheads are allocated to production cost centres, service department cost centres or general overhead cost centres. General overheads are then apportioned to production and service department cost centres using an appropriate basis. The service department cost centre overheads are then apportioned to production cost centres.

- There are two main methods of reapportioning service department overheads to production departments.

  - **Direct method** (ignores inter-service department work)
  - **Repeated distribution** (recognises inter-service department work)

- The **absorption rate** is calculated by dividing the budgeted overhead by the budgeted level of activity. For production overheads, the level of activity is often budgeted direct labour hours or budgeted machine hours.

- Management should try to establish an absorption rate that provides a reasonably 'accurate' estimate of overhead costs for jobs, products or services.

- The overhead absorption rate is **predetermined** using figures from the budget and so actual costs of production include overheads based on this predetermined recovery rate. As a consequence there will be a discrepancy between overheads incurred and overheads absorbed. If overheads absorbed exceed overheads incurred, the cost of production (or sales), will have been too high. The amount of over absorption will be written as a **'favourable'** adjustment to the profit and loss account. Similarly, if overheads absorbed are lower than the amount of overheads incurred, the cost of production (or sales) will have been too low. The amount of under absorption will be written as an **'adverse'** adjustment to the profit and loss account.

- **Under-** or **over-absorbed** overhead is inevitable in estimates of absorption costing because the predetermined overhead absorption rates are based on estimates of overhead expenditure and the level, or volume, of activity. Both estimates are likely to be at least a bit wrong, and overhead under or over absorbed may be due to a combination of estimating the budgeted expenditure wrongly and estimating the volume of activity wrongly.

- All production overhead is thus identified with cost centres engaged directly in production. Administration overhead and selling and distribution overhead are also separately identified.

Quick quiz

1 What is allocation?

2 Match the following overheads with the most appropriate basis of apportionment.

Overhead	**Basis of apportionment**
(a) Depreciation of equipment	(1) Direct machine hours
(b) Heat and light costs	(2) Number of employees
(c) Canteen	(3) Book value of equipment
(d) Insurance of equipment	(4) Floor area

BPP PUBLISHING

3   How do the direct and repeated distribution methods of service cost centre apportionment differ?

4   A direct labour hour basis is most appropriate in which of the following environments?

   A   Machine-intensive
   B   Labour-intensive
   C   When all units produced are identical
   D   None of the above

5   Why might it be a problem to use a single factory overhead absorption rate? What alternative method might be used?

6   Does over absorption occur when absorbed overheads are greater or less than actual overheads?

Answers to quick quiz

1   The process whereby whole cost items are charged direct to a cost unit or cost centre.

2   (a)   (3)
     (b)   (4)
     (c)   (2)
     (d)   (3)

3   The direct method is generally used when inter-service department work is not taken into account. The repeated distribution method is used when inter-service department work is recognised.

4   B

5   Because some products will receive a higher overhead charge than they ought 'fairly' to bear, and other products will be undercharged. A fairer alternative method is to use a separate absorption rate for each department.

6   Greater.

Now try the question below from the Exam Question Bank

Number	Level	Marks	Time
Q6	Examination	25	45 mins

Chapter 6

MARGINAL COSTING AND ABSORPTION COSTING

Topic list	Syllabus reference	Ability required
1 Marginal cost and marginal costing	(i)	Application
2 Contribution	(i), (iv)	Comprehension
3 The principles of marginal costing	(i)	Comprehension
4 Marginal costing and absorption costing compared	(i), (iii)	Application, analysis

Introduction

In Chapter 1 we introduced the idea of **product costs** and **period costs**. **Product costs** are costs identified with goods produced or purchased for resale. Such costs are initially identified as part of the value of stock and only become expenses when the stock is sold. In contrast, **period costs** are costs that are deducted as expenses during the current period without ever being included in the value of stock held. In the previous chapter we saw how product costs are absorbed into the cost of units of output.

This chapter describes **marginal costing** and compares it with **absorption costing**. Whereas absorption costing recognises fixed costs (usually fixed production costs) as part of the cost of a unit of output and hence as product costs, marginal costing treats all fixed costs as period costs. Two such different costing methods obviously each have their supporters and we will be looking at the arguments both in favour of and against each method. Each costing method, because of the different stock valuation used, produces a different profit figure and we will be looking at this particular point in detail.

Learning outcomes covered in this chapter

- **Explain** the contribution concept
- **Calculate** product costs under marginal costing
- **Compare** and **contrast** absorption and marginal costing
- **Prepare** profit and loss accounts from the same data under absorption and marginal costing and reconcile and explain the differences in reported profits

Syllabus content covered in this chapter

- Contribution concept
- Marginal costing
- Marginal and absorption costing profit and loss accounts

1 MARGINAL COST AND MARGINAL COSTING

> **KEY TERMS**
>
> - **Marginal costing** is an alternative method of costing to absorption costing. In marginal costing, only variable costs are charged as a cost of sale and a contribution is calculated which is sales revenue minus the variable cost of sales. Closing stocks of work in progress or finished goods are valued at marginal (variable) production cost. Fixed costs are treated as a period cost, and are charged in full to the profit and loss account of the part of the accounting period in which they are incurred.
>
> - **Marginal cost** is 'The part of one unit of product or service which would be avoided if that unit were not produced, or which would increase if one extra unit were produced'.
>
> CIMA *Official Terminology*

1.1 The marginal production cost per unit of an item usually consists of the following.

- Direct materials
- Direct labour
- Variable production overheads

2 CONTRIBUTION   Pilot paper

> **KEY TERM**
>
> **Contribution** is 'Sales value less variable cost of sales'.
>
> CIMA *Official Terminology*

2.1 **Contribution** is of fundamental importance in marginal costing, and the term 'contribution' is really short for 'contribution towards covering fixed overheads and making a profit'.

3 THE PRINCIPLES OF MARGINAL COSTING

3.1 The principles of marginal costing are as follows.

(a) Period fixed costs are the same, for any volume of sales and production (provided that the level of activity is within the 'relevant range'). Therefore, by selling an extra item of product or service the following will happen.

- Revenue will increase by the sales value of the item sold.
- Costs will increase by the variable cost per unit.
- Profit will increase by the amount of contribution earned from the extra item.

(b) Similarly, if the volume of sales falls by one item, the profit will fall by the amount of contribution earned from the item.

(c) Profit measurement should therefore be based on an analysis of total contribution. Since fixed costs relate to a period of time, and do not change with increases or decreases in sales volume, it is misleading to charge units of sale with a share of fixed costs. Absorption costing is therefore misleading, and it is more appropriate to deduct fixed costs from total contribution for the period to derive a profit figure.

(d) When a unit of product is made, the extra costs incurred in its manufacture are the **variable production costs**. Fixed costs are unaffected, and no extra fixed costs are incurred when output is increased. It is therefore argued that the valuation of closing stocks should be at variable production cost (direct materials, direct labour, direct expenses (if any) and variable production overhead) because these are the only costs properly attributable to the product.

3.2 Before explaining marginal costing principles any further, it will be helpful to look at a numerical example.

3.3 EXAMPLE: MARGINAL COSTING

Water Ltd makes a product, the Splash, which has a variable production cost of £6 per unit and a sales price of £10 per unit. At the beginning of September 20X0, there were no opening stocks and production during the month was 20,000 units. Fixed costs for the month were £45,000 (production, administration, sales and distribution). There were no variable marketing costs.

Required

Calculate the contribution and profit for September 20X0, using marginal costing principles, if sales were as follows.

(a) 10,000 Splashes
(b) 15,000 Splashes
(c) 20,000 Splashes

3.4 SOLUTION

The first stage in the profit calculation must be to identify the variable costs, and then the contribution. Fixed costs are deducted from the total contribution to derive the profit. All closing stocks are valued at marginal production cost (£6 per unit).

	10,000 Splashes		*15,000 Splashes*		*20,000 Splashes*	
	£	£	£	£	£	£
Sales (at £10)		100,000		150,000		200,000
Opening stock	0		0		0	
Variable production cost	120,000		120,000		120,000	
	120,000		120,000		120,000	
Less value of closing stock (at marginal cost)	60,000		30,000		-	
Variable cost of sales		60,000		90,000		120,000
Contribution		40,000		60,000		80,000
Less fixed costs		45,000		45,000		45,000
Profit/(loss)		(5,000)		15,000		35,000
Profit/(loss) per unit		£(0.50)		£1		£1.75
Contribution per unit		£4		£4		£4

3.5 The conclusions which may be drawn from this example are as follows.

(a) The **profit per unit varies** at differing levels of sales, because the average fixed overhead cost per unit changes with the volume of output and sales.

(b) The **contribution per unit is constant** at all levels of output and sales. Total contribution, which is the contribution per unit multiplied by the number of units sold, increases in direct proportion to the volume of sales.

(c) Since the **contribution per unit does not change**, the most effective way of calculating the expected profit at any level of output and sales would be as follows.

  (i)   First calculate the total contribution.
  (ii) Then deduct fixed costs as a period charge in order to find the profit.

(d) In our example the expected profit from the sale of 17,000 Splashes would be as follows.

	£
Total contribution (17,000 × £4)	68,000
Less fixed costs	45,000
Profit	23,000

3.6 (a) If total contribution exceeds fixed costs, a profit is made.

 (b) If total contribution exactly equals fixed costs, no profit and no loss is made and breakeven point is reached.

 (c) If total contribution is less than fixed costs, there will be a loss.

Question 1

Plumber Ltd makes two products, the Loo and the Wash. Information relating to each of these products for April 20X1 is as follows.

	Loo	*Wash*
Opening stock	nil	nil
Production (units)	15,000	6,000
Sales (units)	10,000	5,000
	£	£
Sales price per unit	20	30
Unit costs		
Direct materials	8	14
Direct labour	4	2
Variable production overhead	2	1
Variable sales overhead	2	3

Fixed costs for the month	£
Production costs	40,000
Administration costs	15,000
Sales and distribution costs	25,000

Required

Using marginal costing principles, calculate the profit in April 20X1. Use the approach set out in Paragraph 3.5(d) above.

Answer

	£
Contribution from Loos (unit contribution = £20 − £16 = £4 × 10,000)	40,000
Contribution from Washes (unit contribution = £30 − £20 = £10 × 5,000)	50,000
Total contribution	90,000
Fixed costs for the period	80,000
Profit	10,000

4 MARGINAL COSTING AND ABSORPTION COSTING COMPARED

Pilot paper

> **Exam focus point**
>
> The **Management Accounting Fundamentals** syllabus states that, 'on completion of their studies students should be able to: compare and contrast absorption and marginal costing.' This is a very important section of the chapter – make sure that you work through it very carefully.

4.1 **Marginal costing** as a cost accounting system is significantly different from absorption costing. It is an **alternative method** of accounting for costs and profit, which rejects the principles of absorbing fixed overheads into unit costs.

    (a) **In marginal costing**

        (i)   Closing stocks are valued at **marginal production cost**.

        (ii)   Fixed costs are charged in full against the profit of the period in which they are incurred.

    (b) **In absorption costing** (sometimes referred to as **full costing**)

        (i)   Closing stocks are valued at full production cost, and include a share of fixed production costs.

        (ii)   This means that the cost of sales in a period will include some fixed overhead incurred in a previous period (in opening stock values) and will exclude some fixed overhead incurred in the current period but carried forward in closing stock values as a charge to a subsequent accounting period.

4.2 This distinction between marginal costing and absorption costing is very important and the contrast between the systems must be clearly understood. Work carefully through the following example to ensure that you are familiar with both methods.

4.3 EXAMPLE: MARGINAL AND ABSORPTION COSTING COMPARED

Two Left Feet Ltd manufactures a single product, the Claud. The following figures relate to the Claud for a one-year period.

Activity level	50%	100%
Sales and productions (units)	400	800
	£	£
Sales	8,000	16,000
Production costs: variable	3,200	6,400
fixed	1,600	1,600
Sales and distribution costs:		
variable	1,600	3,200
fixed	2,400	2,400

The normal level of activity for the year is 800 units. Fixed costs are incurred evenly throughout the year, and actual fixed costs are the same as budgeted.

There were no stocks of Claud at the beginning of the year.

In the first quarter, 220 units were produced and 160 units sold.

Required

(a) Calculate the fixed production costs absorbed by Clauds in the first quarter if absorption costing is used.

(b) Calculate the under/over recovery of overheads during the quarter.

(c) Calculate the profit using absorption costing.

(d) Calculate the profit using marginal costing.

(e) Explain why there is a difference between the answers to (c) and (d).

4.4 SOLUTION

(a) $$\frac{\text{Budgeted fixed production costs}}{\text{Budgeted output (normal level of activity)}} = \frac{£1,600}{800 \text{ units}}$$

Absorption rate = £2 per unit produced.

During the quarter, the fixed production overhead absorbed was 220 units × £2 = £440.

(b)

	£
Actual fixed production overhead	400 (¼ of £1,600)
Absorbed fixed production overhead	440
Over absorption of overhead	40

(c) **Profit for the quarter, absorption costing**

	£	£
Sales (160 × £20)		3,200
Production costs		
Variable (220 × £8)	1,760	
Fixed (absorbed overhead (220 × £2))	440	
Total (220 × £10)	2,200	
Less closing stocks (60 × £10)	600	
Production cost of sales	1,600	
Adjustment for over-absorbed overhead	40	
Total production costs		1,560
Gross profit		1,640
Less: sales and distribution costs		
variable (160 × £4)	640	
fixed (¹/₄ of £2,400)	600	
		1,240
Net profit		400

(d) **Profit for the quarter, marginal costing**

	£	£
Sales		3,200
Variable production costs	1,760	
Less closing stocks (60 × £8)	480	
Variable production cost of sales	1,280	
Variable sales and distribution costs	640	
Total variable costs of sales		1,920
Total contribution		1,280
Less:		
Fixed production costs incurred	400	
Fixed sales and distribution costs	600	
		1,000
Net profit		280

(e) The difference in profit is due to the different valuations of closing stock. In absorption costing, the 60 units of closing stock include absorbed fixed overheads of

£120 (60 × £2) , which are therefore costs carried over to the next quarter and not charged against the profit of the current quarter. In marginal costing, all fixed costs incurred in the period are charged against profit.

	£
Absorption costing profit	400
Fixed production costs carried forward in stock values	120
Marginal costing profit	280

4.5 We can draw a number of conclusions from this example.

(a) **Marginal costing** and **absorption costing** are different techniques for assessing profit in a period.

(b) If there are **changes in stocks during a period, marginal costing and absorption costing give different results for profit obtained.**

    (i) **If stock levels increase absorption costing will report the higher profit** because some of the fixed production overhead incurred during the period will be carried forward in closing stock (which reduces cost of sales) to be set against sales revenue in the following period instead of being written off in full against profit in the period concerned (as in the example above).

    (ii) **If stock levels decrease, absorption costing will report the lower profit** because as well as the fixed overhead incurred, fixed production overhead which had been brought forward in opening stock is released and is included in cost of sales.

(c) **If the opening and closing stock volumes and values are the same, marginal costing and absorption costing will give the same profit figure.**

(d) **In the long run, total profit for a company will be the same whether marginal costing or absorption costing is used** because in the long run, total costs will be the same by either method of accounting. Different accounting conventions merely affect the profit of individual accounting periods.

Question 2

The overhead absorption rate for product X is £10 per machine hour. Each unit of product X requires five machine hours. Stock of product X on 1.1.X1 was 150 units and on 31.12.X1 it was 100 units. What is the difference in profit between results reported using absorption costing and results reported using marginal costing?

A   The absorption costing profit would be £2,500 less
B   The absorption costing profit would be £2,500 greater
C   The absorption costing profit would be £5,000 less
A   The absorption costing profit would be £5,000 greater

Answer

Difference in profit = **change** in stock levels × fixed overhead absorption per unit = (150 − 100) × £10 × 5 = £2,500 **lower** profit, because stock levels **decreased**. The correct answer is therefore option A.

The key is the change in the volume of stock. Stock levels have **decreased** therefore absorption costing will report a **lower** profit. This eliminates options B and D.

Option C is incorrect because it is based on the closing stock only (100 units × £10 × 5 hours).

4.6 EXAMPLE: COMPARISON OF TOTAL PROFITS

To illustrate the point in Paragraph 4.5(d), let us suppose that a company makes and sells a single product. At the beginning of period 1, there are no opening stocks of the product, for which the variable production cost is £4 and the sales price £6 per unit. Fixed costs are £2,000 per period, of which £1,500 are fixed production costs.

	Period 1	Period 2
Sales	1,200 units	1,800 units
Production	1,500 units	1,500 units

What would the profit be in each period using the following methods of costing?

(a) Absorption costing. Assume normal output is 1,500 units per period.
(b) Marginal costing.

4.7 SOLUTION

It is important to notice that although production and sales volumes in each period are different (and therefore the profit for each period by absorption costing will be different from the profit by marginal costing), over the full period, total production equals sales volume, the total cost of sales is the same, and therefore the total profit is the same by either method of accounting.

(a) **Absorption costing**: the absorption rate for fixed production overhead is

$$\frac{£1,500}{1,500 \text{ units}} = £1 \text{ per unit}$$

	Period 1		Period 2		Total	
	£	£	£	£	£	£
Sales		7,200		10,800		18,000
Production costs						
Variable	6,000		6,000		12,000	
Fixed	1,500		1,500		3,000	
	7,500		7,500		15,000	
Add opening stock b/f	-		1,500			
	7,500		9,000		15,000	
Less closing stock c/f	1,500		-		-	
Production cost of sales	6,000		9,000		15,000	
(Under-)/over-absorbed overhead	-		-		-	
Total production costs		6,000		9,000		15,000
Gross profit		1,200		1,800		3,000
Other costs		500		500		1,000
Net profit		700		1,300		2,000

(b) **Marginal costing**

	Period 1		Period 2		Total	
	£	£	£	£	£	£
Sales		7,200		10,800		18,000
Variable production cost	6,000		6,000		12,000	
Add opening stock b/f	-		1,200		-	
	6,000		7,200		12,000	
Less closing stock c/f	1,200		-		-	
Variable production cost of sales		4,800		7,200		12,000
Contribution		2,400		3,600		6,000
Fixed costs		2,000		2,000		4,000
Profit		400		1,600		2,000

Note that the total profit over the two periods is the same for each method of costing, but the profit in each period is different.

Question 3

When opening stocks were 8,500 litres and closing stocks 6,750 litres, a firm had a profit of £62,100 using marginal costing.

Assuming that the fixed overhead absorption rate was £3 per litre, what would be the profit using absorption costing?

A £41,850   B £56,850   C £67,350   D £82,350

Answer

Difference in profit = (8,500 – 6,750) × £3 = £5,250

Absorption costing profit = £62,100 – £5,250 = £56,850

The correct answer is B.

Since stock levels reduced, the absorption costing profit will be lower than the marginal costing profit. You can therefore eliminate options C and D.

Exam focus point

The effect on profit of using the two different costing methods can be confusing. You *must* get it straight in your mind before the examination. Remember that if opening stock values are greater than closing stock values, marginal costing shows the greater profit.

Marginal costing and absorption costing compared: which is better?

4.8   There are accountants who favour each costing method.

(a)   Arguments in favour of absorption costing are as follows.

   (i)   Fixed production costs are incurred in order to make output; it is therefore 'fair' to charge all output with a share of these costs.

   (ii)   Closing stock values, by including a share of fixed production overhead, will be valued on the principle required for the financial accounting valuation of stocks by statement of standard accounting practice on stocks and long term contracts (SSAP 9).

   (iii)   A problem with calculating the contribution of various products made by a company is that it may not be clear whether the contribution earned by each product is enough to cover fixed costs, whereas by charging fixed overhead to a product it is possible to ascertain whether it is profitable or not.

(b)   Arguments in favour of marginal costing are as follows.

   (i)   It is simple to operate.

   (ii)   There are no apportionments, which are frequently done on an arbitrary basis, of fixed costs. Many costs, such as the managing director's salary, are indivisible by nature.

   (iii)   Fixed costs will be the same regardless of the volume of output, because they are period costs. It makes sense, therefore, to charge them in full as a cost to the period.

   (iv)   The cost to produce an extra unit is the variable production cost. It is realistic to value closing stock items at this directly attributable cost.

   (v)   Under or over absorption of overheads is avoided.

(vi) Marginal costing information can be used for decision making but (as we will see when we move onto Part C of this Study Text). Absorption costing information is not suitable for decision making.

(vii) Fixed costs (such as depreciation, rent and salaries) relate to a period of time and should be charged against the revenues of the period in which they are incurred.

Exam focus point

In order to give you an idea of the way in which the topics of absorption and marginal costing might be examined, consider the following extract from the **Management Accounting Fundamentals Pilot paper.**

'(a) Prepare profit and loss statements for period 5 using:

(i) Absorption costing
(ii) Marginal costing (15 marks)

(b) Prepare a reconciliation of the difference between the profit/loss under absorption costing *and* under marginal costing and explain the reason for the difference. (4 marks)'

Chapter roundup

- In your examination you may be asked to calculate the profit or produce profit statements for an accounting period using either of the two methods of accounting. **Absorption costing** is most often used for routine profit reporting and must be used for financial accounting purposes. **Marginal costing** provides better management information for planning and decision making.

- **Marginal cost** is the variable cost of one unit of product or service (the cost which would be avoided if that unit were not produced).

- **Contribution** is an important measure in marginal costing, and it is calculated as the difference between sales value and marginal or variable cost.

- In **marginal costing, fixed production costs are treated as period costs** and are written off as they are incurred. In **absorption costing, fixed production costs are absorbed into the cost of units** and are carried forward in stock to be charged against sales for the next period. Stock values using absorption costing are therefore greater than those calculated using marginal costing.

- **Reported profit figures** using marginal costing or absorption costing **will differ if there is any change in the level of stocks** in the period. **If production is equal to sales, there will be no difference in calculated profits** using these costing methods.

- **SSAP 9** recommends the use of absorption costing for the valuation of stocks in financial accounts.

- There are a number of arguments both for and against each of the costing systems.

- The distinction between marginal costing and absorption costing is very important and it is vital that you now understand the contrast between the two systems.

Quick quiz

1   Sales value – marginal cost of sales = ...

2   Marginal costing and absorption costing are different techniques for assessing profit in a period. If there are changes in stock during a period, marginal costing and absorption costing give different results for profit obtained.

Which of the following statements are true?

I   If stock levels increase, marginal costing will report the higher profit.

II   If stock levels decrease, marginal costing will report the lower profit.

III   If stock levels decrease, marginal costing will report the higher profit.

IV   If the opening and closing stock volumes are the same, marginal costing and absorption costing will give the same profit figure.

A   All of the above
B   I, II and IV
C   I and IV
D   III and IV

3   Which of the following are arguments in favour of marginal costing?

(a)   Closing stock is valued in accordance with SSAP 9.
(b)   It is simple to operate.
(c)   There is no under or over absorption of overheads.
(d)   Fixed costs are the same regardless of activity levels.
(e)   The information from this costing method may be used for decision making.

Answers to quick quiz

1   Contribution

2   D

3   (b), (c), (d), (e)

Now try the question below from the Exam Question Bank

Number	Level	Marks	Time
Q7	Examination	15	27 mins

Part B
Costing and accounting systems

Chapter 7

COST BOOKKEEPING

Topic list		Syllabus reference	Ability required
1	Accounting for costs	(iii)	Comprehension
2	Interlocking systems	(iii)	Comprehension
3	Integrated systems	(iii)	Comprehension

Introduction

You now know how to determine the major elements of the cost of a unit of product - **material**, **labour**, **overhead** - and how to build these elements up into a cost unit. What you don't know is how to account for these costs within a cost accounting system. This chapter will teach you the first step, which is **cost bookkeeping**.

The overall bookkeeping routine will vary from organisation to organisation but either an **integrated** or an **interlocking** system will be used. We will be looking at each of these systems in detail, seeing how to record costs in them and how the two systems differ.

Note that the ability required for the contents covered in this chapter is **comprehension**. Whilst it is vital that you understand the workings involved in cost bookkeeping systems, you will only be examined on the **application** of integrated accounting systems using **standard costs**. We will turn our attention to this part of the syllabus later on in the Study Text.

Learning outcome covered in this chapter

- **Explain** the difference between integrated and interlocking accounting systems

Syllabus content covered in this chapter

- Accounting entries for an integrated accounting system
- Interlocking accounting

1   ACCOUNTING FOR COSTS

1.1   There are **no statutory requirements** to keep detailed cost records and so some small firms only keep traditional financial accounts and prepare cost information in an ad-hoc fashion. This approach is, however, unsatisfactory for all but the smallest organisations: most firms therefore maintain some form of cost accounting system.

1.2   **Cost accounting systems** range from simple analysis systems to computer based accounting systems. Often systems are tailored to the users' requirements and therefore incorporate unique features. All systems will incorporate a number of common aspects and all records will be maintained using the **principles of double entry**.

BPP PUBLISHING

Interlocking and integrated accounts

1.3 Recording cost transactions using the self-balancing double entry method of a debit and credit entry for each transaction may be achieved in either of the following ways.

> **KEY TERM**
>
> **Interlocking accounts.** 'A system in which the cost accounts are distinct from the financial accounts, the two sets of accounts being kept continuously in agreement by the use of control accounts or reconciled by other means'.
>
> CIMA *Official Terminology*

1.4 The cost accounts in interlocking systems use the same basic data (purchases, wages and so on) as the financial accounts, but frequently adopt different bases for matters such as depreciation and stock valuation.

> **KEY TERM**
>
> **Integrated accounts.** 'A set of accounting records which provides both financial and cost accounts using a common input of data for all accounting purposes'.
>
> CIMA *Official Terminology*

1.5 With interlocking accounts the same basis for items such as stock valuation and depreciation will be used and there is **no need for a reconciliation** between cost profit and financial profit. Financial profit will simply be the cost profit adjusted by non-cost items such as income from investments and charitable donations.

1.6 The principles of double entry bookkeeping are not described in this chapter, but if you have not yet begun your studies of basic financial accounting, you may not be familiar with the concept of 'debits and credits'. Nevertheless you may still be able to follow the explanations below, provided that you remember the 'golden rule' of double entry bookkeeping, that for every entry made in one account, there must be a corresponding balancing entry in another account.

2 INTERLOCKING SYSTEMS

The principal accounts in a system of interlocking accounts

2.1 These are as follows.

(a) **The resources accounts**
- Materials control account or stores control account
- Wages (and salaries) control account
- Production overhead control account
- Administration overhead control account
- Selling and distribution overhead control account

(b) **Accounts which record the cost of production items from the start of production work through to cost of sales**
- Work in progress control account
- Finished goods control account
- Cost of sales control account

(c)   Sales account

(d)   The costing profit and loss account

(e)   The under-/over-absorbed overhead account

(f)   Cost ledger control account (in the cost ledger)

(g)   Financial ledger control account (in the financial ledger)

How an interlocking system works

2.2   An **interlocking system** features two ledgers.

(a)   The **financial ledger** contains asset, liability, revenue, expense and appropriation (eg dividend) accounts. The trial balance of an enterprise is prepared from the financial ledger.

(b)   The **cost ledger** is where cost information such as the build-up of work in progress is analysed in more detail.

The cost ledger control account

2.3   There are certain items of cost or revenue which are of no interest to the cost accountant because they are **financial accounting items**. These include the following.

- Interest or dividends received
- Dividends paid
- Discounts allowed or received for prompt payment of invoices

2.4   Some financial accounting items are related to costs and profits (and hence interest the cost accountant), although accounts for these items are not included in the separate cost accounting books. The most important of these items are cash, creditors, debtors and profit and loss reserves. To overcome the need to have accounts for cash, creditors and so on in the cost books, a **cost ledger control account** is used. It represents all the accounts in the financial accounting books which are not included in the corresponding cost accounting books.

2.5   Since we are concerned, in this text, with the cost ledger we will not discuss the financial ledger control account at this stage.

Accounting entries in a system of cost ledger accounts

2.6   The accounting entries in a system of cost ledger accounts can be confusing and it is important to keep in mind some general principles.

(a)   When **expenditure** is incurred on materials, wages or overheads, the actual amounts paid or payable are debited to the appropriate **resources accounts**. The credit entries (which in a financial accounting ledger would be in the cash or creditors accounts) are in the **cost ledger control account**.

(b)   When production begins, **resources are allocated to work in progress**. This is recorded by crediting the resources accounts and debiting the work in progress account. In the case of production overheads, the amount credited to the overhead account and debited to work in progress should be the amount of overhead absorbed. If this differs from the amount of overhead incurred, there will be a difference on the overhead control account; this should be written off to an under-/over-absorbed overhead account. (One other point to remember is that when **indirect** materials and labour are allocated to production, the entries are to credit the materials and wages accounts and debit **production overhead account.**)

(c) As **finished goods** are produced, work in progress is reduced. This is recorded by debiting the finished goods control account and crediting the work in progress control account.

(d) To establish the **cost of goods sold,** the balances on finished goods control account, administration overhead control account and selling and distribution overhead control account are transferred to cost of sales control account.

(e) **Sales** are debited to the cost ledger control account and credited to sales account.

(f) **Profit** is established by transferring to the cost profit and loss account the balances on the sales account, cost of sales account and under-/over-absorbed overhead account.

Accounting entries in absorption costing and marginal costing systems

2.7 Cost bookkeeping can appear quite daunting to begin with. You may find the two diagrams on the following pages, which illustrate the (simplified) operation of interlocking systems using absorption costing and marginal costing, useful. Follow the entries through the various control accounts and note the differences between the two diagrams. You will then be ready to work through the following example.

2.8 EXAMPLE: INTERLOCKING ACCOUNTS

Write up the cost ledger accounts of a manufacturing company for the latest accounting period. The following data is relevant.

(a) There is no stock on hand at the beginning of the period.

(b) Details of the transactions for the period received from the financial accounts department include the following.

	£
Sales	420,000
Indirect wages:	
production	25,000
administration	15,000
sales and distribution	20,000
Materials purchased	101,000
Direct factory wages	153,200
Production overheads	46,500
Selling and distribution expenses	39,500
Administration expenses	32,000

(c) Other cost data for the period include the following.

Raw materials issued to production as indirect materials	£15,000
Stores issued to production as direct materials	£77,000
Raw materials of finished production	£270,200
Cost of goods sold at finished goods stock valuation	£267,700
Standard rate of production overhead absorption	50p per operating hour
Rate of administration overhead absorption	20% of production cost of sales
Rate of sales and distribution overhead absorption	10% of sales revenue
Actual operating hours worked	160,000

Cost accounting using absorption costing

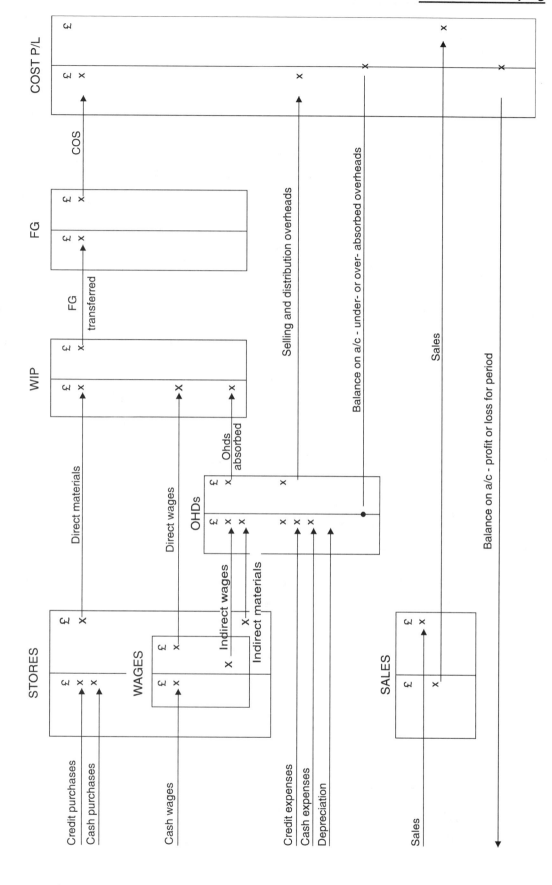

Cost accounting using marginal costing

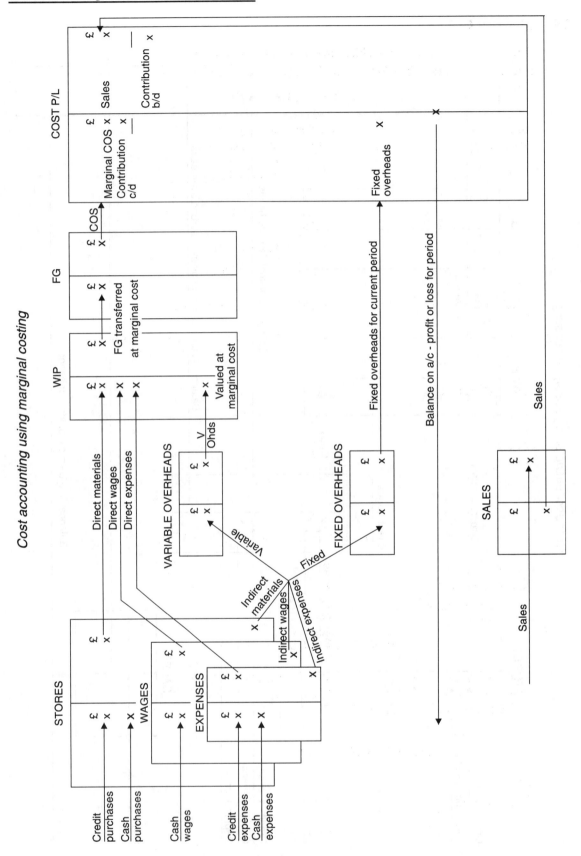

2.9 SOLUTION

The problem should be tackled methodically, in the order suggested by paragraph 2.6 above. The letters in brackets show the sequence in which the various entries are made.

COST LEDGER CONTROL (CLC)

	£		£
Sales (a)	420,000	Wages control (b)	213,200
Balance c/d	51,500	Materials control (c)	101,000
		Prod'n o'hd control (d)	46,500
		S & D o'hd control (e)	39,500
		Admin o'hd control (f)	32,000
		Cost profit and loss a/c	39,300
	471,500		471,500
		Balance b/d	51,500

MATERIALS CONTROL

	£		£
CLC (c) - purchases	101,000	Prod'n o'hd control (k)(indirect materials)	15,000
		WIP control (l)(issues to production)	77,000
		∴Closing stock c/d (bal fig)	9,000
	101,000		101,000
Closing stock b/d	9,000		

WAGES CONTROL

	£		£
CLC (b)	213,200	Prod'n o'hd control (g)	25,000
		Admin o'hd control (h)	15,000
		S & D o'hd control (j)	20,000
		WIP control (m)(direct labour)	153,200
	213,200		213,200

PRODUCTION OVERHEAD CONTROL

	£		£
CLC (d)	46,500	WIP control (p)(160,000 × 50p)	
Wages control (g)	25,000	(overheads absorbed)	80,000
Materials control (k)	15,000	∴ O'hds under-absorbed (bal fig)	6,500
	86,500		86,500

ADMINISTRATION OVERHEAD CONTROL

	£		£
CLC (f)	32,000	Cost of sales control (o/hds absorbed)(q)	
Wages control (h)	15,000	(20% × £267,700)	53,540
∴ O'hds over-absorbed (bal fig)	6,540		
	53,540		53,540

SELLING AND DISTRIBUTION OVERHEAD CONTROL

	£		£
CLC (e)	39,500	Cost of sales control (r)(o/hds absorbed) (10% × £420,000)	42,000
Wages control (j)	20,000	∴ O'hds under-absorbed (bal fig)	17,500
	59,500		59,500

WORK IN PROGRESS CONTROL

	£		£
Materials control (l)	77,000	Finished goods control (n)	270,200
Wages control (m)	153,200	∴ Closing stock of WIP c/d (bal fig)	40,000
Prod'n o'hd control (p)	80,000		
	310,200		310,200
Balance b/d	40,000		

BPP PUBLISHING

FINISHED GOODS CONTROL

	£		£
WIP control (n)	270,200	Cost of sales control (o)	267,700
		∴ Stock of finished goods c/d (bal fig)	2,500
	270,200		270,200
Balance b/d	2,500		

COST OF SALES CONTROL

	£		£
Finished goods control (o)	267,700	Cost profit and loss a/c	363,240
Admin o'hd control (q)	53,540		
S & D o'hd control (r)	42,000		
	363,240		363,240

SALES

	£		£
Cost profit and loss a/c	420,000	CLC (a)	420,000

UNDER-/OVER-ABSORBED OVERHEAD

	£		£
Prod'n o'hd control	6,500	Admin o'hd control	6,540
S & D o'hd control	17,500	∴ Cost profit and loss a/c	17,460
	24,000		24,000

COST PROFIT AND LOSS

	£		£
Cost of sales control	363,240	Sales	420,000
Under-/over-absorbed o'hd	17,460		
CLC (profit for period)	39,300		
	420,000		420,000

2.10 Note how the trial balance can be extracted from the accounts.

TRIAL BALANCE

	Debit £	Credit £
Cost ledger control		51,500
Materials stock	9,000	
Work in progress	40,000	
Finished goods stocks	2,500	
	51,500	51,500

2.11 EXAMPLE: THE WAGES CONTROL ACCOUNT

The following details were extracted from a weekly payroll for 750 employees at a factory.

	Direct workers £	Indirect workers £	Total £
Analysis of gross pay:			
Ordinary time	36,000	22,000	58,000
Overtime: basic wage	8,700	5,430	14,130
premium	4,350	2,715	7,065
Shift allowance	3,465	1,830	5,295
Sick pay	950	500	1,450
Idle time	3,200	-	3,200
	56,665	32,475	89,140
Net wages paid to employees	£45,605	£24,220	£69,825

Required

Prepare the wages control account for the week.

2.12 SOLUTION

(a) The **wages control account** acts as a sort of 'collecting place' for net wages paid and deductions made from gross pay. The gross pay is then analysed between direct and indirect wages.

(b) The first step is to determine which wage costs are direct and which are indirect. The direct wages will be debited to the work in progress account and the indirect wages will be debited to the production overhead account.

(c) There are in fact only two items of direct wages cost in this example - the ordinary time (£36,000) and the basic overtime wage (£8,700) paid to direct workers. All other payments (including the overtime premium) are indirect wages.

(d) The net wages paid are debited to the control account, and the balance then represents the deductions which have been made for income tax, national insurance, and so on.

WAGES CONTROL ACCOUNT

	£		£
Bank: net wages paid	69,825	Work in progress - direct labour	44,700
Deductions control accounts*		Production overhead control:	
(£89,140 – £69,825)	19,315	Indirect labour	27,430
		Overtime premium	7,065
		Shift allowance	5,295
		Sick pay	1,450
		Idle time	3,200
	89,140		89,140

* In practice there would be a separate deductions control account for each type of deduction made (such as PAYE, National Insurance).

2.13 When an organisation maintains separate cost accounts and financial accounts, the cost profit will differ from the financial profit because of differences in the revenue and costs that are included in the respective profit and loss accounts. It is an essential accounting function that the cost profit and financial profit are reconciled in interlocking accounting systems.

2.14 A **memorandum reconciliation account** is not a part of any double entry system of bookkeeping. It is simply a method by which a record can be made of the differences in the cost accounts and the financial accounts, in order to show why their respective profit figures are different.

2.15 Some examples of items creating differences between the cost accounting and financial accounting profits are listed below.

(a) **Items appearing in the financial accounts, but not in the cost accounts.**

(i) Items of income and expenditure which affect the financial accounts profit, but are excluded from the cost accounts. These include the following.

- Interest received or paid
- Discounts received or allowed
- Profits or losses on disposal of fixed assets
- Dividends received
- Fines and penalties

(ii) Appropriations of profit in the financial profit and loss account, including the following.

- Donations

- Income tax
- Dividends paid and proposed

(b) **Items appearing in the cost accounts, but not in the financial accounts** are infrequent, but usually relate to **notional costs**. These are charges made in the cost accounts in order to give a more realistic picture of the cost of an activity. There are two main types of notional cost.

  (i) **Interest on capital**. This represents the nominal cost of capital tied up in production and accounts for the cost of using the capital internally rather than investing it outside the business. The cost accountant makes the charge so that managers are fully aware of the true cost, for example, of holding stocks in the production process. The charge can also help to make the cost of items made with expensive capital equipment more comparable to the cost of items which are not.

  (ii) **Nominal rent charge**. This is a nominal charge raised for the use of premises which are owned. This enables a comparison to be made between the cost of production in a factory which is owned and the costs in one which is rented. The nominal rent charge makes managers more aware of the true cost of occupying the premises.

(c) **Differences may arise between the financial and cost accounts in the calculation of actual overhead costs incurred**. For example if the cost accounting books contain a provision for depreciation account, differences may arise in the choice of depreciation method (for example straight line method, reducing balance method, and so on) or in the expected life of the equipment.

(d) **Valuation of stock on hand is likely to be made according to different bases for the respective accounts**. For the financial accounts the basis of stock valuation will be the lower of cost and net realisable value. For the cost accounts, the basis of stock valuation might be FIFO, LIFO or any basis that is useful to management.

Advantages and disadvantages of interlocking systems

2.16 The main **advantage** of interlocking systems is that they feature two ledgers, each of which **fulfil different purposes**. Having two sets of ledger means that it is less likely that any conflict of needs will arise.

2.17 The main **limitations** of interlocking systems are as follows.

- Profits of separate cost and financial accounts must be reconciled
- They require more administration time
- They are more costly to run

3 INTEGRATED SYSTEMS

3.1 In a system of integrated accounts the financial and cost accounts are combined in **one set of self-balancing ledger accounts**. This eliminates the need to operate financial ledger control accounts and reconcile the respective cost and financial profits.

3.2 There are a few points to note about integrated accounts.

(a) To facilitate the control of costs and assist with management information the same classifications used in the cost ledger of an interlocking system are also used in an integrated system.

(b) All transactions normally excluded from a cost ledger are included in an integrated ledger.

(c) Additional ledger accounts required by an integrated system would be as follows.

- Control accounts for debtors and creditors
- Bank account
- Fixed asset accounts
- Other assets and liabilities accounts
- Share capital account, retained profit account and other reserve accounts

(d) There is no cost ledger control account, because this appears in a system of interlocking accounts only as a substitute for debtors, creditors, bank accounts and so on.

The advantage and disadvantage of integrated systems

3.3 The **advantage** of integrated systems over separate systems for cost and financial accounting is the **saving in administrative effort**. Only one set of accounts needs to be maintained instead of two and the possible confusion arising from having two sets of accounts with different figures (such as for stock values and profits) does not exist.

3.4 The **disadvantage** of integrated accounts is that one set of accounts is expected to fulfil two different purposes.

- Stewardship of the business, and external reporting
- Provision of internal management information

3.5 At times, these different purposes may conflict; for example, the valuation of stocks will conform to the requirements of SSAP 9, whereas for management information purposes it might be preferable to value closing stocks at, say, marginal cost or replacement cost.

3.6 In practice, however, computers have overcome these disadvantages and most modern cost accounting systems are integrated systems, incorporating coding systems which allow basic data to be analysed and presented in different ways for different purposes. The way in which integrated accounts actually work is perhaps best explained by an example.

3.7 EXAMPLE: INTEGRATED ACCOUNTS

KC Ltd manufactures a range of products which are sold through a network of wholesalers and dealers. A set of integrated accounts is kept, and for the year 20X0 the following information is relevant.

(a) Production overhead is absorbed into the cost of products on the basis of a budgeted rate of 80% of direct labour cost.

(b) Finished stocks are valued at factory cost.

(c)

	31 March 20X0 £	30 April 20X0 £
Raw materials stock	17,200	15,160
Work in progress	5,600	4,750
Finished goods stock	10,500	12,090
Debtors for goods sold	9,200	11,140
Creditors for raw materials	7,600	9,420
Fixed assets at net book value	6,000	6,000

(d) Bank transactions for the month of April 20X0 were as follows.

	£
Bank balance at 31 March	1,500
Receipts from debtors	27,560
Payments made	
Direct labour	6,400
Creditors for raw materials	8,960
Production overhead	5,400
Administration overhead	700
Selling and distribution overhead	2,300

Required

(a) Use the information above to write up the following control accounts.

   (i)   Raw materials stock
   (ii)   Work in progress
   (iii)   Finished goods
   (iv)   Production overhead

(b) Prepare the following statements.

   (i)   A profit and loss account for the month of April 20X0
   (ii)   A balance sheet as at 30 April 20X0

3.8 SOLUTION

(a) (i) RAW MATERIALS STOCK

	£		£
Opening balance	17,200	Work in progress	
Creditors (W1)	10,780	(balancing figure)	12,820
		Balance c/d	15,160
	27,980		27,980
Balance b/d	15,160		

(ii) WORK IN PROGRESS

	£		£
Opening balance	5,600	Finished goods	
Raw materials stock	12,820	(balancing figure)	25,190
Direct wages	6,400		
Production overhead (W2)	5,120	Balance c/d	4,750
	29,940		29,940
Balance b/d	4,750		

(iii) FINISHED GOODS

	£		£
Opening balance	10,500	Profit and loss account	
Work in progress	25,190	(cost of sales) (bal fig)	23,600
		Balance c/d	12,090
	35,690		35,690
Balance b/d	12,090		

(iv) PRODUCTION OVERHEAD

	£		£
Cash	5,400	Work in progress	5,120
		Profit and loss account	
		(under-absorbed)	280
	5,400		5,400

(b) (i) PROFIT AND LOSS ACCOUNT
FOR THE MONTH OF APRIL 20X0

	£	£
Sales (W3)		29,500
Production cost of sales		23,600
Gross profit		5,900
Less: administration overhead	700	
sales and distribution overhead	2,300	
under-absorbed production overhead	280	
		3,280
Profit		2,620

(ii) BALANCE SHEET AS AT 30 APRIL 20X0

	£	£
Fixed assets (net book value)		6,000
Current assets		
Raw materials	15,160	
Work in progress	4,750	
Finished goods	12,090	
Debtors	11,140	
Cash (W4)	5,300	
	48,440	
Less current liabilities		
Creditors	9,420	
		39,020
		45,020
Long-term capital £(42,400 (balancing figure)+ 2,620)		45,020

Workings

1

CREDITORS FOR RAW MATERIALS

	£		£
Cash	8,960	Opening balance	7,600
Balance c/f	9,420	Raw materials purchases	
		(balancing figure)	10,780
	18,380		18,380

2	Direct labour	£6,400
	Production overhead absorbed (80%)	£5,120

3

DEBTORS

	£		£
Opening balance	9,200	Cash	27,560
Sales (balancing figure)	29,500	Balance c/f	11,140
	38,700		38,700

4

CASH

	£		£
Opening balance	1,500	Creditors for raw materials	8,960
Debtors	27,560	Direct labour	6,400
		Production overhead	5,400
		Administration overhead	700
		Sales and distribution o'hd	2,300
		Balance c/f	5,300
	29,060		29,060

Question

At the end of a period, in an integrated cost and financial accounting system, the accounting entries for £18,000 overheads under-absorbed would be

A	Debit work-in-progress control account	Credit overhead control account
B	Debit profit and loss account	Credit work-in-progress control account
C	Debit profit and loss account	Credit overhead control account
D	Debit overhead control account	Credit profit and loss account

Answer

Eliminate the incorrect options first. The only overhead charge made to work in progress (WIP) is the overhead absorbed into production based on the predetermined rate. Under or over absorption does not affect WIP. This eliminates A and B. Under-absorbed overhead means that overhead charges have been too low therefore there must be a further debit to profit and loss. This eliminates D, and the correct answer is C.

Exam focus point

The syllabus for **Management Accounting Fundamentals** only expects you to be able to **apply** your cost bookkeeping knowledge to **integrated systems using standard costing.** We shall therefore revisit the topic of cost bookkeeping when we study standard costing in Part D of the Study Text.

Chapter roundup

- There are two types of cost accounting system - **interlocking** and **integrated**.

- Interlocking accounts contain **separate ledgers for cost accounts and for financial accounts**. A **cost ledger control account** is maintained in the cost ledger to complete the costing double entry. It represents the financial ledger accounts which are not maintained in the cost ledger (such as cash, debtors and creditors).

- When an organisation operates an **interlocking accounts system**, it is necessary to **reconcile** the cost accounting profit with the financial accounting profit. Items which create differences between the cost accounting and financial accounting profits include stock valuations, profits and losses on disposal of fixed assets, interest paid and received and appropriations of profit.

- **Integrated systems** combine both financial and cost accounts in one system of ledger accounts. A reconciliation between cost and financial profits is not necessary.

Quick quiz

1   List the principal accounts in a system of interlocking accounts.

2   What is the double entry for the following?

    (a)   Production overhead absorbed in the cost of production
    (b)   Completed work transferred from the production process to stock

3   List five items which might appear in a reconciliation of cost accounting profit and financial accounting profit.

4   What is the main advantage and the main disadvantage of integrated accounts?

Answers to quick quiz

1
- Resources accounts
- Accounts recording cost of production items
- Sales account
- Costing profit and loss account
- Under-/over-absorbed overhead account
- Cost ledger control account (in cost ledger)
- Financial ledger control account (in financial ledger)

2　(a)　Dr　Work in progress control account
　　　　Cr　Production overhead account

　　(b)　Dr　Finished goods control account
　　　　Cr　Work in progress control account

3
- Interest received or paid
- Discounts received or allowed
- Profits or losses on disposal of fixed assets
- Dividends received
- Donations
- Income tax
- Dividends paid and proposed
- Notional costs eg interest on capital

4　**Advantage.** Saving in administrative effort

　Disadvantage. One set of accounts is expected to fulfil two different purposes

Now try the question below from the Exam Question Bank

Number	Level	Marks	Time
Q8	Introductory	n/a	15 mins

Chapter 8

JOB, BATCH AND CONTRACT COSTING

Topic list	Syllabus reference	Ability required
1 Job costing	(iii)	Application
2 Job costing for internal services	(iii)	Application
3 Job costing example	(iii)	Application
4 Batch costing	(iii)	Application
5 Introduction to contract costing	(iii)	Application
6 Recording contract costs	(iii)	Application
7 Contract accounts	(iii)	Application
8 Progress payments	(iii)	Application
9 Profits on contracts	(iii)	Application
10 Losses on incomplete contracts	(iii)	Application
11 Disclosure of long-term contracts in financial accounts	(iii)	Application

Introduction

Having learnt the basics of cost bookkeeping in the previous chapter, we will now apply these basics to particular costing methods.

A **costing method** is designed to suit the way goods are processed or manufactured or the way services are provided. Each organisation's costing method will therefore have unique features but costing methods of firms in the same line of business will more than likely have common aspects. On the other hand, organisations involved in completely different activities, such as hospitals and car part manufacturers, will use very different methods.

This chapter begins by covering **job costing**. We will see the circumstances in which job costing should be used and how the costs of jobs are calculated. We will look at how the **costing of individual jobs** fits in with the recording of total costs in control accounts. The chapter then moves on to **batch costing**, the procedure for which is similar to job costing.

The final costing method considered in this chapter is **contract costing**. Contract costing is similar to job costing but the job is of such importance that a formal contract is made between the supplier and the customer. We will see how to record contract costs, how to account for any profits and losses arising on contracts at the end of an accounting period and we will look briefly at how contract balances are disclosed in financial accounts.

Learning outcome covered in this chapter

- **Prepare** ledger accounts for job, batch and contract costing systems

Syllabus content covered in this chapter

- Job, batch and contract costing

1   JOB COSTING

> **KEY TERMS**
>
> - A **job** is a cost unit which consists of a single order or contract.
>
> - **Job costing** is a costing method applied where work is undertaken to customers' special requirements and each order is of comparatively short duration.

1.1   The work relating to a job is usually carried out within a factory or workshop and moves through processes and operations as a **continuously identifiable unit**.

Procedure for the performance of jobs

1.2   The normal procedure which is adopted in jobbing concerns involves the following.

(a)   The prospective customer approaches the supplier and indicates the requirements of the job.

(b)   A responsible official sees the prospective customer and agrees with him the precise details of the items to be supplied, for example the quantity, quality, size and colour of the goods, the date of delivery and any special requirements.

(c)   The estimating department of the organisation then prepares an estimate for the job. This will include the cost of the materials to be used, the wages expected to be paid, the appropriate amount for factory, administration, selling and distribution overhead, the cost where appropriate of additional equipment needed specially for the job, and finally the supplier's **profit margin**. The total of these items will represent the quoted **selling price**.

(d)   At the appropriate time, the job will be 'loaded' on to the factory floor. This means that as soon as all materials, labour and equipment are available and subject to the scheduling of other orders, the job will be started. In an efficient organisation, the start of the job will be timed to ensure that while it will be ready for the customer by the promised date of delivery it will not be loaded too early, otherwise storage space will have to be found for the product until the date it is required by (and was promised to) the customer.

Collection of job costs

1.3   A separate record must be maintained to show the details of individual jobs. The process of collecting job costs may be outlined as follows.

(a)   **Materials requisitions are sent to stores.** Where a perpetual inventory system is maintained, an advance copy of the requisition is used to appropriate from free stock the relevant quantities of materials. The second copy of the requisition is sent as and when the materials are needed.

(b)   **The material requisition note will be used to cost the materials issued to the job** concerned, and this cost may then be recorded on a **job cost sheet**. The cost may include items already in stock and/or items specially purchased.

(c)   **The job ticket is passed to the worker who is to perform the first operation.** The times of his starting and finishing the operation are recorded on the ticket, which is then passed to the person who is to carry out the second operation, where a similar record of the times of starting and finishing is made.

(d) When the job is completed, the **job ticket is sent to the cost office,** where the time spent will be costed and recorded on the job cost sheet.

(e) The **relevant costs** of materials issued, direct labour performed and direct expenses incurred as recorded on the job cost sheet **are charged to the job account** in the work in progress ledger.

(f) **The job account is debited with the job's share of the factory overhead,** based on the absorption rate(s) in operation. If the job is incomplete at the end of an accounting period, it is valued at factory cost in the closing balance sheet (where a system of absorption costing is in operation).

(g) **On completion of the job,** the job account is charged with the appropriate administration, selling and distribution overhead, after which **the total cost of the job can be ascertained.**

(h) The difference between the agreed selling price and the total actual cost will be the supplier's profit (or loss).

Job cost sheet (or card)

1.4 An example of a job cost sheet is shown on page 117. Job cost sheets show the following.

- Detail of relatively small jobs.
- A summary of direct materials, direct labour and so on for larger jobs.

1.5 When jobs are completed, **job cost sheets** are transferred from the **work in progress** category to **finished goods.** When delivery is made to the customer, the costs become a **cost of sale.** If the completed job was carried out in order to build up finished goods stocks (rather than to meet a specific order) the quantity of items produced and their value are recorded on **finished goods stores ledger cards.**

Rectification costs

KEY TERM

Rectification cost is the cost incurred in rectifying sub-standard output.

1.6 If the finished output is found to be sub-standard, it may be possible to rectify the fault. The sub-standard output will then be returned to the department or cost centre where the fault arose. You should know how to deal with such costs in a job costing system.

1.7 **Rectification costs** can be treated in two ways.

(a) If rectification work is not a frequent occurrence, but arises on occasions with specific jobs to which it can be traced directly, then the rectification costs should be **charged as a direct cost to the jobs concerned.**

(b) If rectification is regarded as a normal part of the work carried out generally in the department, then the rectification costs should be **treated as production overheads.** This means that they would be included in the total of production overheads for the department and absorbed into the cost of all jobs for the period, using the overhead absorption rate.

JOB COST CARD												Job No. B641		
Customer Mr J White				Customer's Order No.								Vehicle make Peugot 205 GTE		
Job Description Repair damage to offside front door												Vehicle reg. no. G 614 50X		
Estimate Ref. 2599				Invoice No.								Date to collect 14.6.X0		
Quoted price £338.68				Invoice price £355.05										

Material						Labour								Overheads			
				Cost			Emp-loyee	Cost Ctre	Hrs.	Rate	Bonus	Cost		Hrs	OAR	Cost	
Date	Req. No.	Qty.	Price	£	p	Date						£	p			£	p
12.6	36815	1	75.49	75	49	12.6	018	B	1.98	6.50	-	12	87	7.9	2.50	19	75
12.6	36816	1	33.19	33	19	13.6	018	B	5.92	6.50	-	38	48				
12.6	36842	5	6.01	30	05						13.65	13	65				
13.6	36881	5	3.99	19	95												
Total C/F				158	68	Total C/F						65	00	Total C/F		19	75

Expenses						Job Cost Summary	Actual		Estimate	
			Cost				£	p	£	p
Date	Ref.	Description	£	p		Direct Materials B/F	158	68	158	68
						Direct Expenses B/F	50	00		
						Direct Labour B/F	65	00	180	00
12.6	-	N. Jolley Panel-beating	50	-		Direct Cost	273	68		
						Overheads B/F	19	75		
							293	43		
						Admin overhead (add 10%)	29	34		
						= Total Cost	322	77	338	68
						Invoice Price	355	05		
Total C/F			50	-		Job Profit/Loss	32	28		

Comments

Job Cost Card Completed by _

BPP PUBLISHING

Job costing and computerisation

1.8 **Job costing cards** exist in **manual** systems, but it is increasingly likely that in large organisations the job costing system will be **computerised**, using accounting software specifically designed to deal with job costing requirements. A computerised job accounting system is likely to contain the following features.

(a) Every job will be given a job code number, which will determine how the data relating to the job is stored.

(b) A separate set of codes will be given for the type of costs that any job is likely to incur. Thus, 'direct wages', say, will have the same code whichever job they are allocated to.

(c) In a sophisticated system, costs can be analysed both by job (for example all costs related to Job 456), but also by type (for example direct wages incurred on all jobs). It is thus easy to perform variance analysis and to make comparisons between jobs.

(d) A job costing system might have facilities built into it which incorporate other factors relating to the performance of the job. In complex jobs, sophisticated planning techniques might be employed to ensure that the job is performed in the minimum time possible. Time management features therefore may be incorporated into job costing software.

Cost plus pricing

1.9 The usual method of fixing selling prices within a jobbing concern is known as **cost plus pricing** where a desired profit margin is added to total costs to arrive at the selling price.

1.10 The **disadvantages** of cost plus pricing are as follows.

(a) There are no incentives to **control costs** as a profit is guaranteed.

(b) There is no motive to tackle **inefficiencies** or **waste**.

(c) It doesn't take into account any significant differences in actual and estimated volumes of activity. Since the overhead absorption rate is based upon estimated volumes, there may be **under-/over-absorbed overheads** not taken into account.

(d) Because overheads are apportioned in an arbitrary way, this may lead to **under and over pricing**.

1.11 The **cost plus system** is often adopted where **one-off jobs** are carried out to **customers' specifications**.

Exam focus point

An exam question about job costing may ask you to accumulate costs to arrive at a job cost, and then to determine a job price by adding a certain amount of profit. To do this, you need to remember the following crucial formula.

	%
Cost of job	100
+ profit	25
= price	125

Profit may be expressed either as a percentage of job cost (such as 25% 25/100 mark up) or as a percentage of price (such as 20% (25/125) margin).

2   JOB COSTING FOR INTERNAL SERVICES

2.1   **Job costing systems** may be used to control the costs of **internal service departments,** eg the maintenance department. A job costing system enables the cost of a specific job to be charged to a user department. Therefore instead of apportioning the total costs of service departments, each job done is charged to the individual user department.

2.2   An **internal job costing system** for service departments will have the following advantages.

(a)   **Realistic apportionment.** The identification of expenses with jobs and the subsequent charging of these to the department(s) responsible means that costs are borne by those who incurred them.

(b)   **Increased responsibility and awareness.** User departments will be aware that they are charged for the specific services used and may be more careful to use the facility more efficiently. They will also appreciate the true cost of the facilities that they are using and can take decisions accordingly.

(c)   **Control of service department costs.** The service department may be restricted to charging a standard cost to user departments for specific jobs carried out. It will then be possible to measure the efficiency or inefficiency of the service department by recording the difference between the standard charges and the actual expenditure.

(d)   **Budget information.** This information will ease the budgeting process, as the purpose and cost of service department expenditure can be separately identified.

Question 1

Twist and Tern Ltd is a company that carries out jobbing work. One of the jobs carried out in February was job 1357, to which the following information relates.

Direct material Y:	400 kilos were issued from stores at a cost of £5 per kilo.
Direct material Z:	800 kilos were issued from stores at a cost of £6 per kilo.
	60 kilos were returned.
Department P:	300 labour hours were worked, of which 100 hours were done in overtime.
Department Q:	200 labour hours were worked, of which 100 hours were done in overtime.

Overtime work is not normal in Department P, where basic pay is £4 per hour plus an overtime premium of £1 per hour. Overtime work was done in Department Q in February because of a request by the customer of another job to complete his job quickly. Basic pay in Department Q is £5 per hour and overtime premium is £1.50 per hour.

Department P had to carry out rectification work which took 20 hours in normal time. These 20 hours are additional to the 300 hours above. This rectification work is normal for a job such as job 1357, and since it was expected, it is included in the direct cost of the job.

Overhead is absorbed at the rate of £3 per direct labour hour in both departments.

Required

Calculate the following.

(a)   The direct materials cost of job 1357
(b)   The direct labour cost of job 1357
(c)   The full production cost of job 1357

Answer

(a)

	£
Direct material Y (400 kilos × £5)	2,000
Direct material Z (800 – 60 kilos × £6)	4,440
Total direct material cost	6,440

(b)

	£
Department P (320 hours × £4)	1,280
Department Q (200 hours × £5)	1,000
Total direct labour cost	2,280

Rectification work, being normal and expected, is included in the direct labour cost of Department P. In Department P, overtime premium will be charged to overhead. In Department Q, overtime premium will be charged to the job of the customer who asked for overtime to be worked.

(c)

	£
Direct material cost	6,440
Direct labour cost	2,280
Production overhead (520 hours × £3)	1,560
	10,280

3 JOB COSTING EXAMPLE

3.1 An example may help to illustrate the principles of job costing, and the way in which the costing of individual jobs fits in with the recording of total costs in control accounts.

3.2 Fateful Morn Ltd is a jobbing company. On 1 June 20X2, there was one uncompleted job in the factory. The job card for this work is summarised as follows.

Job Card, Job No 6832

Costs to date	£
Direct materials	630
Direct labour (120 hours)	350
Factory overhead (£2 per direct labour hour)	240
Factory cost to date	1,220

During June, three new jobs were started in the factory, and costs of production were as follows.

Direct materials	£
Issued to: Job 6832	2,390
Job 6833	1,680
Job 6834	3,950
Job 6835	4,420
Damaged stock written off from stores	2,300

Material transfers	£
Job 6834 to Job 6833	250
Job 6832 to 6834	620

Materials returned to store	£
From Job 6832	870
From Job 6835	170

Direct labour hours recorded	
Job 6832	430 hrs
Job 6833	650 hrs
Job 6834	280 hrs
Job 6835	410 hrs

The cost of labour hours during June 20X2 was £3 per hour, and production overhead is absorbed at the rate of £2 per direct labour hour. Production overheads incurred during the month amounted to £3,800. Completed jobs were delivered to customers as soon as they were completed, and the invoiced amounts were as follows.

Job 6832	£5,500
Job 6834	£8,000
Job 6835	£7,500

Administration and marketing overheads are added to the cost of sales at the rate of 20% of factory cost. Actual costs incurred during June 20X2 amounted to £3,200.

Required

(a) Prepare the job accounts for each individual job during June 20X2; (the accounts should only show the cost of production, and not the full cost of sale).

(b) Prepare the summarised job cost cards for each job, and calculate the profit on each completed job.

(c) Show how the costs would be shown in the company's cost control accounts.

3.3 SOLUTION

(a) **Job accounts**

JOB 6832

	£		£
Balance b/f	1,220	Job 6834 a/c	620
Materials (stores a/c)	2,390	(materials transfer)	
Labour (wages a/c)	1,290	Stores a/c (materials returned)	870
Production overhead (o'hd a/c)	860	Cost of sales a/c (balance)	4,270
	5,760		5,760

JOB 6833

	£		£
Materials (stores a/c)	1,680	Balance c/f	5,180
Labour (wages a/c)	1,950		
Production overhead (o'hd a/c)	1,300		
Job 6834 a/c (materials transfer)	250		
	5,180		5,180

JOB 6834

	£		£
Materials (stores a/c)	3,950	Job 6833 a/c (materials transfer)	250
Labour (wages a/c)	840		
Production overhead (o'hd a/c)	560	Cost of sales a/c (balance)	5,720
Job 6832 a/c (materials transfer)	620		
	5,970		5,970

JOB 6835

	£		£
Materials (stores a/c)	4,420	Stores a/c (materials returned)	170
Labour (wages a/c)	1,230		
Production overhead (o'hd a/c)	820	Cost of sales a/c (balance)	6,300
	6,470		6,470

(b) **Job cards, summarised**

	Job 6832	*Job 6833*	*Job 6834*	*Job 6835*
	£	£	£	
Materials	1,530*	1,930	4,320 **	4,250
Labour	1,640	1,950	840	1,230
Production overhead	1,100	1,300	560	820
Factory cost	4,270	5,180	(c/f) 5,720	6,300
Admin & marketing o'hd (20%)	854		1,144	1,260
Cost of sale	5,124		6,864	7,560
Invoice value	5,500		8,000	7,500
Profit/(loss) on job	376		1,136	(60)

* £(630 + 2,390 – 620 – 870) ** £(3,950 + 620 – 250)

(c) **Control accounts**

STORES CONTROL (incomplete)

	£		£
WIP a/c (returns)	1,040	WIP a/c	
		(2,390 + 1,680 + 3,950 + 4,420)	12,440
		Profit and loss a/c:	
		stock written off	2,300

WORK IN PROGRESS CONTROL

	£		£
Balance b/f	1,220	Stores control a/c (returns)	1,040
Stores control a/c	12,440	Cost of sales a/c	
Wages control a/c	5,310	*(4,270 + 5,720 + 6,300)	16,290
Production o'hd control a/c	3,540	Balance c/f (Job No 6833)	5,180
	22,510		22,510

* 1,770 hours at £3 per hour

COST OF SALES CONTROL

	£		£
WIP control a/c	16,290	Profit and loss	19,548
Admin & marketing o'hd a/c			
(854 + 1,144 + 1,260)	3,258		
	19,548		19,548

SALES

	£		£
Profit and loss	21,000	CLC	21,000
		(5,500 + 8,000 + 7,500)	
	21,000		21,000

PRODUCTION OVERHEAD CONTROL

	£		£
CLC	3,800	WIP a/c	3,540
(overhead incurred)		Under-absorbed o'hd a/c	260
	3,800		3,800

UNDER-/OVER-ABSORBED OVERHEADS

	£		£
Production o'hd control a/c	260	Admin & marketing o'hd a/c	58
		Profit and loss a/c	202
	260		260

ADMIN & MARKETING OVERHEAD CONTROL

	£		£
CLC	3,200	Cost of sales a/c	3,258
(overhead incurred)			
Over absorbed o'hd a/c	58		
	3,258		3,258

PROFIT AND LOSS

	£		£
Cost of sales a/c	19,548	Sales a/c	21,000
Stores a/c (stock written off)	2,300		
Under-absorbed overhead a/c	202	Loss (CLC) - balance	1,050
	22,050		22,050

FINANCIAL LEDGER CONTROL (CLC) (incomplete)

	£		£
Sales a/c	21,000	Production overhead a/c	3,800
P & L a/c (loss)	1,050	Admin and marketing o'hd a/c	3,200

The loss of £1,050 is the sum of the profits/losses on each completed job £(376 + 1,136 – 60) = £1,452, minus the total of under-absorbed overhead (£202) and the stock write-off (£2,300).

Question 2

A furniture-making business manufactures quality furniture to customers' orders. It has three production departments (A, B and C) which have overhead absorption rates (per direct labour hour) of £12.86, £12.40 and £14.03 respectively.

Two pieces of furniture are to be manufactured for customers. Direct costs are as follows.

	Job XYZ	Job MNO
Direct material	£154	£108
Direct labour	20 hours dept A	16 hours dept A
	12 hours dept B	10 hours dept B
	10 hours dept C	14 hours dept C

Labour rates are as follows: £3.80(A); £3.50 (B); £3.40 (C)

The firm quotes prices to customers that reflect a required profit of 25% on selling price. Calculate the total cost and selling price of each job.

Answer

		Job XYZ £		Job MNO £
Direct material		154.00		108.00
Direct labour: dept A	(20 × 3.80)	76.00	(16 × 3.80)	60.80
dept B	(12 × 3.50)	42.00	(10 × 3.50)	35.00
dept C	(10 × 3.40)	34.00	(14 × 3.40)	47.60
Total direct cost		306.00		251.40
Overhead: dept A	(20 × 12.86)	257.20	(16 × 12.86)	205.76
dept B	(12 × 12.40)	148.80	(10 × 12.40)	124.00
dept C	(10 × 14.03)	140.30	(14 × 14.03)	196.42
Total cost		852.30		777.58
Profit (note)		284.10		259.19
Quoted selling price		1,136.40		1,036.77

(*Note*. If profit is 25% on selling price, this is the same as $33^{1}/_{3}$% (25/75) on cost.)

Question 3

A firm uses job costing and recovers overheads on direct labour.

Three jobs were worked on during a period, the details of which are as follows.

	Job 1 £	Job 2 £	Job 3 £
Opening work in progress	8,500	0	46,000
Material in period	17,150	29,025	0
Labour for period	12,500	23,000	4,500

The overheads for the period were exactly as budgeted, £140,000.

Jobs 1 and 2 were the only incomplete jobs.

What was the value of closing work in progress?

A £81,900   B £90,175   C £140,675   D £214,425

Answer

Total labour cost = £12,500 + £23,000 + £4,500 = £40,000

Overhead absorption rate = $\frac{£140,000}{£40,000} \times 100\% = 350\%$ of direct labour cost

Closing work in progress valuation

		Job 1 £		Job 2 £	Total £
Costs given in question		38,150		52,025	90,175
Overhead absorbed	(12,500 × 350%)	43,750	(23,000 × 350%)	80,500	124,250
					214,425

Option D is correct.

We can eliminate option B because £90,175 is simply the total of the costs allocated to Jobs 1 and 2, with no absorption of overheads. Option A is an even lower cost figure, therefore it can also be eliminated.

Option C is wrong because it is a simple total of all allocated costs, including Job 3 which is not incomplete.

4 BATCH COSTING

4.1 The procedures for **costing batches** are very similar to those for costing jobs.

(a) The batch is treated as a **job** during production and the costs are collected in the manner already described in this chapter.

(b) Once the batch has been completed, the **cost per unit** can be calculated as the **total batch cost divided by the number of units in the batch.**

4.2 EXAMPLE: BATCH COSTING

A company manufactures widgets to order and has the following budgeted overheads for the year, based on normal activity levels.

Department	Budgeted overheads £	Budgeted activity
Welding	6,000	1,500 labour hours
Assembly	10,000	1,000 labour hours

Selling and administrative overheads are 20% of factory cost. An order for 250 widgets type X128, made as Batch 5997, incurred the following costs.

Materials   £12,000

Labour   100 hours welding shop at £2.50/hour

         200 hours assembly shop at £1/hour

£500 was paid for the hire of special X-ray equipment for testing the welds.

Required

Calculate the cost per unit for Batch 5997.

4.3 SOLUTION

The first step is to calculate the overhead absorption rate for the production departments.

$$\text{Welding} = \frac{£6,000}{1,500} = £4 \text{ per labour hour}$$

$$\text{Assembly} = \frac{£10,000}{1,000} = £10 \text{ per labour hour}$$

Total cost - Batch no 5997

		£	£
Direct material			12,000
Direct expense			500
Direct labour	$100 \times 2.50 =$	250	
	$200 \times 1.00 =$	200	
			450
Prime cost			12,950
Overheads	$100 \times 4 =$	400	
	$200 \times 10 =$	2,000	
			2,400
Factory cost			15,350
Selling and administrative cost (20% of factory cost)			3,070
Total cost			18,420

$$\text{Cost per unit} = \frac{£18,420}{250} = £73.68$$

5 INTRODUCTION TO CONTRACT COSTING

> **KEY TERMS**
>
> - A **contract** is a cost unit or cost centre which is charged with the direct costs of production and an apportionment of head office overheads.
>
> - **Contract costing** is a method of job costing where the job to be carried out is of such magnitude that a formal contract is made between the customer and supplier. It applies where work is undertaken to customers' special requirements and each order is of long duration (as compared with job costing). The work is usually constructional and in general the method is similar to job costing.

5.1 In industries such as building and construction work, civil engineering and shipbuilding, job costing is not usually appropriate. **Contract costing** is.

Features of contract costing

5.2
- A **formal contract** is made between customer and supplier.
- Work is undertaken to **customers' special requirements**.
- The work is for a **relatively long duration**.
- The work is frequently **constructional in nature**.
- The method of costing is **similar to job costing**.
- The work is frequently **based on site**.
- It is not unusual for a site to have its own cashier and time-keeper.

5.3 The problems which may arise in contract costing are as follows.

(a) **Identifying direct costs**: because of the large size of the job, many cost items which are usually thought of as production overhead are charged as direct costs of the contract (for example supervision, hire of plant, depreciation and so on).

(b) **Low indirect costs**: because many costs normally classed as overheads are charged as direct costs of a contract, the absorption rate for overheads should only apply a share of the cost of those cost items which are not already direct costs.

(c) **Difficulties of cost control**: because of the size of some contracts and some sites, there are often cost control problems (material usage and losses, pilferage, labour supervision, damage to and loss of plant and tools and so on).

(d) **Dividing the profit between different accounting periods**: when a contract covers two or more accounting periods, how should the profit (or loss) on the contract be divided between the periods?

6 RECORDING CONTRACT COSTS

Direct materials

6.1 The **direct materials** used on a contract may be obtained as follows.

- From the company's central stores
- From the company's suppliers (direct)

6.2 The following points concern **materials obtained from the company's central stores.**

(a) A material requisition note must be sent to the store keeper from the contract site.

(b) The contract manager or foreman must sign all material requisition notes, authorising the issue of materials.

(c) The requisition note provides a record of the cost of the materials issued to the contract.

(d) Contract foreman prefer to have too much material, rather than run out. This means that they will often requisition more material than actually needed. The surplus material will need to be returned to stores via a **material returns note**.

(e) The material returns note must be signed by the foreman and checked by the storekeeper. The accounting entry when materials are returned is as follows.

CREDIT   Contract account (work in progress or 'job' account)
DEBIT   Stores account

(f) Materials on site which relate to an incomplete contract should be carried forward as '**closing stock of materials on site**'.

6.3 When materials are delivered directly from the company's suppliers:

(a) a copy of the goods received note will be sent from the site to the accounting department, and checked against the invoice received from the supplier;

(b) the entire invoice cost will then be charged directly to the contract.

Direct labour

6.4 It is usual for **direct labour** on a contract site to be paid on an hourly basis.

- On a **small site,** the foreman will log the hours worked by each employee.
- On a **large site** there will probably be a resident timekeeper.

Since all the work done is spent exclusively on a single contract, the direct labour cost of the contract should be easily identified from the wages sheets.

6.5 Employees who work on several contracts at the same time, will have to record the time spent on each contract on **time sheets**. Each contract will then be charged with the cost of these recorded hours. Any revenue earned from other small jobs done whilst working on a contract should be treated as follows.

DEBIT   Cash (cash received)
CREDIT   Contract account

6.6 **Payment of wages** depends on the following.

(a) If the **site is nearby**, the wages will be calculated in the head office accounting department, and wage packets made up by the head office cashier. The wages may then be transported from head office to the site by security van, and distributed by the site foreman. Unclaimed wages will be returned to the head office cashier.

(b) If the **site is a long way** from head office, the wages may still be calculated by the accounting department at head office, but the job of distributing wage packets might be given to a site cashier. A local bank will be authorised by head office to issue the appropriate amount of wages to the site cashier.

6.7 The **cost of supervision**, which is usually a production overhead in unit costing, job costing and so on, will be a direct cost of a contract.

Subcontractors

6.8 On large contracts, much work may be done by **subcontractors**. The invoices of subcontractors will be treated as a **direct expense to the contract**.

The cost of plant

6.9 A feature of most contract work is the amount of plant used. Plant used on a contract may be **owned** by the company, or **hired** from a plant hire firm.

(a) If the plant is **hired**, the cost will be a direct expense of the contract.
(b) If the plant is **owned**, a variety of accounting methods may be employed.

Method one: charging depreciation

6.10 **The contract may be charged depreciation on the plant, on a straight line or reducing balance basis**. For example if a company has some plant which cost £10,000 and is depreciated at 10% per annum straight line (to a residual value of nil) and a contract makes use of the plant for six months, a depreciation charge of £500 would be made against the contract. The disadvantage of this method of costing for plant is that the contract site foreman is not made directly responsible and accountable for the actual plant in his charge. The foreman must be responsible for receipt of the plant, returning the plant after it has been used and proper care of the plant whilst it is being used.

Method two: charging the contract with current book value

6.11 **A more common method of costing for plant is to charge the contract with the current book value of the plant.**

CREDIT Plant account (fixed asset account) - with the value of the plant net of depreciation

DEBIT Contract account

At the end of an accounting period, the contract account is credited with the written down value of the equipment.

CREDIT Contract account (plant written down value) carried forward as an opening balance at the start of the next period.

When plant is returned from the site to head office (or transferred to another contract site), the contract account is credited with the written down value of the plant.

CREDIT Contract account (written down value)
DEBIT Plant account (or another contract account)

6.12 EXAMPLE : CHARGING THE CONTRACT WITH CURRENT BOOK VALUE

Contract number 123 obtained some plant and loose tools from central store on 1 January 20X2. The book value of the plant was £100,000 and the book value of the loose tools was £8,000. On 1 October 20X2, some plant was removed from the site: this plant had a written down value on 1 October of £20,000. At 31 December 20X2, the plant remaining on site had a written down value of £60,000 and the loose tools had a written down value of £5,000.

CONTRACT 123 ACCOUNT

	£		£
1 January 20X2		*1 October 20X2*	
Plant issued to site	100,000	Plant transferred	20,000
Loose tools issued to site	8,000	*31 December 20X2*	
		Plant value c/f	60,000
		Loose tools value c/f	5,000
		Depreciation (bal fig)	23,000
	108,000		108,000

The difference between the values on the debit and the credit sides of the account (£20,000 for plant and £3,000 for loose tools) is the depreciation cost of the equipment for the year.

Method three: using a plant account

6.13 A third method of accounting for plant costs is to **open a plant account, which is debited with the depreciation costs and the running costs** (repairs, fuel and so on) **of the equipment**. A notional hire charge is then made to contracts using the plant. For example suppose that a company owns some equipment which is depreciated at the rate of £100 per month. Running costs in May 20X3 are £300. The plant is used on 20 days in the month, 12 days on Contract X and 8 days on Contract Y. The accounting entries would be as follows.

PLANT ACCOUNT

	£		£
Depreciation (cost ledger control account)	100	Contract X (hire for 12 days)	240
		Contract Y (hire for 8 days)	160
Running costs (cost ledger control a/c, wages a/c and stores a/c)	300		
	400		400

CONTRACT X

	£		£
Plant account (notional hire)	240		

CONTRACT Y

	£		£
Plant account (notional hire)	160		

Overhead costs

6.14 **Overhead costs** are added periodically (for example at the end of an accounting period) and are based on predetermined overhead absorption rates for the period. You may come across examples where a share of head office general costs is absorbed as an overhead cost to the contract, but this should not happen if the contract is unfinished at the end of the period, because only production overheads should be included in the value of any closing work in progress.

7 CONTRACT ACCOUNTS

7.1 The account for a contract is a **job account**, or **work in progress account**, and is a record of the direct materials, direct labour, direct expenses and overhead charges on the contract. If we ignore, for the moment, profits on a part-finished contract, a typical contract account might appear as shown below. Check the items in the account carefully, and notice how the cost (or value) of the work done emerges as work in progress. On an unfinished contract, where no profits are taken mid-way through the contract, this cost of work in progress is carried forward as a closing stock balance.

7.2 EXAMPLE: A CONTRACT ACCOUNT

CONTRACT 794 - LUTTERBINS HOLIDAY CAMP

	£		£
Materials requisition from stores	15,247	Materials returned to stores or	
Materials and equipment purchased	36,300	transferred to other sites	2,100
Maintenance and operating costs		Proceeds from sale of materials	
of plant and vehicles	14,444	on site and jobbing work for	
Hire charges for plant and		other customers	600
vehicles not owned	6,500	Book value of plant transferred	4,800
Tools and consumables	8,570	Materials on site c/d	7,194
Book value of plant on site b/d	14,300	Book value of plant on site c/d	6,640
Direct wages	23,890		21,334
Supervisors' and engineers' salaries			
(proportion relating to time spent		Cost of work done c/d	
on the contract)	13,000	(balancing item)	139,917
Other site expenses	12,000		
Overheads (apportioned perhaps on			
the basis of direct labour hours)	17,000		
	161,251		161,251
Materials on site b/d	7,194		
Book value of plant on site b/d	6,640		
Cost of work done b/d	139,917		

8 PROGRESS PAYMENTS

8.1 A customer is likely to be required under the terms of the contract to make **progress payments** to the contractor throughout the course of the work. The amount of the payments will be based on the **value of work done** (as a proportion of the contract price) as assessed by the architect or surveyor (for a building contract) or qualified engineer in his certificate. A **certificate** provides confirmation that work to a certain value has been completed, and that some payment to the contractor is now due. The amount of the payment will be calculated as follows.

The value of work done and certified by the architect or engineer

minus **a retention (commonly 10%)**
minus **the payments made to date**
equals **payment due.**

8.2 Thus, if an architect's certificate assesses the value of work done on a contract to be £125,000 and if the retention is 10%, and if £92,000 has already been paid in progress payments the current payment = £125,000 – £12,500 – £92,000 = £20,500

8.3 When **progress payments** are received from the customer, the accounting entry is as follows.

DEBIT   Bank (or financial ledger control account)
CREDIT   Cash received on account, or contractee account.

8.4 **Retention monies** are released when the contract is completed and accepted by the customer.

9 PROFITS ON CONTRACTS

9.1 You may have noticed that the progress payments do not necessarily give rise to profit immediately because of **retentions. So how are profits calculated on contracts?**

9.2 EXAMPLE: PROFITS ON CONTRACTS COMPLETED IN ONE ACCOUNTING PERIOD

If a contract is started and completed in the same accounting period, the calculation of the profit is straightforward, sales minus the cost of the contract. Suppose that a contract, No 6548, has the following costs.

	£
Direct materials (less returns)	40,000
Direct labour	35,000
Direct expenses	8,000
Plant costs	6,000
Overhead	11,000
	100,000

The work began on 1 February 20X3 and was completed on 15 November 20X3 in the contractor's same accounting year.

The contract price was £120,000 and on 20 November the inspecting engineer issued the final certificate of work done. At that date the customer had already paid £90,000 and the remaining £30,000 was still outstanding at the end of the contractor's accounting period. The accounts would appear as follows.

CONTRACT 6548 ACCOUNT

	£		£
Materials less returns	40,000	Cost of sales (P&L)	100,000
Labour	35,000		
Expenses	8,000		
Plant cost	6,000		
Overhead	11,000		
	100,000		100,000

WORK CERTIFIED ACCOUNT

	£		£
Turnover (P&L)	120,000	Contractee account	120,000
	120,000		120,000

CONTRACTEE (CUSTOMER) ACCOUNT

	£		£
Work certified a/c - value of work certified	120,000	Cash	90,000
		Balance c/f (debtor in balance sheet)	30,000
	120,000		120,000

The profit on the contract will be treated in the profit and loss account as follows.

	£
Turnover	120,000
Cost of sales	100,000
	20,000

Taking profits on incomplete contracts

9.3 A more difficult problem emerges when a contract is **incomplete** at the end of an accounting period. The contractor may have spent considerable sums of money on the work, and received substantial progress payments, and even if the work is not finished, the contractor will want to claim some profit on the work done so far.

9.4 Suppose that a company starts four new contracts in its accounting year to 31 December 20X1, but at the end of the year, none of them has been completed. All of the contracts are eventually completed in the first few months of 20X2 and they make profits of £40,000, £50,000, £60,000 and £70,000 respectively, £220,000 in total. If profits are not taken until the contracts are finished, the company would make no profits at all in 20X1, when most of the work was done, and £220,000 in 20X2. Such violent fluctuations in profitability would be confusing not only to the company's management, but also to shareholders and the investing public at large.

9.5 The problem arises because **contracts are for long-term work,** and it is a well-established practice that some profits should be taken in an accounting period, even if the contract is incomplete.

9.6 EXAMPLE: PROFITS ON INCOMPLETE CONTRACTS

Suppose that contract 246 is started on 1 July 20X2. Costs to 31 December 20X2, when the company's accounting year ends, are derived from the following information.

	£
Direct materials issued from store	18,000
Materials returned to store	400
Direct labour	15,500
Plant issued, at book value 1 July 20X2	32,000
Written-down value of plant 31 December 20X2	24,000
Materials on site, 31 December 20X2	1,600
Overhead costs	2,000

As at 31 December, certificates had been issued for work valued at £50,000 and the contractee had made progress payments of £45,000. The company has calculated that more work has been done since the last certificates were issued, and that the cost of work done but not yet certified is £8,000.

9.7 SOLUTION

The contract account would be prepared as follows.

CONTRACT 246 ACCOUNT

	£	£		£
Materials	18,000		Value of plant c/d	24,000
Less returns	400		Materials on site c/d	1,600
		17,600	Cost of work done not	
Labour		15,500	certified c/d	8,000
Plant issued at book value		32,000	Cost of sales (P&L)	33,500
Overheads		2,000		
		67,100		67,100

WORK CERTIFIED ACCOUNT

	£		£
Turnover (P&L)	50,000	Contractee account	50,000
	50,000		50,000

CONTRACTEE ACCOUNT

	£		£
Work certified account	50,000	Cash (progress payment)	45,000
		Balance c/f	5,000
	50,000		50,000

Points to note

(a) **The work done, but not yet certified, must be valued at cost,** and not at the value of the unissued certificates. It would be imprudent to suppose that the work has been done to the complete satisfaction of the architect or engineer, who may not issue certificates until further work is done.

(b) It would appear that £50,000 should be recognised as turnover and £33,500 as cost of sales leaving £16,500 as net profit. However it is often considered imprudent to claim this full amount of profit, and it is commonly argued that the profit taken should be a more conservative figure (in our example, less than £16,500, so that amounts taken to turnover and cost of sales relating to the contract should be less than £50,000 and £33,500 respectively).

(c) We have ignored retentions here.

Estimating the size of the profit

Exam focus point

The method of calculating profit on an incomplete contract may vary, and you should check any examination question carefully to find out whether a specific method is stated in the text of the question.

9.8 The **concept of prudence** should be applied when estimating the size of the profit on an incomplete contract and the following guidelines should be noted.

(a) **If the contract is in its early stages, no profit should be taken.** Profit should only be taken when the outcome of the contract can be assessed with reasonable accuracy.

(b) **For a contract on which substantial costs have been incurred, but which is not yet near completion** (that is, it is in the region of 35% to 85% complete) a formula which has often been used in the past is as follows.

Profit taken = $^2/_3$ (or $^3/_4$) of the notional profit

where notional profit = (the value of work certified to date) − (the cost of the work certified).

In the example above, the notional profit for contract 246 is £16,500 (£(50,000 − 33,500)) and the profit taken for the period using the above formula would be calculated as follows.

$^2/_3$ of £16,500 = £11,000 (or $^3/_4$ of £16,500 = £12,375)

(c) **Where the contractee withholds a retention, or where progress payments are not made as soon as work certificates are issued,** it would be more prudent to reduce the profit taken by the proportion of retentions to the value of work certified.

$$\textbf{Profit taken} = {^2/_3}\textbf{(or }{^3/_4}\textbf{)} \times \textbf{notional profit} \times \frac{\text{cash received on account}}{\text{value of work certified}}$$

In our example of contract 246, this would be:

$$^2/_3 \times £16,500 \times \frac{£45,000}{£50,000} = £9,900$$

(d) **If the contract is nearing completion, the size of the eventual profit should be foreseeable with reasonable certainty and there is no need to be excessively prudent.** The profit taken may be calculated by one of three methods.

(i) **Work certified to date minus the cost of work certified.** In our example, this would be the full £16,500.

(ii) $\dfrac{\textbf{Cost of work done}}{\textbf{Estimated total cost of contract}} \times \textbf{estimated total profit on contract}$

In our example, if the estimated total cost of the contract 246 is £64,000 and the estimated total profit on the contract is £18,000, the profit taken would be:

$$\frac{£(33,500+8,000)}{£64,000} \times £18,000 = £11,672$$

(iii) **Profit taken =** $\dfrac{\textbf{Value of work certified}}{\textbf{contract price}} \times \textbf{estimated total profit}$

This is perhaps the most-favoured of the three methods. In our example of contract 246, if the final contract price is £82,000 and the estimated total profit is £18,000 the profit taken would be:

$$\frac{£50,000}{£82,000} \times £18,000 = £10,976$$

Some companies may feel that it is prudent to reduce the profit attributed to the current accounting period still further, to allow for retentions of cash by the contractee. In our example, the profit taken would now be:

$$\frac{£50,000}{£82,000} \times £18,000 \times \frac{£45,000}{£50,000} = £9,878$$

This formula simplifies to:

$$\frac{\text{cash received to date}}{\text{contract price}} \times \text{estimated total profit from the contract}$$

(e) **A loss on the contract may be foreseen.** The method of dealing with losses is covered in the next section.

9.9 It should be apparent from these different formulae that the profit taken on an incomplete contract will depend on two things.

- The degree of completion
- The choice of formula

Question 4

Landy Stroyers plc is a construction company. Data relating to one of its contracts, XYZ, for the year to 31 December 20X2, are as follows.

	£'000
Value of work certified to 31 December 20X1	500
Cost of work certified to 31 December 20X1	360
Plant on site b/f at 1 January 20X2	30
Materials on site b/f at 1 January 20X2	10
Cost of contract to 1 January 20X2 b/f	370
Materials issued from store	190
Sub-contractors' costs	200
Wages and salaries	200
Overheads absorbed by contract in 20X2	100
Plant on site c/f at 31 December 20X2	15
Materials on site c/f at 31 December 20X2	5
Value of work certified to 31 December 20X2	1,200
Cost of work certified to 31 December 20X2	950

No profit has been taken on the contract prior to 20X2. There are no retentions.

Required

(a) Calculate the total cumulative cost of contract XYZ to the end of December 20X2.

(b) Turnover on the contract is taken as the value of work certified. Calculate the gross profit for the contract for the year to 31 December 20X2.

Answer

(a)

CONTRACT ACCOUNT

	£'000		£'000
Cost of contract b/f	370	Plant on site c/f	15
Plant on site b/f	30	Materials on site c/f	5
Materials on site b/f	10	Cost of contract c/f (balance)	1,080
Materials from stores	190		
Sub-contractors' costs	200		
Wages and salaries	200		
Overheads	100		
	1,100		1,100

(b) No profit had been taken on the contract prior to 20X2, and so profit is quite simply calculated as follows.

	£'000
Value of work certified to 31.12.X2	1,200
Cost of work certified to 31.12.X2	950
Gross profit to 31.12.X2	250

10 LOSSES ON INCOMPLETE CONTRACTS

10.1 At the end of an accounting period, it may be that instead of finding that the contract is profitable, a loss is expected. When this occurs, the **total expected loss should be taken into account as soon as it is recognised, even though the contract is not yet complete.** The contract account should be debited with the **anticipated future loss** (final cost of contract – full contract price – (cost of work at present – value of work certified at present)) and the profit and loss account debited with the total expected loss (final cost of contract – full contract price).

The same accounting procedure would be followed on completed contracts, as well as incomplete contracts, but it is essential that the full amount of the loss on the total contract, if foreseeable, should be charged against company profits at the earliest opportunity, even if a contract is incomplete. This means that in the next accounting period, the contract should break even, making neither a profit nor a loss, because the full loss has already been charged to the profit and loss account.

10.2 EXAMPLE: LOSS ON CONTRACT

Contract 257 was begun on 22 March 20X3. By 31 December 20X3, the end of the contractor's accounting year, costs incurred were as follows.

	£
Materials issued	24,000
Materials on site, 31 December	2,000
Labour	36,000
Plant issued to site 22 March	40,000
Written-down value of plant, 31 December	28,000
Overheads	6,000

The contract is expected to end in February 20X4 and at 31 December 20X3, the cost accountant estimated that the final cost of the contract would be £95,000. The full contract price is £90,000. Work certified at 31 December was valued at £72,000. The contractee has made progress payments up to 31 December of £63,000.

Required

Prepare the contract account.

10.3 SOLUTION

CONTRACT 257 ACCOUNT

	£		£
Materials issued	24,000	Materials on site c/f	2,000
Labour	36,000	Plant at written-down value, c/f	28,000
Plant issued, written-down value	40,000	Cost of work c/d (balancing figure)	76,000
Overheads	6,000		
	106,000		106,000
Cost of work done, b/d	76,000	Cost of sales (P&L)	77,000
Anticipated future loss*	1,000		
	77,000		77,000

* The total estimated loss on the contract is £5,000 (£90,000 – £95,000). Of this amount £4,000 has been lost in the current period (£76,000 – £72,000) and so £1,000 is anticipated as arising in the future: the company will invoice £18,000 (£90,000 – £72,000) and will incur costs of £19,000 (£95,000 – £76,000). This is taken as a loss in the current period.

The loss is posted £72,000 to turnover and £77,000 to cost of sales (£5,000 net).

Question 5

Jibby Ltd's year end is 30 April. At 30 April 20X4 costs of £43,750 have been incurred on contract N53. The value of work certified at the period end is £38,615. The contract price is £57,500 but it is anticipated that the final costs at 30 September 20X4, when the contract is expected to end, will be £63,111.

Required

(a) Prepare the contract account.
(b) Calculate the figures for turnover and cost of sales for the period to 30 April 20X4.

Answer

(a)

CONTRACT N53

	£		£
Cost of work done b/d	43,750	Cost of sales (P&L)	44,226
Anticipated future loss*	476		
	44,226		44,226

*£[(63,111 – 57,500) – (43,750 – 38,615)] = £476.

(b) Turnover = £38,615

Cost of sales = £44,226

---

11 DISCLOSURE OF LONG-TERM CONTRACTS IN FINANCIAL ACCOUNTS

11.1 **SSAP 9** defines how **stocks** and **work in progress** should be valued in the financial accounts, and makes particular reference to long-term contract work in progress and profits. Although there is no requirement that cost accounting procedures should be the same as financial accounting procedures and standards, it is generally thought that conformity between the financial and cost accounts is desirable in contract costing.

11.2 SSAP 9 makes the following requirements with relation to the profit and loss account.

(a) The profit and loss account will contain turnover and related costs deemed to accrue to the contract over the period, so that the profit and loss account reflects the net profit on the contract taken in the period.

(b) The profit taken needs to reflect the proportion of the work carried out at the accounting date, and to take account of any known inequalities of profitability at the various stages of a contract.

(c) Where the outcome of a contract cannot be reasonably assessed before its completion, no profits should be taken on the incomplete contract.

(d) The amount of profit taken to the profit and loss account for an incomplete contract should be judged with prudence.

(e) If it is expected that there will be a loss on the contract as a whole, provision needs to be made for the whole of the loss as soon as it is recognised (in accordance with the prudence concept). The amount of the loss should be deducted from the amounts for long-term contracts included under stocks, and where a credit balance results, it should be disclosed separately under creditors or provisions for liabilities and charges.

11.3 **SSAP 9** requires the following **disclosures** in the balance sheet.

Balances relating to long-term contracts are split into two elements.

(a) Work done on long-term contracts not yet recognised in the profit and loss account is disclosed under 'stocks' as 'long-term contract balances'.

(b) The difference between

(i)	amounts recognised as turnover	X
(ii)	progress payments received	(X)
		X

will be recognised in debtors as 'amounts recoverable on long-term contracts' if (i) is greater than (ii), or will be offset against the balances in (a) above if (ii) is greater than (i).

Chapter roundup

- **Job costing** is the costing method used where each cost unit is separately identifiable.

- Each job is given a **number** to distinguish it from other jobs.

- Costs for each job are collected on a **job cost sheet** or **job card**.

- Material costs for each job are determined from **material requisition notes**.

- Labour times on each job are recorded on a **job ticket**, which is then costed and recorded on the job cost sheet. Some labour costs, such as overtime premium or the cost of rectifying sub-standard output, might be charged either directly to a job or else as an overhead cost, depending on the circumstances in which the costs have arisen.

- **Overhead** is absorbed into the cost of jobs using the predetermined overhead absorption rates.

- The usual method of fixing prices within a jobbing concern is **cost plus pricing**.

- An **internal job costing system** can be used for costing the work of service departments.

- **Batch costing** is similar to job costing in that each batch of similar articles is separately identifiable. The **cost per unit** manufactured in a batch is the total batch cost divided by the number of units in the batch.

- **Contract costing** is a form of job costing which applies where the job is on a large scale and for a long duration. The majority of costs relating to a contact are direct costs.

- Contract costs are collected in a **contract account**.

- A customer is likely to be required to make **progress payments** which are calculated as the value of work done and certified by the architect or engineer minus a retention minus the payments made to date.

- The long duration of a contract usually means that an estimate must be made of the profit earned on each incomplete contract at the end of the accounting period. There are several different ways of calculating contract profits, but the overriding consideration must be the application of the prudence concept. **If a loss is expected on a contract, the total expected loss should be taken into account as soon as it is recognised, even if the contract is not complete.**

- The loss should be deducted from the amounts for long-term contracts included under stocks in the balance sheet. If the resulting balance is a credit, it should be disclosed separately under creditors or provisions for liabilities and charges.

- **SSAP 9** requires the following disclosures in the balance sheet.

  - Work done on long-term contracts which has yet to be recognised in the profit and loss account in disclosed under 'stocks' as 'long-term contract balances'.

  - The difference between (a) 'amounts recognised as turnover' and (b) 'progress payments received' will be recognised in debtors as 'amounts recoverable on long-term contracts' if (a) > (b), but will be offset against the stock balance mentioned above if (b) > (a).

Quick quiz

1   Which of the following are not characteristics of job costing?

    I   Customer driven production
    II   Complete production possible within a single accounting period
    III   Homogeneous products

    A   I and II only
    B   I and III only
    C   II and III only
    D   III only

2   The cost of a job is £100,000

    (a)   If profit is 25% of the job cost, the price of the job = £.................

    (b)   If there is a 25% margin, the price of the job = £....................

3   List six features of contract costing

    •   ....

    •   ....

    •   ....

    •   ....

    •   ....

    •   ....

4   When progress payments are received from a customer for a contract, what is the accounting entry?

    DEBIT..

    CREDIT..

5   What are the three methods of calculating profit on a contract which is nearing completion?

6   How would you account for a loss on an incomplete contract?

Answers to quick quiz

1 D

2 (a) £100,000 + (25% × £100,000) = £100,000 + £25,000 = £125,000

   (b) Let price of job = x

   $$\therefore \text{Profit} = 25\% \times x \text{ (selling price)}$$
   $$\text{If profit} = 0.25x$$
   $$x - 0.25x = \text{cost of job}$$
   $$0.75x = £100,000$$
   $$x = \frac{£100,000}{0.75}$$
   $$= £133,333$$

3 • A formal contract is made between customer and supplier
   • Work is undertaken to customers' special requirements
   • The work is for a relatively long duration
   • The work is frequently constructional in nature
   • The method of costing is similar to job costing
   • The work is frequently based on site

4 DEBIT   BANK/CASH

   CREDIT   CASH RECEIVED ON ACCOUNT/CONTRACTEE ACCOUNT

5 (a) Work certified to date – cost of work certified

   (b) $\dfrac{\text{Cost of work done}}{\text{Estimated total cost of contract}} \times$ estimated total profit on contract

   (c) $\dfrac{\text{Value of work certified}}{\text{Contract price}} \times$ estimated total profit

6 If a loss is expected on an incomplete contract, the total expected loss should be taken into account as soon as it is recognised, even though the contract is not yet complete.

Now try the questions below from the Exam Question Bank

Number	Level	Marks	Time
Q9	Introductory	n/a	30 mins
Q10	Examination	15	27 mins
Q11	Introductory	n/a	30 mins

Chapter 9

PROCESS COSTING

Topic list	Syllabus reference	Ability required
1 The distinguishing features of process costing	(iii)	Application
2 The basics of process costing	(iii)	Application
3 Dealing with losses in process	(iii)	Application
4 Accounting for scrap	(iii)	Application
5 Valuing closing work in progress	(iii)	Application
6 Valuing opening work in progress	(iii)	Application

Introduction

We have looked at three cost accounting methods, **job costing**, **batch costing** and **contract costing**, in the previous chapter. In this chapter we will consider another, **process costing**. We will begin from basics and look at how to account for the most simple of processes. We will then move on to how to account for any **losses** which might occur, as well as what to do with any **scrapped units** which are sold. Next we will consider how to deal with **closing work in progress** before examining situations involving closing work in progress and losses. We will then go on to have a look at situations involving opening work in progress and finally we shall consider how to deal with situations where we have both opening and closing stock and losses. Throughout the chapter we will be looking at how to record process costs in **process accounts** which are simply WIP ledger accounts.

Learning outcome covered in this chapter

* **Prepare** ledger accounts for process costing systems

    NB. The average cost method will only be used for process costing and students must be able to calculate normal loss and abnormal loss/gains and deal with opening and closing stocks.

Syllabus content covered in this chapter

* Process costing

1   THE DISTINGUISHING FEATURES OF PROCESS COSTING

1.1 It is common to identify process costing with **continuous production** such as the following.

- Oil refining
- The manufacture of soap
- Paint
- Food and drink

1.2 The features of process costing which make it different from job or batch costing are as follows.

(a) The continuous nature of production in many processes means that there will usually be **closing work in progress which must be valued**. In process costing it is not possible to build up cost records of the cost of each individual unit of output because production in progress is an **indistinguishable homogeneous mass**.

(b) There is often a **loss in process** due to spoilage, wastage, evaporation and so on.

(c) The **output** of one process becomes the **input** to the next until the finished product is made in the final process.

(d) Output from production may be a single product, but there may also be a **by-product** (or by-products) and/or **joint products**.

2 THE BASICS OF PROCESS COSTING

2.1 Before tackling the more complex areas of process costing, we will begin by looking at a very simple process costing example which will illustrate the basic techniques which we will build upon in the remainder of this chapter.

2.2 Suppose that Purr and Miaow Ltd make squeaky toys for cats. Production of the toys involves two processes, shaping and colouring. During the year to 31 March 20X3, 1,000,000 units of material worth £500,000 were input to the first process, shaping. Direct labour costs of £200,000 and production overhead costs of £200,000 were also incurred in connection with the shaping process. There were no opening or closing stocks in the shaping department. The process account for shaping for the year ended 31 March 20X3 is as follows.

PROCESS 1 (SHAPING) ACCOUNT

	Units	£		Units	£
Direct materials	1,000,000	500,000	Output to Process 2	1,000,000	900,000
Direct labour		200,000			
Production overheads		200,000			
	1,000,000	900,000		1,000,000	900,000

2.3 You will see that a **process account** is nothing more than a **ledger account** with debit and credit entries although it does have an additional column on both the debit and credit sides showing **quantity**. When preparing process accounts you are advised to include these memorandum quantity columns and to balance them off (ie ensure they total to the same amount on both sides) **before** attempting to complete the monetary value columns since they will help you to check that you have missed nothing out. This becomes increasingly important as more complications are introduced into questions.

2.4 Because process accounts are simply ledger accounts, the double entry works as it does for any other ledger account. For example, the corresponding credit entry of £200,000 for labour in the process 1 account above will be in the **wages and salaries control account**. Students often think process costing is difficult but if you bear in mind that you are simply completing a normal ledger account which is part of a system of double entry cost bookkeeping you will find this topic much more straightforward.

2.5 After that slight digression let us go back to Purr and Miaow Ltd. When using process costing, if a series of separate processes is needed to manufacture the finished product, the output of one process becomes the input to the next until the final output is made in the final process. In our example, all output from shaping was transferred to the second process, colouring, during the year to 31 March 20X3. An additional 500,000 units of material, costing £300,000, were input to the colouring process. Direct labour costs of £150,000 and production overhead costs of £150,000 were also incurred. There were no opening or closing stocks in the colouring department. The process account for colouring for the year ended 31 March 20X3 is as follows.

PROCESS 2 (COLOURING) ACCOUNT

	Units	£		Units	£
Materials from process 1	1,000,000	900,000	Output to finished		
Added materials		300,000	goods	1,000,000	1,500,000
Direct labour		150,000			
Production overhead		150,000			
	1,000,000	1,500,000		1,000,000	1,500,000

2.6 Direct labour and production overhead may be treated together in an examination question as **conversion cost**.

2.7 **Added** materials, labour and overhead in Process 2 are usually **added gradually** throughout the process. Materials from Process 1, in contrast, will often be **introduced in full at the start of the second process**.

Framework for dealing with process costing

2.8 Process costing is centred around **four key steps**. The exact work done at each step will depend on the circumstances of the question, but the approach can always be used. Don't worry about the terms used. We will be looking at their meaning as we work through the chapter.

Step 1. **Determine output and losses**

- Determine expected output.
- Calculate normal loss and abnormal loss and gain.
- Calculate equivalent units if there is closing work in progress.

Step 2. **Calculate cost per unit of output, losses and WIP**

Calculate cost per unit or cost per equivalent unit.

Step 3. **Calculate total cost of output, losses and WIP**

In some examples this will be straightforward. In cases where there is work in progress, a **statement of evaluation** will have to be prepared.

Step 4. **Complete accounts**

- Complete the process account.
- Write up the other accounts required by the question

3 DEALING WITH LOSSES IN PROCESS

3.1 During a production process, a loss may occur due to wastage, spoilage, evaporation, and so on.

KEY TERMS

- **Normal loss** is the loss expected during a process. It is not given a cost.

- **Abnormal loss** is the extra loss resulting when actual loss is greater than normal or expected loss, and it is given a cost.

- **Abnormal gain** is the gain resulting when actual loss is less than the normal or expected loss, and it is given a 'negative cost'.

3.2 Since normal loss is not given a cost, the cost of producing these units is borne by the 'good' units of output.

3.3 Abnormal loss and gain units are valued at the same unit rate as 'good' units. Abnormal events do not therefore affect the cost of good production. Their costs are **analysed separately** in an **abnormal loss or abnormal gain account**.

3.4 EXAMPLE: ABNORMAL LOSSES AND GAINS

Suppose that input to a process is 1,000 units at a cost of £4,500. Normal loss is 10% and there are no opening or closing stocks. Determine the accounting entries for the cost of output and the cost of the loss if actual output were as follows.

(a) 860 units (so that actual loss is 140 units)
(b) 920 units (so that actual loss is 80 units)

3.5 SOLUTION

Before we demonstrate the use of the 'four-step framework' we will summarise the way that the losses are dealt with.

(a) Normal loss is given no share of cost.

(b) The cost of output is therefore based on the **expected** units of output, which in our example amount to 90% of 1,000 = 900 units.

(c) Abnormal loss is given a cost, which is written off to the profit and loss account via an abnormal loss/gain account.

(d) Abnormal gain is treated in the same way, except that being a gain rather than a loss, it appears as a **debit** entry in the process account (whereas a loss appears as a **credit** entry in this account).

(a) **Output is 860 units**

Step 1. **Determine output and losses**

If actual output is 860 units and the actual loss is 140 units:

	Units
Actual loss	140
Normal loss (10% of 1,000)	100
Abnormal loss	40

Step 2. **Calculate cost per unit of output and losses**

The cost per unit of output and the cost per unit of abnormal loss are based on expected output.

$$\frac{\text{Costs incurred}}{\text{Expected output}} = \frac{£4,500}{900 \text{ units}} = £5 \text{ per unit}$$

Step 3. **Calculate total cost of output and losses**

Normal loss is not assigned any cost.

	£
Cost of output (860 × £5)	4,300
Normal loss	0
Abnormal loss (40 × £5)	200
	4,500

Step 4. **Complete accounts**

PROCESS ACCOUNT

	Units	£		Units		£
Cost incurred	1,000	4,500	Normal loss	100		0
			Output (finished goods a/c)	860	(× £5)	4,300
			Abnormal loss	40	(× £5)	200
	1,000	4,500		1,000		4,500

ABNORMAL LOSS ACCOUNT

	Units	£		Units	£
Process a/c	40	200	Profit and loss a/c	40	200

(b) **Output is 920 units**

Step 1. **Determine output and losses**

If actual output is 920 units and the actual loss is 80 units:

	Units
Actual loss	80
Normal loss (10% of 1,000)	100
Abnormal gain	20

Step 2. **Calculate cost per unit of output and losses**

The cost per unit of output and the cost per unit of abnormal **gain** are based on **expected** output.

$$\frac{\text{Costs incurred}}{\text{Expected output}} = \frac{£4,500}{900 \text{ units}} = £5 \text{ per unit}$$

(Whether there is abnormal loss or gain does not affect the valuation of units of output. The figure of £5 per unit is exactly the same as in the previous paragraph, when there were 40 units of abnormal loss.)

Step 3. **Calculate total cost of output and losses**

	£
Cost of output (920 × £5)	4,600
Normal loss	0
Abnormal gain (20 × £5)	(100)
	4,500

Step 4. **Complete accounts**

PROCESS ACCOUNT

	Units	£		Units	£
Cost incurred	1,000	4,500	Normal loss	100	0
Abnormal gain a/c	20 (× £5)	100	Output (finished goods a/c)	920 (× £5)	4,600
	1,020	4,600		1,020	4,600

ABNORMAL GAIN

	Units	£		Units	£
Profit and loss a/c	20	100	Process a/c	20	100

3.6 EXAMPLE: ABNORMAL LOSSES AND GAINS AGAIN

During a four-week period, period 3, costs of input to a process were £29,070. Input was 1,000 units, output was 850 units and normal loss is 10%.

During the next period, period 4, costs of input were again £29,070. Input was again 1,000 units, but output was 950 units.

There were no units of opening or closing stock.

Required

Prepare the process account and abnormal loss or gain account for each period.

3.7 SOLUTION

Step 1. **Determine output and losses**

Period 3

	Units
Actual output	850
Normal loss (10% × 1,000)	100
Abnormal loss	50
Input	1,000

Period 4

	Units
Actual output	950
Normal loss (10% × 1,000)	100
Abnormal gain	(50)
Input	1,000

Step 2. **Calculate cost per unit of output and losses**

For each period the cost per unit is based on expected output.

$$\frac{\text{Cost of input}}{\text{Expected units of output}} = \frac{£29,070}{900} = £32.30 \text{ per unit}$$

Step 3. **Calculate total cost of output and losses**

Period 3

	£
Cost of output (850 × £32.30)	27,455
Normal loss	0
Abnormal loss (50 × £32.30)	1,615
	29,070

Period 4

	£
Cost of output (950 × £32.30)	30,685
Normal loss	0
Abnormal gain (50 × £32.30)	1,615
	29,070

Step 4. **Complete accounts**

PROCESS ACCOUNT

	Units	£		Units	£
Period 3					
Cost of input	1,000	29,070	Normal loss	100	0
			Finished goods a/c	850	27,455
			(× £32.30)		
			Abnormal loss a/c	50	1,615
			(× £32.30)		
	1,000	29,070		1,000	29,070
Period 4					
Cost of input	1,000	29,070	Normal loss	100	0
Abnormal gain a/c	50	1,615	Finished goods a/c	950	30,685
(× £32.30)			(× £32.30)		
	1,050	30,685		1,050	30,685

ABNORMAL LOSS OR GAIN ACCOUNT

	£		£
Period 3		*Period 4*	
Abnormal loss in process a/c	1,615	Abnormal gain in process a/c	1,615

A nil balance on this account will be carried forward into period 5.

3.8 If there is a closing balance in the abnormal loss or gain account when the profit for the period is calculated, this balance is taken to the profit and loss account: an abnormal gain will be a credit to profit and loss and an abnormal loss will be a debit to profit and loss.

Question 1

Charlton Ltd manufactures a product in a single process operation. Normal loss is 10% of input. Loss occurs at the end of the process. Data for June are as follows.

Opening and closing stocks of work in progress	Nil
Cost of input materials (3,300 units)	£59,100
Direct labour and production overhead	£30,000
Output to finished goods	2,750 units

The full cost of finished output in June was

A £74,250   B £81,000   C £82,500   D £89,100

Answer

Step 1. Determine output and losses

	Units
Actual output	2,750
Normal loss (10% × 3,300)	330
Abnormal loss	220
	3,300

Step 2. Calculate cost per unit of output and losses

$$\frac{\text{Cost of input}}{\text{Expected units of output}} = \frac{£89,100}{3,300-330} = £30 \text{ per unit}$$

Step 3. Calculate total cost of output and losses

	£
Cost of output (2,750 × £30)	82,500 **(The correct answer is C)**
Normal loss	0
Abnormal loss (220 × £30)	6,600
	89,100

If you were reduced to making a calculated guess, you could have eliminated option D. This is simply the total input cost, with no attempt to apportion some of the cost to the abnormal loss.

Option A is incorrect because it results from allocating a full unit cost to the normal loss: remember that normal loss does not carry any of the process cost.

Option B is incorrect because it results from calculating a 10% normal loss based on *output* of 2,750 units (275 units normal loss), rather than on *input* of 3,300 units.

---

4 ACCOUNTING FOR SCRAP

4.1 **Loss may have a scrap value**. The following basic rules are applied in accounting for this value in the process accounts.

(a) **Revenue from scrap** is treated, not as an addition to sales revenue, but as a **reduction in costs**.

(b) The scrap value of **normal loss** is therefore used to reduce the material costs of the process.

DEBIT   Scrap account
CREDIT   Process account

with the scrap value of the normal loss.

(c) The scrap value of **abnormal loss** is used to reduce the cost of abnormal loss.

DEBIT   Scrap account
CREDIT   Abnormal loss account

with the scrap value of abnormal loss, which therefore reduces the write-off of cost to the profit and loss account.

(d) The scrap value of **abnormal gain** arises because the actual units sold as scrap will be less than the scrap value of normal loss. Because there are fewer units of scrap than expected, there will be less revenue from scrap as a direct consequence of the abnormal gain. The abnormal gain account should therefore be debited with the scrap value.

DEBIT   Abnormal gain account
CREDIT   Scrap account

with the scrap value of abnormal gain.

(e) The **scrap account** is completed by recording the **actual cash received** from the sale of scrap.

DEBIT   Cash received
CREDIT   Scrap account

with the cash received from the sale of the actual scrap.

4.2 The same basic principle therefore applies that only **normal losses** should affect the cost of the good output. The scrap value of **normal loss only** is credited to the process account. The scrap values of abnormal losses and gains are analysed separately in the abnormal loss or gain account.

4.3 EXAMPLE: SCRAP AND ABNORMAL LOSS OR GAIN

A factory with two production processes. Normal loss in each process is 10% and scrapped units sell for £0.50 each from process 1 and £3 each from process 2. Relevant information for costing purposes relating to period 5 is as follows.

Direct materials added:	*Process 1*	*Process 2*
units	2,000	1,250
cost	£8,100	£1,900
Direct labour	£4,000	£10,000
Production overhead	150% of direct labour cost	120% of direct labour cost
Output to process 2/finished goods	1,750 units	2,800 units
Actual production overhead	£17,800	

Required

Prepare the accounts for process 1, process 2, scrap, abnormal loss or gain and production overhead.

4.4 SOLUTION

Step 1. **Determine output and losses**

	Process 1 Units	*Process 2* Units
Output	1,750	2,800
Normal loss (10% of input)	200	300
Abnormal loss	50	-
Abnormal gain	-	(100)
	2,000	3,000*

★ 1,750 units from Process 1 + 1,250 units input to process.

Step 2. **Calculate cost per unit of output and losses**

		Process 1 £		Process 2 £
Cost of input				
- material		8,100		1,900
- from Process 1		-	(1,750 × £10)	17,500
- labour		4,000		10,000
- overhead	(150% × £4,000)	6,000	(120% × £10,000)	12,000
		18,100		41,400
less: scrap value of **normal loss** (200 × £0.50)		(100)	(300 × £3)	(900)
		18,000		40,500
Expected output				
90% of 2,000		1,800		
90% of 3,000				2,700
Cost per unit				
£18,000 ÷ 1,800		£10		
£40,500 ÷ 2,700				£15

Step 3. **Calculate total cost of output and losses**

	Process 1 £		Process 2 £
Output (1,750 × £10)	17,500	(2,800 × £15)	42,000
Normal loss (200 × £0.50)★	100	(300 × £3)★	900
Abnormal loss (50 × £10)	500		-
	18,100		42,900
Abnormal gain	-	(100 × £15)	(1,500)
	18,100		41,400

★ Remember that normal loss is valued at scrap value only.

Step 4. **Complete accounts**

PROCESS 1 ACCOUNT

	Units	£		Units	£
Direct material	2,000	8,100	Scrap a/c (normal loss)	200	100
Direct labour		4,000	Process 2 a/c	1,750	17,500
Production overhead a/c		6,000	Abnormal loss a/c	50	500
	2,000	18,100		2,000	18,100

PROCESS 2 ACCOUNT

	Units	£		Units	£
Direct materials					
From process 1	1,750	17,500	Scrap a/c (normal loss)	300	900
Added materials	1,250	1,900	Finished goods a/c	2,800	42,000
Direct labour		10,000			
Production overhead		12,000			
	3,000	41,400			
Abnormal gain	100	1,500			
	3,100	42,900		3,100	42,900

ABNORMAL LOSS ACCOUNT

	£		£
Process 1 (50 units)	500	Scrap a/c: sale of scrap of	
		extra loss (50 units)	25
		Profit and loss a/c	475
	500		500

ABNORMAL GAIN ACCOUNT

	£		£
Scrap a/c (loss of scrap revenue due to abnormal gain, 100 units × £3)	300	Process 2 abnormal gain (100 units)	1,500
Profit and loss a/c	1,200		
	1,500		1,500

SCRAP ACCOUNT

	£		£
Scrap value of normal loss		Cash a/c - cash received	
Process 1 (200 units)	100	Loss in process 1 (250 units)	125
Process 2 (300 units)	900	Loss in process 2 (200 units)	600
Abnormal loss a/c (process 1)	25	Abnormal gain a/c (process 2)	300
	1,025		1,025

PRODUCTION OVERHEAD ACCOUNT

	£		£
Overhead incurred	17,800	Process 1 a/c	6,000
Over-absorbed overhead a/c		Process 2 a/c	12,000
(or P & L a/c)	200		
	18,000		18,000

Question 2

Parks Ltd operates a processing operation involving two stages, the output of process 1 being passed to process 2. The process costs for period 3 were as follows.

Process 1

Material	3,000 kg at £0.25 per kg
Labour	£120

Process 2

Material	2,000 kg at £0.40 per kg
Labour	£84

General overhead for period 3 amounted to £357 and is absorbed into process costs at a rate of 375% of direct labour costs in process 1 and 496% of direct labour costs in process 2.

The normal output of process 1 is 80% of input and of process 2, 90% of input. Waste matter from process 1 is sold for £0.20 per kg and that from process 2 for £0.30 per kg.

The output for period 3 was as follows.

Process 1	2,300 kgs
Process 2	4,000 kgs

There was no stock of work in progress at either the beginning or the end of the period and it may be assumed that all available waste matter had been sold at the prices indicated.

Required

Show how the foregoing data would be recorded in a system of cost accounts.

Answer

Step 1.   Determine output and losses

	Process 1 kgs		Process 2 kgs
Output	2,300		4,000
Normal loss (20% of 3,000 kgs)	600	(10% of 4,300)	430
Abnormal loss	100		-
Abnormal gain	-		(130)
	3,000		4,300*

* From process 1 (2,300 kgs) + 2,000 kgs added

Step 2. **Determine cost per unit of output and losses**

	Process 1 £		Process 2 £
Material (3,000 × £0.25)	750	(2,000 × £0.40)	800
From process 1	-	(2,300 × £0.50)	1,150
Labour	120		84
Overhead (375% × £120)	450	(496% × £84)	417
less: scrap value of **normal** loss			
(600 × £0.20)	(120)	(430 × £0.3)	(129)
	1,200		2,322

Expected output

	Process 1		Process 2
3,000 × 80%	2,400	4,300 × 90%	3,870
	Process 1		Process 2
Cost per unit ($\dfrac{£1,320 - £120}{3,000 - 600}$)	£0.50	($\dfrac{£2,451 - £129}{4,300 - 430}$)	£0.60

Step 3. **Determine total cost of output and losses**

	Process 1 £		Process 2 £
Output (2,300 × £0.50)	1,150	(4,000 × £0.60)	2,400
Normal loss (scrap)			
(600 × £0.20)	120	(430 × £0.30)	129
Abnormal loss (100 × £0.50)	50		-
	1,320		2,529
Abnormal gain	-	(130 × £0.60)	(78)
	1,320		2,451

Step 4. **Complete accounts**

PROCESS 1 ACCOUNT

	kg	£		kg	£
Material	3,000	750	Normal loss to scrap a/c		
Labour		120	(20%)	600	120
General overhead		450	Production transferred to		
			process 2	2,300	1,150
			Abnormal loss a/c	100	50
	3,000	1,320		3,000	1,320

PROCESS 2 ACCOUNT

	kg	£		kg	£
Transferred from					
process 1	2,300	1,150	Normal loss to scrap a/c		
Material added	2,000	800	(10%)	430	129
Labour		84	Production transferred to		
General overhead		417	finished stock	4,000	2,400
	4,300	2,451			
Abnormal gain	130	78			
	4,430	2,529		4,430	2,529

FINISHED STOCK ACCOUNT

	kg	£
Process 2	4,000	2,400

SCRAP ACCOUNT

	kg	£		kg	£
Normal loss (process 1)	600	120	Abnormal gain (process 2)	130	39
Normal loss (process 2)	430	129	Cash	1,000	230
Abnormal loss					
(process 1)	100	20			
	1,130	269		1,130	269

ABNORMAL LOSS AND GAIN ACCOUNT

	kg	£		kg	£
Process 1 (loss)	100	50	Scrap value of		
Scrap value of abnormal			abnormal loss	100	20
gain	130	39	Process 2 (gain)	130	78
Profit and loss		9			
	230	98		230	98

(*Note.* In this answer, a single account has been prepared for abnormal loss/gain. Your solution will probably have separated this single account into two separate accounts, one for abnormal gain and one for abnormal loss.)

5   VALUING CLOSING WORK IN PROGRESS

5.1   In the examples we have looked at so far we have assumed that opening and closing stocks of work in process have been nil. We must now look at more realistic examples and consider how to allocate the costs incurred in a period between completed output (ie finished units) and partly completed closing stock.

5.2   Some examples will help to illustrate the problem, and the techniques used to share out (apportion) costs between finished output and closing work in progress.

5.3   EXAMPLE: VALUATION OF CLOSING STOCK

Trotter Ltd is a manufacturer of processed goods. In March 20X3, in one process, there was no opening stock, but 5,000 units of input were introduced to the process during the month, at the following cost.

	£
Direct materials	16,560
Direct labour	7,360
Production overhead	5,520
	29,440

Of the 5,000 units introduced, 4,000 were completely finished during the month and transferred to the next process. Closing stock of 1,000 units was only 60% complete with respect to materials and conversion costs.

5.4   SOLUTION

(a)   The problem in this example is to **divide the costs of production** (£29,440) between the finished output of 4,000 units and the closing stock of 1,000 units. It is argued, with good reason, that a division of costs in proportion to the number of units of each (4,000:1,000) would not be 'fair' because closing stock has not been completed, and has not yet 'received' its full amount of materials and conversion costs, but only 60% of the full amount. The 1,000 units of closing stock, being only 60% complete, are the equivalent of 600 fully worked units.

(b)   To apportion costs fairly and proportionately, units of production must be converted into the equivalent of completed units, ie into **equivalent units of production**.

> **KEY TERM**
>
> **Equivalent units** are notional whole units which represent incomplete work, and which are used to apportion costs between work in process and completed output.

Step 1. **Determine output**

For this step in our framework we need to prepare a statement of equivalent units.

STATEMENT OF EQUIVALENT UNITS

	Total units	Completion	Equivalent units
Fully worked units	4,000	100%	4,000
Closing stock	1,000	60%	600
	5,000		4,600

Step 2. **Calculate cost per unit of output, and WIP**

For this step in our framework we need to prepare a statement of costs per equivalent unit because equivalent units are the basis for apportioning costs.

STATEMENT OF COSTS PER EQUIVALENT UNIT

$$\frac{\text{Total cost}}{\text{Equivalent units}} = \frac{£29,440}{4,600}$$

Cost per equivalent unit £6.40

Step 3. **Calculate total cost of output and WIP**

For this stage in our framework a statement of evaluation may now be prepared, to show how the costs should be apportioned between finished output and closing stock.

STATEMENT OF EVALUATION

Item	Equivalent units	Cost per equivalent unit	Valuation £
Fully worked units	4,000	£6.40	25,600
Closing stock	600	£6.40	3,840
	4,600		29,440

Step 4. **Complete accounts**

The process account would be shown as follows.

PROCESS ACCOUNT

		Units	£		Units	£
(Stores a/c)	Direct materials	5,000	16,560	Output to next process	4,000	25,600
(Wages a/c)	Direct labour		7,360	Closing stock c/f	1,000	3,840
(O'hd a/c)	Production o'hd		5,520			
		5,000	29,440		5,000	29,440

5.5 When preparing a process 'T' account, it might help to make the entries as follows.

(a) **Enter the units first.** The units columns are simply memorandum columns, but they help you to make sure that there are no units unaccounted for (for example as loss).

(b) **Enter the costs of materials, labour and overheads next.** These should be given to you.

(c) **Enter your valuation of finished output and closing stock next.** The value of the credit entries should, of course, equal the value of the debit entries.

Different rates of input

5.6 In many industries, materials, labour and overhead may be added at **different rates** during the course of production.

(a) Output from a previous process (for example the output from process 1 to process 2) may be introduced into the subsequent process all at once, so that closing stock is 100% complete in respect of these materials.

(b) Further materials may be **added gradually** during the process, so that closing stock is only **partially complete** in respect of these added materials.

(c) Labour and overhead may be 'added' at yet another different rate. When production overhead is absorbed on a labour hour basis, however, we should expect the degree of completion on overhead to be the same as the degree of completion on labour.

5.7 When this situation occurs, equivalent units, and a cost per equivalent unit, should be **calculated separately for each type of material, and also for conversion costs**.

5.8 EXAMPLE: EQUIVALENT UNITS AND DIFFERENT DEGREES OF COMPLETION

Suppose that Shaker Ltd is a manufacturer of processed goods, and that results in process 2 for April 20X3 were as follows.

Opening stock	nil
Material input from process 1	4,000 units

Costs of input:	£
material from process 1	6,000
added materials in process 2	1,080
conversion costs	1,720

Output is transferred into the next process, process 3.

Closing work in process amounted to 800 units, complete as to:	
process 1 material	100%
added materials	50%
conversion costs	30%

Required

Prepare the account for process 2 for April 20X3.

5.9 SOLUTION

Step 1. **Determine output and losses**

STATEMENT OF EQUIVALENT UNITS (OF PRODUCTION IN THE PERIOD)

			\multicolumn{6}{c}{*Equivalent units of production*}
			\multicolumn{2}{c}{*Process 1 material*}	\multicolumn{2}{c}{*Added materials*}	\multicolumn{2}{c}{*Labour and overhead*}
Input	*Output*	*Total*						
Units		Units	Units	%	Units	%	Units	%
4,000	Completed production	3,200	3,200	100	3,200	100	3,200	100
	Closing stock	800	800	100	400	50	240	30
4,000		4,000	4,000		3,600		3,440	

Step 2. **Calculate cost per unit of output, losses and WIP**

STATEMENT OF COST (PER EQUIVALENT UNIT)

Input	Cost £	Equivalent production in units	Cost per unit £
Process 1 material	6,000	4,000	1.50
Added materials	1,080	3,600	0.30
Labour and overhead	1,720	3,440	0.50
	8,800		2.30

Step 3. **Calculate total cost of output, losses and WIP**

STATEMENT OF EVALUATION (OF FINISHED WORK AND CLOSING STOCKS)

Production	Cost element	Number of equivalent units	Cost per equivalent unit £	Total £	Cost £
Completed production		3,200	2.30		7,360
Closing stock:	process 1 material	800	1.50	1,200	
	added material	400	0.30	120	
	labour and overhead	240	0.50	120	
					1,440
					8,800

Step 4. **Complete accounts**

PROCESS ACCOUNT

	Units	£		Units	£
Process 1 material	4,000	6,000	Process 3 a/c	3,200	7,360
Added material		1,080	(finished output)		
Conversion costs		1,720	Closing stock c/f	800	1,440
	4,000	8,800		4,000	8,800

Closing work in progress and losses

5.10 The previous paragraphs have dealt separately with the following.

(a) The treatment of loss and scrap.

(b) The use of equivalent units as a basis for apportioning costs between units of output and units of closing stock.

We must now look at a situation where both problems occur together. We shall begin with an example where loss has no scrap value.

5.11 The rules are as follows.

(a) Costs should be divided between finished output, closing stock and abnormal loss/gain using **equivalent units** as a basis of apportionment.

(b) Units of abnormal loss/gain are often taken to be **one full equivalent unit each**, and are valued on this basis, ie they carry their full 'share' of the process costs.

(c) **Abnormal loss units are an addition** to the total equivalent units produced but **abnormal gain units are subtracted** in arriving at the total number of equivalent units produced.

(d) Units of **normal loss are valued at zero equivalent units,** ie they do not carry any of the process costs.

5.12 EXAMPLE: CHANGES IN STOCK LEVEL AND LOSSES

The following data have been collected for a process.

Opening stock	none	Output to finished goods	2,000 units
Input units	2,800 units	Closing stock	450 units, 70% complete
Cost of input	£16,695	Total loss	350 units
Normal loss	10%; nil scrap value		

Required

Prepare the process account for the period.

5.13 SOLUTION

Step 1. **Determine output and losses**

STATEMENT OF EQUIVALENT UNITS

	Total units		Equivalent units of work done this period
Completely worked units	2,000	(× 100%)	2,000
Closing stock	450	(× 70%)	315
Normal loss	280		0
Abnormal loss	70	(× 100%)	70
	2,800		2,385

Step 2. **Calculate cost per unit of output, losses and WIP**

STATEMENT OF COST PER EQUIVALENT UNIT

$$\frac{\text{Costs incurred}}{\text{Equivalent units of work done}} = \frac{16,695}{2,385}$$

Cost per equivalent unit = £7

Step 3. **Calculate total cost of output, losses and WIP**

STATEMENT OF EVALUATION

	Equivalent units	£
Completely worked units	2,000	14,000
Closing stock	315	2,205
Abnormal loss	70	490
	2,385	16,695

Step 4. **Complete accounts**

PROCESS ACCOUNT

	Units	£		Units	£
Opening stock	-	-	Normal loss	280	0
Input costs	2,800	16,695	Finished goods a/c	2,000	14,000
			Abnormal loss a/c	70	490
			Closing stock c/d	450	2,205
	2,800	16,695		2,800	16,695

Closing work in progress, loss and scrap

5.14 When loss has a **scrap value**, the accounting procedures are the same as those previously described. However, if the equivalent units are a different percentage (of the total units) for materials, labour and overhead, it is a convention that the **scrap value of normal loss** is **deducted from the cost of materials** before a cost per equivalent unit is calculated.

Question 3

Prepare a process account from the following information.

Opening stock	Nil
Input units	10,000
Input costs	
Material	£5,150
Labour	£2,700
Normal loss	5% of input
Scrap value of units of loss	£1 per unit
Output to finished goods	8,000 units
Closing stock	1,000 units
Compl0etion of closing stock	80% for material
	50% for labour

Answer

Step 1. **Determine output and losses**

STATEMENT OF EQUIVALENT UNITS

		Equivalent units			
	Total	*Material*		*Labour*	
	Units	%	Units	%	Units
Completed production	8,000	100	8,000	100	8,000
Closing stock	1,000	80	800	50	500
Normal loss	500				
Abnormal loss	500	100	500	100	500
	10,000		9,300		9,000

Step 2. **Calculate cost per unit of output, losses and WIP**

STATEMENT OF COST PER EQUIVALENT UNIT

	Cost	*Equivalent units*	*Cost per equivalent unit*
	£		£
Material (£(5,150 – 500))	4,650	9,300	0.50
Labour	2,700	9,000	0.30
	7,350		0.80

Step 3. **Calculate total cost of output, losses and WIP**

STATEMENT OF EVALUATION

	Equivalent units	*Cost per equivalent unit*	*Total*	
		£	£	£
Completed production	8,000	0.80		6,400
Closing stock: material	800	0.50	400	
labour	500	0.30	150	
				550
Abnormal loss	500	0.80		400
				7,350

Step 4. Complete accounts

PROCESS ACCOUNT

	Units	£		Units	£
Material	10,000	5,150	Completed production	8,000	6,400
Labour		2,700	Closing stock	1,000	550
			Normal loss	500	500
			Abnormal loss	500	400
	10,000	7,850		10,000	7,850

6 VALUING OPENING WORK IN PROGRESS

6.1 The weighted average cost method of stock valuation is a stock valuation method that calculates a weighted average cost of units produced from both opening stock and units introduced in the current period. (We studied this method earlier in the Study Text in Chapter 3.)

By this method no distinction is made between units of opening stock and new units introduced to the process during the current period. The cost of opening stock is added to costs incurred during the period, and **completed units of opening stock are each given a value of one full equivalent unit of production.**

6.2 EXAMPLE: WEIGHTED AVERAGE COST METHOD

Magpie Ltd produces an item which is manufactured in two consecutive processes. Information relating to process 2 during September 20X3 is as follows.

Opening stock 800 units
Degree of completion:		£
process 1 materials	100%	4,700
added materials	40%	600
conversion costs	30%	1,000
		6,300

During September 20X3, 3,000 units were transferred from process 1 at a valuation of £18,100. Added materials cost £9,600 and conversion costs were £11,800.

Closing stock at 30 September 20X3 amounted to 1,000 units which were 100% complete with respect to process 1 materials and 60% complete with respect to added materials. Conversion cost work was 40% complete.

Magpie Ltd uses a weighted average cost system for the valuation of output and closing stock.

Required

Prepare the process 2 account for September 20X3.

6.3 SOLUTION

Step 1. **Determine output and losses**

Opening stock units count as a full equivalent unit of production when the weighted average cost system is applied. Closing stock units are assessed in the usual way.

STATEMENT OF EQUIVALENT UNITS

	Total units		Process 1 material		Added material		Conversion costs
				Equivalent units			
Output to finished goods*	2,800	(100%)	2,800		2,800		2,800
Closing stock	1,000	(100%)	1,000	(60%) 600		(40%) 400	
	3,800		3,800		3,400		3,200

* 3,000 units from Process 1 minus closing stock of 1,000 units plus opening stock of 800 units.

Step 2. Calculate cost per unit of output and WIP

The cost of opening stock is added to costs incurred in September 20X3, and a cost per equivalent unit is then calculated.

STATEMENT OF COSTS PER EQUIVALENT UNIT

	Process 1 Material £	Added materials £	Conversion costs £
Opening stock	4,700	600	1,000
Added in September 20X3	18,100	9,600	11,800
Total cost	22,800	10,200	12,800
Equivalent units	3,800 units	3,400 units	3,200 units
Cost per equivalent unit	£6	£3	£4

Step 3. Calculate total cost of output and WIP

STATEMENT OF EVALUATION

	Process 1 material £	Added materials £	Conversion costs £	Total cost £
Output to finished goods (2,800 units)	16,800	8,400	11,200	36,400
Closing stock	6,000	1,800	1,600	9,400
				45,800

Step 4. Complete accounts

PROCESS 2 ACCOUNT

	Units	£		Units	£
Opening stock b/f	800	6,300	Finished goods a/c	2,800	36,400
Process 1 a/c	3,000	18,100			
Added materials		9,600			
Conversion costs		11,800	Closing stock c/f	1,000	9,400
	3,800	45,800		3,800	45,800

6.4 Question 4 involves the following process costing situations.

- Normal loss (with and without sale of scrap)
- Abnormal loss
- Abnormal gain
- Opening work in progress
- Closing work in progress

Take time to work through this question carefully and to check your workings against the answer given below. This is an excellent question which should help you to consolidate all of the process costing knowledge that you have acquired whilst studying this chapter.

Question 4

Watkins Ltd has a financial year which ends on 30 April. It operates in a processing industry in which a single product is produced by passing inputs through two sequential processes. A normal loss of 10% of input is expected in each process.

The following account balances have been extracted from its ledger at 31 March 20X0.

	Debit £	Credit £
Process 1 (Materials £4,400; Conversion costs £3,744)	8,144	
Process 2 (Process 1 £4,431; Conversion costs £5,250)	9,681	
Abnormal loss	1,400	
Abnormal gain		300
Overhead control account		250
Sales		585,000
Cost of sales	442,500	
Finished goods stock	65,000	

Watkins Ltd uses the weighted average method of accounting work in process.

During April 20X0 the following transactions occurred.

Process 1	Materials input	4,000 kg costing	£22,000
	Labour cost		£12,000
	Transfer to process 2	2,400 kg	
Process 2	Transfer from process 1	2,400 kg	
	Labour cost		£15,000
	Transfer to finished goods	2,500 kg	

Overhead costs incurred amounted to	£54,000
Sales to customer were	£52,000

Overhead costs are absorbed into process costs on the basis of 150% of labour cost.

The losses which arise in process 1 have no scrap value: those arising in process 2 can be sold for £2 per kg.

Details of opening and closing work in process for the month of April 20X0 are as follows.

	Opening	Closing
Process 1	3,000 kg	3,400 kg
Process 2	2,250 kg	2,600 kg

In both processes closing work in process is fully complete as to material cost and 40% complete as to conversion cost.

Stocks of finished goods at 30 April 20X0 were valued at cost of £60,000.

Required

Prepare the Process 1 and Process 2 accounts for April 20X0 for Watkins Ltd.

Answer

(a)   **Process 1**

STATEMENT OF EQUIVALENT UNITS

	Total units	Equivalent units Material costs	Conversion costs
Transfers to process 2	2,400	2,400	2,400
Closing WIP	3,400	(100%) 3,400	(40%) 1,360
Normal loss (10% × 4,000)	400	0	0
Abnormal loss	800	800	800
	7,000	6,600	4,560

STATEMENT OF COSTS PER EQUIVALENT UNIT

$$\frac{\text{Costs incurred}}{\text{Equivalent units}} = \text{Cost per equivalent unit}$$

$$\therefore \text{Materials cost per equivalent unit} \quad = \quad \frac{\pounds4,400 + \pounds22,000}{6,600}$$

$$= \quad \frac{\pounds26,400}{6,600} = \pounds4$$

$$\therefore \text{Conversion costs per equivalent unit} \quad = \quad \frac{\pounds3,744 + \pounds12,000 + \pounds18,000}{4,560}$$

$$= \quad \frac{\pounds33,744}{4,560} = \pounds7.40$$

STATEMENT OF EVALUATION

	Materials	Conversion costs	Total
	£	£	£
Transfers to process 2	9,600	17,760	27,360
Abnormal loss	3,200	5,920	9,120
Closing WIP	13,600	10,064	23,664
	26,400	33,744	60,144

PROCESS 1 ACCOUNT

	Kg	£		Kg	£
WIP materials	3,000	4,400	Process 2	2,400	27,360
WIP conversion costs	-	3,744	Normal loss	400	-
Materials	4,000	22,000	Abnormal loss	800	9,120
Labour	-	12,000	WIP materials	3,400	13,600
Overhead	-	18,000	WIP conversion costs	-	10,064
	7,000	60,144		7,000	60,144

(b) **Process 2**

STATEMENT OF EQUIVALENT UNITS

	Total units	Process 1	Conversion costs
Finished goods	2,500	2,500	2,500
Normal loss	240	0	0
Abnormal gain	(690)	(690)	(690)
Closing WIP	*2,600*	2,600	1,040 **
	4,650	4,410	2,850

* Total input units = opening WIP + input = 2,250 + 2,400 = 4,650

Total output units = finished goods + closing WIP + normal loss – abnormal gain
= 2,500 + 2,600 + 240 – 690
= 4,650

** 2,600 × 40% = 1,040

STATEMENT OF COSTS PER EQUIVALENT UNIT

$$\textbf{Process 1} \quad = \quad \frac{\pounds4,431 + \pounds27,360 - 480}{4,410} = \pounds7.10$$

$$\textbf{Conversion costs} \quad = \quad \frac{\pounds5,250 + \pounds15,000 + \pounds22,500}{2,850} = \pounds15.00$$

STATEMENT OF EVALUATION

	Process 1	Conversion costs	Total
Finished goods	17,750	37,500	55,250
Abnormal gain	4,899	10,350	15,249
Closing WIP	18,460	15,600	34,060
	41,109	63,450	104,559

PROCESS 2 ACCOUNT

	Kg	£		Kg	£
WIP Process 1	2,250	4,431	Finished goods	2,500	55,250
WIP conversion costs	-	5,250	Normal loss	240	480
Process 1	2,400	27,360	WIP Process 1	2,600	18,460
Labour	-	15,000	WIP conversion costs	-	15,600
Overhead	-	22,500			
Abnormal gain	690	15,249			
	5,340	89,790		5,340	89,790

Exam focus point

Of the twenty five multiple choice questions contained within the Pilot paper for **Management Accounting Fundamentals,** six examined the topic of process costing. Six MCQs are worth 12% of the paper – proof that the contents of this chapter are very important!

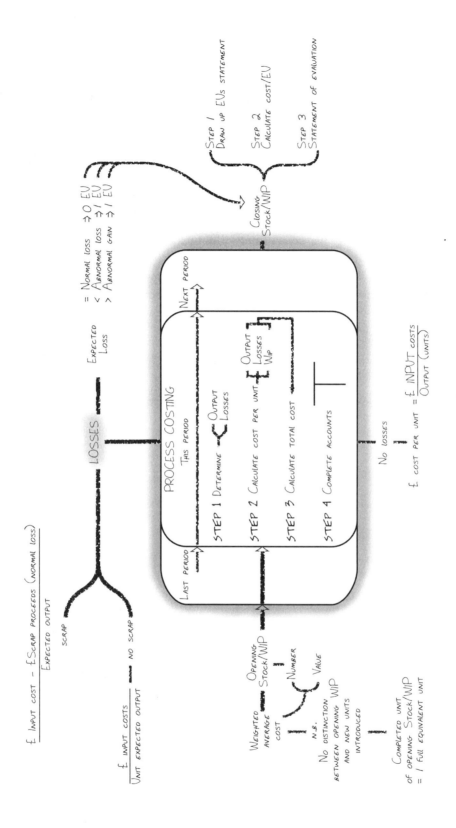

LOSSES

$$\frac{£ \text{ Input cost} - £ \text{ Scrap proceeds (normal loss)}}{\text{Expected output}}$$

Scrap

$$\frac{£ \text{ input costs}}{\text{Unit expected output}}$$ No scrap

Expected Loss

= Normal loss → O EU
< Abnormal loss → / EU
> Abnormal gain → / EU

Step 1
Draw up EUs statement

Step 2
Calculate cost/EU

Step 3
Statement of evaluation

Closing Stock/WIP

PROCESS COSTING
This period

Next period

Step 1 Determine ⟨ Output / Losses

Step 2 Calculate cost per unit ⟨ Output / Losses / WIP

Step 3 Calculate total cost

Step 4 Complete accounts

Last period

Weighted average cost — Opening Stock/WIP ⟨ Number / Value

N.B.
No distinction between opening WIP and new units introduced

Completed unit of opening Stock/WIP = 1 full equivalent unit

No losses

$$£ \text{ cost per unit} = \frac{£ \text{ INPUT costs}}{\text{Output (units)}}$$

Chapter roundup

- Use our suggested four-step approach when dealing with process costing questions.

  Step 1.   Determine output and losses
  Step 2.   Calculate cost per unit of output, losses and WIP
  Step 3.   Calculate total cost of output, losses and WIP
  Step 4.   Complete accounts

- **Process costing** is used where there is a continuous flow of identical units.

- **Losses** may occur in process. If a certain level of loss is expected, this is known as **normal loss**. If losses are greater than expected, the extra loss is **abnormal loss**. If losses are less than expected, the difference is known as **abnormal gain**.

- The **valuation of normal loss is either at scrap value or nil**.

- It is conventional for the **scrap value of normal loss to be deducted from the cost of materials** before a cost per equivalent unit is calculated.

- Abnormal losses and gains never affect the cost of good units of production. The scrap value of abnormal losses is not credited to the process account, and abnormal loss and gain units carry the same full cost as a good unit of production.

- When units are partly completed at the end of a period (ie when there is **closing work in progress**) it is necessary to calculate the **equivalent units of production** in order to determine the cost of a completed unit.

- If there is **opening work in progress** at the beginning of a period, this syllabus requires that you account for it using the **weighted average cost method of stock valuation.** By this method, no distinction is made between units of opening stock and new units introduced to the process during the current period.

Quick quiz

1   Define process costing.

2   Process costing is centred around four key steps.

  Step 1.   ....

  Step 2.   ....

  Step 3.   ....

  Step 4.   ....

3   Abnormal gains result when actual loss is less than normal or expected loss.

  True   ☐

  False   ☐

4   Normal loss (no scrap value)   Same value as good output (positive cost)

  Abnormal loss   ?   No value

  Abnormal gain   Same value as good output (negative cost)

5   How is revenue from scrap treated?

  A   As an addition to sales revenue
  B   As a reduction in costs of processing
  C   As a bonus to employees
  D   Any of the above

6   When there is closing WIP at the end of a process, what is the first step in the four-step approach to process costing questions and why must it be done?

7   What is the weighted average cost method of stock valuation?

Answers to quick quiz

1. **Process costing** is a costing method used where it is not possible to identify separate units of production, or jobs, usually because of the continuous nature of the production processes involved.

2. **Step 1.** Determine output and losses
   Step 2. Calculate cost per unit of output, losses and WIP
   Step 3. Calculate total cost of output, losses and WIP
   Step 4. Complete accounts

3. True

4.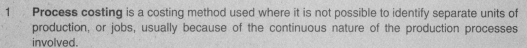

   Normal loss (no scrap value) → Same value as good output (positive cost)

   Abnormal loss → No value

   Abnormal gain → Same value as good output (negative cost)

5. B

6. **Step 1.** It is necessary to calculate the equivalent units of production (by drawing up a statement of equivalent units). Equivalent units of production are notional whole units which represent incomplete work and which are used to apportion costs between work in progress and completed output.

7. A method where no distinction is made between units of opening stock and new units introduced to the process during the current period.

Now try the question below from the Exam Question Bank

Number	Level	Marks	Time
Q12	Examination	15	27 mins

BPP PUBLISHING

Chapter 10

SERVICE COSTING

Topic list	Syllabus reference	Ability required
1 Service industry costing	(iii)	Application
2 Service department costing	(iii)	Application
3 Job costing and services	(iii)	Application

Introduction

So far in this Study Text we have looked at different types of cost and different cost accounting systems and the inference has been that we have been discussing a **manufacturing** organisation. Many of the cost accounting principles we have looked at so far can be applied to **service organisations** also.

In this chapter we will therefore look at the costing method used by service organisations which we will call **service costing**. As you study this chapter, you will see how the knowledge you have built up can be applied easily to service organisations.

Service costing is the last costing method on your syllabus. Apart from being used by organisations operating in a service industry that wish to cost their services, it can also be applied when **internal services** are provided within an organisation.

Learning outcome covered in this chapter

- **Prepare** and contrast cost statements for service and manufacturing organisations

Syllabus content covered in this chapter

- Cost accounting statements for services and service industries

1   SERVICE INDUSTRY COSTING

KEY TERM

Service costing is 'Cost accounting for services or functions, eg canteens, maintenance, personnel. These may be referred to as service centres, departments or functions'.

CIMA *Official Terminology*

What are service organisations?

1.1   Service organisations do not make or sell tangible goods. Profit-seeking service organisations include accountancy firms, law firms, management consultants, transport companies, banks, insurance companies and hotels. Almost all not-for-profit organisations - hospitals, schools, libraries and so on - are also service organisations.

1.2 Service costing differs from the other costing methods (product costing methods) for a number of reasons.

(a) With many services, the cost of direct materials consumed will be relatively small compared to the labour, direct expenses and overheads cost. In product costing the direct materials are often a greater proportion of the total cost.

(b) The output of most service organisations is often intangible and hence difficult to define. A unit cost is therefore difficult to calculate.

(c) The service industry includes such a wide range of organisations which provide such different services and have such different cost structures that costing will vary considerably from one service to another.

1.3 Specific characteristics of services are **intangibility, simultaneity, perishability** and **heterogeneity.** Consider the service of providing a haircut.

(a) A haircut is **intangible** in itself, and the performance of the service comprises many other intangible factors, like the music in the salon, the personality of the hairdresser, the quality of the coffee.

(b) The production and consumption of a haircut are **simultaneous,** and therefore it cannot be inspected for quality in advance, nor can it be returned if it is not what was required.

(c) Haircuts are **perishable,** that is, they cannot be stored. You cannot buy them in bulk, and the hairdresser cannot do them in advance and keep them stocked away in case of heavy demand. The incidence of work in progress in service organisations is less frequent than in other types of organisation.

(d) A haircut is **heterogeneous** and so the exact service received will vary each time: not only will two hairdressers cut hair differently, but a hairdresser will not consistently deliver the same standard of haircut.

Unit cost measures

1.4 A particular problem with service costing is the difficulty in defining a realistic cost unit that represents a suitable measure of the service provided. Frequently, a **composite cost unit** may be deemed more appropriate if the service is a function of two activity variables. Hotels, for example, may use the 'occupied bed-night' as an appropriate unit for cost ascertainment and control. You may remember that we discussed such cost units in Chapter 1.

1.5 Typical cost units used by companies operating in a service industry are shown below.

Service	Cost unit
Road, rail and air transport services	Passenger/ kilometre, tonne/kilometre
Hotels	Occupied bed-night
Education	Full-time student
Hospitals	Patient-day
Catering establishments	Meal served

1.6 Each organisation will need to ascertain the cost unit most appropriate to its activities. If a number of organisations within an industry use a common cost unit, valuable **comparisons** can be made between similar establishments. This is particularly applicable to hospitals, educational establishments and local authorities. Unit costs are also useful control measures as we shall see in the examples that follow.

Exam focus point

Make sure that you are familiar with suitable composite costs units for common forms of service operation eg transport.

1.7 Whatever cost unit is decided upon, the calculation of a cost per unit is as follows.

FORMULA TO LEARN

$$\text{Cost per service unit} = \frac{\text{Total costs for period}}{\text{Number of service units in the period}}$$

1.8 The following examples will illustrate the principles involved in service industry costing and the further considerations to bear in mind when costing services.

1.9 EXAMPLE: COSTING AN EDUCATIONAL ESTABLISHMENT

A university offers a range of degree courses. The university organisation structure consists of three faculties each with a number of teaching departments. In addition, there is a university administrative/management function and a central services function.

(a) The following cost information is available for the year ended 30 June 20X3.

(i) **Occupancy costs**
Total £1,500,000

Such costs are apportioned on the basis of area used which is as follows.

	Square metres
Faculties	7,500
Teaching departments	20,000
Administration/management	7,000
Central services	3,000

(ii) **Administrative/management costs**
Direct costs: £1,775,000
Indirect costs: an apportionment of occupancy costs

Direct and indirect costs are charged to degree courses on a percentage basis.

(iii) **Faculty costs**

Direct costs: £700,000
Indirect costs: an apportionment of occupancy costs and central service costs

Direct and indirect costs are charged to teaching departments.

(iv) **Teaching departments**

Direct costs: £5,525,000
Indirect costs: an apportionment of occupancy costs and central service costs plus all faculty costs

Direct and indirect costs are charged to degree courses on a percentage basis.

(v) **Central services**

Direct costs: £1,000,000

Indirect costs: an apportionment of occupancy costs

(b) Direct and indirect costs of central services have, in previous years, been charged to users on a percentage basis. A study has now been completed which has estimated what user areas would have paid external suppliers for the same services on an individual basis. For the year ended 30 June 20X3, the apportionment of the central services cost is to be recalculated in a manner which recognises the cost savings achieved by using the central services facilities instead of using external service companies. This is to be done by apportioning the overall savings to user areas in proportion to their share of the estimated external costs.

The estimated external costs of service provision are as follows.

	£'000
Faculties	240
Teaching departments	800
Degree courses:	
Business studies	32
Mechanical engineering	48
Catering studies	32
All other degrees	448
	1,600

(c) Additional data relating to the degree courses is as follows.

		Degree course	
	Business studies	Mechanical engineering	Catering studies
Number of graduates	80	50	120
Apportioned costs (as % of totals)			
Teaching departments	3.0%	2.5%	7%
Administration/management	2.5%	5.0%	4%

Central services are to be apportioned as detailed in (b) above.

The total number of undergraduates from the university in the year to 30 June 20X3 was 2,500.

Required

(a) Calculate the average cost per undergraduate for the year ended 30 June 20X3.

(b) Calculate the average cost per undergraduate for each of the degrees in business studies, mechanical engineering and catering studies, showing all relevant cost analysis.

1.10 SOLUTION

(a) The average cost per undergraduate is as follows.

	Total costs for university £'000
Occupancy	1,500
Admin/management	1,775
Faculty	700
Teaching departments	5,525
Central services	1,000
	10,500

		2,500
Number of undergraduates		2,500
Average cost per undergraduate for year ended 30 June 20X3		£4,200

(b) Average cost per undergraduate for each course is as follows.

	Business studies £	*Mechanical engineering* £	*Catering studies* £
Teaching department costs			
(W1 and using % in question)	241,590	201,325	563,710
Admin/management costs			
(W1 and using % in question)	51,375	102,750	82,200
Central services (W2)	22,400	33,600	22,400
	315,365	337,675	668,310
Number of undergraduates	80	50	120
Average cost per undergraduate for year ended 30 June 20X3	£3,942	£6,754	£5,569

Workings

1 Cost allocation and apportionment

Cost item	*Basis of apportionment*	*Teaching departments* £'000	*Admin/ management* £'000	*Central services* £'000	*Faculties* £'000
Direct costs	allocation	5,525	1,775	1,000	700
Occupancy costs	area used	800	280	120	300
Central services reapportioned	(W2)	560	-	(1,120)	168
Faculty costs reallocated	allocation	1,168	-	-	(1,168)
		8,053	2,055		

2 Apportioning savings to user areas on the basis given in the question gives the same result as apportioning internal costs in proportion to the external costs.

	External costs £'000	*Apportionment of internal central service costs* £'000
Faculties	240	168.0
Teaching	800	560.0
Degree courses:		
Business studies	32	22.4
Mechanical engineering	48	33.6
Catering studies	32	22.4
All other degrees	448	313.6
	1,600	1,120.0

Question 1

Briefly describe cost units that are appropriate to a transport business.

Answer

The cost unit is the basic measure of control in an organisation, used to monitor cost and activity levels. The cost unit selected must be measurable and appropriate for the type of cost and activity. Possible cost units which could be suggested are as follows.

Cost per kilometre

- Variable cost per kilometre
- Fixed cost per kilometre

This is not particularly useful for control purposes because it will tend to vary with the kilometres run.

- Total cost of each vehicle per kilometre
- Maintenance cost of each vehicle per kilometre

Cost per tonne-kilometre

This can be more useful than a cost per kilometre for control purposes, because it combines the distance travelled and the load carried, both of which affect cost.

Cost per operating hour

Once again, many costs can be related to this cost unit, including the following.

- Total cost of each vehicle per operating hour
- Variable costs per operating hour
- Fixed costs per operating hour

Question 2

Carry Ltd operates a small fleet of delivery vehicles. Expected costs are as follows.

Loading	1 hour per tonne loaded
Loading costs:	
Labour (casual)	£2 per hour
Equipment depreciation	£80 per week
Supervision	£80 per week
Drivers' wages (fixed)	£100 per man per week
Petrol	10p per kilometre
Repairs	5p per kilometre
Depreciation	£80 per week per vehicle
Supervision	£120 per week
Other general expenses (fixed)	£200 per week

There are two drivers and two vehicles in the fleet.

During a slack week, only six journeys were made.

Journey	Tonnes carried (one way)	One-way distance of journey Kilometres
1	5	100
2	8	20
3	2	60
4	4	50
5	6	200
6	5	300

Required

Calculate the expected average full cost per tonne/kilometre for the week.

Answer

Variable costs

Journey	1	2	3	4	5	6
	£	£	£	£	£	£
Loading labour	10	16	4	8	12	10
Petrol (both ways)	20	4	12	10	40	60
Repairs (both ways)	10	2	6	5	20	30
	40	22	22	23	72	100

Total costs

	£
Variable costs (total for journeys 1 to 6)	279
Loading equipment depreciation	80
Loading supervision	80
Drivers' wages	200
Vehicles depreciation	160
Drivers' supervision	120
Other costs	200
	1,119

Journey	Tonnes	One-way distance Kilometres	Tonne/kilometres
1	5	100	500
2	8	20	160
3	2	60	120
4	4	50	200
5	6	200	1,200
6	5	300	1,500
			3,680

Cost per tonne/kilometre $\dfrac{£1,119}{3,680} = £0.304$

Note that the large element of fixed costs may distort this measure but that a variable cost per tonne/kilometre of £279/3,680 = £0.076 may be useful for budgetary control.

Question 3

Mary Manor Hotel has 80 rooms and these are all either double or twin-bedded rooms offered for either holiday accommodation or for private hire for conferences and company gatherings.

In addition the hotel has a recreation area offering swimming pool, sauna and so on. This area is for the use of all residents with some days being available for paying outside customers.

The restaurant is highly regarded and widely recommended. This is used by the guests and is also open to the general public.

Required

Discuss the possible features of an accounting information system that might be used in this organisation.

Answer

The accounting information system that might be used in this organisation would require the following features.

(a) The hotel should be divided into a number of responsibility centres, with one manager responsible for the performance of each centre. Examples of such centres could be rooms, recreation area and restaurant.

(b) The costing system must be capable of identifying the costs and revenues to be allocated to each responsibility centre.

(c) The system must also include a fair method of apportioning those costs and revenues which cannot be directly allocated to a specific centre.

(d) Each responsibility centre would have a detailed budget against which the actual results would be compared for management control purposes.

(e) The information system must be capable of providing rapid feedback of information to managers so that prompt control action can be taken where appropriate.

(f) Key control measures should also be used, perhaps with standard targets set in advance. Examples include the following.

   • Cost per bed per night

- Cost per sauna hour
- Cost per meal in the restaurant

These control measures would also provide the basic information from which a pricing decision can be made.

2 SERVICE DEPARTMENT COSTING

2.1 Service department costing is used to establish a specific cost for an '**internal service**' which is a service provided by one department for another, rather than sold externally to customers. Examples of some internal service departments include the following.

- Canteen
- Data processing
- Maintenance

The purposes of service department costing

2.2 The costing of internal services has two basic purposes.

(a) **To control the costs and efficiency in the service department.** If we establish a distribution cost per tonne/km, a canteen cost per employee, a maintenance cost per machine hour, job cost per repair, or a mainframe computer operating cost per hour, we can do the following in order to establish control measures.

(i) Compare actual costs against a target or standard

(ii) Compare actual costs in the current period against actual costs in previous periods

(b) **To control the costs of the user departments, and prevent the unnecessary use of services.** If the costs of services are charged to the user departments in such a way that the charges reflect the use actually made by each user department of the service department's services then the following will occur.

(i) The overhead costs of user departments will be established more accurately. Some service department variable costs might be identified as costs which are directly attributable to the user department.

(ii) If the service department's charges for a user department are high, the user department might be encouraged to consider whether it is making an excessively costly and wasteful use of the service department's service.

(iii) The user department might decide that it can obtain a similar service at a lower cost from an external service company and so the service department will have priced itself out of the market. This is clearly not satisfactory from the point of view of the organisation as a whole.

2.3 Service costing also provides a **fairer basis** for charging service costs to user departments, instead of charging service costs as overheads on a broad direct labour hour basis, or similar arbitrary apportionment basis. This is because service costs are related more directly to **use**.

2.4 Some examples of situations where the costing of internal services would be useful are as follows.

(a) If repair costs in a factory are costed as jobs with each bit of repair work being given a job number and costed accordingly, repair costs can be charged to the departments on the basis of repair jobs actually undertaken, instead of on a more generalised basis, such as apportionment according to machine hour capacity in each department. Departments with high repair costs could then consider their high incidence of repairs, the age and reliability of their machines, or the skills of the machine operators.

(b)   If mainframe computer costs are charged to a user department on the basis of a cost per hour, the user department would make the following assessment.

(i)   Whether it was getting good value from its use of the mainframe computer.

(ii)   Whether it might be better to hire the service of a computer bureau, or perhaps install a stand-alone microcomputer system in the department.

The bases for charging service costs to user departments

2.5   The charges to user departments for their use of support services could use any of the following bases.

- No charge at all
- Total actual cost
- Standard absorption cost
- Variable cost

No charge at all

2.6   If service costs are not charged directly to the user departments, they will be either:

(a)   apportioned on a more **arbitrary basis** between production departments, in a system of absorption costing; or

(b)   charged against profit as a **period charge** in a system of marginal costing,

There may be no attempt to recognise that some departments are using services more than others.

Total actual cost

2.7   By this method, the total costs of the service department are accumulated over a period of time. No distinction is made between fixed and variable costs in the department.

The charge to the user departments will then be:

$$\frac{\text{Total actual cost}}{\text{Total activity (eg hours worked)}} \times \text{work done for user department}$$

2.8   For example, a distribution department might charge production departments for road haulage (carriage inwards). If actual distribution costs are £200,000 per month and 400,000 tonne/miles are delivered, the charge to the production departments would be £0.50 per tonne mile (£200,000 ÷ 400,000).

2.9   This method might be suitable in the following circumstances.

- If it is difficult to separate fixed and variable costs
- If it is difficult to establish standard costs

2.10   There are several problems with this method.

(a)   If actual service costs are charged to user departments, then user departments will be charged for any overspending and inefficiency in the service departments. The user departments 'suffer' from poor cost control in the service departments.

(b) If the service department is not working at full capacity, the charge per unit of service would be higher than if the department is more busy. This might discourage user departments from using the service, to avoid high service charges.

(c) The fluctuation charges which can result from the use of actual costs would make it difficult for the user departments to plan and control costs.

Standard absorption cost

2.11 By this method, the charge to user departments for support services is based on a standard, predetermined cost for the service. This service cost will consist of variable costs plus a share of fixed costs for the service department.

2.12 Standard cost has an advantage over actual cost. The standard charge is a predetermined rate based on:

$$\frac{\text{Standard (budgeted) total costs}}{\text{Standard (budgeted) service activity}}$$

The user departments would therefore **not** be penalised for either of the following.

- Overspending and inefficiency in the service departments
- Under-capacity in the service department

2.13 There are, however, two problems with using standard absorption costs as a basis for charging for services.

(a) It is necessary to review the standard cost regularly and frequently, so that user departments do not get a false impression of the cost of the service.

(b) There is a problem in deciding what the standard activity level ought to be.

Variable cost

2.14 By this method of charging, support services are costed at marginal or variable cost only. This could be either standard or actual variable cost. The **advantage** of this method is that user departments are charged for the extra costs incurred by using more of the service, which would help to provide better costing information within a system of marginal costing.

2.15 There are a number of **weaknesses** or problems with this system.

(a) The user departments would be under a false impression as to the true full cost of the service that they are using, because they would be charged with just the marginal costs.

(b) If actual variable costs are used, there would be no control of overspending and inefficiency in the service department because the service department would simply 'pass on' its overspending in higher charges to the user department.

(c) If standard variable costs are used it will be necessary to revise the standard regularly.

Question 4

Identify three different reasons for the charging of service department costs to user departments and comment on the charging methods which may be relevant in the case of maintenance, computer services, and health, safety and welfare service departments.

Answer

Service department costs are charged to user departments for the following reasons.

(a)   User departments which use most of the services are made responsible for them.

(b)   Service costs are included in production costs, where appropriate. Overheads related to production are included in many stock valuations.

(c)   The 'true' cost of each user department is known to management.

(d)   User departments are encouraged to use the service (if they are being charged for it) as opposed to external contractors.

Maintenance might be easy to allocate, especially if machines are in definite locations, and there is a distinct chain of responsibility. Maintenance costs could be charged out in the budget as part of production overhead at a predetermined rate, or in an activity based costing system. This would be for budgetary purposes only. In practice, during the budget period, maintenance jobs could be charged out on an individual basis, directly to user departments.

Computer services cost could be charged on the basis of computer time for normal processing, and any computer projects which are directly attributable to user departments could be charged directly. Some estimate would be needed of any system enhancements required during the year.

Health, safety and welfare department's costs could be allocated to user departments on the basis of employee numbers in the case of nursing care, or floor space in the case of fire prevention equipment, alarm systems and so forth.

---

3   JOB COSTING AND SERVICES

3.1   Service costing is one of the subdivisions of **continuous operation costing** and as such should theoretically be applied when the services result from a sequence of continuous or repetitive operations or processes. Service costing is therefore ideal for catering establishments, road, rail and air transport services and hotels. However, just because an organisation provides a service, it does not mean that service costing should automatically be applied.

3.2   Remember that job costing applies where work is undertaken to customers' special requirements. An organisation may therefore be working in the service sector but may supply one-off services which meet particular customers' special requirements; in such a situation job costing may be more appropriate than service costing. For example, a consultancy business, although part of the service sector, could use job costing.

(a)   Each job could be given a separate number.

(b)   Time sheets could be used to record and analyse consultants' time.

(c)   The time spent against each job number would be shown as well as, for example, travelling time and mileage.

(d)   Other costs such as stationery could be charged direct to each job as necessary.

Chapter roundup

- **Service costing** can be used by companies operating in a **service industry** or by companies wishing to establish the **cost of services carried out by some of their departments**.

- Service organisations do not make or sell tangible goods.

- **Specific characteristics of services**

  o Intangibility
  o Simultaneity
  o Perishability
  o Heterogeneity

- One main problem with service costing is being able to define a realistic **cost unit** that represents a suitable measure of the service provided. If the service is a function of two activity variables, a **composite cost unit** may be more appropriate.

- **Cost per service unit** = $\dfrac{\text{Total costs for period}}{\text{Number of service units in the period}}$

- Service department costing is also used to establish a specific cost for an **internal service** which is a service provided by one department for another, rather than sold externally to customers eg canteen, maintenance.

Quick quiz

1   Define service costing

2   Match up the following services with their typical cost units

Service		Cost unit
Hotels		Patient-day
Education	?	Meal served
Hospitals		Full-time student
Catering organisations		Occupied bed-night

3   What is the advantage of organisations within an industry using a common cost unit?

4   Cost per service units = ──────────────

5   Service department costing is used to establish a specific cost for an 'internal service' which is a service provided by one department for another.

    True   ☐
    False ☐

Answers to quick quiz

1 Cost accounting for services or functions eg canteens, maintenance, personnel (service centres/functions).

2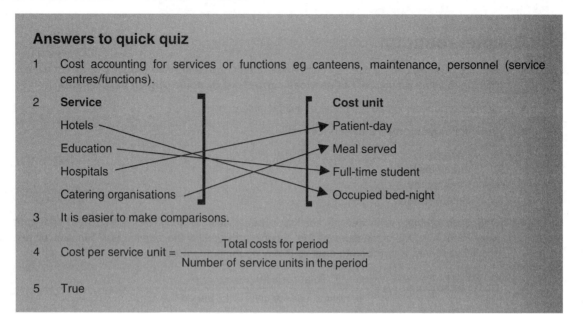

Service	Cost unit
Hotels	Patient-day
Education	Meal served
Hospitals	Full-time student
Catering organisations	Occupied bed-night

3 It is easier to make comparisons.

4 $\text{Cost per service unit} = \dfrac{\text{Total costs for period}}{\text{Number of service units in the period}}$

5 True

Now try the question below from the Exam Question Bank

Number	Level	Marks	Time
Q13	Examination	15	27 mins

Part C
Marginal costing and decision making

Chapter 11

RELEVANT COSTING AND DECISION MAKING

Topic list	Syllabus reference	Ability required
1 Relevant costs	(iv)	Comprehension
2 Choice of product (product mix) decisions	(iv)	Application
3 Make or buy decisions	(iv)	Application
4 Discontinuing a product	(iv)	Application
5 Acceptance of a special order	(iv)	Application

Introduction

Cost accounting was defined in Chapter 1 and so far we have been looking at it as a means of establishing profits, balance sheet items and stock valuations but there is more to cost accounting than that. One of the other reasons for the existence of cost accounting is to assist management in **decision making**.

Management at all levels within an organisation take decisions. The overriding requirement of the information that should be supplied by the cost accountant to aid decision making is that of **relevance.** This chapter therefore begins by looking at the costing technique required in decision-making situations, that of **relevant costing**, and explains how to decide which costs need taking into account when a decision is being made and which costs do not.

We then go on to see how to apply relevant costing to some specific decision-making scenarios.

Learning outcomes covered in this chapter

- **Identify** relevant costs and revenues
- **Calculate** the profit-maximising sales mix for a company with a single resource constraint which has total freedom of action

Syllabus content covered in this chapter

- Relevant cost concepts, including sunk costs, committed costs and opportunity costs
- Limiting factor analysis

BPP
PUBLISHING

1 RELEVANT COSTS

Relevant costs

KEY TERM

A **relevant cost** is a future cash flow arising as a direct consequence of a decision.

1.1 Decision making should be based on relevant costs.

(a) **Relevant costs are future costs**.

(i) A decision is about the future; it cannot alter what has been done already. Costs that have been incurred in the past are totally irrelevant to any decision that is being made 'now'. Such costs are **past costs** or **sunk costs**.

(ii) Costs that have been incurred include not only costs that have already been paid, but also **committed costs** (a future cash flow that will be incurred anyway, regardless of the decision taken now).

(b) **Relevant costs are cash flows**. Only cash flow information is required. This means that costs or charges which do not reflect additional cash spending (such as depreciation and notional costs) should be ignored for the purpose of decision making.

(c) **Relevant costs are incremental costs**. For example, if an employee is expected to have no other work to do during the next week, but will be paid his basic wage (of, say, £100 per week) for attending work and doing nothing, his manager might decide to give him a job which earns the organisation £40. The net gain is £40 and the £100 is irrelevant to the decision because although it is a future cash flow, it will be incurred anyway whether the employee is given work or not.

1.2 Other terms are sometimes used to describe relevant costs.

KEY TERM

Differential cost is 'the difference in total cost between alternatives.'

CIMA *Official Terminology*

1.3 For example, if decision option A costs £300 and decision option B costs £360, the differential cost is £60.

KEY TERM

An **opportunity cost** is 'The value of the benefit sacrificed when one course of action is chosen, in preference to an alternative'.

CIMA *Official Terminology*

1.4 Suppose for example that there are three options, A, B and C, only one of which can be chosen. The net profit from each would be £80, £100 and £70 respectively.

Since only one option can be selected option B would be chosen because it offers the biggest benefit.

	£
Profit from option B	100
Less opportunity cost (ie the benefit from the most profitable alternative, A)	80
Differential benefit of option B	20

The decision to choose option B would not be taken simply because it offers a profit of £100, but because it offers a differential profit of £20 in excess of the next best alternative.

Sunk costs

> **KEY TERM**
>
> A **sunk cost** is a past cost which is not directly relevant in decision making.

1.5 The principle underlying decision accounting is that **management decisions can only affect the future.** In decision making, managers therefore require information about **future costs and revenues** which would be affected by the decision under review, and they must not be misled by events, costs and revenues in the past, about which they can do nothing. Therefore **sunk costs**, which have been charged already as a cost of sales in a previous accounting period or will be charged in a future accounting period although the expenditure has already been incurred (or the expenditure decision irrevocably taken), are irrelevant to decision making.

An example of this type of cost is **depreciation**. If a fixed asset has been purchased, depreciation may be charged for several years but the cost is a **sunk cost**, about which nothing can now be done.

1.6 Another example of sunk costs are development costs which have already been incurred. Suppose that a company has spent £250,000 in developing a new service for customers, but the marketing department's most recent findings are that the service might not gain customer acceptance and could be a commercial failure. The decision whether or not to abandon the development of the new service would have to be taken, but the £250,000 spent so far should be ignored by the decision makers because it is a **sunk cost**.

Fixed and variable costs

> **Exam focus point**
>
> Unless you are given an indication to the contrary, you should assume the following.
>
> - Variable costs will be relevant costs.
> - Fixed costs are irrelevant to a decision.
>
> This need not be the case, however, and you should analyse variable and fixed cost data carefully. Do not forget that 'fixed' costs may only be fixed in the short term.

Non-relevant variable costs

1.7 There might be occasions when a variable cost is in fact a sunk cost. For example, suppose that a company has some units of raw material in stock. They have been paid for already, and originally cost £2,000. They are now obsolete and are no longer used in regular production, and they have no scrap value. However, they could be used in a special job which the company is trying to decide whether to undertake. The special job is a 'one-off' customer order, and would use up all these materials in stock.

In deciding whether the job should be undertaken, the relevant cost of the materials to the special job is nil. Their original cost of £2,000 is a **sunk cost**, and should be ignored in the decision.

However, if the materials did have a scrap value of, say, £300, then their relevant cost to the job would be the **opportunity cost** of being unable to sell them for scrap, ie £300.

Attributable fixed costs

1.8   There might be occasions when a fixed cost is a relevant cost, and you must be aware of the distinction between 'specific' or 'directly attributable' fixed costs, and general fixed overheads.

(a)   **Directly attributable fixed costs** are those costs which, although fixed within a relevant range of activity level are relevant to a decision for either of the following reasons.

   (i)   They could increase if certain extra activities were undertaken. For example, it may be necessary to employ an extra supervisor if a particular order is accepted. The extra salary would be an attributable fixed cost.

   (ii)   They would decrease or be eliminated entirely if a decision were taken either to reduce the scale of operations or shut down entirely.

(b)   **General fixed overheads** are those fixed overheads which will be unaffected by decisions to increase or decrease the scale of operations, perhaps because they are an apportioned share of the fixed costs of items which would be completely unaffected by the decisions. An apportioned share of head office charges is an example of general fixed overheads for a local office or department. General fixed overheads are not relevant in decision making.

Absorbed overhead

1.9   **Absorbed overhead** is a **notional** accounting cost and hence should be ignored for decision-making purposes. It is overhead *incurred* which *may* be relevant to a decision.

The relevant cost of materials

1.10   The relevant cost of raw materials is generally their **current replacement cost,** *unless* the materials have already been purchased and would not be replaced once used. In this case the relevant cost of using them is the **higher** of the following.

•   Their current resale value
•   The value they would obtain if they were put to an alternative use

If the materials have no resale value and no other possible use, then the relevant cost of using them for the opportunity under consideration would be nil.

You should test your knowledge of the relevant cost of materials by attempting the following question.

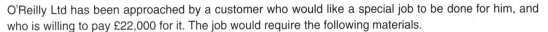

Question 1

O'Reilly Ltd has been approached by a customer who would like a special job to be done for him, and who is willing to pay £22,000 for it. The job would require the following materials.

Material	Total units required	Units already in stock	Book value of units in stock £/unit	Realisable value £/unit	Replacement cost £/unit
A	1,000	0	-	-	6
B	1,000	600	2	2.50	5
C	1,000	700	3	2.50	4
D	200	200	4	6.00	9

Material B is used regularly by O'Reilly Ltd, and if units of B are required for this job, they would need to be replaced to meet other production demand.

Materials C and D are in stock as the result of previous over-buying, and they have a restricted use. No other use could be found for material C, but the units of material D could be used in another job as substitute for 300 units of material E, which currently costs £5 per unit (of which the company has no units in stock at the moment).

Required

Calculate the relevant costs of material for deciding whether or not to accept the contract.

Answer

(a) **Material A** is not yet owned. It would have to be bought in full at the replacement cost of £6 per unit.

(b) **Material B** is used regularly by the company. There are existing stocks (600 units) but if these are used on the contract under review a further 600 units would be bought to replace them. Relevant costs are therefore 1,000 units at the replacement cost of £5 per unit.

(c) 1,000 units of **material C** are needed and 700 are already in stock. If used for the contract, a further 300 units must be bought at £4 each. The existing stocks of 700 will not be replaced. If they are used for the contract, they could not be sold at £2.50 each. The realisable value of these 700 units is an opportunity cost of sales revenue forgone.

(d) The required units of **material D** are already in stock and will not be replaced. There is an opportunity cost of using D in the contract because there are alternative opportunities either to sell the existing stocks for £6 per unit (£1,200 in total) or avoid other purchases (of material E), which would cost 300 x £5 = £1,500. Since substitution for E is more beneficial, £1,500 is the opportunity cost.

(e) **Summary of relevant costs**

	£
Material A (1,000 × £6)	6,000
Material B (1,000 × £5)	5,000
Material C (300 × £4) plus (700 × £2.50)	2,950
Material D	1,500
Total	15,450

1.11 It is important that you should be able to identify the relevant costs which are appropriate to a decision. In many cases, this is a fairly straightforward problem, but there are cases where great care should be taken. Attempt the following question.

Question 2

A company has been making a machine to order for a customer, but the customer has since gone into liquidation, and there is no prospect that any money will be obtained from the winding up of the company.

Costs incurred to date in manufacturing the machine are £50,000 and progress payments of £15,000 had been received from the customer prior to the liquidation.

The sales department has found another company willing to buy the machine for £34,000 once it has been completed.

To complete the work, the following costs would be incurred.

(a)   Materials: these have been bought at a cost of £6,000. They have no other use, and if the machine is not finished, they would be sold for scrap for £2,000.

(b)   Further labour costs would be £8,000. Labour is in short supply, and if the machine is not finished, the work force would be switched to another job, which would earn £30,000 in revenue, and incur direct costs of £12,000 and absorbed (fixed) overhead of £8,000.

(c)   Consultancy fees £4,000. If the work is not completed, the consultant's contract would be cancelled at a cost of £1,500.

(d)   General overheads of £8,000 would be added to the cost of the additional work.

Required

Assess whether the new customer's offer should be accepted.

Answer

(a)   Costs incurred in the past, or revenue received in the past are not relevant because they cannot affect a decision about what is best for the future. Costs incurred to date of £50,000 and revenue received of £15,000 are 'water under the bridge' and should be ignored.

(b)   Similarly, the price paid in the past for the materials is irrelevant. The only relevant cost of materials affecting the decision is the opportunity cost of the revenue from scrap which would be forgone - £2,000.

(c)   **Labour costs**

	£
Labour costs required to complete work	8,000
Opportunity costs: contribution forgone by losing other work £(30,000 – 12,000)	18,000
Relevant cost of labour	26,000

(d)   The incremental cost of consultancy from completing the work is £2,500.

	£
Cost of completing work	4,000
Cost of cancelling contract	1,500
Incremental cost of completing work	2,500

(e)   Absorbed overhead is a notional accounting cost and should be ignored. Actual overhead incurred is the only overhead cost to consider. General overhead costs (and the absorbed overhead of the alternative work for the labour force) should be ignored.

(f)   Relevant costs may be summarised as follows.

	£	£
Revenue from completing work		34,000
Relevant costs		
Materials: opportunity cost	2,000	
Labour: basic pay	8,000	
opportunity cost	18,000	
Incremental cost of consultant	2,500	
		30,500
Extra profit to be earned by accepting the order		3,500

---

2   CHOICE OF PRODUCT (PRODUCT MIX) DECISIONS   **Pilot paper**

2.1   One of the more common decision-making problems is a situation where there are not enough resources to meet the potential sales demand, and so a decision has to be made about what mix of products to produce, using what resources there are as effectively as possible.

> ### KEY TERM
>
> A **limiting factor** is a factor which limits the organisation's activities.

2.2 A **limiting factor** could be sales if there is a limit to sales demand but any one of the organisation's resources (labour, materials and so on) may be insufficient to meet the level of production demanded.

2.3 It is assumed in limiting factor accounting that management wishes to maximise profit and that **profit will be maximised when contribution is maximised** (given no change in fixed cost expenditure incurred). In other words, **marginal costing ideas are applied**.

2.4 **Contribution will be maximised by earning the biggest possible contribution from each unit of limiting factor.** For example if grade A labour is the limiting factor, contribution will be maximised by earning the biggest contribution from each hour of grade A labour worked.

2.5 The limiting factor decision therefore involves the determination of the contribution earned by each different product from each unit of the limiting factor.

2.6 EXAMPLE: LIMITING FACTOR

AB Ltd makes two products, the Ay and the Be. Unit variable costs are as follows.

	Ay	*Be*
	£	£
Direct materials	1	3
Direct labour (£3 per hour)	6	3
Variable overhead	1	1
	8	7

The sales price per unit is £14 per Ay and £11 per Be. During July 20X2 the available direct labour is limited to 8,000 hours. Sales demand in July is expected to be 3,000 units for Ays and 5,000 units for Bes.

Required

Determine the profit-maximising production mix, assuming that monthly fixed costs are £20,000, and that opening stocks of finished goods and work in progress are nil.

2.7 SOLUTION

Step 1. Confirm that the limiting factor is something other than sales demand.

	Ays	*Bes*	*Total*
Labour hours per unit	2 hrs	1 hr	
Sales demand	3,000 units	5,000 units	
Labour hours needed	6,000 hrs	5,000 hrs	11,000 hrs
Labour hours available			8,000 hrs
Shortfall			3,000 hrs

Labour is the limiting factor on production.

Step 2. Identify the contribution earned by each product per unit of limiting factor, that is per labour hour worked.

	Ays	*Bes*
	£	£
Sales price	14	11
Variable cost	8	7
Unit contribution	6	4
Labour hours per unit	2 hrs	1 hr
Contribution per labour hour (= unit of limiting factor)	£3	£4

Although Ays have a higher unit contribution than Bes, two Bes can be made in the time it takes to make one Ay. Because labour is in short supply it is more profitable to make Bes than Ays.

Step 3. Determine the **optimum production plan**. Sufficient Bes will be made to meet the full sales demand, and the remaining labour hours available will then be used to make Ays.

(a)

Product	*Demand*	*Hours required*	*Hours available*	*Priority of manufacture*
Bes	5,000	5,000	5,000	1st
Ays	3,000	6,000	3,000 (bal)	2nd
		11,000	8,000	

(b)

Product	*Units*	*Hours needed*	*Contribution per unit*	*Total*
			£	£
Bes	5,000	5,000	4	20,000
Ays	1,500	3,000	6	9,000
		8,000		29,000
Less fixed costs				20,000
Profit				9,000

2.8 In conclusion.

(a) Unit contribution is *not* the correct way to decide priorities.

(b) Labour hours are the scarce resource, and therefore contribution **per labour hour** is the correct way to decide priorities.

(c) The Be earns £4 contribution per labour hour, and the Ay earns £3 contribution per labour hour. Bes therefore make more profitable use of the scarce resource, and should be manufactured first.

Exam focus point

If an examination question asks you to determine the optimum production plan, follow the five-step approach shown below.

Step 1. Identify the limiting factor
Step 2. Calculate contribution per unit for each product
Step 3. Calculate contribution per unit of limiting factor
Step 4. Rank products (make product with highest contribution per unit of limiting factor first)
Step 5. Make products in rank order until scare resource is used up **(optimal production plan)**

There were 15 marks available in the Pilot paper for **Management Accounting Fundamentals** for determining the optimum production plan of a company that manufactured three products.

---

3 MAKE OR BUY DECISIONS

3.1 A **make or buy problem** involves a decision by an organisation about whether it should make a product/carry out an activity with its own internal resources, or whether it should pay another organisation to make the product/carry out the activity. Examples of make or buy decisions would be as follows.

(a) Whether a company should manufacture its own components, or buy the components from an outside supplier.

(b) Whether a construction company should do some work with its own employees, or whether it should subcontract the work to another company.

(c) Whether the design and development of a new computer system should be entrusted to in-house data processing staff or whether an external software house should be hired to do the work.

3.2 The 'make' option should give management more direct control over the work, but the 'buy' option often has the benefit that the external organisation has a specialist skill and expertise in the work. Make or buy decisions should certainly not be based exclusively on cost considerations.

3.3 If an organisation has the freedom of choice about whether to make internally or buy externally and has no scarce resources that put a restriction on what it can do itself, the relevant costs for the decision will be the **differential costs** between the two options.

3.4 EXAMPLE: MAKE OR BUY

Buster Ltd makes four components, W, X, Y and Z, for which costs in the forthcoming year are expected to be as follows.

	W	*X*	*Y*	*Z*
Production (units)	1,000	2,000	4,000	3,000
Unit marginal costs	£	£	£	£
Direct materials	4	5	2	4
Direct labour	8	9	4	6
Variable production overheads	2	3	1	2
	14	17	7	12

Directly attributable fixed costs per annum and committed fixed costs are as follows.

	£
Incurred as a direct consequence of making W	1,000
Incurred as a direct consequence of making X	5,000
Incurred as a direct consequence of making Y	6,000
Incurred as a direct consequence of making Z	8,000
Other fixed costs (committed)	30,000
	50,000

A subcontractor has offered to supply units of W, X, Y and Z for £12, £21, £10 and £14 respectively.

Required

Decide whether Buster Ltd should make or buy the components.

3.5 SOLUTION

(a) The relevant costs are the differential costs between making and buying, and they consist of differences in unit variable costs plus differences in directly attributable fixed costs. Subcontracting will result in some fixed cost savings.

	W	X	Y	Z
	£	£	£	£
Unit variable cost of making	14	17	7	12
Unit variable cost of buying	12	21	10	14
	(2)	4	3	2
Annual requirements (units)	1,000	2,000	4,000	3,000
	£	£	£	£
Extra variable cost of buying (per annum)	(2,000)	8,000	12,000	6,000
Fixed costs saved by buying	1,000	5,000	6,000	8,000
Extra total cost of buying	(3,000)	3,000	6,000	(2,000)

(b) The company would save £3,000 pa by subcontracting component W (where the purchase cost would be less than the marginal cost per unit to make internally) and would save £2,000 pa by subcontracting component Z (because of the saving in fixed costs of £8,000).

(c) In this example, relevant costs are the variable costs of in-house manufacture, the variable costs of subcontracted units, and the saving in fixed costs.

(d) Important further considerations would be as follows.

(i) If components W and Z are subcontracted, the company will have spare capacity. How should that spare capacity be profitably used? Are there hidden benefits to be obtained from subcontracting? Would the company's workforce resent the loss of work to an outside subcontractor, and might such a decision cause an industrial dispute?

(ii) Would the subcontractor be reliable with delivery times, and would he supply components of the same quality as those manufactured internally?

(iii) Does the company wish to be flexible and maintain better control over operations by making everything itself?

(iv) Are the estimates of fixed cost savings reliable? In the case of Product W, buying is clearly cheaper than making in-house. In the case of product Z, the decision to buy rather than make would only be financially beneficial if the fixed cost savings of £8,000 could really be 'delivered' by management. All too often in practice, promised savings fail to materialise!

Question 3

BB Limited makes three components - S, T and W. The following costs have been recorded.

	Component S Unit cost	Component T Unit cost	Component W Unit cost
	£	£	£
Variable cost	2.50	8.00	5.00
Fixed cost	2.00	8.30	3.75
Total cost	4.50	16.30	8.75

Another company has offered to supply the components to BB Limited at the following prices.

	Component S	Component T	Component W
Price each	£4	£7	£5.50

Which component(s), if any, should BB Limited consider buying in?

A   Buy in all three components
B   Do not buy any
C   Buy in S and W
D   Buy in T only

Answer

BB Ltd should buy the component if the variable cost of making the component is more than the variable cost of buying the component.

	Component S	Component T	Component W
	£	£	£
Variable cost of making	2.50	8.00	5.00
Variable cost of buying	4.00	7.00	5.50
	(1.50)	1.00	(0.50)

The variable cost of making component T is greater than the variable cost of buying it.

∴ BB Ltd should consider buying in component T only.

The correct answer is D.

Make or buy decisions and limiting factors

3.6   In a situation where a company must subcontract work to make up a shortfall in its own production capability, its total costs are minimised if those components/products subcontracted are those with the lowest extra variable cost of buying per unit of limiting factor saved by buying.

3.7   EXAMPLE: MAKE OR BUY AND LIMITING FACTORS

Green Ltd manufactures two components, the Alpha and the Beta, using the same machines for each. The budget for the next year calls for the production and assembly of 4,000 of each component. The variable production cost per unit of the final product, the gamma, is as follows.

	Machine hours	Variable cost
		£
1 unit of Alpha	3	20
1 unit of Beta	2	36
Assembly		20
		76

Only 16,000 hours of machine time will be available during the year, and a sub-contractor has quoted the following unit prices for supplying components: Alpha £29; Beta £40. Advise Green Ltd.

3.8   SOLUTION

(a)   There is a shortfall in machine hours available, and some products must be sub-contracted.

Product	Units		Machine hours
Alpha	4,000		12,000
Beta	4,000		8,000
		Required	20,000
		Available	16,000
		Shortfall	4,000

(b) The assembly costs are not relevant costs because they are unaffected by the make or buy decision. The units subcontracted should be those which will add least to the costs of Green Ltd. Since 4,000 hours of work must be sub-contracted, the cheapest policy is to subcontract work which adds the least extra costs (the least extra variable costs) per hour of own-time saved.

(c)

	Alpha	*Beta*
	£	£
Variable cost of making	20	36
Variable cost of buying	29	40
Extra variable cost of buying	9	4
Machine hours saved by buying	3 hrs	2 hrs
Extra variable cost of buying, per hour saved	£3	£2

It is cheaper to buy Betas than to buy Alphas and so the priority for making the components in-house will be in the reverse order to the preference for buying them from a subcontractor.

(d)

Component	*Hrs per unit to make in-house*	*Hrs required in total*	*Cumulative hours*
Alpha	3 hrs	12,000	12,000
Beta	2 hrs	8,000	20,000
		20,000	
Hours available		16,000	
Shortfall		4,000	

There are enough machine hours to make all 4,000 units of Alpha and 2,000 units of Beta. 4,000 hours production of Beta must be sub-contracted. This will be the cheapest production policy available

(e)

Component	*Machine hours*	*Number of units*	*Unit variable cost*	*Total variable cost*
Make			£	£
Alpha	12,000	4,000	20	80,000
Beta (balance)	4,000	2,000	36	72,000
	16,000			152,000
Buy	*Hours saved*			
Beta (balance)	4,000	2,000	40	80,000
		Total variable costs of components		232,000
		Assembly costs (4,000 × £20)		80,000
		Total variable costs		312,000

4   DISCONTINUING A PRODUCT

4.1 Suppose that a company manufactures three products, Corfus, Cretes and Zantes. The present net profit from these is as follows.

	Corfus	*Cretes*	*Zantes*	*Total*
	£	£	£	£
Sales	50,000	40,000	60,000	150,000
Variable costs	30,000	25,000	35,000	90,000
Contribution	20,000	15,000	25,000	60,000
Fixed costs	17,000	18,000	20,000	55,000
Profit/loss	3,000	(3,000)	5,000	5,000

The company is concerned about its poor profit performance, and is considering whether or not to cease selling Cretes. It is felt that selling prices cannot be raised or lowered without adversely affecting net income. £5,000 of the fixed costs of Cretes are attributable fixed costs which would be saved if production ceased. All other fixed costs would remain the same.

4.2   By stopping production of Cretes, the consequences would be a £10,000 fall in profits.

	£
Loss of contribution	(15,000)
Savings in fixed costs	5,000
Incremental loss	(10,000)

4.3   Suppose, however, it were possible to use the resources realised by stopping production of Cretes and switch to producing a new item, Rhodes, which would sell for £50,000 and incur variable costs of £30,000 and extra direct fixed costs of £6,000. A new decision is now required.

	Cretes	*Rhodes*
	£	£
Sales	40,000	50,000
Less variable costs	25,000	30,000
Contribution	15,000	20,000
Less direct fixed costs	5,000	6,000
Contribution to shared fixed costs and profit	10,000	14,000

It would be more profitable to shut down production of Cretes and switch resources to making Rhodes, in order to boost profits to £9,000.

5   ACCEPTANCE OF A SPECIAL ORDER

5.1   This type of decision-making situation will concern an order which would utilise an organisation's spare capacity but which would have to be accepted at a price lower than that normally required by the organisation. In general you can assume that an order will probably be accepted if it increases contribution and hence profit, and rejected if it reduces profit. Let us consider an example.

5.2   EXAMPLE: ACCEPT OR REJECT

Belt and Braces Ltd makes a single product which sells for £20. It has a full cost of £15 which is made up as follows.

	£
Direct material	4
Direct labour (2 hours)	6
Variable overhead	2
General fixed overhead	3
	15

The labour force is currently working at 90% of capacity and so there is a spare capacity for 2,000 units. A customer has approached the company with a request for the manufacture of a special order of 2,000 units for which he is willing to pay £25,000. Assess whether the order should be accepted.

5.3   SOLUTION

	£	£
Value of order		25,000
Cost of order		
Direct materials (£4 × 2,000)	8,000	
Direct labour (£6 × 2,000)	12,000	
Variable overhead (£2 × 2,000)	4,000	
Relevant cost of order		24,000
Profit from order acceptance		1,000

Fixed costs will be incurred regardless of whether the order is accepted and so are not relevant to the decision. The order should be accepted since it increases contribution to profit by £1,000.

5.4 There are, however, several other factors which would need to be considered before a final decision is taken.

(a) The acceptance of the order at a lower price may lead other customers to demand lower prices as well.

(b) There may be more profitable ways of using the spare capacity.

(c) Accepting the order may lock up capacity that could be used for future full-price business.

(d) Fixed costs may, in fact, alter if the order is accepted.

Chapter roundup

- **Relevant costs** are future cash flows arising as a direct consequence of a decision.

  - Relevant costs are **future costs**
  - Relevant costs are **cashflows**
  - Relevant costs are **incremental costs**

- Relevant costs are also **differential costs** and **opportunity costs.**

  - **Differential cost** is the difference in total cost between alternatives.

  - An **opportunity cost** is the value of the benefit sacrificed when one course of action is chosen in preference to an alternative.

- A **sunk cost** is a past cost which is not directly relevant in decision making.

- The principle underlying decision accounting is that management decisions can only affect the **future**. Management therefore require information about **future costs and revenues.**

- **In general**, variable costs will be relevant costs and fixed costs will be irrelevant to a decision.

- A **limiting factor** is a factor which limits the organisation's activities.

- In a **limiting factor situation,** contribution will be maximised by earning the biggest possible contribution per unit of limiting factor.

1 In a make or buy situation with no limiting factors, the relevant costs for the decision are the **differential costs** between the two options.

2 The decision to accept or reject an order should be made on the basis of whether or not the order **increases contribution and profit**.

Quick quiz

1 Relevant costs are:

(a)
(b)
(c)
(d)
(e)

2 Sunk costs are directly relevant in decision making.

True ☐

False ☐

3   A limiting factor is a factor which ....

4   When determining the optimum production plan, what five steps are involved?

Step 1.   ....

Step 2   ....

Step 3.   ....

Step 4.   ....

Step 5.   ....

5   A sunk cost is:

A   a cost committed to be spent in the current period

B   a cost which is irrelevant for decision making

C   a cost connected with oil exploration in the North Sea

D   a cost unaffected by fluctuations in the level of activity

Answers to quick quiz

1   (a)   Future costs
     (b)   Cash flows
     (c)   Incremental costs
     (d)   Differential costs
     (e)   Opportunity costs

2   False

3   Limits the organisation's activities.

4   *Step 1.*   Identify the limiting factor
     Step 2.   Calculate contribution per unit for each product
     Step 3.   Calculate contribution per unit of limiting factor
     Step 4.   Rank products (make product with highest contribution per unit of limiting factor first)
     Step 5.   Make products in rank order until scare resource is used up **(optimal production plan)**

5   B

Now try the question below from the Exam Question Bank

Number	Level	Marks	Time
Q14	Examination	25	45 mins

BPP
PUBLISHING

Chapter 12

BREAKEVEN ANALYSIS

Topic list	Syllabus reference	Ability required
1 CVP analysis and breakeven point	(iv)	Application, analysis
2 The Contribution/Sales (C/S) ratio	(iv)	Application, analysis
3 The margin of safety	(iv)	Application, analysis
4 Breakeven arithmetic and profit targets	(iv)	Application, analysis
5 Breakeven charts and profit/volume graphs	(iv)	Application
6 Limitations of CVP analysis	(iv)	Analysis

Introduction

You should by now realise that the cost accountant needs estimates of **fixed** and **variable costs**, and **revenues**, at various output levels. The cost accountant, must also be fully aware of **cost behaviour** because, to be able to estimate costs, he must know what a particular cost will do given particular conditions.

An understanding of cost behaviour is not all that you may need to know, however. The application of **cost-volume-profit analysis**, which is based on the cost behaviour principles and marginal costing ideas, is sometimes necessary so that the appropriate decision-making information can be provided. As you may have guessed, this chapter is going to look at that very topic, **cost-volume-profit analysis** or **breakeven analysis.**

Learning outcomes covered in this chapter

- **Calculate** and **interpret** the breakeven point, profit target, margin of safety and profit/volume ratio for a single product

- **Prepare** breakeven charts and profit/volume graphs for a single product

- **Discuss** CVP analysis

Syllabus content covered in this chapter

- Breakeven charts, profit volume graphs, breakeven point, profit target, margin of safety, contribution/sales ratio

1   CVP ANALYSIS AND BREAKEVEN POINT   Pilot paper

> **KEY TERM**
>
> **Cost-volume-profit (CVP)/breakeven analysis** is the study of the interrelationships between costs, volume and profit at various levels of activity

1.1 The management of an organisation usually wishes to know the profit likely to be made if the aimed-for production and sales for the year are achieved. Management may also be interested to know the following.

(a) The **breakeven** point which is the activity levels at which there is neither profit nor loss.

(b) The **amount** by which actual **sales can fall** below anticipated sales, **without** a **loss** being incurred.

1.2 The breakeven point (BEP) can be calculated arithmetically.

FORMULA TO LEARN

$$\text{Breakeven point} = \frac{\text{Total fixed costs}}{\text{Contribution per unit}} = \frac{\text{Contribution required to break even}}{\text{Contribution per unit}}$$

$$= \text{Number of units of sale required to break even.}$$

1.3 **EXAMPLE: BREAKEVEN POINT**

Expected sales	10,000 units at £8 = £80,000
Variable cost	£5 per unit
Fixed costs	£21,000

Required

Compute the breakeven point.

1.4 **SOLUTION**

The contribution per unit is £(8–5)	=	£3
Contribution required to break even	=	fixed costs = £21,000
Breakeven point (BEP)	=	21,000 ÷ 3
	=	7,000 units
In revenue, BEP	=	(7,000 × £8) = £56,000

Sales above £56,000 will result in profit of £3 per unit of additional sales and sales below £56,000 will mean a loss of £3 per unit for each unit by which sales fall short of 7,000 units. In other words, profit will improve or worsen by the amount of contribution per unit.

	7,000 units		*7,001 units*
	£		£
Revenue	56,000		56,008
Less variable costs	35,000		35,005
Contribution	21,000		21,003
Less fixed costs	21,000		21,000
Profit	0	(= breakeven)	3

2 **THE CONTRIBUTION/SALES (C/S) RATIO**

2.1 An alternative way of calculating the breakeven point to give an answer in terms of sales revenue is as follows.

FORMULA TO LEARN

$$\frac{\text{Required contribution} = \text{Fixed costs}}{\text{C/S ratio}} = \textbf{Sales revenue at breakeven point}$$

(The **C/S (contribution/sales) ratio** is also sometimes called a profit/volume or P/V ratio).

2.2 In the example in Paragraph 1.3 the C/S ratio is $\frac{£3}{£8} = 37.5\%$

Breakeven is where sales revenue equals $\frac{£21,000}{37.5\%} = £56,000$

At a price of £8 per unit, this represents 7,000 units of sales.

The C/S ratio is a measure of how much contribution is earned from each £1 of sales. The C/S ratio of 37.5% in the above example means that for every £1 of sales, a contribution of 37.5p is earned. Thus, in order to earn a total contribution of £21,000 and if contribution increases by 37.5p per £1 of sales, sales must be:

$$\frac{£1}{37.5p} \times £21,000 = £56,000$$

Question 1

The C/S ratio of product W is 20%. IB Ltd, the manufacturer of product W, wishes to make a contribution of £50,000 towards fixed costs. How many units of product W must be sold if the selling price is £10 per unit?

Answer

$$\frac{\text{Required contribution}}{\text{C/S ratio}} = \frac{£50,000}{20\%} = £250,000$$

∴ Number of units = £250,000 ÷ £10 = 25,000.

3 THE MARGIN OF SAFETY   Pilot paper

KEY TERM

The **margin of safety** is the difference in units between the budgeted sales volume and the breakeven sales volume and it is sometimes expressed as a percentage of the budgeted sales volume.

3.1 The margin of safety may also be expressed as the difference between the budgeted sales revenue and breakeven sales revenue, expressed as a percentage of the budgeted sales revenue.

3.2 EXAMPLE: MARGIN OF SAFETY

Mal de Mer Ltd makes and sells a product which has a variable cost of £30 and which sells for £40. Budgeted fixed costs are £70,000 and budgeted sales are 8,000 units.

Required

Calculate the breakeven point and the margin of safety.

3.3 SOLUTION

(a) Breakeven point $= \dfrac{\text{Total fixed costs}}{\text{Contribution per unit}} = \dfrac{£70,000}{£(40-30)}$

$= 7,000 \text{ units}$

(b) Margin of safety $= 8,000 - 7,000 \text{ units} = 1,000 \text{ units}$

which may be expressed as $\dfrac{1,000 \text{ units}}{8,000 \text{ units}} \times 100\% = 12\frac{1}{2}\% \text{ of budget}$

(c) The margin of safety indicates to management that actual sales can fall short of budget by 1,000 units or 12½% before the breakeven point is reached and no profit at all is made.

4 BREAKEVEN ARITHMETIC AND PROFIT TARGETS

FORMULA TO LEARN

At the **breakeven point**, sales revenue equals total costs and there is no profit.

	S	= V + F
where	S	= Sales revenue
	V	= Total variable costs
	F	= Total fixed costs

Subtracting V from each side of the equation, we get:

S – V = F, that is, **total contribution = fixed costs**

4.1 EXAMPLE: BREAKEVEN ARITHMETIC

Butterfingers Ltd makes a product which has a variable cost of £7 per unit.

Required

If fixed costs are £63,000 per annum, calculate the selling price per unit if the company wishes to break even with a sales volume of 12,000 units.

4.2 SOLUTION

			£
Contribution required to break even (= Fixed costs)	=	£63,000	
Volume of sales	=	12,000 units	
Required contribution per unit (S – V)	=	£63,000 ÷ 12,000 =	5.25
Variable cost per unit (V)	=		7.00
Required sales price per unit (S)	=		12.25

BPP
PUBLISHING

Target profits

4.3 A similar formula may be applied where a company wishes to achieve a certain profit during a period. To achieve this profit, sales must cover all costs and leave the required profit.

> **FORMULA TO LEARN**
>
> The **target profit** is achieved when: $S = V + F + P$,
>
> where P = required profit
>
> Subtracting V from each side of the equation, we get:
>
> $$S - V = F + P, \text{ so}$$
> $$\text{Total contribution required} = F + P$$

4.4 EXAMPLE: TARGET PROFITS

Riding Breeches Ltd makes and sells a single product, for which variable costs are as follows.

	£
Direct materials	10
Direct labour	8
Variable production overhead	6
	24

The sales price is £30 per unit, and fixed costs per annum are £68,000. The company wishes to make a profit of £16,000 per annum.

Required

Determine the sales required to achieve this profit.

4.5 SOLUTION

Required contribution = fixed costs + profit = £68,000 + £16,000 = £84,000

Required sales can be calculated in one of two ways.

(a) $\dfrac{\text{Required contribution}}{\text{Contribution per unit}} = \dfrac{£84,000}{£(30-24)} = 14,000$ units, or £420,000 in revenue

(b) $\dfrac{\text{Required contribution}}{\text{C/S ratio}} = \dfrac{£84,000}{20\%\,\star} = £420,000$ of revenue, or 14,000 units.

$\star$ C/S ratio $= \dfrac{£30-£24}{£30} = \dfrac{£6}{£30} = 0.2 = 20\%.$

Question 2

Seven League Boots Ltd wishes to sell 14,000 units of its product, which has a variable cost of £15 to make and sell. Fixed costs are £47,000 and the required profit is £23,000.

Required

Calculate the sales price per unit.

Answer

Required contribution	=	fixed costs plus profit
	=	£47,000 + £23,000
	=	£70,000
Required sales		14,000 units

	£
Required contribution per unit sold	5
Variable cost per unit	15
Required sales price per unit	20

Decisions to change sales price or costs

4.6 You may come across a problem in which you will be expected to offer advice as to the effect of altering the selling price, variable cost per unit or fixed cost. Such problems are slight variations on basic breakeven arithmetic.

4.7 EXAMPLE: CHANGE IN SELLING PRICE

Stomer Cakes Ltd bake and sell a single type of cake. The variable cost of production is 15p and the current sales price is 25p. Fixed costs are £2,600 per month, and the annual profit for the company at current sales volume is £36,000. The volume of sales demand is constant throughout the year.

The sales manager, Ian Digestion, wishes to raise the sales price to 29p per cake, but considers that a price rise will result in some loss of sales.

Required

Ascertain the minimum volume of sales required each month to raise the price to 29p.

4.8 SOLUTION

The minimum volume of demand which would justify a price of 29p is one which would leave total profit at least the same as before, ie £3,000 per month. Required profit should be converted into required contribution, as follows.

	£
Monthly fixed costs	2,600
Monthly profit, minimum required	3,000
Current monthly contribution	5,600
Contribution per unit (25p – 15p)	10p
Current monthly sales	56,000 cakes

The minimum volume of sales required after the price rise will be an amount which earns a contribution of £5,600 per month, no worse than at the moment. The contribution per cake at a sales price of 29p would be 14p.

$$\text{Required sales} = \frac{\text{required contribution}}{\text{contribution per unit}} = \frac{£5,600}{14p} = 40,000 \text{ cakes per month.}$$

4.9 EXAMPLE: CHANGE IN PRODUCTION COSTS

Close Brickett Ltd makes a product which has a variable production cost of £8 and a variable sales cost of £2 per unit. Fixed costs are £40,000 per annum, the sales price per unit is £18, and the current volume of output and sales is 6,000 units.

The company is considering whether to have an improved machine for production. Annual hire costs would be £10,000 and it is expected that the variable cost of production would fall to £6 per unit.

Required

(a) Determine the number of units that must be produced and sold to achieve the same profit as is currently earned, if the machine is hired.

(b) Calculate the annual profit with the machine if output and sales remain at 6,000 units per annum.

4.10 SOLUTION

The current unit contribution is £(18 − (8+2)) = £8

(a)
	£
Current contribution (6,000 × £8)	48,000
Less current fixed costs	40,000
Current profit	8,000

With the new machine fixed costs will go up by £10,000 to £50,000 per annum. The variable cost per unit will fall to £(6 + 2) = £8, and the contribution per unit will be £10.

	£
Required profit (as currently earned)	8,000
Fixed costs	50,000
Required contribution	58,000
Contribution per unit	£10
Sales required to earn £8,000 profit	5,800 units

(b) **If sales are 6,000 units**

	£	£
Sales (6,000 × £18)		108,000
Variable costs: production (6,000 × £6)	36,000	
sales (6,000 × £2)	12,000	
		48,000
Contribution (6,000 × £10)		60,000
Less fixed costs		50,000
Profit		10,000

	£
Alternative calculation	
Profit at 5,800 units of sale (see (a))	8,000
Contribution from sale of extra 200 units (× £10)	2,000
Profit at 6,000 units of sale	10,000

Sales price and sales volume

4.11 It may be clear by now that, given no change in fixed costs, **total profit is maximised when the total contribution is at its maximum**. Total contribution in turn depends on the unit contribution and on the sales volume.

4.12 An increase in the sales price will increase unit contribution, but sales volume is likely to fall because fewer customers will be prepared to pay the higher price. A decrease in sales price will reduce the unit contribution, but sales volume may increase because the goods on offer are now cheaper. The **optimum combination** of sales price and sales volume is arguably the one which **maximises total contribution**.

4.13 EXAMPLE: PROFIT MAXIMISATION

C Ltd has developed a new product which is about to be launched on to the market. The variable cost of selling the product is £12 per unit. The marketing department has estimated that at a sales price of £20, annual demand would be 10,000 units.

However, if the sales price is set above £20, sales demand would fall by 500 units for each 50p increase above £20. Similarly, if the price is set below £20, demand would increase by 500 units for each 50p stepped reduction in price below £20.

Required

Determine the price which would maximise C Ltd's profit in the next year.

4.14 SOLUTION

At a price of £20 per unit, the unit contribution would be £(20 − 12) = £8. Each 50p increase (or decrease) in price would raise (or lower) the unit contribution by 50p. The total contribution is calculated at each sales price by multiplying the unit contribution by the expected sales volume.

	Unit price £	Unit contribution £	Sales volume Units	Total contribution £
	20.00	8.00	10,000	80,000
(a) **Reduce price**				
	19.50	7.50	10,500	78,750
	19.00	7.00	11,000	77,000
(b) **Increase price**				
	20.50	8.50	9,500	80,750
	21.00	9.00	9,000	81,000
	21.50	9.50	8,500	80,750
	22.00	10.00	8,000	80,000
	22.50	10.50	7,500	78,750

The total contribution would be maximised, and therefore profit maximised, at a sales price of £21 per unit, and sales demand of 9,000 units.

Quadratic equations and breakeven points

4.15 In the problems that we have looked at so far, the relationships have all been linear. We shall now look at relationships which are expressed as quadratic equations.

4.16 EXAMPLE: QUADRATICS AND BREAKEVEN ANALYSIS

A company manufactures a product. Total fixed costs are £75 and the variable cost per unit is £5x, where x is the quantity of the product produced and sold. The total revenue function is given by $R = (25 − x)x$.

Required

Find the breakeven point.

4.17 SOLUTION

Total costs (C) = fixed costs + variable costs
= £(75 + 5x)

Total revenue (R) = $25x - x^2$

Breakeven point occurs when C = R

    ie when $75 + 5x = 25x - x^2$

    ie when $0 = x^2 - 20x + 75$

    $x = \dfrac{20 \pm \sqrt{400 - (4 \times 1 \times 75)}}{2} = \dfrac{20 \pm 10}{2} = 5 \text{ or } 15$

Therefore the company will breakeven when it produces either 5 or 15 units.

Question 3

Betty Battle Ltd manufactures a product which has a selling price of £20 and a variable cost of £10 per unit. The company incurs annual fixed costs of £29,000. Annual sales demand is 9,000 units.

New production methods are under consideration, which would cause a £1,000 increase in fixed costs and a reduction in variable cost to £9 per unit. The new production methods would result in a superior product and would enable sales to be increased to 9,750 units per annum at a price of £21 each.

If the change in production methods were to take place, the breakeven output level would be:

A   400 units higher
B   400 units lower
C   100 units higher
D   100 units lower

Answer

	Current	*Revised*	*Difference*
	£	£	
Selling price	20	21	
Variable costs	10	9	
Contribution per unit	10	12	
Fixed costs	£29,000	£30,000	
Breakeven point (units)	2,900	2,500	**400 lower**

$$\text{Breakeven point} = \frac{\text{Total fixed costs}}{\text{Contribution per unit}}$$

$$\text{Current BEP} = \frac{£29,000}{£10} = 2,900 \text{ units}$$

$$\text{Revised BEP} = \frac{£30,000}{£12} = 2,500 \text{ units}$$

The correct answer is therefore B.

5   BREAKEVEN CHARTS AND PROFIT/VOLUME GRAPHS   Pilot paper

Exam focus point

Remember that you can pick up easy marks in an examination for drawing graphs neatly and accurately. Always use a ruler, label your axes and use an appropriate scale.

Breakeven charts

5.1 **The breakeven point can also be determined graphically using a breakeven chart.** This is a chart which shows approximate levels of profit or loss at different sales volume levels within a limited range.

5.2 A breakeven chart has the following axes.

- A **horizontal** axis showing the **sales/output** (in value or units)
- A **vertical axis** showing £ for **sales revenues** and **costs**

5.3 The following lines are drawn on the breakeven chart.

(a) The **sales line**

- Starts at the origin
- Ends at the point signifying expected sales

(b) The **fixed costs line**

- Runs parallel to the horizontal axis
- Meets the vertical axis at a point which represents total fixed costs

(c) The **total costs line**

- Starts where the fixed costs line meets the vertical axis
- Ends at the point which represents anticipated sales on the horizontal axis and total costs of anticipated sales on the vertical axis

5.4 The **breakeven point** is the **intersection** of the **sales line** and the **total costs line**.

5.5 The distance between the **breakeven point** and the **expected (or budgeted) sales**, in units, indicates the **margin of safety**.

5.6 EXAMPLE: A BREAKEVEN CHART

The budgeted annual output of a factory is 120,000 units. The fixed overheads amount to £40,000 and the variable costs are 50p per unit. The sales price is £1 per unit.

Required

Construct a breakeven chart showing the current breakeven point and profit earned up to the present maximum capacity.

5.7 SOLUTION

We begin by calculating the profit at the budgeted annual output.

	£
Sales (120,000 units)	120,000
Variable costs	60,000
Contribution	60,000
Fixed costs	40,000
Profit	20,000

Breakeven chart (1) is shown on the following page.

The chart is drawn as follows.

(a) The **vertical axis** represents **money** (costs and revenue) and the **horizontal axis** represents the **level of activity** (production and sales).

(b) The fixed costs are represented by a **straight line parallel to the horizontal axis** (in our example, at £40,000).

(c) The **variable costs** are added 'on top of' fixed costs, to give **total costs**. It is assumed that fixed costs are the same in total and variable costs are the same per unit at all levels of output.

The line of costs is therefore a straight line and only two points need to be plotted and joined up. Perhaps the two most convenient points to plot are total costs at zero output, and total costs at the budgeted output and sales.

- At zero output, costs are equal to the amount of fixed costs only, £40,000, since there are no variable costs.

- At the budgeted output of 120,000 units, costs are £100,000.

	£
Fixed costs	40,000
Variable costs 120,000 × 50p	60,000
Total costs	100,000

(d) The sales line is also drawn by plotting two points and joining them up.

- At zero sales, revenue is nil.
- At the budgeted output and sales of 120,000 units, revenue is £120,000.

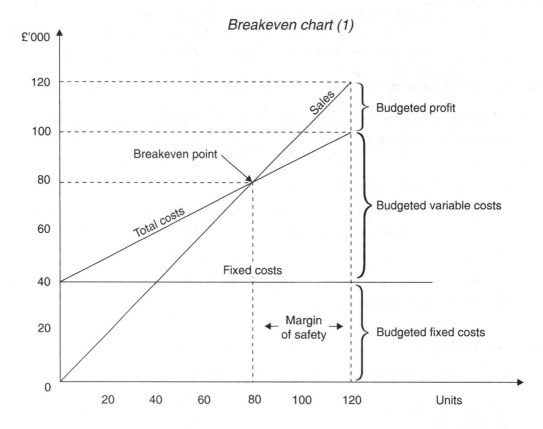

Breakeven chart (1)

5.8 **The breakeven point is where total costs are matched exactly by total revenue.** From the chart, this can be seen to occur at output and sales of 80,000 units, when revenue and costs are both £80,000. This breakeven point can be proved mathematically as:

$$\frac{\text{Required contribution} (= \text{fixed costs})}{\text{Contribution per unit}} = \frac{£40,000}{50\text{p per unit}} = 80,000 \text{ units}$$

5.9 The margin of safety can be seen on the chart as the difference between the budgeted level of activity and the breakeven level.

The value of breakeven charts

5.10 Breakeven charts are used as follows.

- To **plan** the production of a company's products
- To **market** a company's products
- To give a **visual display** of breakeven arithmetic

5.11 EXAMPLE: VARIATIONS IN THE USE OF BREAKEVEN CHARTS

Breakeven charts can be used to **show variations** in the possible **sales price, variable costs** or **fixed costs**. Suppose that a company sells a product which has a variable cost of £2 per unit. Fixed costs are £15,000. It has been estimated that if the sales price is set at £4.40 per unit, the expected sales volume would be 7,500 units; whereas if the sales price is lower, at £4 per unit, the expected sales volume would be 10,000 units.

Required

Draw a breakeven chart to show the budgeted profit, the breakeven point and the margin of safety at each of the possible sales prices.

5.12 SOLUTION

Workings	*Sales price £4.40 per unit* £		*Sales price £4 per unit* £
Fixed costs	15,000		15,000
Variable costs (7,500 × £2.00)	15,000	(10,000 × £2.00)	20,000
Total costs	30,000		35,000
Budgeted revenue (7,500 × £4.40)	33,000	(10,000 × £4.00)	40,000

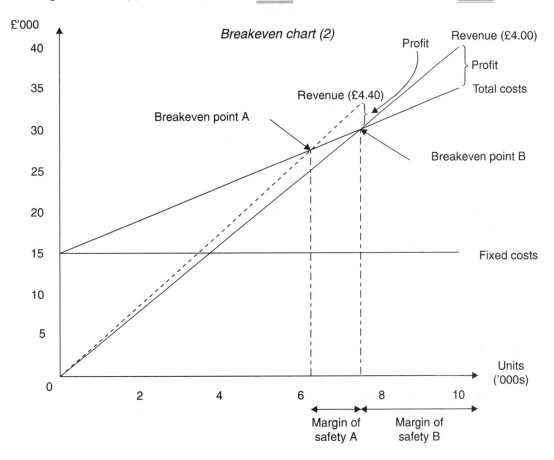

BPP
PUBLISHING

(a) **Breakeven point A** is the breakeven point at a sales price of £4.40 per unit, which is 6,250 units or £27,500 in costs and revenues.

(check: $\dfrac{\text{Required contribution to breakeven}}{\text{Contribution per unit}}$ $\dfrac{£15,000}{£2.40 \text{ per unit}} = 6,250$ units)

The **margin of safety (A)** is 7,500 units – 6,250 units = 1,250 units or 16.7% of expected sales.

(b) **Breakeven point B** is the breakeven point at a sales price of £4 per unit which is 7,500 units or £30,000 in costs and revenues.

(check: $\dfrac{\text{Required contribution to breakeven}}{\text{Contribution per unit}}$ $\dfrac{£15,000}{£2 \text{ per unit}} = 7,500$ units)

The **margin of safety (B)** = 10,000 units – 7,500 units = 2,500 units or 25% of expected sales.

5.13   Since a price of £4 per unit gives a higher expected profit and a wider margin of safety, this price will probably be preferred even though the breakeven point is higher than at a sales price of £4.40 per unit.

The Profit/Volume (P/V) chart

> **KEY TERM**
>
> The **profit/volume (P/V) chart** is a variation of the breakeven chart which illustrates the relationship of costs and profit to sales, and the margin of safety.

5.14   A P/V chart is constructed as follows (look at the chart in the example that follows as you read the explanation).

(a) 'P' is on the y axis and actually comprises not only 'profit' but contribution to profit (in monetary value), extending above and below the x axis with a zero point at the intersection of the two axes, and the negative section below the x axis representing fixed costs. This means that at zero production, the firm is incurring a loss equal to the fixed costs.

(b) 'V' is on the x axis and comprises either volume of sales or value of sales (revenue).

(c) The profit-volume line is a straight line drawn with its starting point (at zero production) at the intercept on the y axis representing the level of fixed costs, and with a gradient of contribution/unit (or the C/S ratio if sales value is used rather than units). The P/V line will cut the x axis at the breakeven point of sales volume. Any point on the P/V line above the x axis represents the profit to the firm (as measured on the vertical axis) for that particular level of sales.

5.15   EXAMPLE: P/V CHART

Let us draw a P/V chart for our example. At sales of 120,000 units, total contribution will be $120,000 \times £(1 - 0.5) = £60,000$ and total profit will be £20,000.

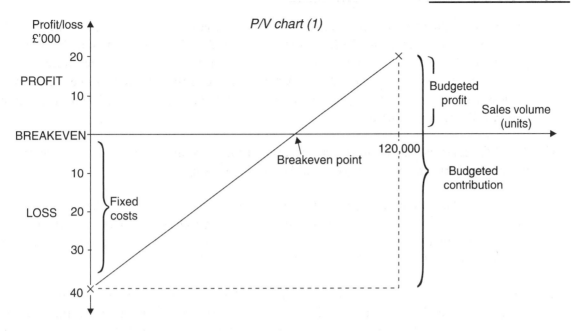

P/V chart (1)

The advantage of the P/V chart

5.16 **The P/V chart shows clearly the effect on profit and breakeven point of any changes in selling price, variable cost, fixed cost and/or sales demand.** If the budgeted selling price of the product in our example is increased to £1.20, with the result that demand drops to 105,000 units despite additional fixed costs of £10,000 being spent on advertising, we could add a line representing this situation to our P/V chart.

5.17 At sales of 105,000 units, contribution will be $105,000 \times £(1.20 - 0.50) = £73,500$ and total profit will be £23,500 (fixed costs being £50,000).

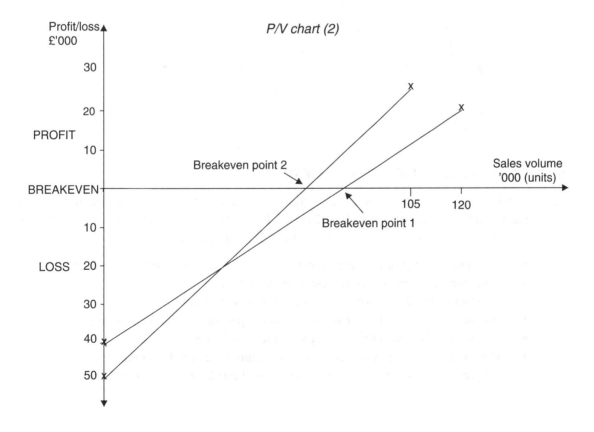

P/V chart (2)

5.18 The diagram shows that if the selling price is increased, the breakeven point occurs at a lower level of sales revenue (71,429 units instead of 80,000 units), although this is not a particularly large increase when viewed in the context of the projected sales volume. It is also possible to see that for sales above 50,000 units, the profit achieved will be higher (and the loss achieved lower) if the price is £1.20. For sales volumes below 50,000 units the first option will yield lower losses.

5.19 The P/V chart is the clearest way of presenting such information; two conventional breakeven charts on one set of axes would be very confusing.

5.20 Changes in the variable cost per unit or in fixed costs at certain activity levels can also be easily incorporated into a P/V chart. The profit or loss at each point where the cost structure changes should be calculated and plotted on the graph so that the profit/volume line becomes a series of straight lines.

5.21 For example, suppose that in our example, at sales levels in excess of 120,000 units the variable cost per unit increases to £0.60 (perhaps because of overtime premiums that are incurred when production exceeds a certain level). At sales of 130,000 units, contribution would therefore be $130,000 \times £(1 - 0.60) = £52,000$ and total profit would be £12,000.

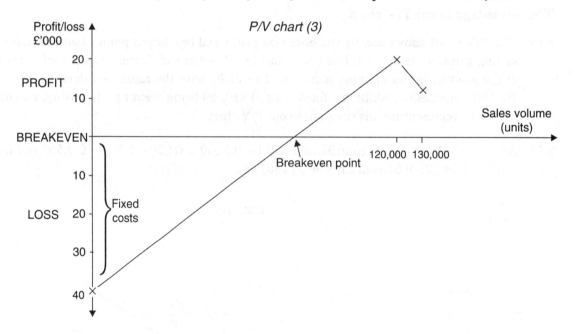

6 LIMITATIONS OF CVP ANALYSIS

6.1 Breakeven analysis is a useful technique for managers. Breakeven arithmetic can provide **simple** and **quick** estimates. **Breakeven charts** provide a **graphical representation** of breakeven arithmetic. Breakeven analysis has a number of limitations.

- It **can only apply to a single product** or a single mix of a group of products.
- A breakeven chart may be **time-consuming** to prepare.
- It **assumes** fixed costs are constant at all levels of output.
- It **assumes** that **variable costs** are the **same** per unit at all levels of output.
- It **assumes** that **sales prices** are **constant** at all levels of output.
- It assumes **production** and **sales** are the **same** (stock levels are ignored).
- It **ignores** the **uncertainty** in the estimates of fixed costs and variable cost per unit.

Exam focus point

There were four marks available in the Pilot paper for **Management Accounting Fundamentals** for preparing a profit-volume chart showing the breakeven point and margin of safety.

There were a further two marks available for using breakeven arithmetic to calculate the breakeven point (and demonstrate the accuracy of the profit-volume graph drawn earlier).

Chapter roundup

- **Cost-volume- profit (CVP)/breakeven analysis** is the study of the interrelationships between costs, volume and profits at various levels of activity.

- **Breakeven point** = **Number of units of sale** required to breakeven

$$= \frac{\text{Fixed costs}}{\text{Contribution per unit}}$$

$$= \frac{\text{Contribution required to break even}}{\text{Contribution per unit}}$$

- **Breakeven point** = **Sales revenue** required to break even

$$= \frac{\text{Contribution required to break even}}{\text{C/S ratio}}$$

$$= \frac{\text{Fixed costs}}{\text{C/S ratio}}$$

- The **C/S ratio** (or **P/V ratio**) is a measure of how much contribution is earned form each £1 of sales.

- The **margin of safety** is the difference in units between the **budgeted sales volume** and the **breakeven sales volume.** It is sometimes expressed as a percentage of the budgeted sales volume.

- Alternatively, the **margin of safety** can be expressed as the difference between the **budgeted sales revenue** and the **breakeven sales revenue** expressed as a percentage of the budgeted sales revenue.

- At the **breakeven point**, sales revenue = total costs and there is no profit. At the breakeven point **total contribution = fixed costs.**

- The **target profit** is achieved when S = V + F + P. Therefore the **total contribution required** for a target profit = **fixed costs + required profit.**

- The breakeven point can also be determined graphically using a **breakeven chart.**

- The **profit/volume (PV) chart** is a variation of the breakeven chart which illustrates the relationship of costs and profits to sales and the margin of safety.

- The **P/V chart** shows clearly the effect on profit and breakeven point of any changes in selling price, variable cost, fixed cost and/or sales demand.

- **Breakeven analysis** is a useful technique for managers as it can provide simple and quick estimates. **Breakeven charts** provide a graphical representation of breakeven arithmetic. Breakeven analysis does, however, have a number of **limitations.**

Quick quiz

1   What does CVP analysis study?

2   The **breakeven point** is the .... or.. ....

3   Use the following to make up three formulae which can be used to calculate the breakeven point.

Contribution per unit
Contribution per unit
Fixed costs
Fixed costs
Contribution required to breakeven
Contribution required to breakeven
C/S ratio
C/S ratio

(a)   Breakeven points (sales units)   = _____

or   _____

(b)   Breakeven point (sales revenue)   = _____

or   _____

4   The P/V ratio is a measure of how much profit is earned from each £1 of sales.

   True   ☐

   False   ☐

5   The **margin of safety** is the difference in units between the budgeted sales volume and the breakeven sales volume. How is it sometimes expressed?

6   Profits are maximised at the breakeven point.

   True   ☐

   False   ☐

7   At the breakeven point, total contribution = ...

8   The total contribution required for a **target profit** = ...

9   Give three uses of breakeven charts.

10   Breakeven charts show approximate levels of profit or loss at different sales volume levels within a limited range. Which of the following are true?

   I   The sales line starts at the origin
   II   The fixed costs line runs parallel to the vertical axis
   III   Breakeven charts have a horizontal axis showing the sales/output (in value or units)
   IV   Breakeven charts have a vertical axis showing £ for revenues and costs
   V   The breakeven point is the intersection of the sales line and the fixed cost line

   A   I and II
   B   I and III
   C   I, III and IV
   D   I, III, IV, and V

11   On a breakeven chart, the distance between the breakeven point and the expected (or budgeted) sales, in units, indicates the ....

12   Give seven limitations of CVP analysis.

- ....
- ....
- ....
- ....
- ....
- ....
- ....

Answers to quick quiz

1   The interrelations between **costs, volume** and **profits** of a product at various activity levels.

2   The **breakeven point** is the number of units of sale required to breakeven or the sales revenue required to breakeven.

3   (a)   Breakeven points (sales units)   = $\dfrac{\text{Fixed costs}}{\text{Contribution per unit}}$

or $\dfrac{\text{Contribution required to break even}}{\text{Contribution per unit}}$

(b)   Breakeven point (sales revenue)   = $\dfrac{\text{Fixed costs}}{\text{C/S ratio}}$

or $\dfrac{\text{Contribution required to break even}}{\text{C/S ratio}}$

4   False. The P/V ratio is a measure of how much **contribution** is earned from each £1 of sales.

5   As a **percentage** of the budgeted sales volume.

6   False. At the breakeven point there is no profit.

7   At the breakeven point, total contribution = fixed costs

8   Fixed costs + required profit

9   - To plan the production of a company's products
    - To market a company's products
    - To give a visual display of breakeven arithmetic

10   B

11   Margin of safety

12   - It **can only apply to a single product** or a single mix of a group of products.
     - A breakeven chart may be **time-consuming** to prepare.
     - It **assumes** fixed costs are constant at all levels of output.
     - It **assumes** that **variable costs** are the **same** per unit at all levels of output.
     - It **assumes** that **sales prices** are **constant** at all levels of output.
     - It assumes **production** and **sales** are the **same** (stock levels are ignored).
     - It **ignores** the **uncertainty** in the estimates of fixed costs and variable cost per unit.

Now try the questions below from the Exam Question Bank

Number	Level	Marks	Time
Q15	Examination	25	45 mins
Q16	Examination	25	45 mins

Part D
Standard costing and budgeting

Chapter 13

PREPARING THE MASTER BUDGET

Topic list	Syllabus reference	Ability required
1 The purposes of a budget	(v)	Comprehension
2 Steps in the preparation of a budget	(v)	Comprehension
3 Functional budgets	(v)	Application
4 Cash budgets	(v)	Application
5 Budgeted profit and loss account and balance sheet	(v)	Application

Introduction

This chapter is the first of two on a new topic, **budgeting**. It is a topic which you will meet at all stages of your examination studies so it is vital that you get a firm grasp of the basics now. The chapter begins by explaining the **reasons** why an organisation might prepare a budget and goes on to detail the **steps in the preparation of a budget**. The method of preparing and the relationship between the various **functional budgets** is then set out.

The chapter also considers the construction of **cash budgets** and **budgeted profit and loss accounts and balance sheets**, the budgeted profit and loss account and balance sheet making up what is known as a **master budget**.

In Chapter 14 we will build on the general awareness of budgeting gained in this chapter and look at more specific budgeting issues.

Learning outcomes covered in this chapter

- **Explain** why organisations prepare budgets
- **Explain** how organisations prepare budgets
- **Prepare** functional budgets, profit and loss account, balance sheet and a simple cash budget

Syllabus content covered in this chapter

- Budget theory
- Budget preparation

1   THE PURPOSES OF A BUDGET

> **KEY TERM**
>
> A **budget** is 'A quantitative statement, for a defined period of time, which may include planned revenues, expenses, assets, liabilities and cash flows'.
>
> (CIMA *Official Terminology*)

1.1   A budget has four main purposes.

- To **coordinate** the activities of different departments towards a single plan
- To **communicate targets** to the managers responsible for achieving them
- To **establish a system of control** by comparing budgeted and actual results
- To **compel planning**

2   STEPS IN THE PREPARATION OF A BUDGET

2.1   Having seen why organisations prepare budgets we will turn our attention to the mechanics of budget preparation.

Budget committee

2.2   The **coordination** and **administration** of budgets is usually the responsibility of a **budget committee** (with the managing director as chairman). The budget committee is assisted by a **budget officer** who is usually an accountant. Every part of the organisation should be represented on the committee, so there should be a representative from sales, production, marketing and so on. Functions of the budget committee include the following.

- **Coordination and allocation of responsibility** for the preparation of budgets
- Issuing of the **budget manual**
- **Timetabling**
- **Provision of information** to assist in the preparation of budgets
- **Communication** of final budgets to the appropriate managers
- **Monitoring** the budgeting process by **comparing actual and budgeted results**

Responsibility for budgets

2.3   The responsibility for preparing the budgets should, ideally, lie with the managers who are responsible for implementing them. For example, the preparation of particular budgets might be allocated as follows.

(a)   The **sales manager** should draft the **sales budget** and the selling overhead cost centre budgets.

(b)   The **purchasing manager** should draft the **material purchases budget**.

(c)   The **production manager** should draft the **direct production cost budgets**.

Question 1

Which of the following is the budget committee *not* responsible for?

A   Preparing functional budgets
B   Timetabling the budgeting operation
C   Allocating responsibility for the budget preparation
D   Monitoring the budgeting process

Answer

A is correct because it is the manager responsible for implementing the budget that must prepare it, not the budget committee.

If you don't know the answer, remember not to fall for the common pitfall of thinking, 'Well, we haven't had a D for a while, so I'll guess that'.

It is good practice to guess if you don't know the answer (never leave out a multiple choice question) but first eliminate some of the options if you can.

Since the committee is a co-ordinating body we can definitely say that they are responsible for B and D. Similarly, a co-ordinating body is more likely to allocate responsibility than to actually undertake the budget preparation, so eliminate C and select A as the correct answer.

The budget manual

> **KEY TERM**
>
> The **budget manual** is 'A detailed set of documents providing guidelines and information about the budget process'.
>
> CIMA *Official Terminology*

2.4 A budget manual may contain the following.

(a) An explanation of the **objectives** of the budgetary process

- The purpose of budgetary planning and control
- The objectives of the various stages of the budgetary process
- The importance of budgets in the long-term planning of the business

(b) **Organisational structures**

- An organisation chart
- A list of individuals holding budget responsibilities

(c) An **outline of the principal budgets** and the **relationship between them**

(d) **Administrative details of budget preparation**

- Membership and terms of reference of the budget committee
- The sequence in which budgets are to be prepared
- A timetable

(e) **Procedural matters**

- Specimen forms and instructions for their completion
- Specimen reports
- Account codes (or a chart of accounts)
- The name of the budget officer to whom enquiries must be sent

Steps in budget preparation

2.5 The procedures for preparing a budget will differ from organisation to organisation but the steps described below will be indicative of the steps followed by many organisations. The preparation of a budget may take weeks or months and the **budget committee** may meet several times before the **master budget** (budgeted profit and loss account and budgeted balance sheet) is finally agreed. **Functional budgets** (sales budgets, production budgets, direct labour budgets and so on), which are amalgamated into the master budget, may need to be amended many times over as a consequence of discussions between departments, changes in market conditions and so on during the course of budget preparation.

Identifying the principal budget factor

> **KEY TERM**
>
> The **principal budget factor** is the factor which limits the activities of an organisation.

2.6 The first task in the budgetary process is to identify the **principal budget factor**. This is also known as the **key budget factor** or **limiting budget factor**.

2.7 The **principal budget factor** is usually **sales demand**: a company is usually restricted from making and selling more of its products because there would be no sales demand for the increased output at a price which would be acceptable/profitable to the company. The principal budget factor may also be machine capacity, distribution and selling resources, the availability of key raw materials or the availability of cash. Once this factor is defined then the remainder of the budgets can be prepared. For example, if sales are the principal budget factor then the production manager can only prepare his budget after the sales budget is complete.

2.8 Assuming that the principal budget factor has been identified as being sales, the stages involved in the preparation of a budget can be summarised as follows.

(a) The **sales budget** is prepared in units of product and sales value. The **finished goods stock budget** can be prepared at the same time. This budget decides the planned increase or decrease in finished goods stock levels.

(b) With the information from the sales and stock budgets, the **production budget** can be prepared. This is, in effect, the sales budget in units plus (or minus) the increase (or decrease) in finished goods stock. The production budget will be stated in terms of units.

(c) This leads on logically to budgeting the **resources for production**. This involves preparing a **materials usage budget, machine usage budget and a labour budget**.

(d) In addition to the materials usage budget, a **materials stock budget** will be prepared, to decide the planned increase or decrease in the level of stocks held. Once the raw materials usage requirements and the raw materials stock budget are known, the purchasing department can prepare a **raw materials purchases budget** in quantities and value for each type of material purchased.

(e) During the preparation of the sales and production budgets, the managers of the cost centres of the organisation will prepare their draft budgets for the department **overhead costs**. Such overheads will include maintenance, stores, administration, selling and research and development.

(f) From the above information a **budgeted profit and loss account** can be produced.

(g) In addition several other budgets must be prepared in order to arrive at the **budgeted balance sheet**. These are the **capital expenditure budget** (for fixed assets), the **working capital budget** (for budgeted increases or decreases in the level of debtors and creditors as well as stocks), and a **cash budget**.

3 FUNCTIONAL BUDGETS

3.1 Having seen the theory of budget preparation, let us look at **functional** (or **departmental**) budget preparation.

3.2 EXAMPLE: PREPARING A MATERIALS PURCHASES BUDGET

ECO Ltd manufactures two products, S and T, which use the same raw materials, D and E. One unit of S uses 3 litres of D and 4 kilograms of E. One unit of T uses 5 litres of D and 2 kilograms of E. A litre of D is expected to cost £3 and a kilogram of E £7.

Budgeted sales for 20X2 are 8,000 units of S and 6,000 units of T; finished goods in stock at 1 January 20X2 are 1,500 units of S and 300 units of T, and the company plans to hold stocks of 600 units of each product at 31 December 20X2.

Stocks of raw material are 6,000 litres of D and 2,800 kilograms of E at 1 January and the company plans to hold 5,000 litres and 3,500 kilograms respectively at 31 December 20X2.

The warehouse and stores managers have suggested that a provision should be made for damages and deterioration of items held in store, as follows.

Product S :	loss of 50 units
Product T :	loss of 100 units
Material D :	loss of 500 litres
Material E :	loss of 200 kilograms

Required

Prepare a material purchases budget for the year 20X2.

3.3 SOLUTION

To calculate material purchases requirements it is first necessary to calculate the material usage requirements. That in turn depends on calculating the budgeted production volumes.

	Product S Units	*Product T* Units
Production required		
To meet sales demand	8,000	6,000
To provide for stock loss	50	100
For closing stock	600	600
	8,650	6,700
Less stock already in hand	1,500	300
Budgeted production volume	7,150	6,400

	Material D Litres	*Material E* Kgs
Usage requirements		
To produce 7,150 units of S	21,450	28,600
To produce 6,400 units of T	32,000	12,800
To provide for stock loss	500	200
For closing stock	5,000	3,500
	58,950	45,100
Less stock already in hand	6,000	2,800
Budgeted material purchases	52,950	42,300
Unit cost	£3	£7
Cost of material purchases	£158,850	£296,100
Total cost of material purchases		£454,950

3.4 The basics of the preparation of each functional budget are similar to those above. Work carefully through the following question which covers the preparation of a number of different types of functional budget.

Question 2

XYZ company produces three products X, Y and Z. For the coming accounting period budgets are to be prepared based on the following information.

Budgeted sales

Product X   2,000 at £100 each
Product Y   4,000 at £130 each
Product Z   3,000 at £150 each

Budgeted usage of raw material

	RM11	RM22	RM33
Product X	5	2	-
Product Y	3	2	2
Product Z	2	1	3
Cost per unit of material	£5	£3	£4

Finished stocks budget

	Product X	Product Y	Product Z
Beginning	500	800	700
End	600	1,000	800

Raw materials stock

	RM11	RM22	RM33
Beginning	21,000	10,000	16,000
End	18,000	9,000	12,000

	Product X	Product Y	Product Z
Expected hours per unit	4	6	8
Expected hourly rate (labour)	£3	£3	£3

Required

Draw up the following functional budgets.

(a)   Sales budget in terms of both quantity and value
(b)   Production budget
(c)   Material usage budget
(d)   Material purchases budget
(e)   Labour budget

Answer

(a)

Sales budget

	Product X	Product Y	Product Z	Total
Sales quantity	2,000	4,000	3,000	
Sales price	£100	£130	£150	
Sales value	£200,000	£520,000	£450,000	£1,170,000

(b)

Production budget

	Product X Units	Product Y Units	Product Z Units
Sales quantity	2,000	4,000	3,000
Closing stocks	600	1,000	800
	2,600	5,000	3,800
Less opening stocks	500	800	700
Budgeted production	2,100	4,200	3,100

(c)

Material usage budget

	Production Units	RM11 Units	RM22 Units	RM33 Units
Product X	2,100	10,500	4,200	-
Product Y	4,200	12,600	8,400	8,400
Product Z	3,100	6,200	3,100	9,300
Budgeted material usage		29,300	15,700	17,700

(d)

	Material purchases budget		
	RM11	RM22	RM33
	Units	Units	Units
Budgeted material usage	29,300	15,700	17,700
Closing stocks	18,000	9,000	12,000
	47,300	24,700	29,700
Less opening stocks	21,000	10,000	16,000
Budgeted material purchases	26,300	14,700	13,700
Standard cost per unit	£5	£3	£4
Budgeted material purchases	£131,500	£44,100	£54,800

(e)

		Labour budget			
Product	Production	Hours required per unit	Total hours	Rate per hour	Cost
	Units			£	£
X	2,100	4	8,400	3	25,200
Y	4,200	6	25,200	3	75,600
Z	3,100	8	24,800	3	74,400
Budgeted total wages					175,200

4 CASH BUDGETS

4.1 A **cash budget** is a statement in which estimated **future cash receipts and payments** are tabulated in such a way as to show the forecast cash balance of a business at defined intervals. For example, in December 20X2 an accounts department might wish to estimate the cash position of the business during the three following months, January to March 20X3. A cash budget might be drawn up in the following format.

	Jan £	Feb £	Mar £
Estimated cash receipts			
From credit customers	14,000	16,500	17,000
From cash sales	3,000	4,000	4,500
Proceeds on disposal of fixed assets		2,200	
Total cash receipts	17,000	22,700	21,500
Estimated cash payments			
To suppliers of goods	8,000	7,800	10,500
To employees (wages)	3,000	3,500	3,500
Purchase of fixed assets		16,000	
Rent and rates			1,000
Other overheads	1,200	1,200	1,200
Repayment of loan	2,500		
	14,700	28,500	16,200
Net surplus/(deficit) for month	2,300	(5,800)	5,300
Opening cash balance	1,200	3,500	(2,300)
Closing cash balance	3,500	(2,300)	3,000

4.2 In the example above (where the figures are purely for illustration) the accounts department has calculated that the cash balance at the beginning of the budget period, 1 January, will be £1,200. Estimates have been made of the cash which is likely to be received by the business (from cash and credit sales, and from a planned disposal of fixed assets in February). Similar estimates have been made of cash due to be paid out by the business (payments to suppliers and employees, payments for rent, rates and other overheads, payment for a planned purchase of fixed assets in February and a loan repayment due in January).

4.3 From these estimates it is a simple step to calculate the excess of cash receipts over cash payments in each month. In some months cash payments may exceed cash receipts and there will be a **deficit** for the month; this occurs during February in the above example because of the large investment in fixed assets in that month.

4.4 The last part of the cash budget above shows how the business's estimated cash balance can then be rolled along from month to month. Starting with the opening balance of £1,200 at 1 January a cash surplus of £2,300 is generated in January. This leads to a closing January balance of £3,500 which becomes the opening balance for February. The deficit of £5,800 in February throws the business's cash position into **overdraft** and the overdrawn balance of £2,300 becomes the opening balance for March. Finally, the healthy cash surplus of £5,300 in March leaves the business with a favourable cash position of £3,000 at the end of the budget period.

The usefulness of cash budgets

4.5 The cash budget is one of the most important planning tools that an organisation can use. It shows the **cash effect of all plans made within the budgetary process** and hence its preparation can lead to a **modification of budgets** if it shows that there are insufficient cash resources to finance the planned operations.

4.6 It can also give management an indication of **potential problems** that could arise and allows them the opportunity to take action to avoid such problems. A cash budget can show **four positions**. Management will need to take appropriate action depending on the potential position.

Cash position	Appropriate management action
Short-term surplus	• Pay creditors early to obtain discount • Attempt to increase sales by increasing debtors and stocks • Make short-term investments
Short-term deficit	• Increase creditors • Reduce debtors • Arrange an overdraft
Long-term surplus	• Make long-term investments • Expand • Diversify • Replace/update fixed assets
Long-term deficit	• Raise long-term finance (such as via issue of share capital) • Consider shutdown/disinvestment opportunities

Exam focus point

A cash budgeting question in an examination could ask you to recommend appropriate action for management to take once you have prepared the cash budget. Ensure your advice takes account both of whether there is a surplus or deficit and whether the position is long or short term.

4.7 EXAMPLE: CASH BUDGET

Peter Blair has worked for some years as a sales representative, but has recently been made redundant. He intends to start up in business on his own account, using £15,000 which he currently has invested with a building society. Peter maintains a bank account showing a small credit balance, and he plans to approach his bank for the necessary additional finance. Peter asks you for advice and provides the following additional information.

(a) Arrangements have been made to purchase fixed assets costing £8,000. These will be paid for at the end of September and are expected to have a five-year life, at the end of which they will possess a nil residual value.

(b) Stocks costing £5,000 will be acquired on 28 September and subsequent monthly purchases will be at a level sufficient to replace forecast sales for the month.

(c) Forecast monthly sales are £3,000 for October, £6,000 for November and December, and £10,500 from January 20X4 onwards.

(d) Selling price is fixed at the cost of stock plus 50%.

(e) Two months' credit will be allowed to customers but only one month's credit will be received from suppliers of stock.

(f) Running expenses, including rent but excluding depreciation of fixed assets, are estimated at £1,600 per month.

(g) Blair intends to make monthly cash drawings of £1,000.

Required

Prepare a cash budget for the six months to 31 March 20X4.

4.8 SOLUTION

The opening cash balance at 1 October will consist of Peter's initial £15,000 less the £8,000 expended on fixed assets purchased in September. In other words, the opening balance is £7,000. Cash receipts from credit customers arise two months after the relevant sales.

Payments to suppliers are a little more tricky. We are told that cost of sales is 100/150 × sales. Thus for October cost of sales is 100/150 × £3,000 = £2,000. These goods will be purchased in October but not paid for until November. Similar calculations can be made for later months. The initial stock of £5,000 is purchased in September and consequently paid for in October.

Depreciation is not a cash flow and so is *not* included in a cash budget.

4.9 The cash budget can now be constructed.

CASH BUDGET FOR THE SIX MONTHS ENDING 31 MARCH 20X4

	Oct £	Nov £	Dec £	Jan £	Feb £	Mar £
Payments						
Suppliers	5,000	2,000	4,000	4,000	7,000	7,000
Running expenses	1,600	1,600	1,600	1,600	1,600	1,600
Drawings	1,000	1,000	1,000	1,000	1,000	1,000
	7,600	4,600	6,600	6,600	9,600	9,600
Receipts						
Debtors	-	-	3,000	6,000	6,000	10,500
Surplus/(shortfall)	(7,600)	(4,600)	(3,600)	(600)	(3,600)	900
Opening balance	7,000	(600)	(5,200)	(8,800)	(9,400)	(13,000)
Closing balance	(600)	(5,200)	(8,800)	(9,400)	(13,000)	(12,100)

Question 3

You are presented with the budgeted data shown in Annex A for the period November 20X1 to June 20X2 by your firm. It has been extracted from the other functional budgets that have been prepared.

You are also told the following.

(a) Sales are 40% cash, 60% credit. Credit sales are paid two months after the month of sale.
(b) Purchases are paid the month following purchase.
(c) 75% of wages are paid in the current month and 25% the following month.
(d) Overheads are paid the month after they are incurred.
(e) Dividends are paid three months after they are declared.
(f) Capital expenditure is paid two months after it is incurred.
(g) The opening cash balance is £15,000.

The managing director is pleased with the above figures as they show sales will have increased by more than 100% in the period under review. In order to achieve this he has arranged a bank overdraft with a ceiling of £50,000 to accommodate the increased stock levels and wage bill for overtime worked.

Annex A

	Nov X1	Dec X1	Jan X2	Feb X2	Mar X2	Apr X2	May X2	June X2
	£	£	£	£	£	£	£	£
Sales	80,000	100,000	110,000	130,000	140,000	150,000	160,000	180,000
Purchases	40,000	60,000	80,000	90,000	110,000	130,000	140,000	150,000
Wages	10,000	12,000	16,000	20,000	24,000	28,000	32,000	36,000
Overheads	10,000	10,000	15,000	15,000	15,000	20,000	20,000	20,000
Dividends		20,000						40,000
Capital Expenditure			30,000			40,000		

Required

(a) Prepare a cash budget for the 6 month period January to June 20X2.
(b) Comment upon your results in the light of your managing director's comments and offer advice.

Answer

Cash budget for January to June 20X2

(a)

	January £'000	February £'000	March £'000	April £'000	May £'000	June £'000
Receipts						
Sales revenue						
Cash	44	52	56	60	64	72
Credit	48	60	66	78	84	90
	92	112	122	138	148	162
Payments						
Purchases	60	80	90	110	130	140
Wages						
75%	12	15	18	21	24	27
25%	3	4	5	6	7	8
Overheads	10	15	15	15	20	20
Dividends			20			
Capital expenditure			30			40
	85	114	178	152	181	235
b/f	15	22	20	(36)	(50)	(83)
Net cash flow	7	(2)	(56)	(14)	(33)	(73)
c/f	22	20	(36)	(50)	(83)	(156)

(b) The overdraft arrangements are quite inadequate to service the cash needs of the business over the six month period. If the figures are realistic then action should be taken now to avoid difficulties in the near future. The following are possible courses of action.

(i) Activities could be curtailed.

(ii) Other sources of cash could be explored, for example a long-term loan to finance the capital expenditure and a factoring arrangement to provide cash due from debtors more quickly.

(iii) Efforts to increase the speed of debt collection could be made.

(iv) Payments to creditors could be delayed.

(v) The dividend payments could be postponed (the figures indicate that this is a small company, possibly owner-managed).

(vi) Staff might be persuaded to work at a lower rate in return for, say, an annual bonus or a profit-sharing agreement.

(vii) Extra staff might be taken on to reduce the amount of overtime paid.

(viii) The stockholding policy should be reviewed: it may be possible to meet demand from current production and minimise cash tied up in stocks.

5 BUDGETED PROFIT AND LOSS ACCOUNT AND BALANCE SHEET

5.1 As well as wishing to forecast its cash position, a business might want to estimate its profitability and its financial position for a coming period. This would involve the preparation of a budgeted profit and loss account and balance sheet, both of which form the **master budget**.

5.2 EXAMPLE: PREPARING A BUDGETED PROFIT AND LOSS ACCOUNT AND BALANCE SHEET

Using the information in Paragraph 4.7, you are required to prepare Peter Blair's budgeted profit and loss account for the six months ending on 31 March 20X4 and a budgeted balance sheet as at that date.

5.3 SOLUTION

The profit and loss account is straightforward. The first figure is sales, which can be computed very easily from the information in Paragraph 4.7(c). It is sufficient to add up the monthly sales figures given there; for the profit and loss account there is no need to worry about any closing debtor. Similarly, cost of sales is calculated directly from the information on gross margin contained in Paragraph 4.7 (d).

FORECAST TRADING AND PROFIT AND LOSS ACCOUNT
FOR THE SIX MONTHS ENDING 31 MARCH 20X4

	£	£
Sales $(3,000 + (2 \times 6,000) + (3 \times 10,500))$		46,500
Cost of sales $(^2/_3 \times £46,500)$		31,000
Gross profit		15,500
Expenses		
Running expenses $(6 \times £1,600)$	9,600	
Depreciation $(£8,000 \times 20\% \times 6/12)$	800	
		10,400
Net profit		5,100

Items will be shown in the balance sheet as follows.

(a) Stock will comprise the initial purchases of £5,000.

(b) Debtors will comprise sales made in February and March (not paid until April and May respectively).

(c)   Creditors will comprise purchases made in March (not paid for until April).

(d)   The bank overdraft is the closing cash figure computed in the cash budget.

FORECAST BALANCE SHEET AT 31 MARCH 20X4

	£	£
Fixed assets £(8,000 – 800)		7,200
Current assets		
Stocks	5,000	
Debtors (2 × £10,500)	21,000	
	26,000	
Current liabilities		
Bank overdraft	12,100	
Trade creditors (March purchases)	7,000	
	19,100	
Net current assets		6,900
		14,100
Proprietor's interest		
Capital introduced		15,000
Profit for the period	5,100	
Less drawings	6,000	
Deficit retained		(900)
		14,100

5.4   Budget questions are often accompanied by a large amount of sometimes confusing detail. This should not blind you to the fact that many figures can be entered very simply from the logic of the trading situation described. For example in the case of Blair you might feel tempted to begin a T-account to compute the closing debtors figure. This kind of working is rarely necessary, since you are told that debtors take two months to pay. Closing debtors will equal total credit sales in the last two months of the period.

5.5   Similarly, you may be given a simple statement that a business pays rates at £1,500 a year, followed by a lot of detail to enable you to calculate a prepayment at the beginning and end of the year. If you are preparing a budgeted profit and loss account for the year do not lose sight of the fact that the rates expense can be entered as £1,500 without any calculation at all.

Chapter roundup

- The **purposes** of a budget are as follows.

    o   To **coordinate** activities
    o   To **communicate** targets
    o   To **establish a system of control**
    o   To **compel planning**

- A **budget** is a financial or quantitative plan of operations for a forthcoming accounting period.

- The **budget committee** is the **coordinating** body in the preparation and administration of budgets.

- The manager responsible for preparing each budget should ideally be the manager responsible for carrying out the budget.

- The **budget manual** is a collection of instructions governing the responsibilities of persons and the procedures, forms and records relating to the preparation and use of budgetary data.

- The sales budget is usually the first functional budget prepared because sales is usually the **principal budget factor**. The order of preparation of the remaining budgets could be finished goods stock budget, production budget, budgets for resources of production, materials stock budget, raw materials purchases budget and overhead cost budgets.

- **Cash budgets** show the expected receipts and payments during a budget period. The usefulness of cash budgets is that they enable management to make any **forward planning decisions** that may be needed, such as advising their bank of estimated overdraft requirements or strengthening their credit control procedures to ensure that debtors pay more quickly.

- The **master budget** consists of a budgeted profit and loss account and a budgeted balance sheet.

Quick quiz

1   Budgets have four main purposes. Fill in the key words which are missing from the statements below.

    (a)   To .... the activities of different departments towards a single plan.

    (b)   To .... targets to managers responsible for achieving them.

    (c)   To establish a system of .... by comparing budgeted and actual results.

    (d)   To compel ....

2   Which of the following is unlikely to be contained with a budget manual?

    A   Organisational structures
    B   Objectives of the budgetary process
    C   Selling overhead budget
    D   Administrative details of budget preparation

3   The factor which limits the activities of an organisation is known as:

    I   The key factor budget
    II   The limiting budget factor
    III   The principal budget factor
    IV   The main budget factor

    A   I,II and IV
    B   I and III
    C   II and III
    D   I, II and III

4   If the principal budget factor is sales demand, in which order would the following budgets be prepared?

Materials usage	Materials purchase	Production	Sales	Cash

1st   [   ]

2nd   [   ]

3rd   [   ]

4th   [   ]

5th   [   ]

5   Match the following cash positions with the appropriate management action.

Short-term surplus   Increase creditors

Long-term surplus   Replace/update fixed assets

Short-term deficit   ?   Issue share capital

Long-term deficit   Increase debtors and stock

6   Depreciation has an effect on net profit and is therefore included in a cash budget.

True   [   ]

False   [   ]

7   Which of the following are included in the master budget?

I   Budgeted profit and loss account
II   Budgeted balance sheet
III   Cash budget
IV   Functional budgets

A   I and II
B   II and III
C   II, III and IV
D   IV only

Answers to quick quiz

1   (a)   Coordinate
    (b)   Communicate
    (c)   Control
    (d)   Planning

2   C

3   D

4   1st | Sales |
    2nd | Production |
    3rd | Materials usage |
    4th | Materials purchase |
    5th | Cash |

5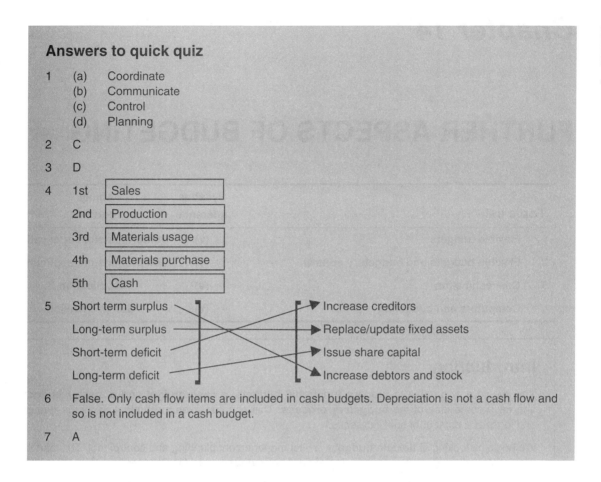

    Short term surplus   Increase creditors

    Long-term surplus   Replace/update fixed assets

    Short-term deficit   Issue share capital

    Long-term deficit   Increase debtors and stock

6   False. Only cash flow items are included in cash budgets. Depreciation is not a cash flow and so is not included in a cash budget.

7   A

Now try the question below from the Exam Question Bank

Number	Level	Marks	Time
Q17	Examination	15	27 mins

Chapter 14

FURTHER ASPECTS OF BUDGETING

Topic list	Syllabus reference	Ability required
1 Flexible budgets	(v)	Comprehension, application
2 Flexible budgets and budgetary control	(v)	Comprehension, application
3 Cost estimation	(v)	Application
4 Computers and budgeting	(v)	Comprehension

Introduction

You should now be able to **prepare functional budgets, a cash budget and a master budget** and have some idea of the **budgetary process**. This chapter takes the budgeting theme further and looks at a number of specific issues.

We begin by looking at **flexible budgets**, a vital management planning and control tool. This part of the chapter relies on your understanding of **cost behaviour** covered in Chapter 2.

We then move on to methods of **estimating** the costs to be included in budgets and conclude with a look at how **computers** can assist the budgeting process.

This chapter ends our study of budgeting. You will, however, come across **variances** again, which are mentioned in this chapter in relation to flexible budgets, in Chapters 15 to 17, which look at a new topic and consider the use of **standard costing** and **variance analysis**.

Learning outcomes covered in this chapter

- **Prepare** simple reports showing actual and budgeted results
- **Explain** the differences between fixed and flexible budgets
- **Prepare** a fixed and flexible budget
- **Calculate** simple cost estimates using high-low method and line of best fit
- **Explain** the use of IT in the budget process
- **Calculate** expenditure, volume and total budget variances

Syllabus content covered in this chapter

- Reporting of actual against budget
- Fixed and flexible budgeting
- IT and budgeting

1 FLEXIBLE BUDGETS

> ### KEY TERM
>
> - A **fixed budget** is a budget which is set for a single activity level.
>
> - A **flexible budget** is 'A budget which, by recognising different cost behaviour patterns, is designed to change as volume of activity changes'.
>
>   (CIMA *Official Terminology*)

1.1 **Master budgets** are based on planned volumes of production and sales but do not include any provision for the event that actual volumes may differ from the budget. In this sense they may be described as **fixed budgets**.

1.2 A **flexible budget** has two advantages.

   (a) At the **planning** stage, it may be helpful to know what the effects would be if the actual outcome differs from the prediction. For example, a company may budget to sell 10,000 units of its product, but may prepare flexible budgets based on sales of, say, 8,000 and 12,000 units. This would enable **contingency plans** to be drawn up if necessary.

   (b) At the end of each month or year, actual results may be compared with the relevant activity level in the flexible budget as a **control** procedure.

1.3 Flexible budgeting uses the principles of marginal costing. In estimating future costs it is often necessary to begin by looking at cost behaviour in the past. For costs which are wholly fixed or wholly variable no problem arises. But you may be presented with a cost which appears to have behaved in the past as a semi-variable cost (partly fixed and partly variable). A technique for estimating the level of the cost for the future is called the high/low method. We looked at this technique in Chapter 2: attempt the following question to ensure that you can remember what to do.

Question 1

The cost of factory power has behaved as follows in past years.

	Units of output produced	Cost of factory power £
20X1	7,900	38,700
20X2	7,700	38,100
20X3	9,800	44,400
20X4	9,100	42,300

Budgeted production for 20X5 is 10,200 units. Estimate the cost of factory power which will be incurred. Ignore inflation.

Answer

	Units	£
20X3 (highest output)	9,800	44,400
20X2 (lowest output)	7,700	38,100
	2,100	6,300

The variable cost per unit is therefore £6,300/2,100 = £3.

The level of fixed cost can be calculated by looking at any output level.

	£
Total cost of factory power in 20X3	44,400
Less variable cost of factory power (9,800 × £3)	29,400
Fixed cost of factory power	15,000

An estimate of costs is 20X5 is as follows.

	£
Fixed cost	15,000
Variable cost of budgeted production (10,200 × £3)	30,600
Total budgeted cost of factory power	45,600

1.4   We can now look at a full example of preparing a flexible budget.

1.5   EXAMPLE: PREPARING A FLEXIBLE BUDGET

(a) Prepare a budget for 20X6 for the direct labour costs and overhead expenses of a production department at the activity levels of 80%, 90% and 100%, using the information listed below.

   (i)   The direct labour hourly rate is expected to be £3.75.

   (ii)   100% activity represents 60,000 direct labour hours.

   (iii)   Variable costs

Indirect labour	£0.75 per direct labour hour
Consumable supplies	£0.375 per direct labour hour
Canteen and other welfare services	6% of direct and indirect labour costs

   (iv)   Semi-variable costs are expected to relate to the direct labour hours in the same manner as for the last five years.

Year	Direct labour hours	Semi-variable costs £
20X1	64,000	20,800
20X2	59,000	19,800
20X3	53,000	18,600
20X4	49,000	17,800
20X5	40,000 (estimate)	16,000 (estimate)

   (v)   *Fixed costs*

	£
Depreciation	18,000
Maintenance	10,000
Insurance	4,000
Rates	15,000
Management salaries	25,000

   (vi)   Inflation is to be ignored.

(b) Calculate the budget cost allowance (ie expected expenditure) for 20X6 assuming that 57,000 direct labour hours are worked.

1.6 SOLUTION

(a)

	80% level 48,000 hrs £'000	90% level 54,000 hrs £'000	100% level 60,000 hrs £'000
Direct labour	180.00	202.50	225.0
Other variable costs			
Indirect labour	36.00	40.50	45.0
Consumable supplies	18.00	20.25	22.5
Canteen etc	12.96	14.58	16.2
Total variable costs (£5.145 per hour)	246.96	277.83	308.7
Semi-variable costs (W)	17.60	18.80	20.0
Fixed costs			
Depreciation	18.00	18.00	18.0
Maintenance	10.00	10.00	10.0
Insurance	4.00	4.00	4.0
Rates	15.00	15.00	15.0
Management salaries	25.00	25.00	25.0
Budgeted costs	336.56	368.63	400.7

Working

Using the high/low method:

	£
Total cost of 64,000 hours	20,800
Total cost of 40,000 hours	16,000
Variable cost of 24,000 hours	4,800
Variable cost per hour (£4,800/24,000)	£0.20

	£
Total cost of 64,000 hours	20,800
Variable cost of 64,000 hours (× £0.20)	12,800
Fixed costs	8,000

Semi-variable costs are calculated as follows.

			£
60,000 hours	(60,000 × £0.20) + £8,000	=	20,000
54,000 hours	(54,000 × £0.20) + £8,000	=	18,800
48,000 hours	(48,000 × £0.20) + £8,000	=	17,600

(b) The budget cost allowance for 57,000 direct labour hours of work would be as follows.

		£
Variable costs	(57,000 × £5.145)	293,265
Semi-variable costs	(£8,000 + (57,000 × £0.20))	19,400
Fixed costs		72,000
		384,665

Exam focus point

You must be able to analyse the fixed and variable elements of cost to be able to produce a flexible budget.

---

2 FLEXIBLE BUDGETS AND BUDGETARY CONTROL　　　Pilot paper

2.1 **Budgetary control** is the practice of establishing budgets which identify areas of responsibility for individual managers (for example production managers, purchasing managers and so on) and of regularly comparing actual results against expected results. The most important method of budgetary control, for the purpose of your examination, is

variance analysis, which involves the comparison of actual results achieved during a control period (usually a month, or four weeks) with a flexible budget. The differences between actual results and expected results are called **variances** and these are used to provide a guideline for **control action** by individual managers. We will be looking at variances in some detail in Chapter 16.

2.2 The wrong approach to budgetary control is to compare actual results against a fixed budget. Consider the following example.

Windy Ltd manufactures a single product, the cloud. Budgeted results and actual results for June 20X2 are shown below.

	Budget	*Actual results*	*Variance*
Production and sales of the cloud (units)	2,000	3,000	
	£	£	£
Sales revenue (a)	20,000	30,000	10,000 (F)
Direct materials	6,000	8,500	2,500 (A)
Direct labour	4,000	4,500	500 (A)
Maintenance	1,000	1,400	400 (A)
Depreciation	2,000	2,200	200 (A)
Rent and rates	1,500	1,600	100 (A)
Other costs	3,600	5,000	1,400 (A)
Total costs (b)	18,100	23,200	5,100
Profit (a) – (b)	1,900	6,800	4,900 (F)

2.3 (a) In this example, the variances are meaningless for purposes of control. Costs were higher than budget because the **volume of output was also higher**; variable costs would be expected to increase above the budgeted costs in the fixed budget. There is no information to show whether control action is needed for any aspect of costs or revenue.

(b) For control purposes, it is necessary to know the answers to questions such as the following.

- Were actual costs higher than they should have been to produce and sell 3,000 clouds?

- Was actual revenue satisfactory from the sale of 3,000 clouds?

2.4 The correct approach to budgetary control is as follows.

- Identify fixed and variable costs.
- Produce a flexible budget using marginal costing techniques.

2.5 In the previous example of Windy Ltd, let us suppose that we have the following estimates of cost behaviour.

(a) Direct materials, direct labour and maintenance costs are variable.

(b) Rent and rates and depreciation are fixed costs.

(c) Other costs consist of fixed costs of £1,600 plus a variable cost of £1 per unit made and sold.

2.6 The budgetary control analysis should be as follows.

	Fixed budget (a)	Flexible budget (b)	Actual results (c)	Budget variance (b) - (c)
Production & sales (units)	2,000	3,000	3,000	
	£	£	£	£
Sales revenue	20,000	30,000	30,000	0
Variable costs				
Direct materials	6,000	9,000	8,500	500 (F)
Direct labour	4,000	6,000	4,500	1,500 (F)
Maintenance	1,000	1,500	1,400	100 (F)
Semi-variable costs				
Other costs	3,600	4,600	5,000	400 (A)
Fixed costs				
Depreciation	2,000	2,000	2,200	200 (A)
Rent and rates	1,500	1,500	1,600	100 (A)
Total costs	18,100	24,600	23,200	1,400 (F)
Profit	1,900	5,400	6,800	1,400 (F)

Note. (F) denotes a **favourable** variance and (A) an **adverse** or unfavourable variance. Adverse variances are sometimes denoted as (U) for 'unfavourable'.

Exam focus point

Variances are calculated by comparing actual results and the flexible budget, *not* actual results and the original budget.

2.7 We can analyse the above as follows.

(a) In selling 3,000 units the expected profit should have been, not the fixed budget profit of £1,900, but the flexible budget profit of £5,400. Instead, actual profit was £6,800 ie £1,400 more than we should have expected. The reason for this £1,400 improvement is that, given output and sales of 3,000 units, overall costs were lower than expected (and sales revenue was exactly as expected). For example the direct material cost was £500 lower than expected.

(b) Another reason for the improvement in profit above the fixed budget profit is the **sales volume**. Windy Ltd sold 3,000 clouds instead of 2,000 clouds, with the following result.

	£	£
Budgeted sales revenue increased by		10,000
Budgeted variable costs increased by:		
direct materials	3,000	
direct labour	2,000	
maintenance	500	
variable element of other costs	1,000	
Budgeted fixed costs are unchanged		6,500
Budgeted profit increased by		3,500

Budgeted profit was therefore increased by £3,500 because sales volume increased.

(c) A full variance analysis statement would be as follows.

	£	£
Fixed budget profit		1,900
Variances		
Sales volume	3,500 (F)	
Direct materials cost	500 (F)	
Direct labour cost	1,500 (F)	
Maintenance cost	100 (F)	
Other costs	400 (A)	
Depreciation	200 (A)	
Rent and rates	100 (A)	
		4,900 (F)
Actual profit		6,800

2.8 If management believes that any of these variances are large enough to justify it, they will investigate the reasons for them to see whether any corrective action is necessary.

Question 2

The budgeted variable cost per unit was £2.75. When output was 18,000 units, total expenditure was £98,000 and it was found that fixed overheads were £11,000 over budget whilst variable costs were in line with budget.

What was the amount budgeted for fixed costs?

A £37,500 B £48,500 C £49,500 D £87,000

Answer

	£
Total expenditure	98,000
Budgeted variable cost (18,000 × £2.75)	49,500
Actual fixed costs incurred	48,500
Fixed overhead expenditure variance	11,000
Budgeted fixed costs	37,500

The correct answer is A.

Option D is incorrect: it is simply the £98,000 total expenditure less the £11,000 fixed overhead expenditure variance.

Option C is also incorrect, being the budgeted variable cost (£2.75 × 18,000).

Option B is incorrect: £48,000 is the actual fixed costs incurred (see working above).

3 COST ESTIMATION

3.1 It should be obvious that the production of a budget calls for the preparation of **cost estimates** and **sales forecasts**. In fact, budgeting could be said to be as much a test of estimating and forecasting skills than anything else. In this section we will consider the two cost estimation techniques that you need to know about for **Management Accounting Fundamentals**.

Cost estimation methods

3.2 Cost estimation involves the measurement of **historical costs** to predict **future costs**. Some estimation techniques are more sophisticated than others and are therefore likely to be more reliable but, in practice, the simple techniques are more commonly found and should give estimates that are sufficiently accurate for their purpose.

High/low method

3.3 We met the **high/low method** again earlier in this chapter. The major drawback to the high/low method is that **only two historical cost records from previous periods are used** in the cost estimation. Unless these two records are a reliable indicator of costs throughout the relevant range of output, which is unlikely, only a 'loose approximation' of fixed and variable costs will be obtained. The advantage of the method is its relative **simplicity**.

The scattergraph method

3.4 You should recall from Chapter 2 that a **graph** can be plotted of the historical costs from previous periods, and from the resulting scatter diagram, a '**line-of-best-fit**' can be drawn by visual estimation.

3.5 The advantage of the scattergraph over the high/low method is that a **greater quantity of historical data is used** in the estimation, but its disadvantage is that the cost line is drawn by visual judgement and so is a **subjective approximation**.

4 COMPUTERS AND BUDGETING

4.1 The examples we have looked at so far have demonstrated the need for a great number of **numerical manipulations** to produce a budget, be it a cash budget or a master budget. It is highly unlikely that the execution of the steps in the process will be problem free. Functional budgets will be out of balance with each other and will require modification so that they are **compatible**. The revision of one budget may well lead to the revision of all of the budgets. The manual preparation of a master budget and a cash budget in the real world would therefore be daunting to say the very least.

4.2 Computers, however, can take the hard work out of budgeting: a computerised system will have four basic advantages over a manual system.

- A computer has the ability to process a **larger volume of data**.
- A computerised system can **process data more rapidly** than a manual system.
- Computerised systems tend to be **more accurate** than manual systems.
- Computers have the ability to **store large volumes of data** in a readily accessible form.

4.3 Such advantages make computers ideal for taking over the manipulation of numbers, leaving staff to get involved in the real planning process.

4.4 Budgeting is usually computerised using either a **computer program written specifically for the organisation** or by a commercial **spreadsheet package**.

4.5 Both methods of computerisation of the budgeting process will involve a **mathematical model** which represents the real world in terms of financial values. The model will consist of several, or many, **interrelated variables**, a variable being an item in the model which has a value. For example a cash budgeting model would include variables for sales, credit periods, purchases, wages and salaries and so on.

4.6 Once the planning model has been constructed, the same model can be used again and again, simply by changing the values of the variables to produce new results for cash inflows, cash outflows, net cash flows and cash/bank balance.

4.7 A major advantage of **budget models** is the ability to evaluate different options and carry out '**what if' analysis**. By changing the value of certain variables (for example altering the ratio of cash sales to credit sales, increasing the amount of bad debts or capital expenditure, increasing the annual pay award to the workforce and so on) management are able to assess the effect of potential changes in their environment.

4.8 Computerised models can also incorporate **actual results**, period by period, and carry out the necessary calculations to produce **budgetary control reports**.

4.9 The use of a model also allows the **budget for the remainder of the year to be adjusted** once it is clear that the circumstances on which the budget was originally based have changed.

Spreadsheets

4.10 Most organisations do not have budgeting programs written for them but use standard spreadsheet packages.

> ### KEY TERM
>
> 'Spreadsheet' is defined in CIMA *Computing Terminology* as 'the term commonly used to describe many of the modelling packages available for microcomputers, being loosely derived from the likeness to a 'spreadsheet of paper' divided into rows and columns'.

4.11 The idea behind a spreadsheet is that the model builder should construct a model in rows and columns format.

 (a) Variables are represented by a row or column of items, or even by just one 'cell' in the spreadsheet.

 (b) Numerical values for the **variables** are derived as follows.

   (i) They can be inserted into the model via **keyboard input**.

   (ii) They can be calculated from other data in the model using **formulae** specified within the construction of the model itself. In other words formulae can be included in the cells of the spreadsheet and referenced to other cells containing numerical information.

   (iii) They can be obtained from data held on **disk file** - in another spreadsheet, for example.

 (c) **Text** can also be entered and manipulated to some extent.

4.12 The more sophisticated modern packages can handle information in '**3D' format** (a 'pad' of paper, as it were, rather than a single sheet) and can present results as charts or graphs.

4.13 To assess the **use of spreadsheets in budgeting** let us consider a cash budget. A cash budget needs frequent updating to reflect current and forecast conditions, changes in credit behaviour and so on. Each period (week, month or whatever) up-to-date information is input and in combination with brought forward file data, the cash budget will be automatically projected forward by the spreadsheet program. Surpluses and deficiencies may well be highlighted.

4.14 Both abbreviated and detailed versions of the cash budget may be produced along with graphical representations of the same information.

	A	B	C	D	E	F	G	H
2			Summary Cash Budget (Ref. Details Budgets A-L)					
3								
4			Jan	Feb	Mar	Apr	May	June
5			£'000	£'000	£'000	£'000	£'000	£'000
6	Opening balance		15	22	20	-36	-50	-83
7	add							
8	Total receipts		92	112	122	138	148	162
9	less							
10	Total payments		-85	-114	-178	-152	-181	-235
11	equals							
12	Closing balance		22	20	-36	-50	-83	-156
13								
14	Current overdraft limit		40	40	40	40	60	120
15								
16	Warning indicator					*	*	*
17						*	*	*
18							*	*
19								*

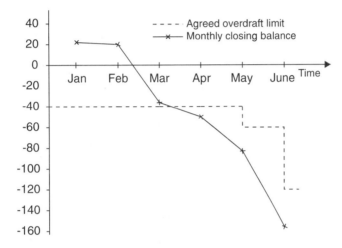

4.15 Perhaps the greatest benefit that can be obtained from a spreadsheet package is its facility to perform **'what if' calculations** at great speed. For example, the consequences throughout the organisation of sales growth per month of nil, $\frac{1}{2}$%, 1%, $1\frac{1}{2}$% and so on can be calculated at the touch of a button.

Chapter roundup

- A **Fixed budget** is a budget which is set for a single activity level.

- A **flexible budget** is a budget which recognises different cost behaviour patterns and is designed to change as volume of activity changes.

- **Budgetary control** is the practice of establishing budgets which identify areas of responsibility for individual managers and of regularly comparing actual results against expected results.

- **Variance analysis** involves the comparison of actual results achieved during a control period with a flexible budget. **Variances** are the differences between actual results and expected results.

- **Budget variances** are calculated by comparing the **flexible budget** with actual results. Budget variances may be divided into **expenditure** and **volume** variances.

- **(F)** denotes a **favourable** variance and **(A)** denotes an **adverse** or **unfavourable** variance.

- A prerequisite of flexible budgeting is a knowledge of **cost behaviour patterns**. The production of a budget also calls for the preparation of **cost estimation** and **sales forecasts**. Simple cost estimation techniques include the **high-low method** and the **scattergraph method.**

- Computers can take the hard work out of budgeting. **Computerised systems** have the following advantages over manual systems.

  - The ability to process a **larger volume of data**
  - The ability to **process data more rapidly** than manual systems
  - They tend to be **more accurate** than manual systems
  - The ability to **store large volumes of data** in a readily accessible form

- A major advantage of budget models is the ability to evaluate different options and carry out 'what if' analysis. Computerised models can incorporate budgeted results and actual results, and carry out the necessary calculations to produce **budgetary control reports.**

Quick quiz

1   What are the advantages of a flexible budget over a fixed budget?

2   Flexible budgets are normally prepared on a marginal costing basis.

   True   ☐

   False ☐

3   Define budgetary control.

4   What is the wrong approach to budgetary control?

5   What is the correct approach to budgetary control?

6   In what way is the scattergraph method more reliable than the high/low method of cost estimation?

7   The main weakness of the scattergraph method of cost estimation is

   A   It only uses two historical cost records
   B   It is a subjective approximation
   C   It is a relatively simple method
   D   It uses vast amounts of historical data

8   List four advantages of a computerised system over a manual system.

9   What is a spreadsheet?

Answers to quick quiz

1   (a)   At the planning stage, a flexible budget can show what the effects would be if the actual outcome differs from the prediction.

    (b)   At the end of each period, actual results may be compared with the relevant activity level in the flexible budget as a control procedure.

2   True

3   Budgetary control is the practice of establishing budgets which identify areas of responsibility for individual managers and of regularly comparing actual results against expected results.

4   To compare actual results against a fixed budget.

5   •   To identify fixed and variable costs
    •   To produce a flexible budget using marginal costing techniques

6   A greater quantity of historical data is used in the estimation.

7   B

8   •   The ability to process a larger volume of data
    •   To process data more rapidly than a manual system
    •   To tend to be more accurate than manual systems
    •   To store larger volumes of data in a readily accessible form

9   A term commonly used to describe many of the modelling packages available for computers, being loosely derived from the likeness to a 'spreadsheet of paper' divided into rows and columns.

Now try the question below from the Exam Question Bank

Question to try	Level	Marks	Time
Q18	Introductory	n/a	30 mins

Chapter 15

INTRODUCTION TO STANDARD COSTING

Topic list	Syllabus reference	Ability required
1 What is standard costing?	(ii)	Comprehension
2 Setting standards	(ii)	Application

Introduction

Just as there are **standards** for most things in our daily lives (cleanliness in hamburger restaurants, educational achievement of nine year olds, number of trains running on time), there are standards for the costs of products and services. Moreover, just as the standards in our daily lives are not always met, the standards for the costs of products and services are not always met. We will not, however, be considering the standards of cleanliness of hamburger restaurants in this chapter but we will be looking at standards for **costs**, what they are used for and how they are set.

In the next chapter we will see how **standard costing** forms the basis of a process called **variance analysis**, a vital management control tool.

Learning outcomes covered in this chapter

- **Explain** the principles of standard costing

- **Prepare** the standard cost for a product/service

Syllabus content covered in this chapter

- Principles of standard costing

- Preparation of standard costs under absorption and marginal costing

1   WHAT IS STANDARD COSTING?

1.1   The building blocks of standard costing are standard costs and so before we look at standard costing in any detail you really need to know what a standard cost is.

Standard cost

1.2   The standard cost of product 1234 is set out below.

STANDARD COST CARD - PRODUCT 1234

	£	£
Direct materials		
Material X – 3 kg at £4 per kg	12	
Material Y – 9 litres at £2 per litre	18	
		30
Direct labour		
Grade A – 6 hours at £1.50 per hour	9	
Grade B – 8 hours at £2 per hour	16	
		25
Standard direct cost		55
Variable production overhead – 14 hours at £0.50 per hour		7
Standard variable cost of production		62
Fixed production overhead – 14 hours at £4.50 per hour		63
Standard full production cost		125
Administration and marketing overhead		15
Standard cost of sale		140
Standard profit		20
Standard sales price		160

KEY TERM

A **standard cost** is a planned unit cost.

1.3 Notice how the total standard cost is built up from standards for each cost element: standard quantities of materials at standard prices, standard quantities of labour time at standard rates and so on. It is therefore determined by management's estimates of the following.

- The expected prices of materials, labour and expenses
- Efficiency levels in the use of materials and labour
- Budgeted overhead costs and budgeted volumes of activity

We will see how management arrives at these estimates in Section 2.

1.4 But why should management want to prepare standard costs? Obviously to assist with standard costing, but what is the point of standard costing?

The uses of standard costing

1.5 **Standard costing** has a variety of uses but its two principal ones are as follows.

(a) To **value stocks** and **cost production** for cost accounting purposes. It is an alternative method of valuation to methods like FIFO and LIFO which we looked at in Chapter 3.

(b) To act as a **control device** by establishing standards (planned costs), highlighting (via **variance analysis** which we will cover in the next chapter) activities that are not conforming to plan and thus **alerting management** to areas which may be out of control and in need of corrective action.

Question 1

Bloggs Ltd makes one product, the joe. Two types of labour are involved in the preparation of a joe, skilled and semi-skilled. Skilled labour is paid £10 per hour and semi-skilled £5 per hour. Twice as many skilled labour hours as semi-skilled labour hours are needed to produce a joe, four semi-skilled labour hours being needed.

A joe is made up of three different direct materials. Seven kilograms of direct material A, four litres of direct material B and three metres of direct material C are needed. Direct material A costs £1 per kilogram, direct material B £2 per litre and direct material C £3 per metre.

Variable production overheads are incurred at Bloggs Ltd at the rate of £2.50 per direct labour (skilled) hour.

A system of absorption costing is in operation at Bloggs Ltd. The basis of absorption is direct labour (skilled) hours. For the forthcoming accounting period, budgeted fixed production overheads are £250,000 and budgeted production of the joe is 5,000 units.

Administration, selling and distribution overheads are added to products at the rate of £10 per unit.

A mark-up of 25% is made on the joe.

Required

Using the above information draw up a standard cost card for the joe.

Answer

STANDARD COST CARD - PRODUCT JOE

	£	£
Direct materials		
A - 7 kgs × £1	7	
B - 4 litres × £2	8	
C - 3 m × £3	9	
	—	
		24
Direct labour		
Skilled - 8 × £10	80	
Semi-skilled - 4 × £5	20	
	—	
		100
Standard direct cost		124
Variable production overhead - 8 × £2.50		20
Standard variable cost of production		144
Fixed production overhead - 8 × £6.25 (W)		50
Standard full production cost		194
Administration, selling and distribution overhead		10
Standard cost of sale		204
Standard profit (25% × 204)		51
Standard sales price		255

Working

Overhead absorption rate $= \dfrac{£250,000}{5,000 \ \times 8} = £6.25$ per skilled labour hour

---

1.6 Although the use of standard costs to simplify the keeping of cost accounting records should not be overlooked, we will be concentrating on the **control** and **variance analysis** aspect of standard costing.

KEY TERM

Standard costing is 'A control technique which compares standard costs and revenues with actual results to obtain variances which are used to stimulate improved performance'.

CIMA *Official Terminology*

1.7 Notice that the above definition highlights the control aspects of standard costing.

Standard costing as a control technique

1.8 **Standard costing** therefore involves the following.

- The establishment of predetermined estimates of the costs of products or services
- The collection of actual costs
- The comparison of the actual costs with the predetermined estimates.

1.9 The predetermined costs are known as **standard costs** and the difference between standard and actual cost is known as a **variance**. The process by which the total difference between standard and actual results is analysed in known as **variance analysis**.

1.10 Although standard costing can be used in a variety of costing situations (batch and mass production, process manufacture, jobbing manufacture (where there is standardisation of parts) and service industries (if a realistic cost unit can be established)), the greatest benefit from its use can be gained if there is a **degree of repetition** in the production process. It is therefore most suited to **mass production** and **repetitive assembly work**.

2 SETTING STANDARDS

2.1 Standard costs may be used in both absorption costing and in marginal costing systems. We shall, however, confine our description to standard costs in absorption costing systems.

2.2 As we noted earlier, the standard cost of a product (or service) is made up of a number of different standards, one for each cost element, each of which has to be set by management. We have divided this section into two: the first part looks at setting the monetary part of each standard, whereas the second part looks at setting the resources requirement part of each standard.

Standard rates

Direct material prices

2.3 **Direct material prices** will be estimated by the purchasing department from their knowledge of the following.

- Purchase contracts already agreed
- Pricing discussions with regular suppliers
- The forecast movement of prices in the market
- The availability of bulk purchase discounts

2.4 Price inflation can cause difficulties in setting realistic standard prices. Suppose that a material costs £10 per kilogram at the moment and during the course of the next twelve months it is expected to go up in price by 20% to £12 per kilogram. What standard price should be selected?

- The current price of £10 per kilogram
- The average expected price for the year, say £11 per kilogram

2.5 Either would be possible, but neither would be entirely satisfactory.

  (a) If the **current price** were used in the standard, the reported price variance will become adverse as soon as prices go up, which might be very early in the year. If prices go up gradually rather than in one big jump, it would be difficult to select an appropriate time for revising the standard.

BPP PUBLISHING

(b) If an **estimated mid-year price** were used, price variances should be favourable in the first half of the year and adverse in the second half of the year, again assuming that prices go up gradually throughout the year. Management could only really check that in any month, the price variance did not become excessively adverse (or favourable) and that the price variance switched from being favourable to adverse around month six or seven and not sooner.

Direct labour rates

2.6 **Direct labour rates per hour** will be set by discussion with the personnel department and by reference to the payroll and to any agreements on pay rises with trade union representatives of the employees.

(a) A separate hourly rate or weekly wage will be set for each different labour grade/type of employee.

(b) An average hourly rate will be applied for each grade (even though individual rates of pay may vary according to age and experience).

2.7 Similar problems when dealing with inflation to those described for material prices can be met when setting labour standards.

Overhead absorption rates

2.8 When standard costs are fully absorbed costs, the **absorption rate** of fixed production overheads will be **predetermined**, usually each year when the budget is prepared, and based in the usual manner on budgeted fixed production overhead expenditure and budgeted production.

For selling and distribution costs, standard costs might be absorbed as a percentage of the standard selling price.

2.9 Standard costs under marginal costing will, of course, not include any element of absorbed overheads.

Standard resource requirements

2.10 To estimate the materials required to make each product (**material usage**) and also the labour hours required (**labour efficiency**), **technical specifications** must be prepared for each product by production experts (either in the production department or the work study department).

(a) The 'standard product specification' for materials must list the quantities required per unit of each material in the product. These standard input quantities must be made known to the operators in the production department so that control action by management to deal with **excess material wastage** will be understood by them.

(b) The 'standard operation sheet' for labour will specify the expected hours required by each grade of labour in each department to make one unit of product. These standard times must be carefully set (for example by work study) and must be understood by the labour force. Where necessary, **standard procedures** or **operating methods** should be stated.

Performance standards

2.11 The quantity of material and labour time required will depend on the level of performance required by management. There are two types of **performance standard** which might be used. Standards may be set at '**attainable levels** which assume efficient levels of operation, but which include **allowances** for normal loss, waste and machine downtime, or at **ideal levels**, which make **no allowance** for the above losses, and are only attainable under the most favourable conditions' (CIMA *Official Terminology*).

2.12 **Ideal standards** are sometimes thought to have a negative motivational impact, because employees will often feel that the goals are unattainable and not work so hard. When setting standards, managers must be aware of two requirements.

- The need to establish a useful control measure
- The need to set a standard which will have the desired motivational effect.

These two requirements are often conflicting, so that the final standard cost might be a compromise between the two.

Taking account of wastage, losses etc

2.13 If, during processing, the quantity of material input to the process is likely to reduce (due to wastage, evaporation and so on), the quantity input must be greater than the quantity in the finished product and a material standard must take account of this.

2.14 Suppose that the fresh raspberry juice content of a litre of Purple Pop is 100ml and that there is a 10% loss of raspberry juice during process due to evaporation. The standard material usage of raspberry juice per litre of Purple Pop will be:

$$100ml \times \frac{100\%}{(100-10)\%} = 100ml \times \frac{100\%}{90\%} = 111.11ml$$

Exam focus point

Make sure that you understand how to account for wastage and losses etc when calculating standard costs. Examination questions could well ask you to calculate the standard cost of a product given that there is loss due to evaporation or idle time and so on. Have a go at question 2 below.

Question 2

A unit of product X requires 24 active labour hours for completion. It is anticipated that there will be 20% idle time which is to be incorporated into the standard times for all products. If the wage rate is £10 per hour, what is the standard labour cost of one unit of product X?

A £192   B £240   C £288   D £300

Answer

The basic labour cost for 24 hours is £240. However with idle time it will be necessary to pay for more than 24 hours in order to achieve 24 hours of actual work Therefore options A and B are incorrect.

Standard labour cost = active hours for completion $\times \dfrac{125}{100} \times$ £10

$= 24 \times 1.25 \times$ £10   =   <u>£300</u>

BPP PUBLISHING

Option D is correct.

Option C is incorrect because it results from simply adding an extra 20 per cent to the labour hours. However the idle hours are 20 per cent of the *total* hours worked, therefore we need to add 25 per cent to the required active hours, as shown in the working.

Problems in setting standards

Question 3

What sort of problems can you envisage arising when setting standards?

Answer

(a) Deciding how to incorporate **inflation** into planned unit costs

(b) Agreeing on a **performance standard** (attainable or ideal)

(c) Deciding on the **quality** of materials to be used (a better quality of material will cost more, but perhaps reduce material wastage)

(d) Estimating materials **prices** where seasonal price variations or bulk purchase discounts may be significant

(e) Finding sufficient **time** to construct accurate standards as standard setting can be a **time-consuming process**

(f) Incurring the **cost of setting up and maintaining a system** for establishing standards

(g) Dealing with possible **behavioural problems**, managers responsible for the achievement of standards possibly resisting the use of a standard costing control system for fear of being blamed for any adverse variances

2.15 Note that standard costing is most difficult in times of inflation but it is still worthwhile.

(a) **Usage** and **efficiency** variances will still be meaningful

(b) **Inflation is measurable**: there is no reason why its effects cannot be removed from the variances reported.

(c) Standard costs can be **revised** so long as this is **not done too frequently**.

The advantages of standard costing

Question 4

What do you think are the benefits to be gained from using standard costing?

Answer

The advantages for **control** in having a standard costing system in operation can be summarised as follows.

(a) Carefully planned standards are an **aid to more accurate budgeting**.

(b) Standard costs provide a **yardstick** against which actual costs can be measured.

(c) The **setting of standards** involves determining the best materials and methods which may lead to **economies**.

(d) A **target of efficiency** is set for employees to reach and **cost consciousness** is stimulated.

(e) Variances can be calculated which enable the principle of '**management by exception**' to be operated. Only the variances which exceed acceptable tolerance limits need to be investigated by management with a view to control action.

(f) Standard costs **simplify the process of bookkeeping** in cost accounting, because they are easier to use than LIFO, FIFO and weighted average costs.

(g) Standard times **simplify the process of production scheduling**.

(h) Standard performance levels might provide an **incentive for individuals** to achieve targets for themselves at work.

Chapter roundup

- A **standard cost** is a **predetermined estimated unit cost**, used for stock valuation and control.

- A **standard cost card** shows full details of the standard cost of each product.

- Differences between actual and standard cost are called **variances**.

- **Performance standards** are used to set efficiency targets. There are basically two types: **attainable and ideal**.

- A standard cost is an **average** expected unit cost. The actual cost of individual items may fluctuate around this average.

- Management should only receive information of **significant** variances. This is known as '**management by exception**'.

- There are a number of advantages and disadvantages associated with standard costing.

Quick quiz

1   A standard cost is ……………………………………………………….. .

2   What are two main uses of standard costing?

3   A control technique which compares standard costs and revenues with actual results to obtain variances which are used to stimulate improves performance is known as:

    A   Standard costing
    B   Variance analysis
    C   Budgetary control
    D   Budgeting

4   Standard costs may only be used in absorption costing.

    True   ☐

    False   ☐

5   Two types of performance standard are

    (a)   …………………………..
    (b)   …………………………..

6   List three problems in setting standards.

7   List three advantages of using standard costing.

Answers to quick quiz

1   A planned unit cost.

2   (a) To value stocks and cost production for cost accounting purposes.

    (b) To act as a control device by establishing standards and highlighting activities that are not conforming to plan and bringing these to the attention of management.

3   A

4   False

5   (a) Attainable
    (b) Ideal

6   See answer to Question 3.

7   See answer to Question 4.

Now try the question below from the Exam Question Bank

Question to try	Level	Marks	Time
Q19	Examination	15	27 mins

Chapter 16

BASIC VARIANCE ANALYSIS

Topic list		Syllabus reference	Ability required
1	Variances	(ii)	Application, analysis
2	Direct material cost variances	(ii)	Application, analysis
3	Direct labour cost variances	(ii)	Application, analysis
4	Variable production overhead variances	(ii)	Application, analysis
5	Fixed production overhead variances	(ii)	Application, analysis
6	The reasons for cost variances	(ii)	Application, analysis
7	The significance of cost variances	(ii)	Application, analysis

Introduction

The actual results achieved by an organisation during a reporting period (week, month, quarter, year) will, more than likely, be different from the expected results (the expected results being the standard costs and revenues which we looked at in the previous chapter). Such differences may occur between individual items, such as the cost of labour and the volume of sales, and between the total expected profit/contribution and the total actual profit/contribution.

Management will have spent considerable time and trouble setting standards. Actual results have differed from the standards. The wise manager will consider the differences that have occurred and use the results of these considerations to assist in attempts to attain the standards. The wise manager will use **variance analysis** as a method of **control**.

This chapter examines **variance analysis** and sets out the method of calculating the following variances.

- Direct material cost variances
- Direct labour cost variances
- Variable production overhead variances
- Fixed production overhead variances

We will then go on to look at the reasons for and significance of cost variances.

Chapter 17 of this **Management Accounting Fundamentals** Study Text will build on the basics set down in this chapter by introducing **sales variances** and **operating statements.**

Learning outcomes covered in this chapter

- **Calculate** and **interpret** variances for materials, labour, variable overheads and fixed overheads

Syllabus content covered in this chapter

- Variances: materials: total, price and usage; labour: total, rate and efficiency; variable overhead: total, expenditure and efficiency; fixed overhead: total, expenditure and volume (absorption costing); fixed overhead: expenditure (marginal costing).

BPP PUBLISHING

1 VARIANCES

> **KEY TERM**
>
> A **variance** is 'The difference between a planned, budgeted, or standard cost and the actual cost incurred. The same comparisons may be made for revenues.'
>
> CIMA *Official Terminology*

1.1 The process by which the **total** difference between standard and actual results is analysed is known as **variance analysis**.

> **KEY TERM**
>
> **Variance analysis** is defined as 'The evaluation of performance by means of variances, whose timely reporting should maximise the opportunity for managerial action'.
>
> CIMA *Official Terminology*

1.2 When actual results are better than expected results, we have a **favourable variance** (F). If, on the other hand, actual results are worse than expected results, we have an **adverse variance** (A).

1.3 Variances can be divided into three main groups.

- Variable cost variances
- Sales variances
- Fixed production overhead variances.

In the remainder of this chapter we will consider, in detail, variable cost variances and fixed production overhead variances.

2 DIRECT MATERIAL COST VARIANCES

2.1 The **direct material total variance** (the difference between what the output actually cost and what it should have cost, in terms of material) can be divided into two sub-variances.

(a) **The direct material price variance**

This is the **difference between the standard cost and the actual cost for the actual quantity of material used or purchased.** In other words, it is the difference between what the material did cost and what it should have cost.

(b) **The direct material usage variance**

This is the **difference between the standard quantity of materials that should have been used for the number of units actually produced, and the actual quantity of materials used, valued at the standard cost per unit of material.** In other words, it is the difference between how much material should have been used and how much material was used, valued at standard cost.

2.2 EXAMPLE: DIRECT MATERIAL VARIANCES

Product X has a standard direct material cost as follows.

10 kilograms of material Y at £10 per kilogram = £100 per unit of X.

During period 4, 1,000 units of X were manufactured, using 11,700 kilograms of material Y which cost £98,600.

Required

Calculate the following variances.

(a) The direct material total variance
(b) The direct material price variance
(c) The direct material usage variance

2.3 SOLUTION

(a) **The direct material total variance**

This is the difference between what 1,000 units should have cost and what they did cost.

	£
1,000 units should have cost ($\times$ £100)	100,000
but did cost	98,600
Direct material total variance	1,400 (F)

The variance is **favourable** because the units cost less than they should have cost.

Now we can break down the direct material total variance into its two constituent parts: the direct material **price** variance and the direct material **usage** variance.

(b) **The direct material price variance**

This is the difference between what 11,700 kgs should have cost and what 11,700 kgs did cost.

	£
11,700 kgs of Y should have cost ($\times$ £10)	117,000
but did cost	98,600
Material Y price variance	18,400 (F)

The variance is **favourable** because the material cost less than it should have.

(c) **The direct material usage variance**

This is the difference between how many kilograms of Y should have been used to produce 1,000 units of X and how many kilograms were used, valued at the standard cost per kilogram.

1,000 units should have used ($\times$ 10 kgs)	10,000 kgs
but did use	11,700 kgs
Usage variance in kgs	1,700 kgs (A)
$\times$ standard cost per kilogram	$\times$ £10
Usage variance in £	£17,000 (A)

The variance is **adverse** because more material than should have been used was used.

(d) **Summary**

	£
Price variance	18,400 (F)
Usage variance	17,000 (A)
Total variance	1,400 (A)

Materials variances and opening and closing stock

2.4 Suppose that a company uses raw material P in production, and that this raw material has a standard price of £3 per metre. During one month 6,000 metres are bought for £18,600, and

5,000 metres are used in production. At the end of the month, stock will have been increased by 1,000 metres. In variance analysis, the problem is to decide the **material price variance**. Should it be calculated on the basis of **materials purchased** (6,000 metres) or on the basis of **materials used** (5,000 metres)?

2.5 The answer to this problem depends on how **closing stocks** of the raw materials will be valued.

(a) If they are valued at **standard cost**, (1,000 units at £3 per unit) the price variance is calculated on material **purchases** in the period.

(b) If they are valued at **actual cost** (FIFO) (1,000 units at £3.10 per unit) the price variance is calculated on materials **used in production** in the period.

2.6 A **full standard costing system** is usually in operation and therefore the price variance is usually calculated on **purchases** in the period. The variance on the full 6,000 metres will be written off to the costing profit and loss account, even though only 5,000 metres are included in the cost of production.

2.7 There are two main advantages in extracting the material price variance at the time of **receipt**.

(a) If variances are extracted at the time of receipt they will be **brought to the attention of managers earlier** than if they are extracted as the material is used. If it is necessary to correct any variances then management action can be more timely.

(b) Since variances are extracted at the time of receipt, **all stocks will be valued at standard price**. This is administratively easier and it means that all issues from stocks can be made at standard price. If stocks are held at actual cost it is necessary to calculate a separate price variance on each batch as it is issued. Since issues are usually made in a number of small batches this can be a time-consuming task, especially with a manual system.

2.8 The price variance would be calculated as follows.

	£
6,000 metres of material P purchased should cost (× £3)	18,000
but did cost	18,600
Price variance	600 (A)

3 DIRECT LABOUR COST VARIANCES

3.1 The calculation of **direct labour variances** is very similar to the calculation of direct material variances.

The **direct labour total variance** (the difference between what the output should have cost and what it did cost, in terms of labour) can be divided into two sub-variances.

(a) **The direct labour rate variance**

This is similar to the direct material price variance. If is the **difference between the standard cost and the actual cost for the actual number of hours paid for.**

In other words, it is the difference between what the labour did cost and what it should have cost.

(b) **The direct labour efficiency variance**

This is similar to the direct material usage variance. It is the **difference between the hours that should have been worked for the number of units actually produced, and the actual number of hours worked, valued at the standard rate per hour.**

In other words, it is the difference between how many hours should have been worked and how many hours were worked, valued at the standard rate per hour.

3.2 EXAMPLE: DIRECT LABOUR VARIANCES

The standard direct labour cost of product X is as follows.

2 hours of grade Z labour at £5 per hour = £10 per unit of product X.

During period 4, 1,000 units of product X were made, and the direct labour cost of grade Z labour was £8,900 for 2,300 hours of work.

Required

Calculate the following variances.

(a) The direct labour total variance
(b) The direct labour rate variance
(c) The direct labour efficiency (productivity) variance

3.3 SOLUTION

(a) **The direct labour total variance**

This is the difference between what 1,000 units should have cost and what they did cost.

	£
1,000 units should have cost (× £10)	10,000
but did cost	8,900
Direct labour total variance	1,100 (F)

The variance is **favourable** because the units cost less than they should have done.

Again we can analyse this total variance into its two constituent parts.

(b) **The direct labour rate variance**

This is the difference between what 2,300 hours should have cost and what 2,300 hours did cost.

	£
2,300 hours of work should have cost (× £5 per hr)	11,500
but did cost	8,900
Direct labour rate variance	2,600 (F)

The variance is **favourable** because the labour cost less than it should have cost.

(c) **The direct labour efficiency variance**

1,000 units of X should have taken (× 2 hrs)	2,000 hrs
but did take	2,300 hrs
Efficiency variance in hours	300 hrs (A)
× standard rate per hour	× £5
Efficiency variance in £	£1,500 (A)

The variance is **adverse** because more hours were worked than should have been worked.

(d) **Summary**

	£
Rate variance	2,600 (F)
Efficiency variance	1,500 (A)
Total variance	1,100 (F)

Idle time variance

3.4   A company may operate a costing system in which any **idle time** is recorded. Idle time may be caused by machine breakdowns or not having work to give to employees, perhaps because of bottlenecks in production or a shortage of orders from customers. When idle time occurs, the labour force is still paid wages for time at work, but no actual work is done. Time paid for without any work being done is unproductive and therefore inefficient. In variance analysis, **idle time is always an adverse efficiency variance**.

3.5   When idle time is recorded separately, it is helpful to provide control information which identifies the cost of idle time separately, and in variance analysis, there will be an idle time variance **as a separate part of the total labour efficiency variance**. The remaining efficiency variance will then relate only to the productivity of the labour force during the hours spent **actively working**.

3.6   EXAMPLE: LABOUR VARIANCES WITH IDLE TIME

Refer to the standard cost data in Paragraph 3.2. During period 5, 1,500 units of product X were made and the cost of grade Z labour was £17,500 for 3,080 hours. During the period, however, there as a shortage of customer orders and 100 hours were recorded as idle time.

Required

Calculate the following variances.

(a)   The direct labour total variance
(b)   The direct labour rate variance
(c)   The idle time variance
(d)   The direct labour efficiency variance

3.7   SOLUTION

(a)   **The direct labour total variance**

	£
1,500 units of product X should have cost (× £10)	15,000
but did cost	17,500
Direct labour total variance	2,500 (A)

Actual cost is greater than standard cost. The variance is therefore **adverse**.

(b)   **The direct labour rate variance**

The rate variance is a comparison of what the hours paid should have cost and what they did cost.

	£
3,080 hours of grade Z labour should have cost (× £5)	15,400
but did cost	17,500
Direct labour rate variance	2,100 (A)

Actual cost is greater than standard cost. The variance is therefore **adverse**.

(c)   **The idle time variance**

The idle time variance is the hours of idle time, valued at the standard rate per hour.

Idle time variance = 100 hours (A) × £5 = £500 (A)

Idle time is **always** an adverse variance.

(d) **The direct labour efficiency variance**

The efficiency variance considers the hours actively worked (the difference between hours paid for and idle time hours). In our example, there were (3,080 – 100) = 2,980 hours when the labour force was not idle. The variance is calculated by taking the amount of output produced (1,500 units of product X) and comparing the time it should have taken to make them, with the actual time spent **actively** making them (2,980 hours). Once again, the variance in hours is valued at the **standard rate per labour hour.**

1,500 units of product X should take (× 2hrs)	3,000 hrs
but did take (3,080 – 100)	2,980 hrs
Direct labour efficiency variance in hours	20 hrs (F)
× standard rate per hour	× £5
Direct labour efficiency variance in £	£100 (F)

(e) **Summary**

	£
Direct labour rate variance	2,100 (A)
Idle time variance	500 (A)
Direct labour efficiency variance	100 (F)
Direct labour total variance	2,500 (A)

3.8 Remember that, if idle time is recorded, the actual hours used in the efficiency variance calculation are the **hours worked and not the hours paid for**.

Question 1

Growler Ltd is planning to make 100,000 units per period of product AA. Each unit of AA should require 2 hours to produce, with labour being paid £11 per hour. Attainable work hours are less than clock hours, so 250,000 hours have been budgeted in the period.

Actual data for the period was:

Units produced	120,000
Direct labour cost	£3,200,000
Clock hours	280,000

Required

Calculate the following variances.

(a) Labour rate variance
(b) Labour efficiency variance
(c) Idle time variance

Answer

The information means that clock hours have to be multiplied by $\dfrac{200,000}{250,000}$ (80%) in order to arrive at a realistic efficiency variance.

(a) **Labour rate variance**

	£'000	
280,000 hours should have cost (× £11)	3,080	
but did cost	3,200	
Labour rate variance	120	(A)

(b) **Labour efficiency variance**

120,000 units should have taken (× 2 hours)	240,000	Hrs
but did take (280,000 × 80%)	224,000	Hrs
	16,000	hrs (F)
	× £11	
Labour efficiency variance	£176,000	(F)

(c)   **Idle time variance**

280,000 × 20%

	56,000	hrs
	× £11	
	£616,000	(A)

---

4   VARIABLE PRODUCTION OVERHEAD VARIANCES

4.1   Suppose that the variable production overhead cost of product X is as follows.

2 hours at £1.50 = £3 per unit

During period 6, 400 units of product X were made. The labour force worked 820 hours, of which 60 hours were recorded as idle time. The variable overhead cost was £1,230.

Calculate the following variances.

(a)   The variable overhead total variance
(b)   The variable production overhead expenditure variance
(c)   The variable production overhead efficiency variance

4.2   Since this example relates to variable production costs, the total variance is based on actual units of production. (If the overhead had been a variable selling cost, the variance would be based on sales volumes.)

	£
400 units of product X should cost (× £3)	1,200
but did cost	1,230
Variable production overhead total variance	30 (A)

4.3   In many variance reporting systems, the variance analysis goes no further, and expenditure and efficiency variances are not calculated. However, the adverse variance of £30 may be explained as the sum of two factors.

(a)   The hourly rate of spending on variable production overheads was higher than it should have been, that is there is an **expenditure variance**.

(b)   The labour force worked inefficiently, and took longer to make the output than it should have done. This means that spending on variable production overhead was higher than it should have been, in other words there is an **efficiency (productivity) variance**. The variable production overhead efficiency variance is exactly the same, in hours, as the direct labour efficiency variance, and occurs for the same reasons.

4.4   It is usually assumed that **variable overheads are incurred during active working hours,** but are not incurred during idle time (for example the machines are not running, therefore power is not being consumed, and no direct materials are being used). This means in our example that although the labour force was paid for 820 hours, they were actively working for only 760 of those hours and so variable production overhead spending occurred during 760 hours.

4.5   (a)   **The variable production overhead expenditure variance**

This is the difference between the amount of variable production overhead that should have been incurred in the actual hours actively worked, and the actual amount of variable production overhead incurred.

	£
760 hours of variable production overhead should cost (× £1.50)	1,140
but did cost	1,230
Variable production overhead expenditure variance	90 (A)

(b) **The variable production overhead efficiency variance**

If you already know the direct labour efficiency variance, the variable production overhead efficiency variance is exactly the same in hours, but priced at the variable production overhead rate per hour. In our example, the efficiency variance would be as follows.

400 units of product X should take (× 2hrs)	800 hrs
but did take (active hours)	760 hrs
Variable production overhead efficiency variance in hours	40 hrs (F)
× standard rate per hour	× £1.50
Variable production overhead efficiency variance in £	£60 (F)

(c) **Summary**

	£
Variable production overhead expenditure variance	90 (A)
Variable production overhead efficiency variance	60 (F)
Variable production overhead total variance	30 (A)

5 FIXED PRODUCTION OVERHEAD VARIANCES

5.1 You may have noticed that the method of calculating cost variances for variable cost items is essentially the same for labour, materials and variable overheads. Fixed production overhead variances are very different. In an **absorption costing system**, they are an attempt to explain the **under- or over-absorption of fixed production overheads** in production costs.

5.2 The fixed production overhead total variance (ie the under- or over-absorbed fixed production overhead) may be broken down into two parts as usual.

- An expenditure variance
- A volume variance

5.3 The fixed production overhead volume variance sometimes causes confusion and may need more explanation. The most important point is that the **volume variance applies to fixed production overhead costs only and not to variable production overheads.**

(a) Variable production overheads incurred change with the volume of activity. Thus, if the budget is to work for 300 hours and variable production overheads are incurred and absorbed at a rate of £6 per hour, the variable production overhead budget will be £1,800. If, however, actual hours worked turn out to be only 200 hours, the variable production overhead absorbed will be £1,200, but the expected expenditure will also be £1,200, so that there will be no under- or over-absorption of variable production overhead because of volume changes.

(b) Fixed production overheads are different because the **level of expenditure does not change as the number of hours worked varies**. Thus if the budget is to work for 300 hours and fixed production overheads are budgeted to be £2,400, the fixed production overhead absorption rate will be £8 per hour. Now if actual hours worked are only 200 hours, the fixed production overhead absorbed will be £1,600, whereas expected expenditure will be unchanged at £2,400. There is an under absorption of £800 because of the volume variance of 100 hours shortfall multiplied by the absorption rate of £8 per hour.

5.4　You will find it easier to calculate and understand fixed production overhead variances if you keep in mind the whole time the fact that **you are trying to explain the reasons for any under- or over-absorbed fixed production overhead**. Remember that the absorption rate is calculated as follows.

$$\textbf{Overhead absorption rate} = \frac{\text{budgeted fixed production overhead}}{\text{budgeted level of activity}}$$

5.5　If either the numerator or the denominator or both in the absorption rate calculation are incorrect then we will have under- or over-absorbed production overhead.

(a)　The fixed production overhead **expenditure variance** measures the under or over absorption caused by the actual **production overhead expenditure** being different from budget, that is the numerator being incorrect.

(b)　The fixed production overhead **volume variance** measures the under or over absorption caused by the **actual production or hours of activity** being different from the budgeted production or budgeted number of hours used in calculating the absorption rate.

How to calculate the variances

5.6　(a)　**Fixed production overhead total variance**

This is the difference between fixed production overhead incurred and fixed production overhead absorbed. In other words, it is the under- or over-absorbed fixed production overhead.

(b)　**Fixed production overhead expenditure variance**

This is the difference between the budgeted fixed production overhead expenditure and actual fixed production overhead expenditure.

(c)　**Fixed production overhead volume variance**

This is the difference between actual and budgeted production/volume multiplied by the standard absorption rate per **unit**.

5.7　You should now be ready to work through an example to demonstrate these fixed overhead variances.

5.8　EXAMPLE: FIXED PRODUCTION OVERHEAD VARIANCES

1,000 units of product X are budgeted to be produced during period 7. The expected time to produce a unit of X is two hours, and the budgeted fixed production overhead is £20,000. The standard fixed production overhead cost per unit of product X will therefore be as follows.

$$2 \text{ hours at} \left(\frac{20,000}{2 \times 1,000} \right) \text{per hour (ie £10)} = \text{£20 per unit}$$

Actual fixed production overhead expenditure in period 7 turns out to be £20,450. The labour force manages to produce 1,100 units of product X in 2,200 hours of work.

Required

Calculate the following variances.

(a) The fixed production overhead total variance
(b) The fixed production overhead expenditure variance
(c) The fixed production overhead volume variance

5.9 SOLUTION

(a) **Fixed production overhead total variance**

	£
Fixed production overhead incurred	20,450
Fixed production overhead absorbed (1,100 units × £20 per unit)	22,000
Fixed production overhead total variance	1,550 (F)

This gives us the total under-/over-absorbed overhead.

The variance is **favourable** because more overheads were absorbed than budgeted.

(b) **Fixed production overhead expenditure variance**

	£
Budgeted fixed production overhead expenditure	20,000
Actual fixed production overhead expenditure	20,450
Fixed production overhead expenditure variance	450 (A)

The variance is **adverse** because actual expenditure was greater than budgeted expenditure.

(c) **Fixed production overhead volume variance**

The production volume achieved was greater than expected. The fixed overhead volume variance measures the difference at the standard rate.

	£
Actual production at standard rate (1,100 × £20 per unit)	22,000
Budgeted production at standard rate (1,000 × £20 per unit)	20,000
Fixed production overhead volume variance	2,000 (F)

The variance is **favourable** because output was greater than expected, leading to a potential over absorption of fixed overhead.

5.10 Do not worry if you find fixed production overhead variances more difficult to grasp than the other variances we have covered. Most students do. Read over this section again and then try the following practice questions.

The following information relates to questions 2, 3 and 4

Barbados Ltd has prepared the following standard cost information for one unit of Product Zeta.

Direct materials	4kg @ £10/kg	£40.00
Direct labour	2 hours @ £4/hour	£8.00
Fixed overheads	3 hours @ £2.50	£7.50

The fixed overheads are based on a budgeted expenditure of £75,000 and budgeted activity of 30,000 hours.

Actual results for the period were recorded as follows.

Production	9,000 units
Materials – 33,600 kg	£336,000
Labour – 16,500 hours	£68,500
Fixed overheads	£320,000

Question 2

The direct material price and usage variances are:

	Material price £	Material usage £
A	-	24,000 (F)
B	-	24,000 (A)
C	24,000 (F)	-
D	24,000 (A)	-

Answer

Material price variance

	£
33,600 kg should have cost (× £10/kg)	336,000
and did cost	336,000
	-

Material usage variance

9,000 units should have used (× 4kg)	36,000 kg
but did use	33,600 kg
	2,400 kg (F)
× standard cost per kg	× £10
	24,000 (F)

The correct answer is therefore A.

Question 3

The direct labour rate and efficiency variances are:

	Labour rate £	Labour efficiency £
A	6,000 (F)	2,500 (A)
B	6,000 (A)	2,500 (F)
C	2,500 (A)	6,000 (F)
D	2,500 (F)	6,000 (A)

Answer

Direct labour rate variance

	£
16,500 hrs should have cost (× £4)	66,000
but did cost	68,500
	2,500 (A)

Direct labour efficiency variance

9,000 units should have taken (× 2 hrs)	18,000 hrs
but did take	16,500 hrs
	1,500 (F)
× standard rate per hour (× £4)	× £4
	6,000 (F)

The correct answer is therefore C.

Question 4

The total fixed production overhead variance is:

A   £5,000 (A)
B   £5,000 (F)
C   £2,500 (A)
D   £2,500 (F)

Answer

	£
Fixed production overhead absorbed (£7.50 × 9,000)	67,500
Fixed production overhead incurred	70,000
	2,500 (A)

The correct answer is therefore C.

Question 5

Brain Ltd produces and sells one product only, the Blob, the standard cost for one unit being as follows.

	£
Direct material A - 10 kilograms at £20 per kg	200
Direct wages – 5 litres at £6 per hour	30
Fixed production overhead	50
Total standard cost	280

The fixed overhead included in the standard cost is based on an expected monthly output of 900 units.

During April 20X3 the actual results were as follows.

Production	800 units
Material A	7,800 kg used, costing £159,900
Direct wages	4,200 hours worked for £24,150
Fixed production overhead	£47,000

Required

(a)   Calculate material price and usage variances.
(b)   Calculate labour rate and efficiency variances.
(c)   Calculate fixed production overhead expenditure and volume variances

Answer

(a)   **Material price variance**

	£
7,800 kgs should have cost (× £20)	156,000
but did cost	159,900
Price variance	3,900 (A)

Material usage variance

800 units should have used (× 10 kgs)	8,000 kgs
but did use	7,800 kgs
Usage variance in kgs	200 kgs (F)
× standard cost per kilogram	× £20
Usage variance in £	£4,000 (F)

(b)   **Labour rate variance**

	£
4,200 hours should have cost (× £6)	25,200
but did cost	24,150
Rate variance	1,050 (F)

Labour efficiency variance

800 units should have taken (× 5 hrs)	4,000 hrs
but did take	4,200 hrs
Efficiency variance in hours	200 hrs (A)
× standard rate per hour	× £6
Efficiency variance in £	£1,200 (A)

(c) **Fixed overhead expenditure variance**

	£
Budgeted expenditure (£50 × 900)	45,000
Actual expenditure	47,000
Expenditure variance	2,000 (A)

Fixed overhead volume variance

	£
Budgeted production at standard rate (900 × £50)	45,000
Actual production at standard rate (800 × £50)	40,000
Volume variance	5,000 (A)

6 THE REASONS FOR COST VARIANCES

6.1 There are many possible reasons for cost variances arising, as you will see from the following list of possible causes.

Exam focus point

This is not an exhaustive list and in an examination question you should review the information given and use your imagination and common sense to suggest possible reasons for variances.

Variance	Favourable	Adverse
(a) Material price	Unforeseen discounts received More care taken in purchasing Change in material standard	Price increase Careless purchasing Change in material standard
(b) Material usage	Material used of higher quality than standard More effective use made of material Errors in allocating material to jobs	Defective material Excessive waste Theft Stricter quality control Errors in allocating material to jobs
(c) Labour rate	Use of apprentices or other workers at a rate of pay lower than standard	Wage rate increase Use of higher grade labour
(d) Idle time	**The idle time variance is always adverse.**	Machine breakdown Non-availability of material Illness or injury to worker
(e) Labour efficiency	Output produced more quickly than expected because of work motivation, better quality of equipment or materials, or better methods Errors in allocating time to jobs	Lost time in excess of standard allowed Output lower than standard set because of deliberate restriction, lack of training, or sub-standard material used Errors in allocating time to jobs

Variance	Favourable	Adverse
(f) Overhead expenditure	Savings in costs incurred More economical use of services	Increase in cost of services used Excessive use of services Change in type of services used
(g) Overhead volume	Production or level of activity greater than budgeted	Production or level of activity less than budgeted

7 THE SIGNIFICANCE OF COST VARIANCES

7.1 Once variances have been calculated, management have to decide whether or not to investigate their causes. It would be extremely time consuming and expensive to investigate every variance therefore managers have to decide which variances are worthy of investigation.

7.2 There are a number of factors which can be taken into account when deciding whether or not a variance should be investigated.

(a) **Materiality.** A standard cost is really only an **average** expected cost and is not a rigid specification. Small variations either side of this average are therefore bound to occur. The problem is to decide whether a variation from standard should be considered **significant** and worthy of investigation. **Tolerance limits** can be set and only variances which exceed such limits would require investigating.

(b) **Controllability.** Some types of variance may not be controllable even once their cause is discovered. For example, if there is a general worldwide increase in the price of a raw material there is nothing that can be done internally to control the effect of this. If a central decision is made to award all employees a 10% increase in salary, staff costs in division A will increase by this amount and the variance is not controllable by division A's manager. Uncontrollable variances call for a change in the plan, not an investigation into the past.

(c) **The type of standard being used.**

(i) The efficiency variance reported in any control period, whether for materials or labour, will depend on the **efficiency level** set. If, for example, an **ideal standard** is used, variances will always be **adverse**.

(ii) A similar problem arises if **average price levels** are used as standards. If inflation exists, favourable price variances are likely to be reported at the beginning of a period, to be offset by adverse price variances later in the period as inflation pushes prices up.

(d) **Interdependence between variances** . Quite possibly, individual variances should not be looked at in isolation. One variance might be inter-related with another, and much of it might have occurred only because the other, inter-related, variance occurred too. We will investigate this issue further in a moment.

(e) **Costs of investigation.** The costs of an investigation should be weighed against the benefits of correcting the cause of a variance.

Interdependence between variances

7.3 When two variances are interdependent (interrelated) one will usually be adverse and the other one favourable. Here are some examples.

Materials price and usage

7.4   It may be decided to purchase cheaper materials for a job in order to obtain a favourable price variance, possibly with the consequence that materials wastage is higher and an adverse usage variance occurs. If the cheaper materials are more difficult to handle, there might be some adverse labour efficiency variance too.

7.5   If a decision is made to purchase more expensive materials, which perhaps have a longer service life, the price variance will be adverse but the usage variance might be favourable.

Labour rate and efficiency

7.6   If employees in a workforce are paid higher rates for experience and skill, using a highly skilled team to do some work would incur an adverse rate variance, but should also obtain a favourable efficiency variance. In contrast, a favourable rate variance might indicate a larger-than-expected proportion of inexperienced workers in the workforce, which could result in an adverse labour efficiency variance, and perhaps poor materials handling and high rates of rejects too (adverse materials usage variance).

Chapter roundup

- **Variances** measure the difference between **actual results** and **expected results**.

- The direct material total variance can be subdivided into the **direct material price** variance and the **direct material usage** variance.

- Direct material price variances are usually extracted at the time of **receipt** of the materials, rather than at the time of usage.

- The direct labour total variance can be subdivided into the **direct labour rate** variance and the **direct labour efficiency** variance.

- If **idle time** arises, it is usual to calculate a separate idle time variance, and to base the calculation of the efficiency variance on **active hours** (when labour actually worked) only. It is always an **adverse** variance.

- The variable production overhead total variance can be subdivided into the variable production overhead **expenditure** variance and the variable production overhead **efficiency** variance **(based on active hours).**

- The fixed production overhead total variance can be subdivided into an **expenditure** variance and a **volume** variance.

- Ensure that you can provide possible **reasons** for cost variances.

- Materiality, controllability, the type of standard being used, the interdependence of variances and the cost of an investigation should be taken into account when deciding whether to investigate reported variances.

Quick quiz

1   Subdivide the following variances.

   (a)   Direct materials cost variance

   (b)   Direct labour cost variance

   (c)   Variable production overhead variance

2   What are the two main advantages in calculating the material price variance at the time of receipt of materials?

3   Idle time variances are always adverse.

True   ☐

False ☐

4   Adverse material usage variances might occur for the following reasons.

I   Defective material
II   Excessive waste
III   Theft
IV   Unforeseen discounts received

A   I
B   I and II
C   I, II and III
D   I, II, III and IV

5   List the factors which should be taken into account when deciding whether or not a variance should be investigated.

Answers to quick quiz

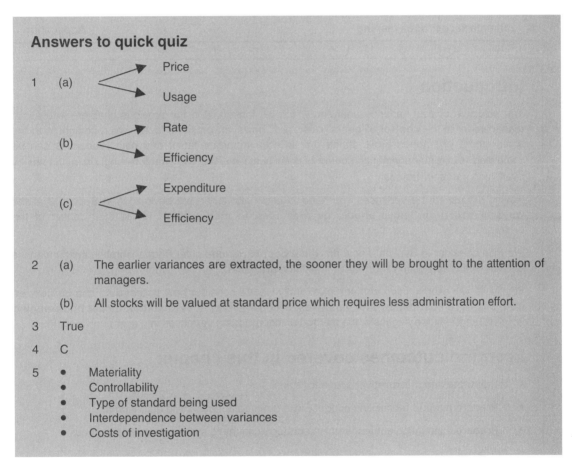

1   (a)   Price / Usage

    (b)   Rate / Efficiency

    (c)   Expenditure / Efficiency

2   (a)   The earlier variances are extracted, the sooner they will be brought to the attention of managers.

    (b)   All stocks will be valued at standard price which requires less administration effort.

3   True

4   C

5   •   Materiality
    •   Controllability
    •   Type of standard being used
    •   Interdependence between variances
    •   Costs of investigation

Now try the questions below from the Exam Question Bank

Questions to try	Level	Marks	Time
Q20	Examination	15	27 mins
Q21	Examination	25	45 mins

Chapter 17

FURTHER VARIANCE ANALYSIS

Topic list	Syllabus reference	Ability required
1 Sales variances	(ii)	Application, analysis
2 Operating statements	(ii)	Application
3 Variances in a standard marginal costing system	(ii)	Application, analysis
4 Deriving actual data from standard cost details and variances	(ii)	Application
5 Standard cost bookkeeping	(ii)	Application

Introduction

The objective of cost variance analysis, which we looked at in the previous chapter, is to assist management in the **control of costs**. Costs are, however, only one factor which contribute to the achievement of planned profit. **Sales** are another important factor and sales variances can be calculated to aid management's control of their business. We will therefore begin this chapter by examining **sales variances**.

Having discussed the variances you need to know about, we will be looking in Section 2 at the **ways in which variances should be presented to management** to aid their control of the organisation.

We then consider in Section 3 how **marginal cost variances** differ from absorption cost variances and how marginal costing information should be presented.

Finally we will examine two further topics: firstly we will consider **how actual data can be derived from standard cost details and variances;** secondly we will look at **standard cost bookkeeping** which is, as the name suggests, the method of incorporating variances into cost bookkeeping.

Learning outcomes covered in this chapter

- **Calculate** and **interpret** variances for sales

- **Prepare** a report reconciling budget gross profit/contribution with actual profit

- **Prepare** accounting entries for an integrated accounting system using standard costs

Syllabus content covered in this chapter

- Variances: sales: total sales margin variance

- Accounting entries for an integrated accounting system

1 SALES VARIANCES

Selling price variance

1.1 The **selling price variance** is a measure of the effect on expected profit of a different selling price to standard selling price. It is calculated as the **difference between what the sales revenue should have been for the actual quantity sold, and what it was.**

1.2 Suppose that the standard selling price of product X is £15. Actual sales in 20X3 were 2,000 units at £15.30 per unit. The selling price variance is calculated as follows.

	£
Sales revenue from 2,000 units should have been (× £15)	30,000
but was (× £15.30)	30,600
Selling price variance	600 (F)

The variance is **favourable** because the price was higher than expected.

Sales volume profit variance

1.3 The **sales volume profit variance** is the difference between the actual units sold and the budgeted quantity, valued at the standard profit per unit. In other words, it measures **the increase or decrease in standard profit as a result of the sales volume being higher or lower than budgeted.**

1.4 Suppose that a company budgets to sell 8,000 units of product J for £12 per unit. The standard full cost per unit is £7. Actual sales were 7,700 units, at £12.50 per unit.

The **sales volume profit variance** is calculated as follows.

Budgeted sales volume	8,000 units
Actual sales volume	7,700 units
Sales volume variance in units	300 units (A)
× standard profit per unit (£(12–7))	× £5
Sales volume variance	£1,500 (A)

The variance is **adverse** because actual sales were less than budgeted.

Question 1

Jasper Ltd has the following budget and actual figures for 20X4.

	Budget	Actual
Sales units	600	620
Selling price per unit	£30	£29

Standard full cost of production = £28 per unit.

Required

Calculate the selling price variance and the sales volume profit variance.

BPP PUBLISHING

Answer

Sales revenue for 620 units should have been (× £30)	18,600
but was (× £29)	17,980
Selling price variance	620 (A)
Budgeted sales volume	600 units
Actual sales volume	620 units
Sales volume variance in units	20 units (F)
× standard profit per unit (£(30 – 28))	× £2
Sales volume profit variance	£40 (F)

The significance of sales variances

1.5 The possible interdependence between sales price and sales volume variances should be obvious to you. A reduction in the sales price might stimulate bigger sales demand, so that an adverse sales price variance might be counterbalanced by a favourable sales volume variance. Similarly, a price rise would give a favourable price variance, but possibly at the cost of a fall in demand and an adverse sales volume variance.

1.6 It is therefore important in analysing an unfavourable sales variance that the overall consequence should be considered, that is, has there been a counterbalancing favourable variance as a direct result of the unfavourable one?

2 OPERATING STATEMENTS

2.1 So far, we have considered how variances are calculated without considering how they combine to reconcile the difference between budgeted profit and actual profit during a period. This reconciliation is usually presented as a report to senior management at the end of each control period. The report is called an operating statement or statement of variances.

> **KEY TERM**
>
> An **operating statement** is 'A regular report for management of actual costs, and revenues, as appropriate. Usually compares actual with budget and shows variances'.
>
> CIMA *Official Terminology*

2.2 An extensive example will now be introduced, both to revise the variance calculations already described, and also to show how to combine them into an operating statement.

2.3 EXAMPLE: VARIANCES AND OPERATING STATEMENTS

Sydney Ltd manufactures one product, and the entire product is sold as soon as it is produced. There are no opening or closing stocks and work in progress is negligible. The company operates a standard costing system and analysis of variances is made every month. The standard cost card for the product, a boomerang, is as follows.

STANDARD COST CARD - BOOMERANG

		£
Direct materials	0.5 kilos at £4 per kilo	2.00
Direct wages	2 hours at £2.00 per hour	4.00
Variable overheads	2 hours at £0.30 per hour	0.60
Fixed overhead	2 hours at £3.70 per hour	7.40
Standard cost		14.00
Standard profit		6.00
Standing selling price		20.00

Selling and administration expenses are not included in the standard cost, and are deducted from profit as a period charge.

Budgeted output for the month of June 20X7 was 5,100 units. Actual results for June 20X7 were as follows.

Production of 4,850 units was sold for £95,600.
Materials consumed in production amounted to 2,300 kgs at a total cost of £9,800.
Labour hours paid for amounted to 8,500 hours at a cost of £16,800.
Actual operating hours amounted to 8,000 hours.
Variable overheads amounted to £2,600.
Fixed overheads amounted to £42,300.
Selling and administration expenses amounted to £18,000.

Required

Calculate all variances and prepare an operating statement for the month ended 30 June 20X7.

2.4 SOLUTION

(a)

	£
2,300 kg of material should cost (× £4)	9,200
but did cost	9,800
Material price variance	600 (A)

(b)

4,850 boomerangs should use (× 0.5 kgs)	2,425 kg
but did use	2,300 kg
Material usage variance in kgs	125 kg (F)
× standard cost per kg	× £4
Material usage variance in £	£ 500 (F)

(c)

	£
8,500 hours of labour should cost (× £2)	17,000
but did cost	16,800
Labour rate variance	200 (F)

(d)

4,850 boomerangs should take (× 2 hrs)	9,700 hrs
but did take (active hours)	8,000 hrs
Labour efficiency variance in hours	1,700 hrs (F)
× standard cost per hour	× £2
Labour efficiency variance in £	£3,400 (F)

(e) Idle time variance 500 hours (A) × £2   £1,000 (A)

(f)

	£
8,000 hours incurring variable o/hd expenditure should cost (× £0.30)	2,400
but did cost	2,600
Variable overhead expenditure variance	200 (A)

(g) Variable overhead efficiency variance in hours is the same as the
labour efficiency variance:

1,700 hours (F) × £0.30 per hour	£ 510 (F)

(h)

	£
Budgeted fixed overhead (5,100 units × 2 hrs × £3.70)	37,740
Actual fixed overhead	42,300
Fixed overhead expenditure variance	4,560 (A)

(i)

	£
Actual production at standard rate (4,850 units × £7.40)	35,890
Budgeted production at standard rate (5,100 units × £7.40)	37,740
Fixed overhead volume variance	1,850 (A)

(j)

	£
Revenue from 4,850 boomerangs should be (× £20)	97,000
but was	95,600
Selling price variance	1,400 (A)

(k)

Budgeted sales volume	5,100 units
Actual sales volume	4,850 units
Sales volume profit variance in units	250 units
× standard profit per unit	× £6 (A)
Sales volume profit variance in £	£1,500 (A)

2.5 There are several ways in which an operating statement may be presented. Perhaps the most common format is one which **reconciles budgeted profit to actual profit**. In this example, sales and administration costs will be introduced at the end of the statement, so that we shall begin with 'budgeted profit before sales and administration costs'.

2.6 Sales variances are reported first, and the total of the budgeted profit and the two sales variances results in a figure for 'actual sales minus the standard cost of sales'. The cost variances are then reported, and an actual profit (before sales and administration costs) calculated. Sales and administration costs are then deducted to reach the actual profit for June 20X7.

SYDNEY LTD - OPERATING STATEMENT JUNE 20X7

		£	£
Budgeted profit before sales and administration costs			30,600
Sales variances:	price	1,400 (A)	
	volume	1,500 (A)	
			2,900 (A)
Actual sales minus the standard cost of sales			27,700

Cost variances	(F)	(A)	
	£	£	
Material price		600	
Material usage	500		
Labour rate	200		
Labour efficiency	3,400		
Labour idle time		1,000	
Variable overhead expenditure		200	
Variable overhead efficiency	510		
Fixed overhead expenditure		4,560	
Fixed overhead volume		1,850	
	4,610	8,210	3,600 (A)
Actual profit before sales and administration costs			24,100
Sales and administration costs			18,000
Actual profit, June 20X7			6,100

Check	£	£
Sales		95,600
Materials	9,800	
Labour	16,800	
Variable overhead	2,600	
Fixed overhead	42,300	
Sales and administration	18,000	
		89,500
Actual profit		6,100

3 VARIANCES IN A STANDARD MARGINAL COSTING SYSTEM

3.1 In all of the examples we have worked through so far, a system of standard absorption costing has been in operation. If an organisation uses **standard marginal costing** instead of standard absorption costing, there will be two differences in the way the variances are calculated.

(a) In marginal costing, fixed costs are not absorbed into product costs and so there are no fixed cost variances to explain any under or over absorption of overheads. There will, therefore, be **no fixed overhead volume variance**. There will be a fixed overhead expenditure variance which is calculated in exactly the same way as for absorption costing systems.

(b) The **sales volume variance** will be valued at **standard contribution margin** (sales price per unit minus variable costs of sale per unit), **not** standard **profit** margin.

Preparing a marginal costing operating statement

3.2 Returning once again to the example of Sydney Ltd, the variances in a system of standard marginal costing would be as follows.

(a) There is **no fixed overhead volume variance**.

(b) The standard contribution per unit of boomerang is £(20 – 6.60) = £13.40, therefore the **sales volume contribution variance** of 250 units (A) is valued at (× £13.40) = £3,350 (A).

3.3 The other variances are unchanged. However, this operating statement differs from an absorption costing operating statement in the following ways.

(a) It begins with the budgeted **contribution** (£30,600 + budgeted fixed production costs £37,740 = £68,340).

(b) The subtotal before the analysis of cost variances is actual sales (£95,600) less the standard **variable** cost of sales (£4,850 × £6.60) = £63,590.

(c) **Actual contribution** is highlighted in the statement.

(d) Budgeted fixed production overhead is adjusted by the fixed overhead expenditure variance to show the **actual** fixed production overhead expenditure.

3.4 Therefore a marginal costing operating statement might look like this.

SYDNEY LTD - OPERATING STATEMENT JUNE 20X7

	£	£	£
Budgeted contribution			68,340
Sales variances: volume		3,350 (A)	
price		1,400 (A)	
			4,750 (A)
Actual sales minus the standard variable cost of sales			63,590

	(F)	(A)	
	£	£	
Variable cost variances			
Material price		600	
Material usage	500		
Labour rate	200		
Labour efficiency	3,400		
Labour idle time		1,000	
Variable overhead expenditure		200	
Variable overhead efficiency	510		
	4,610	1,800	

			£
			2,810 (F)
Actual contribution			66,400
Budgeted fixed production overhead		37,740	
Expenditure variance		4,560 (A)	
Actual fixed production overhead			42,300
Actual profit before sales and administration costs			24,100
Sales and administration costs			18,000
Actual profit			6,100

3.5 Notice that the actual profit is the same as the profit calculated by standard absorption costing because there were no changes in stock levels. Absorption costing and marginal costing do not always produce an identical profit figure.

Question 2

Piglet Ltd, a manufacturing firm, operates a standard marginal costing system. It makes a single product, PIG, using a single raw material LET.

Standard costs relating to PIG have been calculated as follows.

Standard cost schedule – PIG

	Per unit £
Direct material, LET, 100 kg at £5 per kg	500
Direct labour, 10 hours at £8 per hour	80
Variable production overhead, 10 hours at £2 per hour	20
	600

The standard selling price of a PIG is £900 and Piglet Ltd produce 1,020 units a month.

During December 20X0, 1,000 units of PIG were produced. Relevant details of this production are as follows.

Direct material LET

90,000 kgs costing £720,000 were bought and used.

Direct labour

8,200 hours were worked during the month and total wages were £63,000.

Variable production overhead

The actual cost for the month was £25,000.

Stocks of the direct material LET are valued at the standard price of £5 per kg.

Each PIG was sold for £975.

Required

Calculate the following for the month of December 20X0.

(a) Variable production cost variance
(b) Direct labour cost variance, analysed into rate and efficiency variances
(c) Direct material cost variance, analysed into price and usage variances
(d) Variable production overhead variance, analysed into expenditure and efficiency variances
(e) Selling price variance
(f) Sales volume contribution variance

Answer

(a) This is simply a 'total' variance.

	£
1,000 units should have cost (× £600)	600,000
but did cost (see working)	808,000
Variable production cost variance	208,000 (A)

(b) **Direct labour cost variances**

	£
8,200 hours should cost (× £8)	65,600
but did cost	63,000
Direct labour rate variance	2,600 (F)

1,000 units should take (× 10 hours)	10,000 hrs
but did take	8,200 hrs
Direct labour efficiency variance in hrs	1,800 hrs (F)
× standard rate per hour	× £8
Direct labour efficiency variance in £	£14,400 (F)

Summary	£
Rate	2,600 (F)
Efficiency	14,400 (F)
Total	17,000 (F)

(c) **Direct material cost variances**

	£
90,000 kg should cost (× £5)	450,000
but did cost	720,000
Direct material price variance	270,000 (A)

1,000 units should use (× 100 kg)	100,000 kg
but did use	90,000 kg
Direct material usage variance in kgs	10,000 kg (F)
× standard cost per kg	× £5
Direct material usage variance in £	£50,000 (F)

Summary

	£
Price	270,000 (A)
Usage	50,000 (F)
Total	220,000 (A)

(d) **Variable production overhead variances**

	£
8,200 hours incurring o/hd should cost (× £2)	16,400
but did cost	25,000
Variable production overhead expenditure variance	8,600 (A)

Efficiency variance in hrs (from (b))	1,800 hrs (F)
× standard rate per hour	× £2
Variable production overhead efficiency variance	£3,600 (F)

Summary

	£
Expenditure	8,600 (A)
Efficiency	3,600 (F)
Total	5,000 (A)

(e) **Selling price variance**

	£
Revenue from 1,000 units should have been (× £900)	900,000
but was (× £975)	975,000
Selling price variance	75,000 (F)

(f) **Sales volume contribution variance**

Budgeted sales	1,020 units
Actual sales	1,000 units
Sales volume variance in units	20 units (A)
× standard contribution margin (£(900 − 600))	× £300
Sales volume contribution variance in £	£6,000 (A)

Workings

	£
Direct material	720,000
Total wages	63,000
Variable production overhead	25,000
	808,000

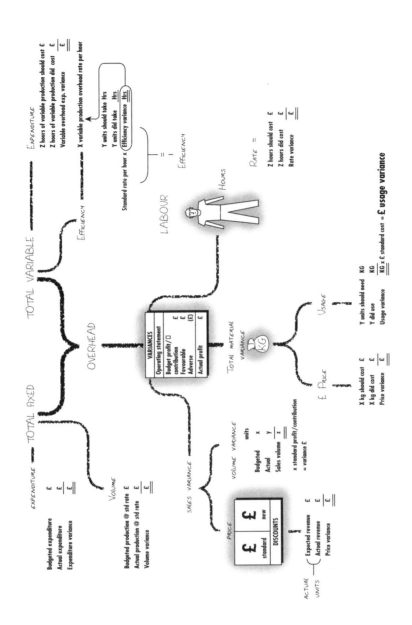

4 DERIVING ACTUAL DATA FROM STANDARD COST DETAILS AND VARIANCES

4.1 EXAMPLE: WORKING BACKWARDS

The standard cost card for the trough, one of the products made by Pig Ltd, is as follows.

	£
Direct material 16 kgs × £6 per kg	96
Direct labour 6 hours × £12 per hour	72
Fixed production overhead 6 hours × £14 per hour	84
	252

Pig Ltd reported the following variances in control period 13 in relation to the trough.

Direct material price: £18,840 favourable
Direct material usage: £480 adverse
Direct labour rate: £10,598 adverse
Direct labour efficiency: £8,478 favourable
Fixed production overhead expenditure: £14,192 adverse
Fixed production overhead volume: £11,592 favourable

Actual fixed production overhead cost £200,000 and direct wages, £171,320. Pig Ltd paid £5.50 for each kg of direct material. There was no opening or closing stocks of the material.

Required

Calculate the following.

(a) Budgeted output
(b) Actual output
(c) Actual hours worked
(d) Average actual wage rate per hour
(e) Actual number of kilograms purchased and used

4.2 SOLUTION

(a) Let budgeted output = q

Fixed production overhead expenditure variance = budgeted overhead – actual overhead = £(84q – 200,000) = £14,192 (A)

$$\therefore 84q - 200,000 = -14,192$$
$$84q = -14,192 + 200,000$$
$$q = 185,808 \div 84$$
$$\therefore q = 2,212 \text{ units}$$

(b)

	£
Total direct wages cost	171,320
Adjust for variances:	
labour rate	(10,598)
labour efficiency	8,478
Standard direct wages cost	169,200

$$\therefore \text{Actual output} = \text{Total standard cost} \div \text{unit standard cost}$$
$$= £169,200 \div £72$$
$$= 2,350 \text{ units}$$

(c)

	£
Total direct wages cost	171,320.0
Less rate variance	(10,598.0)
Standard rate for actual hours	160,722.0
÷ standard rate per hour	÷ £12.0
Actual hours worked	13,393.5 hrs

(d) Average actual wage rate per hour = actual wages/actual hours = £171,320/13,393.5 = £12.79 per hour.

(e) Number of kgs purchased and used = x

	£
x kgs should have cost (× £6)	6.0x
but did cost (× £5.50)	5.5x
Direct material price variance	0.5x

∴ £0.5x = £18,840

∴   x = 37,680 kgs

Question 3

XYZ Ltd uses standard costing. The following data relates to labour grade II.

Actual hours worked	10,400 hours
Standard allowance for actual production	8,320 hours
Standard rate per hour	£5
Rate variance (adverse)	£416

What was the actual rate of pay per hour?

A   £4.95
B   £4.96
C   £5.04
D   £5.05

Answer

Rate variance per hour worked = $\dfrac{£416}{10,400}$ = £0.04 (A)

Actual rate per hour = £(5.00 + 0.04) = £5.04.

The correct answer is C.

You should have been able to eliminate options A and B because they are both below the standard rate per hour. If the rate variance is adverse then the actual rate must be above standard.

Option D is incorrect because it results from basing the calculations on standard hours rather than actual hours.

Question 4

The standard material content of one unit of product A is 10kgs of material X which should cost £10 per kilogram. In June 20X4, 5,750 units of product A were produced and there was an adverse material usage variance of £1,500.

Required

Calculate the quantity of material X used in June 20X4.

Answer

Let the quantity of material X used = Y

5,750 units should have used (× 10kgs)	57,500 kgs
but did use	− Y kgs
Usage variance in kgs	(Y − 57,500) kgs
× standard price per kg	× £10
Usage variance in £	− £1,500 (A)

∴ 10(Y − 57,500) = 1,500
   Y − 57,500   = 150
∴ Y   = 57,650 kgs

---

5 STANDARD COST BOOKKEEPING

5.1 Now that you know how to calculate variances you need to be able to incorporate them into a cost bookkeeping system. We looked at cost bookkeeping in detail in Chapter 7. Glance back at the chapter if you need to remind yourself of the main principles. The syllabus for **Management Accounting Fundamentals** states that you need to be able to prepare accounting entries for an integrated accounting system using standard costs.

5.2 Don't be put off by the sound of standard cost bookkeeping. It is no more complicated than the bookkeeping you have looked at so far. It is simply an extension of the basic system and is used when an organisation runs a standard costing system.

5.3 The general principle in standard cost bookkeeping is that cost variances should be recorded as **early as possible**. They are recorded in the relevant account **where they arise** and the appropriate double entry is taken to a variance account. Examples are as follows.

(a) **Material price variances** are apparent when materials are purchased, and they are therefore recorded in the **stores account**. If a price variance is adverse, we should credit the stores account and debit a variance account with the amount of the variance.

(b) **Material usage variances** do not occur until output is actually produced in the factory, and they are therefore recorded in the **work in progress account**. If a usage variance is favourable, we should debit the work in progress account and credit a variance account with the value of the variance.

5.4 There are some possible variations in accounting method between one organisation's system and others, especially in the method of recording overhead variances, but the following are the basic principles.

(a) The **material price variance** is recorded in the **stores control account**.

(b) The **labour rate variance** is recorded in the **wages control account**.

(c) The following variances are recorded in the **work in progress account**.

- Material usage variance
- Idle time variance
- Labour efficiency variance
- Variable overhead efficiency variance

(d) The **production overhead expenditure variance** will be recorded in the **production overhead control account**.

(e) The **production overhead volume variance** may be recorded in the **fixed production overhead account**. (*Note*. Alternatively, you may find the volume variance recorded in the **work in progress account**.)

(f) **Sales variances do not appear in the books of account.** Sales are recorded in the sales account at actual invoiced value.

(g) The balance of variances in the variance accounts at the end of a period may be **written off to the profit and loss account**.

5.5 The actual process is best demonstrated with an example. Work carefully through the one which follows, ensuring that you know how the various variances are recorded.

5.6 EXAMPLE: COST BOOKKEEPING AND VARIANCES

Zed operates an integrated accounting system and prepares its final accounts monthly. You are provided with the following information.

Balances as at 1 October

	£'000
Issued share capital	1,500
Profit and loss balance	460
Freehold buildings	1,000
Plant and machinery, at cost	500
Plant and machinery: depreciation provision	300
Motor vehicles, at cost	240
Motor vehicles: depreciation provision	80
10% debentures	240
Creditors (materials)	144
Creditors (expenses)	36
Stock - raw materials	520
Wages payable	40
Debtors	246
Bank	162
Stock - finished goods	132

Data for the month of October

Materials purchased	400,000 kgs at £4.90 per kg
Issued to production	328,000 kgs
Paid to creditors	£1,800,000
Direct wages incurred	225,000 hours at £4.20 per hour
Direct wages paid	£920,000
Production overhead incurred on credit	£1,490,000
Expense creditors paid	£1,900,000
Cash received from debtors	£4,800,000
Sales	£4,875,000
Plant and machinery purchased for cash on 1 October	£100,000
Administration and selling o/hd incurred on credit	£895,000
Production and sales	39,000 units

Additional data

Debenture interest	payable monthly
Depreciation provision	plant and machinery, 20% pa on cost
	motor vehicles, 25% pa on cost
Stocks of raw materials and finished goods	maintained at standard

The operation of motor vehicles is regarded as a cost of selling

Standard data

Direct material price	£5.00 per kg
Direct material usage	8 kgs per unit
Direct wages	£4.00 per hour
Direct labour	6 hours per unit
Production overhead	absorbed at 150% of direct wages
Gross profit	calculated at one-sixth of selling price
Budgeted output	10,000 units per week

Required

(a) Calculate the appropriate variances for October. You are not required to calculate sales variances.

(b) Show the following ledger accounts for October.

    (i)   Stores ledger control account
    (ii)   Direct wages control account
    (iii)   Production overhead control account
    (iv)   Administration and selling overhead control account
    (v)   Work in progress control account
    (vi)   Finished goods control account
    (vii)   Cost of sales control account
    (viii) Sales account
    (ix)   Variances account
    (x)   Profit and loss account

5.7 SOLUTION

(a) We will begin by determining the standard unit cost and calculating the variances.

Standard cost per unit	£
Direct materials (8 kgs × £5)	40
Direct labour (6 hrs × £4)	24
Production overhead (150% × £24)	36
	100

Direct material price variance	£'000
400,000 kgs should cost (× £5)	2,000
but did cost (400,000 × £4.90)	1,960
	40 (F)

Direct material usage variance	
39,000 units should use (× 8)	312,000 kgs
but did use	328,000 kgs
Variance in units	16,000 kgs (A)
× standard price per unit	× £5
	£80,000 (A)

Direct labour rate variance	£'000
225,000 hours should cost (× £4)	900
but did cost (225,000 × £4.20)	945
	45 (A)

Direct labour efficiency variance

39,000 units should take (× 6 hrs)		234,000 hrs
but did take		225,000 hrs
Variance in hours		9,000 hrs (F)
× standard cost per hour		× £4
		£36,000 (F)

Production overhead expenditure variance	£'000	£'000
Budgeted expenditure (10,000 × 4 wks × £36)		1,440
Actual expenditure		
Incurred on credit	1,490	
Depreciation (20% × 1/12 × £(500 + 100))	10	
		1,500
		60 (A)

Note. Operation of motor vehicles is a cost of selling and therefore not included in production overhead.

Production overhead volume variance	£'000
Actual production at standard rate (39,000 × £36)	1,404
Budgeted production at standard rate (10,000 × 4 wks × £36)	1,440
	36 (A)

(b) (i)

STORES LEDGER CONTROL ACCOUNT

	£'000		£'000
Balance b/f	520	Work in progress	
Creditors		(328,000 × £5)	1,640
(400,000 × £4.90)	1,960	Balance c/d	880
Material price variance	40		
	2,520		2,520
Balance b/d	880		

Notes

(1) Materials are issued from store at standard price.
(2) The material price variance is recorded in this account.

(ii)

DIRECT WAGES CONTROL ACCOUNT

	£'000		£'000
Bank	920	Balance b/f	40
Balance c/d	65	Work in progress	
		(225,000 hrs × £4)	900
		Labour rate variance	45
	985		985
		Balance b/d	65

Notes

(1) Labour hours are costed to production at the standard rate per hour.
(2) The labour rate variance is recorded in this account.

(iii)

PRODUCTION OVERHEAD CONTROL ACCOUNT

	£'000		£'000
Creditors	1,490	Work in progress	
Depreciation on plant		(39,000 × £36)	1,404
and machinery	10	*Production overhead*	
		expenditure variance	60
		Production overhead	
		volume variance	36
	1,500		1,500

Notes

(1) Production is charged with the standard rate for the hours actively worked.
(2) The production overhead expenditure variance is shown in this account
(3) In this example, the volume variance is shown in the overhead account.

(iv)
ADMIN AND SELLING OVERHEAD CONTROL ACCOUNT

	£'000		£'000
Creditors	895	Profit and loss	900
Motor vehicle depreciation	5		
	900		900

(v)
WORK IN PROGRESS CONTROL ACCOUNT

	£'000		£'000
Stores ledger	1,640	Finished goods	
Direct wages	900	(39,000 × £100)	3,900
Production overhead	1,404	*Direct material usage*	
Direct labour		*variance*	80
efficiency variance	36		
	3,980		3,980

Notes

(1) Output is valued at standard production cost.
(2) The efficiency variances appear in this account.

(vi)
FINISHED GOODS CONTROL ACCOUNT

	£'000		£'000
Balance b/f	132	Cost of sales	3,900
Work in progress	3,900	Balance c/d	132
	4,032		4,032
Balance b/d	132		

(vii)
COST OF SALES CONTROL ACCOUNT

	£'000		£'000
Finished goods	3,900	Profit and loss	3,900

(viii)
SALES ACCOUNT

	£'000		£'000
Profit and loss	4,875	Bank/debtors	4,875

(ix)
VARIANCES ACCOUNT

	£'000		£'000
Wages (labour rate)	45	Stores (material price)	40
Production (expenditure)	60	WIP (labour efficiency)	36
Production (volume)	36	Profit and loss account	145
WIP (material usage)	80		
	221		221

Exam focus point

The variances are recorded in a variances account as part of the double entry system. The balance on the account at the end of the period is written off to the profit and loss account. Sometimes a separate account is used for each variance, but the double entry principles would be the same. In an examination you should prepare a **separate account for each variance** unless you are instructed otherwise.

(x)   PROFIT AND LOSS ACCOUNT

	£'000		£'000
Cost of sales	3,900	Sales	4,875
Administration and selling	900	Loss for month	72
Debenture interest	2		
Variances	145		
	4,947		4,947

5.8 EXAMPLE: JOURNAL ENTRIES

Suppose that 4 kgs of material A are required to make one unit of product TS, each kilogram costing £10. It takes direct labour 5 hours to make one unit of product TS. The labour force is paid £4.50 per hour.

During the period the following results were recorded.

Material A: 8,200 kgs purchased on credit *	£95,000
Material A: kgs issued to production*	8,200 kgs
Units of product TS produced*	1,600
Direct labour hours worked*	10,000
Cost of direct labour*	£32,000

Required

(a) Calculate the following variances for the period.

      (i)   Material price variance
      (ii)   Material usage variance
      (iii)   Labour rate variance
      (iv)   Labour efficiency variance

(b) Prepare journal entries for the transactions marked * above, together with the variances calculated in (a).

      Note

      You should make the following assumptions.

      (i)   An integrated accounting system is maintained.
      (ii)   There are no opening or closing stocks of work in progress.

5.9 SOLUTION

(a)   £

(i)	8,200 kgs should cost (× £10)	82,000
	but did cost	95,000
	Material price variance	13,000 (A)

(ii)	1,600 units of TS should use (× 4 kgs)	6,400 kgs
	but did use	8,200 kgs
	Usage variance in kgs	1,800 kgs (A)
	× standard cost per kg	× £10
	Material usage variance	£18,000 (A)

(iii)		£
	10,000 hours should cost (× £4.50)	45,000
	but did cost	32,000
	Labour rate variance	13,000 (F)

		£	
(iv)	1,600 units of TS should take (× 5 hrs)		8,000 hrs
	but did take		10,000 hrs
	Efficiency variance in hrs		2,000 hrs (A)
	× standard rate per hour		× £4.50
	Labour efficiency variance		£9,000 (A)

(b) (i)

	£	£
Stores ledger control account (8,200 kgs × £10)	82,000	
Material price variance	13,000	
Creditors		95,000

The purchase of materials on credit

(ii)		£	£
	Work in progress control account	82,000	
	Stores ledger control account		82,000

The issue of material A to production

(iii)		£	£
	Material usage variance	18,000	
	Work in progress control account		18,000

The bookkeeping of the material A usage variance

(iv)		£	£
	Work in progress control account (10,000 hrs × £4.50)	45,000	
	Direct labour control account		32,000
	Direct labour rate variance		13,000

The charging of labour to work in progress

(v)		£	£
	Direct labour efficiency variance	9,000	
	Work in progress control account		9,000

The bookkeeping of the labour efficiency variance

(vi)		£	£
	Finished goods control account (1,600 × £62.50 (W))	100,000	
	Work in progress control account		100,000

The transfer of finished goods from work in progress

Working

Standard cost of product TS

	£
Material A (4 kgs × £10)	40.00
Direct labour (5 hrs × £4.50)	22.50
	62.50

Question 5

A company uses raw material J in production. The standard price for material J is £3 per metre. During the month 6,000 metres were purchased for £18,600, of which 5,000 metres were issued to production.

Required

Show the journal entries to record the above transactions in integrated accounts in the following separate circumstances.

(a) When raw material stock is valued at standard cost, that is the direct materials price variance is extracted on receipt.

(b) When raw materials stock is valued at actual cost, that is the direct materials price variance is extracted as the materials are used.

Answer

(a)

	£	£
Raw material stock (6,000 × £3)	18,000	
Direct material price variance	600	
Creditors		18,600
Purchase on credit of 6,000 metres of material J		
Work in progress (5,000 × £3)	15,000	
Raw material stock		15,000
Issue to production of 5,000 metres of J		

(b)

	£	£
Raw material stock	18,600	
Creditors		18,600
Purchase on credit of 6,000 metres of material J		
Work in progress	15,000	
Direct material price variance (5,000 × £(3.10 – 3.00))	500	
Raw material stock		15,500
Issue to production of 5,000 metres of material J		

Note that in both cases the material is charged to work in progress at standard price. In (b) the price variance is extracted only on the material which has been used up, the stock being valued at actual cost.

Question 6

A firm uses standard costing and an integrated accounting system. The double entry for an adverse material usage variance is

A	DR stores control account	CR work-in-progress control account
B	DR material usage variance account	CR stores control account
C	DR work-in-progress control account	CR material usage variance account
D	DR material usage variance account	CR work-in-progress control account

Answer

The usage variance arises during production therefore the correct account to be credited is work-in-progress. Option D is correct.

An adverse variance is debited to the relevant variance account. Therefore we can eliminate the incorrect options A and C.

Option B has the correct debit entry for the adverse variance but the credit entry is incorrect.

Chapter roundup

- The **selling price variance** measures the effect on profit of a different selling price to standard selling price.

- The **sales volume profit variance** measures the effect on profit of sales volume being different to budgeted volume.

- **Operating statements** show how the combination of variances reconcile budgeted profit and actual profit.

- There are two main differences between the variances calculated in an absorption costing system and the variances calculated in a marginal costing system.

  - In a marginal costing system **the only fixed overhead variance is an expenditure variance.**

  - The sales volume variance is **valued at standard contribution margin**, not standard profit margin.

- Variances can be used to derive actual data from standard cost details.

- The general principle in standard cost bookkeeping is that **cost variances should be recorded as early as possible**. They are recorded in the relevant account in which they **arise** and the appropriate double entry is taken to a variance account.

Quick quiz

1   What is the sales volume profit variance?

2   A regular report for management of actual cost, and revenue, and usually comparing actual with budget (and showing variances) is known as

    A   Bank statement
    B   Variance statement
    C   Budget statement
    D   Operating statement

3   If an organisation uses standard marginal costing instead of standard absorption costing, which two variances are calculated differently?

4   The material usage variance is recorded in the stock control account.

    True   ☐

    False   ☐

5   How are sales variances recorded in books of account?

Answers to quick quiz

1   It is a measure of the increase or decrease in standard profit as a result of the sales volume being higher or lower than budgeted.

2   D

3   (a)   In marginal costing there is no fixed overhead volume variance (because fixed costs are not absorbed into product costs).

   (b)   In marginal costing, the sales volume variance will be valued at standard contribution margin and not standard profit margin.

4   False. Material usage variances are recorded in the work in progress account.

5   Sales variances do not appear in the books of account.

Now try the questions below from the Exam Question Bank

Questions to try	Level	Marks	Time
Q22	Introductory	n/a	30 mins
Q23	Introductory	n/a	30 mins

BPP PUBLISHING

Exam question bank

1. DISHWASHERS

The costs listed below have been estimated for the forthcoming year for a company which makes dishwashers.

	£'000
Energy costs and water (heating and general)	20
Electricity for machines	14
Rent and rates	180
Repairs and maintenance: machinery	25
buildings	10
Raw materials	750
Maintenance of patterns and jigs	45
Direct wages	1,040
Direct wages related costs	115
Foremen's wages	83
Indirect wages related costs	10
Production management salaries	133
Depreciation of machinery	150
Security	10
Inspection and commissioning (production)	60
Carriage on raw materials	49
Carriage outwards	88
Salesmen's salaries and commissions	100
Salesmen's expenses	50
Design and estimating related to sales function	75
General management and administration	32
Advertising	40
Accounts	100

REQUIREMENT:

Identify which of these costs are production overheads, which are selling and distribution overheads, which are administration overheads and which overheads are shared between the three categories and calculate the total for each category and for shared costs.

2. COST BEHAVIOUR

Show, by means of a sketch, a separate graph of cost behaviour patterns for each of the listed items of expense. You should label the axes of each graph clearly.

(a) Electricity bill: a standing charge for each period plus a charge for each unit of electricity consumed.

(b) Supervisory labour.

(c) Production bonus, which is payable when output in a period exceeds 10,000 units. The bonus amounts in total to £20,000 plus £50 per unit for additional output above 10,000 units.

(d) Sales commission, which amounts to 2% of sales turnover.

(e) Machine rental costs of a single item of equipment. The rental agreement is that £10 should be paid for every machine hour worked each month, subject to a maximum monthly charge of £480.

3. EFFECTIVE STOCK CONTROL

Describe the essential requirements of an effective material stock control system.

4. STOCK ITEM - CODE NUMBER 988988

The bin card for stock item code no 988988 in a small company's stores contains the following information for the month of June 20X1.

Opening stock 1 June: 60 units, value £360.

Date	Receipts	Supplier's invoice price per unit	Issues
	Units	£	Units
5 June	120	5.90	
10 June			80
14 June	40	6.05	
17 June			80
20 June	20	6.20	
24 June			80
25 June	100	6.30	

The current average market price per unit was £6 on 1 June, rising to £6.20 on 10 June, £6.25 on 15 June and £6.40 on 30 June.

The following methods of stock pricing are being considered.

(a) FIFO
(b) LIFO
(c) Periodic weighted average
(d) Cumulative weighted average
(e) Standard cost
(f) Replacement cost

REQUIREMENT:

Use each of these methods to show the following.

(a) The cost of each batch of materials issued to production
(b) The value of closing stock at 30 June

For the standard cost method of evaluation you should assume that the standard cost per unit of Item No 988988 is £6.

5.   **COMPONENTS A, B AND C**

A factory manufactures three components A, B and C.

During week 26, the following was recorded.

Labour grade	Number of employees	Rate per hour £	Individual hours worked
I	6	4.00	40
II	18	3.20	42
III	4	2.80	40
IV	1	1.60	44

Output and standard times during the same week were as follows.

Component	Output	Standard minutes (each)
A	444	30
B	900	54
C	480	66

The normal working week is 38 hours. Overtime is paid at a premium of 50% of the normal hourly rate.

A group incentive scheme is in operation. The time saved is expressed as a percentage of hours worked and is shared between the group as a proportion of the hours worked by each grade.

The rate paid is 75% of the normal hourly rate.

REQUIREMENT:

Calculate the total payroll showing the basic pay, overtime premium and bonus pay as separate totals for each grade of labour.

6.   **JACK IN THE BOX**   *45 mins*

Jack in the Box Ltd has five cost centres.

(a)   Machining department
(b)   Assembly department
(c)   Finishing department
(d)   Stores department
(e)   Building occupancy - this cost centre is charged with all costs relating to the use of the building

In the cost accounting treatment of the costs of these cost centres, the total costs of building occupancy are apportioned before the stores department costs are apportioned.

Costs incurred during Period 7 of the current year were as follows.

(a)   *Allocated costs*

	Total	*Machining*	*Assembly*	*Finishing*	*Stores*
	£	£	£	£	£
Indirect materials	2,800	500	1,700	600	-
Indirect wages	46,600	11,000	21,900	6,700	7,000
Power	2,000	1,500	400	100	-
Maintenance	2,600	1,900	600	100	-
Other expenses	900	300	100	200	300
	54,900	15,200	24,700	7,700	7,300

(b)   *Other costs*   £
Rent   3,000
Rates   800
Lighting and heating   200
Plant and equipment depreciation   19,800
Insurance on plant and equipment   1,980
Insurance on building   200
Company pension scheme   28,000
Factory administration   12,500
Contract costs of cleaning factory buildings   1,400
Building repairs   400
                                                                                                     68,280

(c)   *General information*

	Machining	*Department Assembly*	*Finishing*	*Stores*
Area occupied (square metres)	3,000	4,000	2,000	1,000
Plant and equipment at cost (£'000)	1,400	380	150	50
Number of employees	100	350	150	25
Direct labour hours	24,000	80,000	35,000	-
Direct wages (£)	24,000	89,400	36,000	-
Number of stores requisitions	556	1,164	270	-

REQUIREMENTS:

(a)   Prepare an overhead analysis sheet showing the basis of apportionments made (calculated to the
      nearest £).   **15 Marks**

(b)   Calculate an overhead absorption rate based on direct labour hours for the assembly department
      and the finishing department.   **4 Marks**

(c)   State brief reasons for your choice of the basis of apportionment for each overhead item or group
      of items.   **6 Marks**

                                                                                    Total Marks = 25

7. MARGINAL AND ABSORPTION

27 mins

X Ltd commenced business on 1 March making one product only. The budgeted cost of one unit is as follows.

	£
Direct labour	5
Direct material	8
Variable production overhead	2
Fixed production overhead	5
Standard production cost	20

The fixed production overhead figure has been calculated on the basis of a budgeted normal output of 36,000 units per annum.

You are to assume that all the budgeted fixed expenses are incurred evenly over the year. March and April are to be taken as equal period months.

Selling, distribution and administration expenses are as follows.

Fixed	£120,000 per annum
Variable	15% of the sales value

The selling price per unit is £35 and the number of units produced and sold was as follows.

	March Units	*April* Units
Production	2,000	3,200
Sales	1,500	3,000

REQUIREMENTS:

(a) Prepare profit statements for each of the months of March and April using the following.

    (i)   Marginal costing

    (ii)   Absorption costing   **10 Marks**

(b) Present a reconciliation of the profit or loss figure given in your answers to (a) (i) and (a) (ii) accompanied by a brief explanation.   **5 Marks**

Total Marks = 15

8. INTEGRATION

Draw a diagram or flowchart to show the flow of accounting entries within an integrated system for the following transactions.

(a) Purchase of raw materials, on credit terms
(b) Issue to production of part of the consignment received in (a) above
(c) Cash payment of wages to direct workers and to indirect workers associated with production
(d) Electricity for production purposes, obtained on credit
(e) Depreciation of machinery used for production
(f) Absorption of production overhead, using a predetermined rate

9. BATCH COSTING

A printing firm is proposing offering a leaflet advertising service to local traders.

The following costs have been estimated for a batch of 10,000 leaflets.

Setting up machine	6 hours at £10 per hour
Artwork	£20 per batch
Paper	£1.80 per 100 sheets
Other printing materials	£15
Direct labour cost	4 hours at £6 per hour

Fixed overheads allocated to this side of the business are £1,000 per annum and recovered on the basis of orders received, which are expected to be two per week for 50 weeks in the year.

The management requires 25% profit on selling price.

REQUIREMENTS:

(a) Calculate a price to be quoted per 1,000 leaflets for batches of 2,000, 5,000, 10,000 and 20,000 leaflets.

(b) Calculate the individual cost per leaflet at the various batch quantities.

10. JOB COSTING

27 mins

A specialist manufacturer of purpose-built plant engaged in three separate jobs in May 20X3. The following costs were incurred.

	Job A	Job B	Job C
Direct materials purchased	£524	£671	£382
Direct labour			
Skilled (hours)	158	170	16
Semi-skilled (hours)	316	190	30
Site expenses	£118	£170	£25
Selling price of job	£3,318	£2,750	£1,950
Completed at 31 May 20X3	100%	80%	25%

The following information is available.

Direct materials for the completion of the jobs have been recorded.

Direct labour rates: skilled £5 per hour; semi-skilled £4 per hour.

Site expenses tend to vary with output.

Administration expenses total £440 per month and are to be allocated to the jobs on a labour hour basis.

On completion of the work the practice of the manufacturer is to divide the calculated profit on each job 20% to site staff as a bonus, 80% to the company. Calculated losses are absorbed by the company in total.

REQUIREMENTS:

(a) Calculate the profit or loss made by the company on Job A.　　　　　　　　**3 Marks**

(b) Project the profit or loss made by the company on Jobs B and C.　　　　　　**8 Marks**

(c) Comment on any matters you think relevant to management as a result of your calculations.

4 Marks

Total Marks = 15

11. BEAVERS LTD

During its financial year ended 30 June 20X7 Beavers Ltd, an engineering company, has worked on several contracts. Information relating to one of them is given below.

Contract X201

Date commenced	1 July 20X6
Original estimate of completion date	30 Sept 20X7
Contract price	£240,000
Proportion of work certified as satisfactorily completed (and invoiced)up to June 20X7	£180,000
Amount received from contractee	£150,000
Costs up to 30 June 20X7	
Wages	£91,000
Materials sent to site	£36,000
Other contract costs	£18,000
Proportion of head office costs	£6,000
Plant and equipment transferred to the site (at book value on 1 July 20X6)	£9,000

The plant and equipment is expected to have a book value of about £1,000 when the contract is completed.

Stock of materials at site on 30 June 20X7	£3,000
Expected additional costs to complete the contract	
Wages	£10,000
Materials (including stock at 30 June 20X7)	£12,000
Other (including head office costs)	£8,000

If the contract is completed one month earlier than originally scheduled, an extra £10,000 will be paid to the contractors. At the end of June 20X7 there seemed to be a good chance that this would happen.

REQUIREMENTS:

(a) Show the account for the contract in the books of Beavers Ltd up to 30 June 20X7 (including any transfer to the profit and loss account which you think is appropriate) and the personal account of the contractee.

(b) Show how the work in progress would be displayed on the balance sheet.

(c) Briefly justify your calculation of the profit (or loss) to be recognised in the 20X6/X7 accounts.

---

12. PROCESS X *27 mins*

Bonto Ltd produces a simple product in two processes, process R and process X. The following information relates to process X for period 4.

Work in progress at start of period - nil.
Material transferred from process R during the period - 2,500 kgs valued at £7,145.
Wages paid - 234½ hours at £4 per hour.
Other direct costs allocated - £463.
Normal waste during processing - 5% of process R input. This has a scrap value of 16p per kg and is credited to the process account.
At the end of period 4 there were 2,100 kgs transferred to finished stock, and 150 kgs remained in work in progress.
The work in progress is 100% complete so far as materials are concerned, but only 80% of labour costs and 60% of other direct costs have been incurred.

REQUIREMENT:

Construct the process X account, showing your workings clearly. **15 Marks**

---

13. TWO HOSPITALS *27 mins*

The following information relates to two hospitals for the year ended 31 December 20X5.

	St Matthew's	St Mark's
Number of in-patients	15,400	710
Average stay per in-patient	10 days	156 days
Total number of out-patient attendances	130,000	3,500
Number of available beds	510	320
Average number of beds occupied	402	307

Cost analysis	In-patients £	Out-patients £	In-patients £	Out-patients £
Patient care services				
Direct treatment services and supplies (eg nursing staff)	6,213,900	1,076,400	1,793,204	70,490
Medical supporting services:				
Diagnostic (eg pathology)	480,480	312,000	22,152	20,650
Other services (eg occupational therapy)	237,160	288,600	77,532	27,790
General services				
Patient related (eg catering)	634,480	15,600	399,843	7,700
General (eg administration)	2,196,760	947,700	1,412,900	56,700

Note. In-patients are those who receive treatment whilst remaining in hospital. Out-patients visit hospital during the day to receive treatment.

REQUIREMENTS:

(a)   Prepare a statement showing the following for each hospital for each cost heading.

   (i)   Cost per in-patient day, in £ to two decimal places
   (ii)   Cost per out-patient attendance, in £ to two decimal places   **8 Marks**

(b)   Calculate for each hospital the bed-occupation percentage.   **2 Marks**

(c)   Comment briefly on your findings.   **5 Marks**

                                                                          Total Marks = 15

14.   **TERRITORIAL (PILOT PAPER)**   *45 mins*

POV Ltd manufactures three products - X, Y and Z - that use the same machines. The budgeted profit and loss statements for the three products are as follows:

	X	Y	Z
	£'000	£'000	£'000
Sales	1,000	1,125	625
Prime costs	(500)	(562.5)	(437.5)
Variable overheads	(250)	(187.5)	(62.5)
Fixed overheads	(200)	(315)	(130)
Profit/(loss)	50	60	(5)
Annual sales demand (units)	5,000	7,500	2,500
Machine hours per unit	20	21	26

Fixed overheads are absorbed on the basis of machine hours. The budgeted machine hours based on normal capacity were 322,500 hours.

However, after the budget had been formulated, an unforeseen condition has meant that during the next period the available machine capacity has been limited to 296,500 hours.

REQUIREMENTS:

(a)   Determine the optimum production plan for the next period and calculate the resulting profit that your production plan will yield.   **15 Marks**

(b)   Discuss problems which may arise as a result of POV Ltd not being able to satisfy demand.

                                                                                          4 Marks

(c)   Comment briefly on the usefulness of marginal costing, as opposed to absorption costing, for decision-making. Illustrate your answer by reference to POV Ltd.   **6 Marks**

                                                                          Total Marks = 25

15.   **FAST FANDANGO LTD**

Fast Fandango Ltd manufactures a single product, a steel poker, which sells for £10. At 75% capacity, which is the normal level of activity for the factory, sales are £600,000.

The cost of these sales are as follows.

Direct cost per unit	£3
Production overhead	£156,000 (including variable costs of £30,000)
Sales costs	£ 80,000
Distribution costs	£ 60,000 (including variable costs of £15,000)
Administration overhead	£ 40,000 (including variable costs of £9,000)

The sales costs are fixed with the exception of sales commission which is 5% of sales value.

REQUIREMENTS:

(a)   Calculate the breakeven volume of sales.

(b)   Prepare statements to show the revenue, contribution and profit in the following circumstances.

   (i)   At the normal level of activity

(ii) If the sales price is reduced by 5% and the sales volume thereby increased by 16²/₃% above the normal level of activity

(iii) If the sales price is reduced by 7% and the sales volume thereby increased by 20% above the normal level of activity

(c) Calculate the C/S ratio in each instance in (b) above.

(d) Calculate what the sales volume would need to be under the sales price arrangements in (b) (iii) for the profit to be the same as in (b) (ii).

16.   ISHAB (PILOT PAPER)   *45 mins*

RJD Ltd uses a standard costing system. The standard cost per unit of product D is as follows:

	£
Direct materials: 5kg × £10/kg	50
Direct labour: 4 hr × £6/hr	24
Production overheads:	
Variable - 4hr × £3/hr	12
Fixed	10
Standard production cost	96
Standard selling price	150

The standard fixed production overhead absorption rate was based on a budgeted activity of 10,000 units.

During period 5, production was 10,000 units as planned but sales were only 8,000 units. There was a total fixed production overhead variance of £10,000 adverse. All units were sold at £150.

There was no opening stock at the beginning of the period.

Other costs incurred during the period were in relation to selling and distribution, and administration.

These were as follows:

Selling and distribution:	Variable	20% of sales
	Fixed	£60,000
Administration:	Fixed	£100,000

REQUIREMENTS:

(a) Prepare a profit and loss statement for period 5 using:

  (i)   absorption costing;
  (ii) marginal costing.   **15 Marks**

(b) Prepare a reconciliation of the difference between the profit/loss under absorption costing *and* under marginal costing and explain the reason for the difference.   **4 Marks**

(c) (i)   Using graph paper, prepare a profit-volume chart based on the budgeted information for period 5, indicating the breakeven point and margin of safety.   **4 Marks**

  (ii) Demonstrate, using the breakeven formula, the accuracy of your answer to (c)(i) above.
                                                                                     2 Marks

                                                                          Total Marks = 25

17.   CASH BUDGET   *27 mins*

A redundant manager who received compensation of £80,000 decides to commence business on 4 January 20X8, manufacturing a product for which he knows there is a ready market. He intends to employ some of his former workers who were also made redundant but they will not all commence on 4 January. Suitable premises have been found to rent and second-hand machinery costing £60,000 has been bought out of the £80,000. This machinery has an estimated life of five years from January 20X8 and no residual value.

Other data

(a) Production will begin on 4 January and 25% of the following month's sales will be manufactured in January. Each month thereafter the production will consist of 75% of the current month's sales and 25% of the following month's sales.

(b) Estimated sales are

	Units	£
January	Nil	Nil
February	3,200	80,000
March	3,600	90,000
April	4,000	100,000
May	4,000	100,000

(c) Variable production cost per unit

	£
Direct materials	7
Direct wages	6
Variable overhead	2
	15

(d) Raw material stocks costing £10,000 have been purchased (out of the manager's £80,000) to enable production to commence and it is intended to buy, each month, 50% of the materials required for the following month's production requirements. The other 50% will be purchased in the month of production. Payment will be made 30 days after purchase.

(e) Direct workers have agreed to have their wages paid into bank accounts on the seventh working day of each month in respect of the previous month's earnings.

(f) Variable production overhead: 60% is to be paid in the month following the month it was incurred and 40% is to be paid one month later.

(g) Fixed overheads are £4,000 per month. One quarter of this is paid in the month incurred, one-half in the following month, and the remainder represents depreciation on the second-hand machinery.

(h) Amounts receivable: a 5% cash discount is allowed for payment in the current month and 20% of each month's sales qualify for this discount. 50% of each month's sales are received in the following month, 20% in the third month and 8% in the fourth month. The balance of 2% represents anticipated bad debts.

REQUIREMENT:

Prepare a cash budget for each of the first four months of 20X8, assuming that overdraft facilities will be available.

15 Marks

18. **TWO THINGS**

(a) Describe briefly the benefits to cash budgeting from the use of a particular type of software package.

(b) Give three reasons why the reported profit figure for a period does not normally represent the amount of cash generated in that period.

19. **DOODLE LTD** *27 mins*

Doodle Ltd manufactures and sells a range of products, one of which is the squiggle.

The following data relates to the expected costs of production and sale of the squiggle.

Budgeted production for the year	11,400 units
Standard details for one unit:	
direct materials	30 metres at £6.10 per metre
direct wages	
Department P	40 hours at £2.20 per hour
Department Q	36 hours at £2.50 per hour
Budgeted costs and hours per annum	
Variable production overhead (factory total)	
Department P	£525,000 : 700,000 hours
Department Q	£300,000 : 600,000 hours

Fixed overheads to be absorbed by the squiggle

Production	£1,083,000 (absorbed on a direct labour hour basis)
Administration	£125,400 (absorbed on a unit basis)
Marketing	£285,000 (absorbed on a unit basis)

REQUIREMENTS:

(a) Prepare a standard cost sheet for the squiggle, to include the following.

    (i)   Standard total direct cost
    (ii)   Standard variable production cost
    (iii) Standard production cost
    (iv) Standard full cost of sale   **13 Marks**

(b) Calculate the standard sales price per unit which allows for a standard profit of 10% on the sales price.   **2 Marks**

Total Marks = 15

20.   **SUMMARY PRODUCTION BUDGET**   *27 mins*

A four-week summary production budget for LB Ltd, an organisation which produces a single product, is as follows.

Production quantity	240,000 units
Production costs	
Material	336,000 kg at £4.10 per kg
Direct labour	216,000 hours at £4.50 per hour
Overheads	£1,920,000

Overheads are absorbed at a predetermined direct labour hour rate.

During the four-week period the actual production was 220,000 units which incurred the following costs.

Material	313,060 kg costing £1,245,980
Direct labour	194,920 hours costing £886,886
Overheads	£1,934,940

REQUIREMENTS:

(a) Calculate the cost variances for the period.   **12 Marks**
(b) Give reasons why the direct labour efficiency variance may have arisen.   **3 Marks**

Total Marks = 15

21.   **HOTELIERS UNITE (PILOT PAPER)**   *45 mins*

A hotel is currently operating at a 55 per cent occupancy level. The hotel's management has traditionally used flexed budget information in the format shown below. The figures given below are for the current year and management intends to use them as the basis for next year's budget.

Occupancy level	55%	75%	85%
	£	£	£
Accommodation:			
Room-cleaning costs	481,800	657,000	744,600
Establishment costs	363,170	477,050	533,990
Sports facilities:			
Recreational facilities costs	180,675	246,375	279,225
Equipment costs	100,000	100,000	100,000

The hotel management expects all variable costs to increase by 3.5 per cent next year. This increase has not been incorporated into the above figures. The hotel's management team has identified a new market, luxury weekend breaks, that it believes will increase the operating level to 80 per cent occupancy for the next year.

The new luxury weekend breaks venture will require an investment in the existing hotel to bring it up to a luxury standard. The cost in relation to upgrading the rooms and the sports facilities is expected to be £50,000 and £75,000 respectively. The management's policy is that the cost of upgrading the rooms and sporting facilities will be charged against profits over the next five years. The amounts to be charged annually are £10,000 for the upgrading of the rooms and £15,000 for the upgrading of the sports facilities.

You have recently been appointed as the management accountant for the hotel.

REQUIREMENTS:

(a) Comment on the format currently used by the hotel management team for the presentation of the budget information. **4 Marks**

(b) Prepare in a more appropriate format the flexed budget statement for next year, assuming that the hotel will operate at 80 per cent occupancy. **8 Marks**

(c) Assuming that over the next year the hotel did achieve an 80 per cent occupancy level, prepare a report for management that compares budget and actual expenditure, calculates appropriate variances and suggests reasons why the variances could have occurred.

Actual expenditure	£
Room-cleaning costs	727,560
Establishment costs	529,258
Recreational facilities costs	275,640
Equipment costs	115,000

Note: All fixed costs actually incurred were as budgeted. The annual charge for upgrading was as expected. **9 Marks**

(d) Briefly discuss two problems which may arise from higher occupancy levels arising from the luxury weekend breaks and the upgraded sporting facilities. **4 Marks**

Total Marks = 25

22. NANOOK OF THE NORTH LTD

Nanook of the North Ltd manufactures a single product, the SK Mow. The standard cost card for this item is as follows.

	£	£
Direct materials:		
P (8 kg at £0.40 per kg)	3.20	
Q (4 kg at £0.70 per kg)	2.80	
		6.00
Direct labour (3 hours at £2.50)		7.50
Variable production overhead (3 hours at £0.50)		1.50
Fixed production overhead (3 hours at £2.00)		6.00
		21.00

The standard sales price per unit is £25. The budgeted production and sales for period 7 were 3,000 units and the budgeted fixed production overhead (from which the fixed cost per unit was derived) was £18,000. Budgeted administration, selling and distribution overheads of £5,000 are excluded from standard costs.

Actual results for period 7 were as follows.

Sales and production	2,800 units	
Sales revenue	£71,200	
Direct materials purchased:		
P	19,000 kg	Cost £7,500	Materials used 24,100 kg
Q	14,000 kg	Cost £10,250	Materials used 10,100 kg
Direct labour	8,600 hours	Cost £24,100

It is known that 300 hours of this labour was recorded as idle time.

Variable production overhead	£4,100
Fixed production overhead	£18,450
Administration, sales and distribution overhead	£5,200

All stocks are valued at standard cost.

REQUIREMENT:

Prepare an operating statement reconciling the budgeted profit in period 7 with the actual profit.

23. BACKE AND SMASH LTD

Backe and Smash Ltd manufactures a brand of tennis racket, the Winsome, and a brand of squash racket, the Boastful. The budget for October was as follows.

		Winsome	Boastful
Production (units)		4,000	1,500
Direct materials:	wood (£0.30 per metre)	7 metres	5 metres
	gut (£1.50 per metre)	6 metres	4 metres
Other materials		£0.20	£0.15
Direct labour (£3 per hour)		30 mins	20 mins

Overheads

	£
Variable:	
power	1,500
maintenance	7,500
	9,000
Fixed:	
supervision	8,000
heating and lighting	1,200
rent	4,800
depreciation	7,000
	21,000

Variable overheads are assumed to vary with standard hours produced.

Actual results for October were as follows.

Production:	Winsome	3,700 units
	Boastful	1,890 units

Direct materials, bought and used:			£
	wood	37,100 metres	11,000
	gut	29,200 metres	44,100
	other materials		1,000
Direct labour		2,200 hours	6,850
Power			1,800
Maintenance			6,900
Supervision			7,940
Heating and lighting			1,320
Rent			4,800
Depreciation			7,000

REQUIREMENT:

Calculate the cost variances which should be incorporated into the operating statement for the month of October. Assume that a standard absorption costing system is in operation.

Exam answer bank

1. DISHWASHERS

	Total £'000	Production £'000	Selling and distribution £'000	Administration £'000	Shared costs £'000
Energy costs and water (heating and general)	20				20
Electricity for machines	14	14			
Rent and rates	180				180
Repairs and maintenance:					
machinery	25	25			
buildings	10				10
Maintenance of patterns and jigs	45	45			
Direct wages related costs	115	115			
Foremen's wages	83	83			
Indirect wages related costs	10	10			
Production management salaries	133	133			
Depreciation of machinery	150	150			
Security	10				10
Inspection and commissioning	60	60			
Carriage outwards	88		88		
Salesmen's salaries and commissions	100		100		
Salesmen's expenses	50		50		
Design and estimating related to sales function	75		75		
General management and administration	32			32	
Advertising	40		40		
Accounts	100			100	
	1,340	635	353	132	220

2. COST BEHAVIOUR

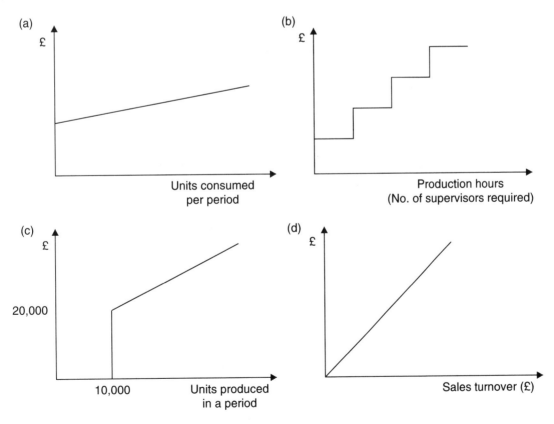

(e)

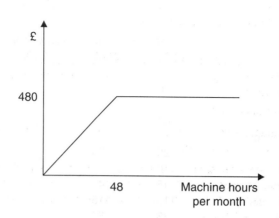

3. **EFFECTIVE STOCK CONTROL**

The requirements of an effective material stock control system may be considered under the headings of physical control, clerical control and stock checks.

(a) **Physical control**

(i) Goods should be kept in a secure place (restricted access, separately identifiable and so on).

(ii) They should be kept in a place where they do not deteriorate too quickly.

(iii) Different types of goods should be kept separately.

(iv) The location of the goods should be clearly labelled.

(v) A maximum stock level for each item should be established; its level should not rise above this.

(vi) A reorder level should be established; when the level is reached, more of the item should be ordered.

(vii) As goods are received into stock, they should be counted and checked for quality.

(b) **Clerical control**

(i) All movements of stock (in and out) should be immediately recorded (this is the essence of good clerical control).

(ii) Usually, such a record is maintained in two ways.

On stores ledger accounts. These give the following detailed information.

(1) Quantity received into stores
(2) Description (such as part numbers)
(3) Date received into stores
(4) Price paid
(5) Reference (so that the corresponding record in the accounting system may be traced)
(6) Details (1), (2), (3) and (5) for issues from stores

The combination of details (1)-(6) gives the balance of stock still held at any moment in time.

On bin cards (not mandatory). These are normally kept at the location of the item. At a minimum the details on these would be as follows.

(1) Date of receipt, and quantity
(2) Date of issue, and quantity
(3) From (1) and (2), the number of units of the item remaining

Either stores ledger accounts or bin cards would also contain information about maximum and reorder levels; comparison of the balance of physical stock to these should trigger the necessary course of action.

(iii) Replacement goods should only be ordered on proper authority; this would normally involve purchase requisition forms signed by a senior manager.

(iv) Replacement goods should only be received into stock once their quality and quantity have been checked; these checks would normally be evidenced by the stores manager's signature on the goods received note.

(v)   Goods should only be issued from stores into production on proper authority; such authority should be properly evidenced.

(c)   **Stock checks**

The efficacy of both physical and clerical controls is considerably enhanced if the stock is physically counted on a regular basis and this amount is then compared to the quantity on the stores ledger accounts.

Four further points should also be made.

(i)   A physical stocktake should occur at least annually (it is often useful to have it coincide with the business year end).

(ii)   However, some firms organise their stocktakes on a cyclical basis: at regular intervals throughout the year a proportion of the items of stock are counted, so that by the end of the year, all elements of stock have been considered. This method of stocktaking is described as continuous.

(iii) Once the physical quantity of stock has been established, the clerical records should immediately be amended if necessary to reflect reality.

(iv)   The reason for the difference between physical and book stock should be established; if it represents a control failure steps should be taken to ensure that such an occurrence does not happen again.

4.   **STOCK ITEM-CODE NUMBER 988988**

The purchase costs in June were as follows.

5 June	120	units at £5.90	708
14 June	40	units at £6.05	242
20 June	20	units at £6.20	124
25 June	100	units at £6.30	630
	280	units	1,704
Value of opening stock	60	units at £6.00	360
	340		2,064

(a)   **FIFO**

			Value £
Issues		*Workings*	
10 June		60 units at £6.00	
	plus	20 units at £5.90	478
17 June		80 units at £5.90	472
24 June		20 units at £5.90	
	plus	40 units at £6.05	
	plus	20 units at £6.20	484
Cost of issues			1,434
Closing stock		100 units at £6.30	630
			2,064

The cost of materials issued plus the value of closing stock are exactly equal to purchase costs plus opening stock (£2,064).

(b)   **LIFO**

			Value £
Issues		*Workings*	
10 June		80 units at £5.90	472
17 June		40 units at £6.05	
	plus	40 units at £5.90	478
24 June		20 units at £6.20	
	plus	60 units at £6.00	484
Cost of issues			1,434
Closing stock		100 units at £6.30	630
			2,064

Once again, the cost of issues plus the value of closing stock equals £2,064.

(c) **Periodic weighted average**

Cost of receipts in the period (June) + cost of opening stock		$\dfrac{£(1,704+360)}{280+60}$
Number of units received in the period + units in opening stock		

Cost per unit issued in the period   £6.0706   per unit

		£	£
Value of opening stock			360
Value of purchases in June			1,704
			2,064
Cost of issues:			
10 June	80 × £6.0706	486	
17 June	80 × £6.0706	486	
24 June	80 × £6.0706	486	
		1,458	
Value of closing stock (balancing figure)			606

There is no discrepancy between the cost of purchases and opening stock and the combined value of materials issued and closing stock.

(d) **Cumulative weighted average**

	Units	Value £	Unit price £
Opening stock	60	360	6.0000
5 June receipts	120	708	5.9000
Average price	180	1,068	5.9333
10 June issues	80	475	5.9333
	100	593	5.9333
14 June receipts	40	242	6.0500
New average price	140	835	5.9643
17 June issues	80	477	5.9643
	60	358	5.9643
20 June receipts	20	124	6.2000
New average price	80	482	6.0250
24 June issues	80	482	6.0250
	0	0	0
25 June receipts	100	630	6.3000

	£
Value of issues	
10 June	475
17 June	477
24 June	482
	1,434
Closing stock value	630
	2,064

There is no discrepancy between the combined value of closing stocks plus materials issued, and the costs of purchases.

(e) **Standard cost**

		£
Issue costs		
10 June	80 × £6	480
17 June	80 × £6	480
24 June	80 × £6	480
		1,440
Value of closing stock	100 × £6	600
		2,040

(f) **Replacement cost**

Issue costs

		£
10 June	80 × £6.20	496
17 June	80 × £6.25	500
24 June	80 × £6.25	500
		1,496
Closing stock, 30 June	100 × £6.40	640
Value of materials plus closing stock		2,136

5. **COMPONENTS A, B AND C**

Calculation of overtime premium

Grade	Overtime premium (50% of basic rate) £/hour (a)	Overtime hours payable (b)	Overtime premium £ ((a) × (b))
I	2.00	2 hrs × 6 = 12	24.00
II	1.60	4 hrs × 18 = 72	115.20
III	1.40	2 hrs × 4 = 8	11.20
IV	0.80	6	4.80

Calculation of standard hours produced

Component		Standard hours
A	$444 \times \dfrac{30}{60}$ hours	222
B	$900 \times \dfrac{54}{60}$ hours	810
C	$480 \times \dfrac{66}{60}$ hours	528
		1,560

Actual time taken

Grade		Hours
I	6 × 40 hrs	240
II	18 × 42 hrs	756
III	4 × 40 hrs	160
IV	1 × 44 hrs	44
		1,200

∴ Time saved = (1,560 − 1,200) hrs = 360 hrs

Time saved as a percentage of hours worked = $\dfrac{360}{1,200} \times 100\% = 30\%$

Calculation of bonus payable

Grade	Bonus hours		75% basic rate £	Bonus payable £
I	240 × 30%	= 72.0	× 3.00	216.00
II	756 × 30%	= 226.8	× 2.40	544.32
III	160 × 30%	= 48.0	× 2.10	100.80
IV	44 × 30%	= 13.2	× 1.20	15.84
				876.96

Calculation of total payroll

Grade	Basic pay			Overtime premium	Bonus	Total
			£	£	£	£
I	240 × £4.00	=	960.00	24.00	216.00	1,200.00
II	756 × £3.20	=	2,419.20	115.20	544.32	3,078.72
III	160 × £2.80	=	448.00	11.20	100.80	560.00
IV	44 × £1.60	=	70.40	4.80	15.84	91.04
			3,897.60	155.20	876.96	4,929.76

6. JACK IN THE BOX

(a) Building occupancy costs

	£
Rent	3,000
Rates	800
Lighting and heating	200
Insurance on building	200
Contract costs of cleaning	1,400
Building repairs	400
	6,000

(i) Overhead analysis sheet - first stage

		Total	Machining	Assembly	Finishing	Stores
		£	£	£	£	£
Allocated costs						
Indirect materials		2,800	500	1,700	600	0
Indirect wages		46,600	11,000	21,900	6,700	7,000
Power		2,000	1,500	400	100	0
Maintenance		2,600	1,900	600	100	0
Other expenses		900	300	100	200	300
		54,900	15,200	24,700	7,700	7,300
Apportioned costs	*Note*					
Plant depreciation	(1)	19,800	14,000	3,800	1,500	500
Plant insurance	(1)	1,980	1,400	380	150	50
Pension scheme	(2)	28,000	5,000	15,900	6,100	1,000
Factory admin	(3)	12,500	2,000	7,000	3,000	500
Building occupancy	(4)	6,000	1,800	2,400	1,200	600
		123,180	39,400	54,180	19,650	9,950

Basis of apportionment

(1) Cost of plant and equipment

(2) Percentage of total direct and indirect labour costs in the four departments:

	£
Direct wages (24,000 + 89,400 + 36,000)	149,400
Indirect wages	46,600
Total wages	196,000

Pension scheme costs (1/7 of wages cost) = £28,000

	Indirect wages	Direct wages	Total wages	Pension costs (1/7 of wages)
	£	£	£	£
Machining	11,000	24,000	35,000	5,000
Assembly	21,900	89,400	111,300	15,900
Finishing	6,700	36,000	42,700	6,100
Stores	7,000	-	7,000	1,000
	46,600	149,400	196,000	28,000

(3) Number of employees (£12,500 ÷ 625 = £20 per employee)

(4) Area occupied (£6,000 ÷ 10,000 square metres = 60p per square metre)

(ii) **Overhead analysis sheet - second stage**

	Total £	Machining £	Assembly £	Finishing £	Stores £
Allocated and apportioned overhead	123,180	39,400	54,180	19,650	9,950
Apportionment of stores costs (see note)		2,780	5,820	1,350	(9,950)
	123,180	42,180	60,000	21,000	0

Note. Stores costs are apportioned on the basis of the number of stores requisitions.

Stores cost $\dfrac{£9,950}{(556+1,164+270)} = £5$ per requisition

(b) **Overhead absorption rates**

	Assembly department	Finishing department
Overhead cost	£60,000	£21,000
Direct labour hours	80,000	35,000
Absorption rate per direct labour hour	£0.75	£0.60

(c) The choice of the basis of apportionment involves an attempt to spread costs on a 'fair' basis, so that each department is burdened with a share of cost which appears to reflect its use of the various shared cost items.

(i) **Plant depreciation.** On the assumption that straight line depreciation is used, and that all items of equipment have the same life and no residual value, apportionment on the basis of historical cost is appropriate.

(ii) **Plant insurance.** On the assumption that the insurance cost relates to the value of the plant and that plant value is in its turn related to plant cost, plant cost would again be the appropriate basis for apportionment.

(iii) **Pension scheme.** Pension scheme costs are almost certainly related to wages and salaries costs, presumably as a percentage of these costs. The only known wages costs are direct and indirect wages in the four departments, and the basis of apportionment was therefore a percentage (or fraction) of these costs.

(iv) **Factory administration**. These costs should be apportioned in relation to the work done by the administration departments (personnel, accounting and so on) for the other departments. Labour hours might be an appropriate basis for apportionment, but given that we are not told the hours of indirect labour in any of the four departments, number of employees is chosen as the most relevant basis available.

(v) **Building occupancy.** Floor area is an apportionment basis commonly used for rent, rates and lighting. It is here assumed that all the other costs may similarly be apportioned.

(vi) **Stores department costs.** The work done by the stores department for each of the three production departments is probably most aptly reflected by the number of requisitions made by each department (on the assumption that requisitions from each department call for roughly equal amounts of stores effort).

7.   MARGINAL AND ABSORPTION

(a) (i)   PROFIT STATEMENTS FOR MARCH AND APRIL
          (Marginal costing basis)

	March £	March £	April £	April £
Sales		52,500		105,000
Opening stock (at £15 per unit)	-		7,500	
Variable costs of production	30,000		48,000	
	30,000		55,500	
Closing stock	7,500		10,500	
		22,500		45,000
		30,000		60,000
Variable selling, distribution and administration costs		7,875		15,750
Contribution		22,125		44,250
Fixed costs				
Production				
(£5 × 36,000 × 1/12)	15,000		15,000	
Selling, distribution and administration	10,000		10,000	
		25,000		25,000
Net (loss)/profit		(2,875)		19,250

(ii) PROFIT STATEMENTS FOR MARCH AND APRIL
      (Absorption costing basis)

	March £	March £	April £	April £
Sales		52,500		105,000
Opening stock (at £20 per unit)	-		10,000	
Standard cost of production	40,000		64,000	
	40,000		74,000	
Closing stock	10,000		14,000	
	30,000		60,000	
Under-/(over-) absorbed production overhead (1,000 × £5; 200 × £5)	5,000		(1,000)	
		35,000		59,000
Gross profit		17,500		46,000
Selling, distribution and administration expenses				
Fixed	10,000		10,000	
Variable	7,875		15,750	
		17,875		25,750
Net (loss)/profit		(375)		20,250

(b) PROFIT RECONCILIATION STATEMENT

	March £	April £
Marginal costing (loss)/profit	(2,875)	19,250
Fixed production overheads b/f in opening stock valuation		(2,500)
Fixed production overhead c/f in closing stock valuation	2,500	3,500
Absorption costing (loss)/profit	(375)	20,250

Under absorption costing, the profit for March is increased because £2,500 of the total fixed production costs incurred is carried forward in the closing stock valuation. This £2,500 results in a corresponding reduction in the April absorption costing profit, but it is outweighed by the £3,500 fixed production costs carried forward in the closing stock valuation.

8. **INTEGRATION**

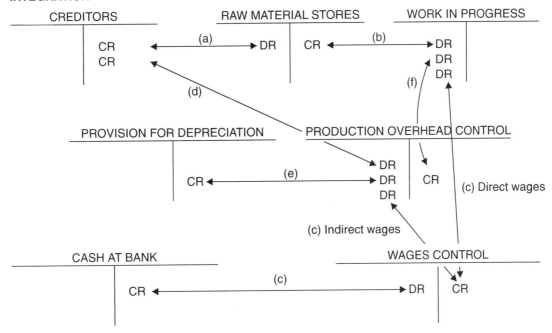

9. **BATCH COSTING**

Expected orders per annum = 2 orders × 50 weeks = 100 orders

∴ Fixed overhead per order = $\dfrac{£1,000}{100}$ = £10

(a) **Calculation of price per 1,000 leaflets**

Batch size: (leaflets)	2,000	5,000	10,000	20,000
	£	£	£	£
Setting up machine	60.00	60.00	60.00	60.00
Artwork	20.00	20.00	20.00	20.00
Paper	36.00	90.00	180.00	360.00
Other printing materials	3.00	7.50	15.00	30.00
Direct labour cost	4.80	12.00	24.00	48.00
Fixed overhead	10.00	10.00	10.00	10.00
Total cost	133.80	199.50	309.00	528.00
Profit	44.60	66.50	103.00	176.00
Selling price	178.40	266.00	412.00	704.00
Price per 1,000 leaflets	89.20	53.20	41.20	35.20

(b) Individual cost per leaflet   £0.0069   £0.0399   £0.0309   £0.0264

The profit is 25% on selling price ie Cost (75) + Profit (25) = Selling price (100), and thus profit = $^1/_3$ cost).

10. **JOB COSTING**

(a) **Job A**

	£	£
Direct materials		524
Direct labour		
Skilled (158 hours at £5)	790	
Semi-skilled (316 hours at £4)	1,264	
		2,054
Site expenses		118
Administrative expenses		
(474 hours at £0.50 (W))		237
		2,933
Selling price		3,318
Calculated profit		385
Divided: staff bonus 20%		77
profit for company 80%		308
		385

Working

Administration expenses absorption rate $= \dfrac{£440}{880}$ per direct labour hour

$= £0.50$ per direct labour hour

(b) It is assumed that direct labour costs, site expenses and administration expenses will increase in proportion to the total labour hours required to complete jobs B and C. There will be no further material costs to complete the jobs.

		Job B			Job C	
		£	£		£	£
Direct materials			671			382.00
Direct labour						
Skilled	170 hrs at £5.00	850		16 hrs at £5.00	80	
Semi-skilled	190 hrs at £4.00	760		30 hrs at £4.00	120	
Site expenses		170			25	
Administration expenses	360 hrs at £0.50	180		46 hrs at £0.50	23	
		1,960			248	
Costs to completion	20/80 × £1,960	490		75/25 × £248	744	
			2,450			992.00
Total costs			3,121			1,374.00
Selling price			2,750			1,950.00
Calculated (loss)/profit			(371)			576.00
Divided: staff bonus (20%)			0			115.20
(Loss)/profit for company			(371)			460.80

(c) Job B is projected to result in a loss, and management should investigate this and negotiate an increase in the selling price if possible. In particular, the relative costs should be examined. It is possible that all of the skilled work has already been carried out and only unskilled labour is required to complete the job. Job B has a higher proportion of skilled labour than jobs A and C, and management should investigate whether this was allowed for in the estimate.

The reasons for the loss should be established.

(i) If it is the result of inadequate estimating, the estimation procedure should be reviewed to prevent recurrence.

(ii) If it is the result of a lack of control over costs, appropriate action should be taken to exercise control in future.

11. BEAVERS LTD

(a)

CONTRACT ACCOUNT X201

	£		£
Wages	91,000	Stock c/d	3,000
Materials	36,000	Plant c/d (£9,000 − £6,400)*	2,600
Other costs	18,000	Costs incurred to date	154,400
Head office costs	6,000		
Plant and equipment	9,000		
	160,000		160,000

* Total expected loss of value of plant = £8,000. Proportion to be allocated to contract to date = 12 months/15 months × £8,000 = £6,400.

CONTRACTEE ACCOUNT

	£		£
Work certified	180,000	Bank	150,000
		Balance c/d	30,000
	180,000		180,000

Working

	£	£	£
Contract price			240,000
Actual costs to date			
Wages	91,000		
Materials	33,000		
Other costs	18,000		
HO costs	6,000		
Plant	6,400		
		154,400	
Expected future costs			
Wages	10,000		
Materials	12,000		
Other costs	8,000		
Plant	1,600		
		31,600	
			186,000
Estimated total profit			54,000

Proportion recognised in the current year:

$$\frac{£180,000}{£240,000} \times £54,000 = £40,500$$

Of this, £180,000 is allocated to turnover and £139,500 is allocated to cost of sales

$$\frac{£180,000}{£240,000} \times £186,000 = £139,500$$

(b)   BALANCE SHEET (EXTRACT)

	£
Fixed assets	
Plant	2,600
Current assets	
Stocks: long term contract balances (W1)	14,900
Debtors: amounts recoverable on long-term contracts (W2)	30,000

Workings

		£
1	Costs incurred to date	154,400
	Less allocated to cost of sales	139,500
		14,900
2	Amounts recognised as turnover	180,000
	Less progress payments received	150,000
		30,000

This is effectively the balance on the contractee account.

(c)   The contract is nearing completion and so credit has been taken for profit in direct proportion to the work certified as completed. The possible bonus has been ignored on the grounds of prudence as there appears to be an element of uncertainty. It is also assumed that profit is accrued evenly in proportion to the completed work and that no provisions have to be made in respect of penalties or other possible contingencies.

12.   PROCESS X

Workings

Loss in process	2,500 kgs – (2,100 + 150)kg	= 250 kg
Normal loss	5% × 2,500 kg	= 125 kg
∴ Abnormal loss		= 125 kg

STATEMENT OF EQUIVALENT UNITS OF PRODUCTION

		Equivalent units					
	Total	Materials		Labour		Other direct costs	
	Units	Units	%	Units	%	Units	%
Normal loss	125	0		0		0	
Abnormal loss	125	125	100	125	100	125	100
Finished stock	2,100	2,100	100	2,100	100	2,100	100
Work in progress	150	150	100	120	80	90	60
	2,500	2,375		2,345		2,315	
Costs		**£7,125		£938		£463	
Cost per equivalent unit	£3.60	£3.00		£0.40		£0.20	

*   £7,145 less scrap value of normal loss £20 = £7,125.

STATEMENT OF EVALUATION OF WORK IN PROGRESS

	Materials	Labour	Other direct costs	Total
Equivalent units	150	120	90	
Cost per equivalent unit	£3	£0.40	£0.20	
Total value	£450	£48	£18	£516

PROCESS B ACCOUNT

	kg	£		kg	£
Process R	2,500	7,145	Finished stock	2,100	7,560
Wages paid		938	Normal loss - scrap	125	20
Other direct costs		463	Abnormal loss	125	450
			Work in progress	150	516
	2,500	8,546		2,500	8,546

13. TWO HOSPITALS

(a) (i) and (ii)

	St Matthew's		St Mark's	
	Cost per in-patient day	Cost per out-patient attendance	Cost per in-patient day	Cost per out-patient attendance
	£	£	£	£
Number of in-patient days *	154,000	-	110,760	-
Number of out-patient attendances	-	130,000	-	3,500
	£	£	£	£
Patient care services				
Direct treatment	40.35	8.28	16.19	20.14
Medical support				
Diagnostic	3.12	2.40	0.20	5.90
Other services	1.54	2.22	0.70	7.94
General services				
Patient related	4.12	0.12	3.61	2.20
General	14.26	7.29	12.76	16.20
Total cost	63.39	20.31	33.46	52.38

* Number of in-patient days = number of in-patients × average stay.

St Matthew's = 15,400 × 10 days = 154,000
St Mark's = 710 × 156 days = 110,760

(b) **Bed-occupation percentages**

St Matthew's $= \dfrac{402}{510} \times 100\% = 78.8\%$

St Mark's $= \dfrac{307}{320} \times 100\% = 95.9\%$

(c) **Cost per in-patient day**

St Mark's has a lower cost than St Matthew's. This is partly due to the fact that St Mark's has a higher bed-occupation percentage, which indicates that this hospital is making more efficient use of the available resources. A higher bed-occupation will mean that the fixed costs are spread over more cost units, thus reducing the unit cost.

Cost per out-patient attendance

St Matthew's has a lower cost in this case, probably owing to the large volume of patients. It is likely that more efficient systems are in operation to cope with the higher activity.

Overview

It is evident from the figures that the two hospitals care for very different types of patient. St Mark's deals with long stays and does not attend to many out-patients. St Matthew's in-patients stay for a short time and are far fewer in number than the out-patients. Despite the use of comparable cost units, caution is therefore necessary before reaching any firm conclusions regarding the relative costs.

14.   **TERRITORIAL (PILOT PAPER)**

(a)   **Contribution per unit of limiting factor (machine hours)**

	X	Y	Z
	£'000	£'000	£'000
Sales revenue	1,000	1,125	625
Total variable costs	(500)	(562.5)	(437.5)
Variable overheads	(250)	(187.5)	(62.5)
Contribution	250	375.0	125.0
Contribution per unit	(÷ 5,000) £50	(÷ 7,500) £50	(÷ 2,500) £50
Contribution per machine hour	(÷ 20) £2.50	(÷ 21) £2.38	(÷ 26) £1.92
Ranking	1st	2nd	3rd

Optimum production plan

Since machine hours is the only limiting factor, the following quantities of Products X, Y and Z should be manufactured in the next period.

Ranking	Product	Demand units	Hours required	Hours available	Production units
1st	X	5,000 (× 20)	100,000	100,000	5,000
2nd	Y	7,500 (× 21)	157,500	157,500	7,500
3rd	Z	2,500 (× 26)	65,000	39,000*	1,500
				296,500	

* Balance (296,500 – 100,000 – 157,500)

OPTIMUM PRODUCTION PLAN – PROFIT

				Total
Contribution per unit	£50	£50	£50	
Units produced	5,000	7,500	1,500	
Total contribution	£250,000	£375,000	£75,000	
Fixed overheads	£200,000	£315,000	£130,000	
Profit/(loss)	£50,000	£60,000	£(55,000)	£55,000

The total profit that the optimum production plan will yield is therefore **£55,000**.

(b)   **Problems which may arise as a result of POV Ltd not being able to satisfy demand**

(i)   Any discounts previously obtained on bulk purchases of material may be lost in the future.

(ii)   If Product Z is a complementary product to either or both of Products X and Y, sales of these products may be affected if the supply of Product Z is inadequate.

(iii)   If there are insufficient quantities of Product Z available, customers may look to obtain this and other products manufactured by POV from other suppliers.

(iv)   If demand for Product Z is not satisfied, it might appear that POV Ltd is in trouble which will in turn have an effect on its reputation and possibly its share price (if applicable). This might provide the right conditions for a competitor to successfully enter the market for Product Z.

(v)   If labour resources used to manufacture Product Z are no longer required at the same level, the relevant staff may need to be retrained to work elsewhere in the company. However, if there is no requirement for their skills within the company, redundancy may be an option (this in turn may have an effect on staff morale and present further staffing problems).

(c)   Management at all levels within an organisation eg POV Ltd take decisions. The overriding requirement of the information that should be supplied by the cost accountant to aid decision making is that of **relevance.**

A **relevant cost** is a future cash flow arising as a direct consequence of a decision. It is generally assumed that **variable costs** will be **relevant costs** and that fixed costs are irrelevant to a decision. Therefore, **marginal costing** is likely to be more useful than absorption costing in decision-making situations since marginal costing makes a clear distinction between fixed and variable costs.

The information supplied on POV Ltd shows that Product Z is budgeted to make a loss of £5,000. When the information is looked at more closely, it reveals that Product Z makes a **positive contribution** of £50 per unit (that is, a contribution towards fixed costs which are unavoidable and generally irrelevant to decision making). When we are faced with a **limiting factor**, such as POV Ltd who have limited machine capacity, it is useful to calculate a contribution per unit of the limiting factor. Such information enables POV Ltd to be able to decide which products should be made first, second and third, and this should allow them to maximise the contribution earned when machine capacity has been reduced to 296,500 hours. It is important to remember that fixed costs will be incurred whatever production level is achieved, and so any **contribution** made will go towards covering these fixed costs. Since marginal costing is based on calculating a 'contribution', it is therefore a useful decision-making tool.

15. **FAST FANDANGO LTD**

(a) Sales are 60,000 units at the normal level of activity. Variable overheads at 60,000 units of production/sales are as follows.

	£	£ per unit
Production overhead	30,000	0.50
Sales costs (5% of £600,000)	30,000	0.50
Distribution costs	15,000	0.25
Administration overhead	9,000	0.15
	84,000	1.40
Direct costs	180,000	3.00
Total variable costs	264,000	4.40
Sales revenue	600,000	10.00
Contribution	336,000	5.60

At breakeven point, the contribution exactly covers fixed costs.

	£
Fixed costs	
Production overhead	126,000
Sales costs	50,000
Distribution costs	45,000
Administration overhead	31,000
	252,000

The contribution/sales ratio is 5.6/10 = 56%.

Breakeven sales can be calculated in two ways.

$$\frac{\text{Contribution required}}{\text{Contribution per unit}} \quad \text{or} \quad \frac{\text{Contribution required}}{\text{C / S ratio}}$$

$$= \frac{£252,000}{£5.60} \quad \text{or} \quad \frac{£252,000}{56\%}$$

$$= \quad 45,000 \text{ units} \quad \text{or} \quad £450,000$$

(b) (i)

	£
Sales	600,000
Variable costs (as in (a))	264,000
Contribution	336,000
Fixed costs (as in (a))	252,000
Profit	84,000

(ii)

	£	£
Sales (70,000 units × £9.50)		665,000
Variable costs		
Direct costs (70,000 × £3)	210,000	
Production overhead (70,000 × £0.50)	35,000	
Sales costs (5% of £665,000)	33,250	
Distribution costs (70,000 × £0.25)	17,500	
Administration overhead (70,000 × £0.15)	10,500	
		306,250
Contribution		358,750
Fixed costs		252,000
Profit		106,750

(iii)

	£	£
Sales (72,000 units × £9.30)		669,600
Variable costs		
Direct costs (72,000 × £3)	216,000	
Production overhead (72,000 × £0.50)	36,000	
Sales costs (5% of £669,600)	33,480	
Distribution costs (72,000 × £0.25)	18,000	
Administration overhead (72,000 × £0.15)	10,800	
		314,280
Contribution		355,320
Fixed costs		252,000
Profit		103,320

(c) The C/S ratio is:

(i) $\dfrac{£336,000}{£600,000}$ = 56%

(ii) $\dfrac{£358,750}{£665,000}$ = 53.95%

(iii) $\dfrac{£355,320}{£669,600}$ = 53.06%

(d) Under the (b)(iii) scheme, if the required profit is £106,750 the required contribution is £358,750.

	£
Profit	106,750
Plus fixed costs	252,000
Required contribution	358,750

Contribution per unit = £355,320 ÷ 72,000 = £4.935

Required sales units = $\dfrac{£358,750}{£4.935}$ = 72,695 units

16.   **ISHAB**

(a) (i)   PROFIT AND LOSS STATEMENT
           PERIOD 5
           ABSORPTION COSTING

		£	£
Sales (£150 × 8,000)			1,200,000
Production costs			
Variable (W1)		860,000	
Fixed (£10 × 10,000)		100,000	
		960,000	
Less closing stock c/f (W2)		(192,000)	
Production cost of sales		768,000	
Adjustment for over-absorbed overhead (W3)		10,000	
Total production costs			778,000
Gross profit			422,000
Less: Selling and distribution costs			
Variable selling costs (20% × £1,200,000)			(240,000)
Fixed selling costs			(60,000)
Fixed administration costs			(100,000)
Net profit			22,000

(ii)   PROFIT AND LOSS STATEMENT
       PERIOD 5
       MARGINAL COSTING

	£	£
Sales		1,200,000
Variable production costs (W1)	860,000	
Less closing stock (W2)	(172,000)	
	688,000	
Variable selling and distribution costs		
(20% × £1,200,000)	240,000	
Total variable costs of sales		928,000
Total contribution		272,000
Less: Fixed costs		
Fixed production costs (W3)	110,000	
Fixed selling and distribution costs	60,000	
Fixed administration costs	100,000	
		270,000
Net profit		2,000

Workings

1   **Variable production costs**

	£
Direct materials	50
Direct labour	24
Production overheads	12
	86

Variable production costs = £86 × 10,000
                          = £860,000

2   **Closing stock**

	Units
Production	10,000
Sales	8,000
Closing stock	2,000

Under **absorption costing**, closing stock is valued at full production cost (variable *plus* fixed costs).

	£
Variable costs	86
Fixed costs	10
	96

Closing stock = £96 × 2,000 = £192,000

Under **marginal costing**, closing stock is valued at variable production cost only (£86)

Closing stock = £86 × 2,000 = £172,000

3   **Under-absorbed fixed production overhead**

	£
Budgeted fixed production overhead (10,000 × £10)	100,000
Actual fixed production overhead	110,000
Fixed production overhead variance	10,000 (A)

	£
Actual fixed production overhead (from above)	110,000
Absorbed fixed production overhead (10,000 × £10)	100,000
Under-absorbed fixed production overhead	10,000

(b)

	£
Absorption costing profit	22,000
Fixed production costs c/f in stock values (2,000 × £10)	20,000
Marginal costing profit	2,000

The difference in profit is due to the different valuations of closing stock. In **absorption costing** the 2,000 units of closing stock include absorbed fixed production overheads of £20,000 (£10 × 2,000), which are carried over to the next period and **not** charged against the profit of the current period. In **marginal** costing, all fixed costs incurred in the period are charged against profit.

(c) (i)

Profit volume chart for period 5

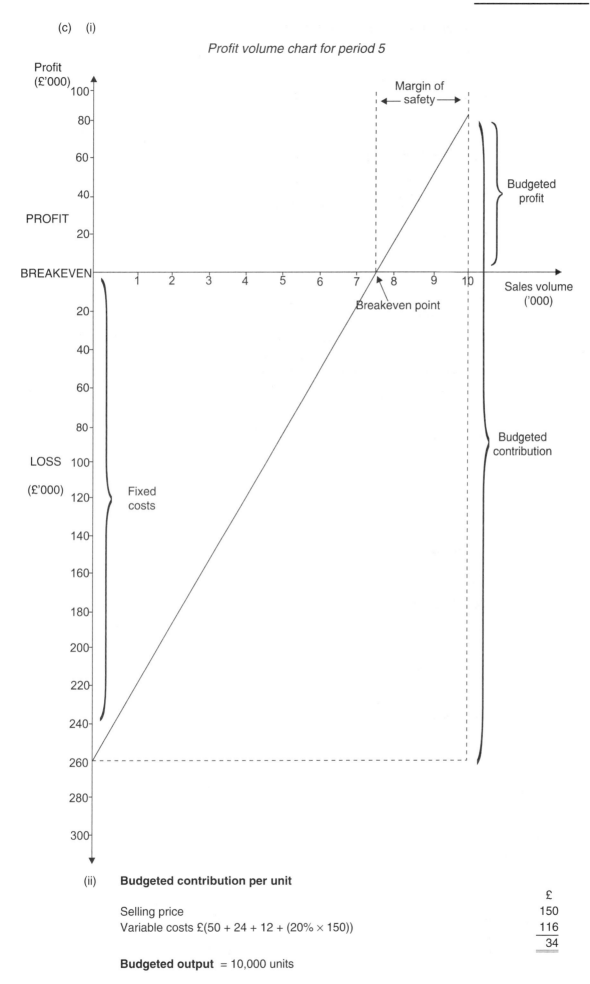

(ii) **Budgeted contribution per unit**

	£
Selling price	150
Variable costs £(50 + 24 + 12 + (20% × 150))	116
	34

Budgeted output = 10,000 units

∴ **Budgeted contribution** = 10,000 × £34 = £340,000

Budgeted fixed costs

	£
Production overhead	100,000
Selling costs	60,000
Administration	100,000
	260,000

Budgeted profit

	£
Budgeted contribution	340,000
Budgeted fixed costs	260,000
Budgeted profit	80,000

To plot the profit volume chart

Step 1. Plot budgeted fixed costs (y axis) against zero sales (x axis). Note that fixed costs are plotted as a negative value (loss).

Step 2. Plot budgeted sales of 10,000 units on x axis against budgeted profit of £80,000 on the y axis.

Step 3. Join the points plotted in Steps 1 and 2 above. The point at which the resulting line cuts the x axis is the breakeven level of sales (**breakeven point**).

The **margin of safety** is represented on the graph as the point between the breakeven point and the budgeted sales activity. Within this range, the company will make a profit, and for this reason, this range is called the **margin of safety.**

(iii) **Breakeven point** = $\dfrac{\text{Total budgeted fixed costs}}{\text{Contribution per unit}}$

Contribution per unit

	£	£
Selling price		150
Variable costs		
Production	86	
Selling (20% × £150)	30	
		116
Contribution		34

Total budgeted fixed costs

	£
Production overheads	100,000
Selling distribution	60,000
Administration	100,000
	260,000

Breakeven point = $\dfrac{£260,000}{£34}$

= **7,647 units**

17. CASH BUDGET

	Jan £	Feb £	Mar £	April £
Receipts				
Sales (W6)	-	15,200	57,100	80,000
Payments				
Purchases (W2)	-	11,550	24,500	26,950
Wages (W3)	-	4,800	19,800	22,200
Variable overhead (W4)	-	960	4,600	7,080
Fixed overhead (W5)	1,000	3,000	3,000	3,000
Total payments	1,000	20,310	51,900	59,230

	Jan	*Feb*	*Mar*	*April*
	£	£	£	£
Balance b/f	10,000	9,000	3,890	9,090
Receipts less payments	(1,000)	(5,110)	5,200	20,770
Balance c/f	9,000	3,890	9,090	29,860

Workings

1 **Production**

		Units
Jan	25% of Feb sales = 3,200 x 25%	800
Feb	(75% x 3,200) + (25% x 3,600) = 2,400 + 900	3,300
Mar	(75% x 3,600) + (25% x 4,000) = 2,700 + 1,000	3,700
April	(75% x 4,000) + (25% x 4,000) = 3,000 + 1,000	4,000

2 **Stock purchases**

£

Jan   50% of Feb production

$$= \frac{3,300}{2} \times £7 \qquad 11,550 \qquad \text{payable Feb}$$

£
11,550

Feb   50% of Feb production
Plus 50% of March production

$$= \frac{3,700}{2} \times £7 \qquad 12,950$$

24,500   payable Mar

£
12,950

Mar   50% of Mar production
Plus 50% of April production

$$= \frac{4,000}{2} \times £7 \qquad 14,000$$

26,950   payable April

£
14,000

April   50% of April production   14,000
Plus 50% of May production   14,000
28,000   payable May

3 **Wages**

			£	
Jan	production	800 x £6	4,800	due Feb
Feb	production	3,300 x £6	19,800	due Mar
Mar	production	3,700 x £6	22,200	due April
April	production	4,000 x £6	24,000	due May

4 **Variable overhead**

£

Jan   nil   -

£

Feb   re Jan (£2 x 800 x 60%)   960

£

Mar   re Jan (£2 x 800 x 40%)   640
re Feb (£2 x 3,300 x 60%)   3,960
4,600

£

April   re Feb (£2 x 3,300 x 40%)   2,640
re Mar (£2 x 3,700 x 60%)   4,440
7,080

5 Fixed overhead payable

		£
Jan	¼ x £4,000	1,000
Feb	(½ × £4,000) + (¼ × £4,000)	3,000
Mar	(½ × £4,000) + (¼ × £4,000)	3,000
April	(½ × £4,000) + (¼ × £4,000)	3,000

6 Sales receipts

		Jan £	*Feb* £	Receivable *Mar* £	*April* £	*May* £
Feb sales	£80,000	-	15,200	40,000	16,000	6,400
March sales	£90,000	-	-	17,100	45,000	18,000
April sales	£100,000	-	-	-	19,000	50,000
May sales	£100,000	-	-	-	-	19,000
Total receipts		-	15,200	57,100	80,000	93,400

18. TWO THINGS

(a) The use of a spreadsheet package (such as Supercalc or Lotus 1-2-3) considerably simplifies cash budgeting. A budget can be set up using the usual format, and can then be altered at will, so that the preparer can see the effects of, for instance, increased sales, different debt collection periods and so on. Time is saved, accuracy is improved, and amendments can be made very speedily and easily.

(b) The principal reasons why profit will not equal cash flow are as follows.

(i) The 'matching concept' means that costs and revenues do not equal payments and receipts. Revenue is recognised in the profit statement when goods are sold, and any revenue not received recorded as a debtor. Similarly, costs are incurred when a resource is acquired or subsequently used, not when it happens to be paid for.

(ii) Some items appearing in the profit statement do not affect cash flow. For example, depreciation is a 'non-cash' deduction in arriving at profit.

(iii) Similarly, items may effect cash flow but not profit. Capital expenditure decisions (apart from depreciation) and stock level adjustments are prime examples.

19. DOODLE LTD

Workings

The budgeted direct labour hours = 11,400 × (40 + 36) = 866,400 direct labour hours.

The fixed production overhead absorption rate = £1.25 per hour (£1,083,000 ÷ 866,400 hours).

The variable production overhead rate (both for costs incurred and absorbed) is:

department P :	75 pence per hour
department Q :	50 pence per hour

STANDARD COST SHEET - THE SQUIGGLE

		£	£
Direct materials: 30 metres at £6.10			183
Direct wages			
Department P: 40 hours at £2.20		88	
Department Q: 36 hours at £2.50		90	
			178
(a) (i) Standard total direct cost			361
Variable production overhead			
Department P: 40 hours at £0.75		30	
Department Q: 36 hours at £0.50		18	
			48
(ii) Standard variable production cost			409
Fixed production overhead: 76 hours at £1.25			95
(iii) Standard production cost			504
Administration overhead (note 1)			11
Marketing overhead (note 2)			25
(iv) Standard cost of sale			540
Standard profit (10% of sales price)			60
(b) Standard sales price			600

Notes

1   £125,400 ÷ 11,400

2   £285,000 ÷ 11,400

20.   SUMMARY PRODUCTION BUDGET

(a)   We need to begin by calculating a standard unit cost.

		£
Materials:	1.4 kg (ie 336,000 kg/240,000) × £4.10	5.74
Direct labour:	0.9 hrs (ie 216,000 hrs/240,000) × £4.50	4.05
Overheads:	0.9 hrs × £8.89 (ie £1,920,000/216,000)	8.00
		17.79

Variances

Material

	£
313,060 kg should have cost (× £4.10)	1,283,546
but did cost	1,245,980
Material price variance	37,566 (F)

220,000 units should have used (× 1.4 kg)	308,000 kg
but did use	313,060 kg
Variance in kgs	5,060 kg (A)
× standard cost per kg	× £4.10
Material usage variance in £	£20,746 (A)

Direct labour

	£
194,920 hrs should have cost (× £4.50)	877,140
but did cost	886,886
Direct labour rate variance	9,746 (A)

220,000 units should have taken (× 0.9 hrs)	198,000 hrs
but did take	194,920 hrs
Variance in hours	3,080 hrs (F)
× standard rate per hour	× £4.50
Direct labour efficiency variance in £	£13,860 (F)

Overheads

	£
Standard overhead absorbed (220,000 × 0.9 × £8.89)	1,760,000
Actual cost	1,934,940
Overhead variance	174,940 (A)

(b) The favourable **direct labour efficiency variance** may have arisen for one of the following reasons.

(i) Better quality material used than anticipated when standard set.

(ii) Better quality equipment used than anticipated when standard set

(iii) Errors in recording labour time (that is, not all labour time recorded)

(iv) Standard too easy to attain

(v) Fewer production delays than anticipated

(vi) More care with material taken than anticipated, resulting in less material loss than included in standard

(vii) Worker motivation

(viii) Use of more skilled labour than anticipated when standard set

21. HOTELIERS UNITE

(a) The format currently used by the hotel management team for the presentation of the budget information does not identify whether the costs are **fixed, variable** or **semi-variable** costs.

A **fixed cost** is a cost which is unaffected by changes in the level of activity (occupancy levels) over the relevant range. In general, fixed costs are **uncontrollable** costs.

A **variable cost** is a cost which tends to vary with the level of activity (occupancy level) over the relevant range. If these costs are identified separately, management should be able to predict the costs for any give occupancy level. In general, variable costs are **controllable** costs.

A **semi-variable cost** contains both fixed and variable components and so is partly affected by changes in the level of activity. If the fixed and variable elements are identified (ie the cost behaviour pattern is identified) future budget information may be prepared much more easily. Fixed and variable elements of mixed costs may be identified by using the **high-low method.**

(b) FLEXED BUDGET STATEMENT OCCUPANCY LEVEL – 80%

	£
Variable costs	
Room cleaning costs (W1)	725,328
Establishment costs (W2)	471,463
Recreational facilities costs (W3)	271,998
Fixed costs	
Establishment costs (W2)	60,000
Equipment costs (W4)	115,000
	1,643,789

Workings

1 **Room cleaning costs**

	Total cost	Occupancy
	£	%
High	744,600	85
Low	481,800	55
	262,800	30

$$\text{Variable cost} = \frac{£262,800}{30} = £8,760$$

Total cost (55%) = Fixed cost + variable cost (55%)

£481,800 = Fixed cost + (£8,760 × 55)

∴ Fixed cost = nil

Room cleaning costs are therefore **variable costs.**

At 80% occupancy, room cleaning costs = 80 × £8,760
= £700,800

However, all variable costs are to increase by 3.5% next year and room cleaning costs will therefore be
£700,800 × 1.035 = £725,328

2   **Establishment costs**

	Total cost £	Occupancy %
High	533,990	85
Low	363,170	55
	170,820	30

Variable cost $= \dfrac{£170,820}{30} = £5,694$

Total cost (55%)	= Fixed cost + variable cost (55%)
£363,170	= Fixed cost + (£5,694 × 55)
∴ Fixed cost	= £363,170 − £313,170
	= £50,000

Establishment costs are therefore **semi-variable.**

	£
Variable element (80%)	
£5,694 × 80 × 1.035	471,463
Fixed element	
£50,000 + £10,000 (upgrade charge)	60,000
	531,463

3   **Recreational facilities costs**

	Total cost £	Occupancy %
High	279,225	85
Low	180,675	55
	98,550	30

Variable cost $= \dfrac{£98,550}{30} = £3,285$

Total cost (55%)	= Fixed cost + variable cost (55%)
£180,675	= Fixed cost + (£3,285 × 55)
∴ Fixed cost	= £nil

Recreational facilities costs are therefore **variable costs.**

At 80% occupancy, room cleaning costs = £3,285 × 80 × 1.035 = £271,998.

4   **Equipment costs**

Equipment costs are £100,000 at 55%, 75% and 85% occupancy levels. Equipment costs are therefore **fixed costs.**

	£
Fixed cost at 80%	100,000
Annual charge for upgrade of sports facilities	15,000
	115,000

(c)   To: Management
      From: Management Accountant
      Subject: Variance analysis
      Date: XX.XX.XX

This report contains a variance schedule which compares budget and actual expenditure for the year under consideration, with appropriate variances calculated. I have also included a list of possible reasons for these variances occurring (though detailed investigations should be carried out if the **actual** cause of the variances is to be identified).

VARIANCE SCHEDULE
YEAR 2000
80% OCCUPANCY

	Flexed budget £	Actual results £	Variance £
Variable costs			
Room cleaning costs	725,328	727,560	2,232 (A)
Establishment costs	471,463	469,258	2,205 (F)
Recreational facilities costs	271,998	275,640	3,642 (A)
Fixed costs			
Establishment costs	60,000	60,000	-
Equipment costs	115,000	115,000	-
	1,643,789	1,647,458	3,669

Possible reasons for the above cost variances arising are as follows.

Room cleaning variance - £2,232 (A)

- Cleaners' weekend working rates are high
- Cleaning products cost more than expected
- Cleaning products have been stolen
- Inefficient purchasing of cleaning products by the purchasing department
- Budget is unrealistic/incorrect

Establishment costs variance - £2,205 (F)

- Efficient purchasing of indirect consumables
- Indirect labour costs less than expected
- Luxury weekend breaks attract higher-quality guests leading to lower maintenance costs
- B0000udget is unrealistic/incorrect.

Recreational costs variance - £3,642 (A)

- Workers' weekend rates are higher than expected
- Sports facility products have been stolen
- Sports facility products cost more than expected
- Inefficient purchasing of sports facility products by the purchasing department
- Budget is unrealistic/incorrect

If you require any further information regarding these variances, please do not hesitate to give me a call.

Signed: Management Accountant

(d) Higher occupancy levels might give rise to the following problems.

- Staff recruitment – additional staff may be required
- Staff training will be required by new staff
- Working anti-social hours (weekends) may be required of staff
- Non-residents using the hotel facilities may have a negative effect on hotel residents
- Competition-rates must be competitive or the hotel's activities might be unprofitable.

22. NANOOK OF THE NORTH

Workings

Budgeted gross profit = 3,000 units × standard profit of £(25 – 21) = £12,000

Other budgeted overheads of £5,000 reduce the budgeted profit to £7,000

Variances

		£	
1	**Selling price**		
	2,800 units of SK Mow should sell for (× £25)	70,000	
	did sell for	71,200	
	Selling price variance	1,200	(F)

2 Sales volume

Budgeted sales volume	3,000	units
Actual sales volume	2,800	units
Sales volume variance in units	200	units (A)
× standard profit per unit	× £4	
Sales volume variance in £	£800	(A)

3 Material price (calculated on purchases where raw material stocks are valued at standard cost)

	£	£	
19,000 kg of P should cost (× 40p)	7,600		
did cost	7,500		
Material P price variance		100	(F)
14,000 kg of Q should cost (× 70p)	9,800		
did cost	10,250		
Material Q price variance		450	(A)
Total material price variance		350	(A)

4 Material usage

Material P

2,800 units of SK Mow should use (× 8 kgs)	22,400	kgs
did use	24,100	kgs
Material P usage variance in kgs	1,700	kgs (A)
× standard price per kg	× £0.40	
Material P usage variance in £	£680	(A)

Material Q

2,800 units of SK Mow should use (× 4 kgs)	11,200	kgs
did use	10,100	kgs
Material Q usage variance in kgs	1,100	kgs (F)
× standard price per kg	× £0.70	
Material Q usage variance in £	£770	(F)
Total material usage variance (£770 − £680)	£90	(F)

5 Direct labour rate

	£	
8,600 hours of labour should cost (× £2.50)	21,500	
did cost	24,100	
Direct labour rate variance	2,600	(A)

6 Idle time variance 300 hours (A) × £2.50 =

	£750	(A)

7 Direct labour efficiency

To make 2,800 units of SK Mow should take (× 3 hrs)	8,400	hrs
did take (active hours)	8,300	hrs
Direct labour variance in hrs	100	hrs (F)
× standard efficiency rate per hour	× £2.50	
Direct labour efficiency variance in £	£250	(F)

8 Variable production overhead efficiency (same as direct labour)

100 hrs (F) × standard rate (£0.50)	£50	(F)

9 Variable production overhead expenditure

	£	
8,300 worked hours should cost (× £0.50)	4,150	
did cost	4,100	
Variable overhead expenditure variance	50	(F)

10   **Fixed production overhead expenditure**

	£	
Budgeted fixed production overhead	18,000	
Actual overhead	18,450	
Overhead expenditure variance	450	(A)

11   **Fixed production overhead volume efficiency**

(Same as labour efficiency) 100 hrs (F) × standard rate (£2 per hr)   £200   (F)

12   **Fixed production overhead volume capacity**

Budgeted worked hours (3,000 × 3 hrs)	9,000	hrs
Actual worked hours	8,300	hrs
Volume capacity variance in hrs	700	hrs (A)
× standard rate per hour	× £2	
Volume capacity variance in £	£1,400	(A)

OPERATING STATEMENT FOR PERIOD 7

	£	£	
Budgeted profit		7,000	
Budgeted sales, distribution, administration overhead		5,000	
Budgeted gross profit		12,000	
Sales variances: volume	800 (A)		
price	1,200 (F)		
		400	(F)
Actual sales less the standard production cost of sales		12,400	

	£	£		
	(F)	(A)		
Cost variances				
Direct material price		350		
Direct material usage	90			
Direct labour rate		2,600		
Direct labour efficiency	250			
Idle time		750		
Variable production overhead efficiency	50			
Variable production overhead expenditure	50			
Fixed production overhead: expenditure		450		
volume efficiency	200			
volume capacity		1,400		
	640	5,550	4,910	(A)
Actual gross profit			7,490	
Less sales, distribution, administration overheads			5,200	
Actual net profit			2,290	

23.   **BACKE AND SMASH LTD**

Materials price variance

	£	£
37,100 metres of wood should cost (× £0.30)	11,130	
but did cost	11,000	
Wood price variance		130 (F)
29,200 metres of gut should cost (× £1.50)	43,800	
but did cost	44,100	
Gut price variance		300 (A)
Wood and gut price variance		170 (A)

Material usage variance

3,700 units of Winsome should use	(× 7m)	25,900 m	(× 6 m)	22,200 m
1,890 units of Boastful should use	(× 5m)	9,450 m	(× 4 m)	7,560 m
		35,350 m		29,760 m
Together they did use		37,100 m		29,200 m
Material usage variance in metres		1,750 m(A)		560 m (F)
× standard cost per metre		× £0.30		× £1.50
Material usage variance				
Wood		£525 (A)		
Gut				£840 (F)

Other materials cost variance

	£
3,700 units of Winsome should cost (× £0.20)	740.00
1,890 units of Boastful should cost (× £0.15)	283.50
	1,023.50
Together they did cost	1,000.00
Other materials cost variance	23.50 (F)

Direct labour rate

	£
2,200 hours of labour should cost (× £3)	6,600
but did cost	6,850
Direct labour rate variance	250 (A)

Direct labour efficiency

3,700 units of Winsome should take (× 30 minutes)	1,850 hrs
1,890 units of Boastful should take (× 20 minutes)	630 hrs
	2,480 hrs
Together they did take	2,200 hrs
Efficiency variance in hrs	280 hrs (F)
× standard rate per hour	× × £3
Direct labour efficiency variance	£840 (F)

Variable overhead costs

	Hours	Units
Budgeted hours: Winsome	2,000	4,000
Boastful	500	1,500
	2,500	

	£
Power cost per standard hour (£1,500 ÷ 2,500 hrs)	0.60
Maintenance cost per standard hour (£7,500 ÷ 2,500 hrs)	3.00
	3.60

Variable overhead efficiency variance		
= (as labour) 280 hours (F) × £3.60 =		£1,008 (F)

	£	£
Variable overhead cost of 2,200 hours should be (× £3.60)		7,920
but was: power	1,800	
maintenance	6,900	
		8,700
Variable overhead expenditure variance		780 (A)

Fixed overhead

Budgeted fixed costs	£21,000
Budgeted hours (see (f))	2,500 hrs
Absorption rate per hour	£8.40

Fixed overhead expenditure variance

	Budgeted expenditure	Actual expenditure	Expenditure variance
	£	£	£
Supervision	8,000	7,940	60 (F)
Heating and lighting	1,200	1,320	120 (A)
Rent	4,800	4,800	-
Depreciation	7,000	7,000	-
Total	21,000	21,060	60 (A)

Fixed overhead volume variance

	£	£
Actual production at standard rates		
Winsome (3,700 × £8.40 × 1/2 hr)	15,540	
Boastful (1,890 × £8.40 ×1/3 hr)	5,292	
Budgeted production at standard rates		20,832
Winsome (4,000 × £8.40 × 1/2 hr)	16,800	
Boastful (1,500 × £8.40 × 1/3 hr)	4,200	21,000
		168 (A)

List of key terms
and index

These are the terms which we have identified throughout the text as being KEY TERMS and the formulae that you must learn. You should make sure that you can define what these terms mean and that you are able to reproduce the formulae correctly; go back to the pages highlighted here if you need to check.

See overleaf for information on other
BPP products and how to order

CIMA Order

To BPP Publishing Ltd, Aldine Place, London W12 8AW
Tel: 020 8740 2211. Fax: 020 8740 1184
www.bpp.com

Mr/Mrs/Ms (Full name)

Daytime delivery address

Postcode

Daytime Tel

E-mail

Date of exam (month/year)

	7/00 Texts	1/01Kits	1/01 Passcards	9/00 Tapes	7/00 Videos	MCQ cards**
FOUNDATION *						
1 Financial Accounting Fundamentals	£19.95	£10.95	£6.95	£12.95	£25.00	£4.50
2 Management Accounting Fundamentals	£19.95	£10.95	£6.95	£12.95	£25.00	£4.50
3A Economics for Business	£19.95	£10.95	£6.95	£12.95	£25.00	£4.50
3B Business Law	£19.95	£10.95	£6.95	£12.95	£25.00	£4.50
3C Business Mathematics	£19.95	£10.95	£6.95	£12.95	£25.00	£4.50
INTERMEDIATE *						
4 Finance	£19.95	£10.95	£6.95	£12.95	£25.00	£4.50
5 Business Tax (FA 2000)	£19.95 (9/00)£10.95	£10.95	£6.95	£12.95	£25.00	£3.50
6 Financial Accounting	£19.95	£10.95	£6.95	£12.95	£25.00	
6I Financial Accounting International	£19.95	£10.95				
7 Financial Reporting	£19.95	£10.95	£6.95	£12.95	£25.00	
7I Financial Reporting International	£19.95	£10.95				
8 Management Accounting - Performance Mgmt	£19.95	£10.95	£6.95	£12.95	£25.00	£3.50
9 Management Accounting - Decision Making	£19.95	£10.95	£6.95	£12.95	£25.00	£3.50
10 Systems and Project Management	£19.95	£10.95	£6.95	£12.95	£25.00	
11 Organisational Management	£19.95	£10.95	£6.95	£12.95	£25.00	
FINAL						
12 Management Accounting - Business Strategy	£20.95	£10.95	£6.95	£12.95	£25.00	
13 Management Accounting - Financial Strategy	£20.95	£10.95	£6.95	£12.95	£25.00	
14 Management Accounting - Information Strategy	£20.95	£10.95	£5.95	£12.95	£25.00	
15 Case Study	£15.95 (1)	£15.95 (2)		£15.95 (12/00)	£15.95 (12/00)	

(1) Workbook   (2) Case Question Book

* There will also be a selection of Master CDs available in 2001

** (FREE WITH TEXT)

* We aim to deliver to all UK addresses inside 5 working days, a signature will be required. Orders to all EU addresses should be delivered within 6 working days. All other orders to overseas addresses should be delivered within 8 working days.

POSTAGE & PACKING

Study Texts

	First	Each extra	
UK	£3.00	£2.00	£
Europe***	£5.00	£4.00	£
Rest of world	£20.00	£10.00	£

Kits/Passcards/Success Tapes

	First	Each extra	
UK	£2.00	£1.00	£
Europe***	£2.50	£1.00	£
Rest of world	£15.00	£8.00	£

Master CDs(2001)/Breakthrough Videos

	First	Each extra	
UK	£2.00	£2.00	£
Europe***	£2.00	£2.00	£
Rest of world	£20.00	£10.00	£
MCQ cards	£1.00	£1.00	£

Grand Total (Cheques to *BPP Publishing*) I enclose a cheque for (incl. Postage)   £

Or charge to Access/Visa/Switch

Card Number

Expiry date

Start Date

Issue Number (Switch Only)

Signature

REVIEW FORM & FREE PRIZE DRAW

All original review forms from the entire BPP range, completed with genuine comments, will be entered into one of two draws on 31 January 2001 and 31 July 2001. The names on the first four forms picked out on each occasion will be sent a cheque for £50.

Name: _____   **Address**: _____

_____

_____

How have you used this Text? *(Tick one box only)*	**During the past six months do you recall seeing/receiving any of the following?** *(Tick as many boxes as are relevant)*

How have you used this Text?
(Tick one box only)

☐ Self study (book only)

☐ On a course: college (please state)_____

_____

☐ With 'correspondence' package

☐ Other _____

Why did you decide to purchase this Text?
(Tick one box only)

☐ Have used BPP Texts in the past

☐ Recommendation by friend/colleague

☐ Recommendation by a lecturer at college

☐ Saw advertising

☐ Other _____

During the past six months do you recall seeing/receiving any of the following?
(Tick as many boxes as are relevant)

☐ Our advertisement in CIMA *Student*

☐ Our advertisement in *Management Accounting*

☐ Our advertisement in *Pass*

☐ Our brochure with a letter through the post

☐ Our website www.bpp.com

Which (if any) aspects of our advertising do you find useful?
(Tick as many boxes as are relevant)

☐ Prices and publication dates of new editions

☐ Information on product content

☐ Facility to order books off-the-page

☐ None of the above

[For foundation only] How did you/will you take the exam for this paper (Tick one box only)

Written exam ☐   Computer based assessment ☐

Your ratings, comments and suggestions would be appreciated on the following areas

	Very useful	Useful	Not useful
Introductory section (Key study steps, personal study)	☐	☐	☐
Chapter introductions	☐	☐	☐
Key terms	☐	☐	☐
Quality of explanations	☐	☐	☐
Case examples and other examples	☐	☐	☐
Questions and answers in each chapter	☐	☐	☐
Chapter roundups	☐	☐	☐
Quick quizzes	☐	☐	☐
Exam focus points	☐	☐	☐
Question bank	☐	☐	☐
Answer bank	☐	☐	☐
List of key terms and index	☐	☐	☐
Icons	☐	☐	☐
Mind maps	☐	☐	☐

	Excellent	Good	Adequate	Poor
Overall opinion of this Study Text	☐	☐	☐	☐

Do you intend to continue using BPP products?   ☐ Yes   ☐ No

Please note any further comments and suggestions/errors on the reverse of this page. The BPP author of this edition can be e-mailed at: lynnwatkins@bpp.com

Please return this form to: Alison McHugh, CIMA range manager BPP Publishing Ltd, FREEPOST, London, W12 8BR

REVIEW FORM & FREE PRIZE DRAW (continued)

Please note any further comments and suggestions/errors below.

FREE PRIZE DRAW RULES

1   Closing date for 31 January 2001 draw is 31 December 2000. Closing date for 31 July 2001 draw is 30 June 2001.

2   Restricted to entries with UK and Eire addresses only. BPP employees, their families and business associates are excluded.

3   No purchase necessary. Entry forms are available upon request from BPP Publishing. No more than one entry per title, per person. Draw restricted to persons aged 16 and over.

4   Winners will be notified by post and receive their cheques not later than 6 weeks after the relevant draw date. Lists of winners will be published in BPP's *focus* newsletter following the relevant draw.

5   The decision of the promoter in all matters is final and binding. No correspondence will be entered into.